PRACTICAL RESEARCH

PRACTICAL RESEARCH

Planning and Design

Third Edition

PAUL D. LEEDY
Professor of Education
The American University
Washington, D.C.

Macmillan Publishing Company
New York
Coller Macmillian Publishers
London

Earlier editions ______________________________

____

copyright © 1974 and 1980
by Paul D. Leedy

Macmillan Publishing Company
866 Third Avenue, New York, New York 10022

Collier Macmillan Canada, Inc.

Library of Congress Cataloging in Publication Data

Leedy, Paul D.
Practical research.

Bibliography: p.
Includes index.
1. Research—Methodology. I. Title.
Q180.55.M4L43 1985 001.4'2 84-731
ISBN 0-02-369220-0

Printing: 2 3 4 5 6 7 8 Year: 5 6 7 8 9 0 1 2 3

ISBN 0-02-369220-0

With special appeciation

to

Two Girls

and

One Boy:

★★★

Renie

Kathy

and

Tom

About This Book (The Third Edition)

In a sense, this is a do-it-yourself, understand-it-yourself manual. It will guide you, step by step, in designing a research project, however large or small it may be. The research of most academic disciplines follows a basic methodological approach. Only the emphasis shifts. The gathering and interpreting of the data may vary from discipline to discipline, but the procedure is basically the same. Whether the research be in education, nursing, sociology, the behavioral sciences, physical education, business administration, accounting, or allied areas, a common substratum of procedure underlies the research projects in *all* of these areas. Those planning to do research in any of these areas should appreciate this basic methodological substratum and, by so doing, may then more adequately fit their particular research endeavor into the general procedural matrix. It is this overview of research methodology that this manual seeks to present. Its broad adoption in the first and second editions across academic and disciplinary boundary lines has been the best evidence for the practicability of this fundamental approach.

The practical nature of this manual has come from years of the author's teaching methodology to both graduate and undergraduate students and from observing all their doubts and uncertainties in the face of a *practical* research undertaking. Many of them knew the *theoretical* aspects of research methodology thoroughly, yet they had difficulty in the *practical* planning of a research project, in the preparing of an acceptable proposal, or in the writing of a passable research report.

The author does not undervalue the importance of a theoretical approach to the understanding of research. Many times such a background is both basic and required. But theoretical methodology does not provide of itself sufficient thrust for many students who need to get their research off the launch pad of theory into the orbit of creativity. This manual, therefore, seeks to give the student the essential theoretical orientation coupled with a *modus operandi* for the carrying out of a realistic research project.

The types of student uncertainties are many. Some students do not know precisely what research is; others are not sure where to find the information they need or, if they find it, are not sure what they should do with it after they have it. There are those who are terrified by statistics, and those who cannot get a proposal accepted or fail to secure approval for the project they have planned.

Many students have labored over a research project only to be told after all their work that "this was not quite what [the instructor] expected" or that "this is just not research." Such a reaction is frustrating, comfortless, and unrewarding.

They who apply for grants or financial assistance to carry out their research projects need to know how to propose their ideas with maximum effectiveness. The third edition has included a digest of guidelines for preparing a research proposal for grants from governmental as well as from private sources as well as a summary for the student and the experienced researcher alike, of the reasons why many proposals fail to merit approval.

One of the unique features of this book is the "Practicum in Research" section which is a part of the end matter. Here, as you pass important milestones in learning the nature of research and how to plan it in the text section of the book, you structure your *own* research project or test your understanding of the basic concepts presented in the text. Nor is the essential thrust of this text restricted to the research endeavors of the graduate or college student. A high school or college student using this book should be able to write better term papers or research reports. Similarly, a graduate student should be able to construct an acceptable proposal for a thesis or dissertation committee. Anyone using it should be able to produce a superior product in research because research is research. Only in degree of sophistication should a high school research report or a college research paper vary from a master's thesis or doctoral dissertation. Of course, in reality one knows that this is not so and that much that is misleading to the student is approved and encouraged under the misnomer of *research.* When one becomes aware of what is involved in applying the scientific method to the solution of research problems, then it is that the student will be led to understand that research is a basic methodology for attacking problems and the scientific method is a way of thinking that is appropriate at all levels of an individual's education.

Underlying the writing of the first edition of *Practical Research:Planning and Design* was the belief that research methodology as a basic method of investigation, under the aegis of the scientific method is *essentially* the same from one academic discipline to another. Every researcher seeking to resolve a researchable problem, every student engaged in dissertational or thesis research follows the same basic steps: the articulation of a problem, the establishment of hypotheses, the collection, the analysis and the interpretation of data, and the resolution of the effort in terms of reportable conclusions.

This belief has been eloquently affirmed in the broad adoption which *Practical Research:Planning and Design* has received. In a brief survey, done for the purpose of eliciting suggestions for the third edition from those who had adopted the text, it was found that *Practical Research:Planning and Design* had been found a suitable text in almost all academic disciplines at the graduate level for students engaged in thesis or dissertational projects.

Every effort has, therefore, been made to make this book of greatest use to students over a broad academic spectrum. Illustrations have been taken from many areas of study. There is actually very little difference between the *methodology* of research in the sciences, the behavioral sciences, and the humanities. In all these areas of learning, the object of the research effort in each discipline is *essentially* the same: to discover undiscovered truth and to extend the frontiers of knowledge in each subject area.

To this text in the third edition, several new features have been added. At the beginning of each chapter a brief overview of the chapter seeks to acquaint the reader with the content and purpose of the chapter and, thus, to make the reading more rewarding.

At the end of each chapter has been added a bibliography for further study. This bibliography is a broad spectrum selection of readings crossing the lines of many academic disciplines and seeking to provide the student with the opportunity of exploring further some of the topics discussed within the chapter.

There have been other aids included embodying the valuable suggestions and recommendations of those who have used the text and assisted in sharing their thoughts with the author at the threshold of the revision process. To all who have thus enriched this edition the author is deeply appreciative and indebted.

The author is, in fact, indebted to so many for so much in this book that he refrains from mentioning any one in particular. To his own teachers who, during his doctoral study, gave him the first insight into the need for a book such as this, he pays much respect and acknowledges himself forever in their debt. Next, he wishes to acknowledge with humility the students who, again and again, have begged him to set down for others what they have found to be most helpful in the seminar sessions they have had with him. The same encouragement has come from faculty colleagues in several universities. Those with whom he has discussed the idea and who are engaged in professional research have also encouraged setting down some of the material in permanent form. For this third edition, other colleagues from widely diversified academic disciplines in colleges and universities all across the nation who found the earlier editions adequately suited to their needs have volunteered valuable suggestions for many parts of this book. All of their critiques were most welcome and, so far as possible, they have been incorporated in this edition.

Those who thus enhanced this edition through the courtesy of their suggestions should have particular mention. Because of the broad spectrum of the academic disciplines which they represent, and the geographical spread of the institutions, their comments have been especially helpful. The author is happy to list them, along with the teaching specialties in which they have found this text helpful: Dr. Jaclyn Card, Assistant Professor, Recreation and Park Administration, University of Missouri–Columbia; Dr. Lynne Faulk, Associate Professor, Nursing, University of South Alabama; Dr. Ruth Heidelbach, Associate Professor, Education, University of Maryland; Dr. Stephen B. Jones, Assistant Professor, Journalism, University of Colorado-Boulder; Dr. Paul R. Raffoul, Assistant Professor, Social Work, University of Houston; Dr. Anthony W. Salerno, Professor, Law and Justice, Glassboro State College; Dr. R. A. Skinner, Associate Professor, Political Science, Old Dominion University; Dr. Ronald L. Spangler, Assistant Professor, Landscape Architecture, Ball State University; Dr. Dennis G. Tesolowski, Assistant Professor, Education, Idaho State University; and Dr. Don Ethridge, Associate Professor, Agricultural Economics, Texas Technological University.

Especially is the author indebted to those colleagues who read the manuscript of this edition just prior to publication and offered many gracious and constructive suggestions. Insofar as possible, their suggestions have been heeded and their assistance has been most helpful. These have been Dr. Robert Blanck, Director of the Graduate Program in Management, University of Redlands; Dr. Fred Dzara, Professor of Education and Dr. Warren B. Fruechtel, Professor of Education, both of the Department of Educational Services, Edinboro University of Pennsylvania; and Dr. F. Andrew Schoolmaster, Assistant Professor, Department of Geography, North Texas State University. Together, their suggestions have greatly improved this edition, and the author is most appreciative of their assistance.

One esteemed colleague sounded the basic theme of the book. "Tell them the obvious," he advised. "It may be exactly what they need to know!" That is what the author has tried to do.

Those of us who have had the mystery of research procedure opened to us by other wise and devoted mentors may forget that the obvious was precisely what *we* needed. *We* know the basic reference works and the "keys" to the library so well that we do not consider is incumbent to tell others about them; the reading of a statistical formula for us is so simple that we would never think of teaching a student how to read one; a proposal for us is such a commonplace document that we would seldom entertain the thought that perhaps the beginning student in research needs explicit instructions on how to write one. All these matters are very obvious—to us! To many of our students they are deep secrets and dark mysteries.

Perhaps it is at the very point of the obvious where many students lose sight of essentials. This book is an attempt to restore academic sight to those who see, either with dim vision or, as in the case of many, with none at all. Deal gently with the author, therefore, at those places in the text where he seems to indulge in the banality of the obvious.

And now, perhaps our first exercise in seeing will be to try to discern what research really is.

P. D. L.

Table of Contents

PRACTICAL RESEARCH

THE RESEARCH PROCESS

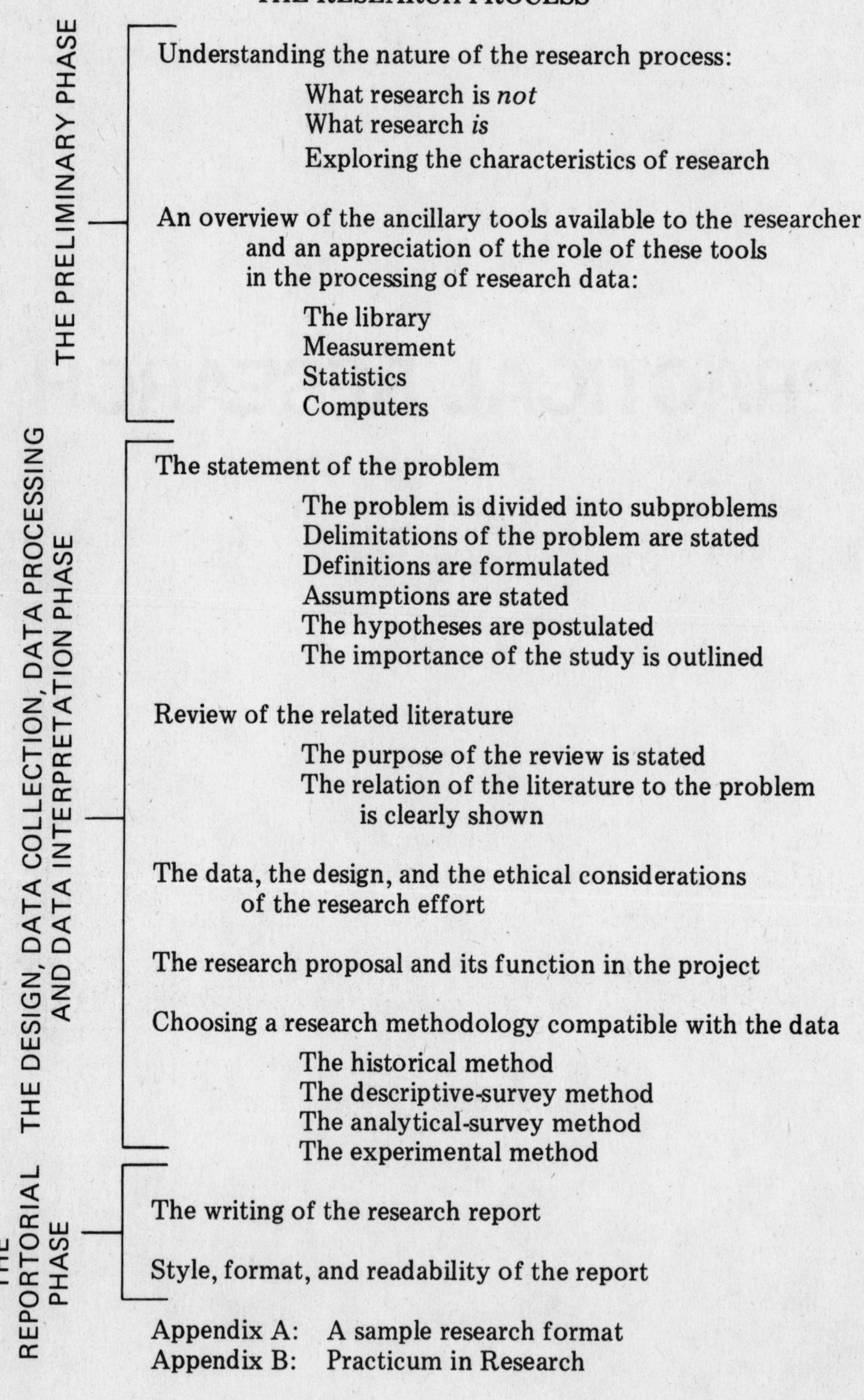

THE PRELIMINARY PHASE
Understanding the nature of the research process:
What research is *not*
What research *is*
Exploring the characteristics of research
An overview of the ancillary tools available to the researcher and an appreciation of the role of these tools in the processing of research data:
The library
Measurement
Statistics
Computers
THE DESIGN, DATA COLLECTION, DATA PROCESSING AND DATA INTERPRETATION PHASE
The statement of the problem
The problem is divided into subproblems
Delimitations of the problem are stated
Definitions are formulated
Assumptions are stated
The hypotheses are postulated
The importance of the study is outlined
Review of the related literature
The purpose of the review is stated
The relation of the literature to the problem is clearly shown
The data, the design, and the ethical considerations of the research effort
The research proposal and its function in the project
Choosing a research methodology compatible with the data
The historical method
The descriptive-survey method
The analytical-survey method
The experimental method
THE REPORTORIAL PHASE
The writing of the research report
Style, format, and readability of the report
Appendix A: A sample research format
Appendix B: Practicum in Research

RESEARCH AND THE TOOLS OF RESEARCH

READ THIS—BEFORE YOU READ THIS CHAPTER

Research is a broadly misunderstood word. First, then, it is important that you get the right orientation to this term as it is used professionally. To that end, this chapter aims at two objectives:

1. To suggest what research is not,
2. To outline what the research process is.

A diagram at the close of the chapter will summarize all that we have said about the research process. It is a cyclical, or helical, process that begins with an unanswered question and strives, through the study of relevant facts, to determine the answer to that question.

At the end of the chapter you will have an opportunity to apply what you have learned. You will also find suggestions for further reading on many of the topics the chapter discusses.

1
What Is Research?

Research is a confusing term.

It has so many meanings that we must understand precisely what it means . We shall discuss in this book what is commonly referred to as *basic* or *pure research*.

Much that is said about basic research will also apply to the several other varieties of research activity: applied research, action research, research and development, and so on. The difference between pragmatic forms and the basic form of research lies in the depth to which basic research probes the underlying causes and meaning of observed phenomena and in the sophistication with which it demands that the collected data of observation be interpreted.

WHAT RESEARCH IS NOT

To understand more readily what research *is*, we begin by considering what research is *not*. Some of the statements that follow may come as a distinct shock to the conventional way in which you may have accepted the meaning of the term *research*. The reason for your surprise may be, in part, because you have been conditioned to the term in so many connotative frameworks that you may not be sure exactly what the term really does mean. Hence, when many students encounter the term for the first time in a truly professional and academic sense, it bewilders them.

Bewilderment is natural. It arises from a misconception—a wrong view that most of us have with respect to the real meaning of the word *research*.

The reason is simple. The word *research* has been so loosely employed in everyday use that few of us have any idea of its real meaning or operative implications. The word has become common jargon. It is used in every situation from an attention-getting phrase to the description of the process whereby a significant discovery is made in a scientific laboratory. The carelessness of its use has robbed it of any real meaning.

Take a case in point. You open an envelope in the morning's mail. As you pull out its contents, a statement greets you that because of "years of *research*" a new product has been developed to clean your car with a miracle shine. The words, "years of *research*," capture your attention. You order the product, and what do you get from "years of *research*"? Liquid soap! No research; merely the employment of the term to attract the reader's attention.

A high school student completes a "research paper" on the role of the "Dark Lady" in the sonnets of Shakespeare. No doubt the student went through some of the motions associated with research, such as gathering information on note cards, collecting a bibliography, and footnoting in prescribed form the material gathered from various documentary sources. To the student, it seemed like an elaborate effort indeed. Furthermore, both the student and the teacher who assigned the paper seem quite serious in thinking of this as a genuine "research project."

But no matter how elaborate the collection of data, the mere accumulation of fact is not research. It is, rather, an exercise in information-gathering, in library-orientation, in ferreting out relevant bits of factual data, in self-enlightenment—but it is not *research*.

Unfortunately, many students have labored under the delusion that looking up a few facts and writing them down in a documented paper constitutes research. Such an activity is, of course, nothing more than *fact finding* and *fact transcribing*. No amount of mere transfer of information from one place to another—even though the act of transportation is done with benefit of note card and is acknowledged by proper footnote form—

can be dignified by the term *research*. *Transfer of information, transportation of fact from one place to another are simply what their activities suggest, nothing more!* Yet, the strange misconception persists that fact-transferral is research; and, what is even more disconcerting, it is aided by the student's teachers and professors as the student moves through the eductional network from grade school to high school, high school to college, and from college to graduate school.

When, therefore, the student comes to graduate study and is faced with a first course in research methodology or a seminar in research design, such a student is usually completely unprepared for the unfamiliar demands of a radically new academic approach. Hence, many students have difficulty in fulfilling the exacting demands required for writing a thesis or producing an acceptable dissertation. In such circumstances, students may either give up in frustration or, after many attempts, write such a mediocre final document that the graduate committee capitulates, despairing of ever getting a piece of real research from such a student. Nor is there any pride nor satisfaction in this bitter experience. Such students have never been taught what research really is. Facts have been glorified as ends in themselves rather than as components of a total process of which the ultimate aim is to reveal new insights and comprehend their meaning in a larger context.

Now, having looked at what research is not, let us look at what research indeed *is*.

WHAT RESEARCH IS

What, then, *is* research? *Research is the manner in which we attempt to solve problems in a systematic effort to push back the frontiers of human ignorance or to confirm the validity of the solutions to problems others have presumably resolved.* Ultimately, research is a way of thinking. It is a way of looking at accumulated fact so that those data become meaningful in the total process of discovering new insights into unsolved problems and revealing new meanings. For those who have never processed data or pursued facts to fresh interpretations, research can be a highly exhilarating experience. Research is the thrill that comes with the making of a new discovery. We shall discuss research as a process that enlists the assistance of the scientific method in solving perplexing problems and resolving unanswered questions.

Characteristics of Research

Research has seven discrete characteristics. Every professional researcher is familiar with these which, taken together, comprise the particular approach to a problem-solving process called *research*.

1. *Research begins with a problem in the form of a question in the mind of the researcher.*[1] The human being is a curious animal. Everywhere we look, we see phenomena that arouse our curiosity, that cause us to wonder, to speculate, and to ask questions. By asking questions we strike the first spark of an inquisitive attitude that is a germinal prerequisite for research. An inquisitive mind is the beginning of research. So much there is that we do not know. The hope of mitigating our ignorance depends upon the questions we ask in the presence of the facts than can dispel that ignorance.

Look around you. Consider the unresolved situations which evoke the questions: "Why?" "What's the cause of that?" "What does it all mean?" Questions like these are the point at which research begins.

---

[1] See Fred N. Kerlinger, *Behavioral Research: A Conceptual Approach* (New York: Holt, Rinehart and Winston, 1979), p. 32: ". . . a scientific research problem is first a question, a sentence in interrogative form. Second, it is a question that usually asks something about the relations among the phenomena or variables. The answer to that question is sought in the research."

2. *Research demands the identification of a problem, stated in clear, unambiguous terms.* Successful research begins with a clear, simple statement of the problem that the researcher seeks to resolve. A question must crystallize at the very beginning of the research effort into a precise and grammatically complete statement setting forth exactly what the ultimate goal of the research is. The reason for this is obvious. We must see clearly at the outset what it is we are attempting to research. Research consists of a three-way triangle: the problem, the researcher, and the facts; and each of these components must be seen clearly and evaluated accurately in order for research to be fruitful and rewarding.

In a later chapter we shall say more about the problem, because the necessity for an unambiguous statement of the problem that the research aims to resolve cannot be overemphasized, nor too well be understood.

3. *Research requires a plan.* Researchers do not hope naively that somehow, in some way, they will discover fortuitously the facts that they need or the truth that they seek. Research is not aimless, undirected activity—merely "looking something up" in the hope that you may "come across" the solution to your problem. Research, rather, demands a definite aggressive plan. It means that your activity must have direction as the result of conscious planning and that the whole research effort must be governed by a purposive and overall design. Consider the title of this book, *Practical Research:Planning and Design*.

4. *Research deals with the main problem through appropriate subproblems.* The first step in planning research is to inspect the main problem for research in terms of its appropriate subproblems. Most researchable problems subsume other problems of lesser breadth and importance which, collectively, are component parts of the whole. The first step in thinking in the manner of a professional researcher is to recognize the subsidiary and integral components within the larger problem.

Because many researchers take neither the time nor the trouble to isolate the lesser problems within the major problem area, they find their research project becoming poorly defined, cumbersome, and unwieldy. From a design standpoint, therefore, it is expedient to divide the main problem into appropriate subproblems, all of which when resolved will result in the solution of the main research problem.

Note how a photographer deals with subproblems in solving a principal problem. He wants to take a picture. Can I capture this scene on film? That's the principal problem. But before he can answer this question, he must resolve three other questions integral to it: (1) Is there sufficient available light? (2) What is the "speed" of the film? (3) What is the "speed" of the lens? They are indeed *sub*problems to his main problem and he cannot resolve the main problem without answers to these several integral parts of which the main problem is composed.

5. *Research seeks direction through appropriate hypotheses and is based upon obvious assumptions.* Having stated the problem and the attendant subproblems, each of the subproblems is then viewed through a logical construct called a *hypothesis.* A hypothesis is a logical supposition, a reasonable guess, an educated conjecture which may give direction to your thinking with respect to the problem and thus aid in solving it.

Hypotheses are a part of everyday life. They represent the natural working of the human mind. Something happens. Immediately, you attempt to account for the event by a series of guesses. In so doing, you are hypothesizing. For example, you turn the key of your car. The starter grinds, but the car does not start. You are confronted with a problem: What's wrong? You now begin a series of reasonable conjectures as to the cause of the trouble. In other words, you hypothesize several possibilities: (1) You have no gasoline in the tank. (2) The spark plugs are worn out. (3) Moisture has condensed in the distributor, causing the electrical system to short-circuit.

Each of these hypotheses *provides a direction for solving the problem*. At this point, you go in search of the facts. You check the fuel tank; it is half full of gasoline. That rules out hypothesis 1. The motor has just been reconditioned and new plugs have been installed. That invalidates hypothesis 2. As you glance out of the window of your car, you note that other automobiles have condensation on them from the humidity and an early morning fog. Hypothesis 3 may lead you to the solution of the problem. To test this hypothesis, you remove the distributor cap, wipe out the moisture that indeed has collected there, and replace it. The car starts. Hypothesis 3 is supported.

Similarly, when you are faced with a problem for research, you make educated guesses to assist you in discovering the solution and to give you direction in looking for the facts.

A distinction should be made here between a hypothesis and an *assumption.* Hypotheses are conjectural suppositions, held in abeyance to determine their validity or invalidity until the facts are available and their interpretation has been made. Ultimately, the facts will either support or fail to support a hypothesis.

An assumption, on the other hand, *is a condition which is taken for granted and without which the research effort would be impossible.* Here is an educational situation. Students are beginning the study of algebra. The question (problem) is: If students are given daily encouragement, will they achieve better than those who are not given such encouragement? Achievement is to be measured by a pre- and post-test evaluation. We may *hypothesize* that such encouragement will produce increased mathematical achievement. We *assume* that the teacher who is teaching the group is capable of giving encouragement to some students and to refrain from giving encouragement to others—that he or she can be totally objective in this aspect of teaching. If the teacher is not able to do this, then the whole basic proposition upon which the research rests is lacking and the research project cannot be effected. *Assumptions are self-evident conditions inherent to the research situation without which the entire research process is nullified.* Assumptions are usually *so* self-evident that many times we consider it unnecessary to mention them; but careful researchers usually do, so that those inspecting the research procedure may see every component within that process and evaluate it accordingly.

6. *Research deals with facts and their meaning.* Having now isolated the problem, subdivided it into appropriate subproblems, posited hypotheses which suggest the direction in which the facts may lie, and recognized the assumptions underlying the entire research project, the next step is to collect whatever facts seem to be appropriate to the problem and to *organize* them into meaningful aggregates, so that they can be *interpreted.* We shall suggest methods of such organization in a later chapter.

Facts, events, happenings, and observations are themselves merely facts, events, happenings, and observations—nothing more. But they are *potentially* meaningful. *The significance of the data depends upon the way in which the facts are regarded.* Different researchers frequently derive entirely different meanings from the same set of data. And, for the researcher, no single rule will guide unerringly to any "correct" interpretation. Two historians study the same series of events. Each is equally competent, both scrupulously honest in their reactions. One reads the meaning of the facts of history one way; the other, viewing precisely the same facts, arrives at an entirely different interpretation. Which one is right? Perhaps both are, or perhaps neither is. And both may have, perhaps, merely posed new problems for future researchers to resolve.

Time was when we considered that clocks measured time and yardsticks measured space, and in one sense they do. We further assumed that time and space were two separate entities. Now we regard both of these factors within a time-space continuum concept. The facts of time and space have not changed. The difference between the earlier and the later concepts is the difference in *the interpretation of the facts.* All research, sooner or later, must arrive at the point where the facts must be made meaningful, and that takes place within the mind of the researcher. It is precisely at this point where all the activities outlined in the opening paragraphs of this chapter fail as fulfilling the requirements of research. None of them demands that the researcher *interpret* any data. Fact-finding and fact-transferral are *not* research; research begins when the researcher reads meaning from the accumulated facts and interprets from the data their message with respect to the problem which initiated the research in the first place.

7. *Research is circular.* The research cycle begins simply: a questioning mind faces a problem situation. To see the target clearly, the researcher isolates and articulates the *central problem.* The central problem is then further divided into subproblems, each of which is an integral part of the principal problem. What we have been calling the "environment out of which the researchable problem arises" is more appropriately called the *research universe,*[2] and it is potentially fact-laden. The researcher seeks from within the universe for those particular facts that seem to be pertinent to the solution of the problem and its attendant subproblems. The search is facilitated by the construction of tentative hypotheses because they point in the direction of relevant facts. The collected facts are organized, analyzed, and interpreted for the purpose of discovering what they mean in terms of the problem. This facilitates the solution of the problem, which satisfies the question that gave rise to the research effort originally. Thus, the cycle is completed. Such is the format of all basic research.

Schematically, the "circle of research" is represented by the diagram on page 8. In a truer sense, this circle might be considered more like a helix than as a circle. Research always gives rise to further unexplored questions. In the helical conception, the solution of the research problem begets still other problems, and thus research becomes a spiral continuing progressively onward. To view research in this way is to invest it with a dynamic quality that is its true nature—a far cry from the common view of research as a one-time act, static, self-contained, and as an end in itself. Every researcher soon learns that research creates more problems than it resolves. Such is the nature of research.

Practical Application ------------------------------------

We learn to do by doing. This book is more than a theoretical discussion of research and its methodology. You become a researcher by the practical application of those principles which form the basis of discussion. Following each major discussion area, you will have an opportunity to turn to the practicum section where you will have an assignment applying those principles which were discussed in the text section of the book. We have been discussing what research is—and what it is not. At this point, you should be able to recognize genuine research when you see it, and also what is not research but masquerades as research. Turn to page 283 where you will find a practical application unit which will give you directions for surveying some research studies and evaluating them in terms of the guidelines suggested in this chapter.

Throughout the book, you will be alerted to the practical applications in the Research Practicum Section by the heading "Practical Application" followed by a dotted line leading to a characteristic wide band of gray screening down the right margin of the text.

----

[2] The term *universe* means simply an "area surrounding the problem which may contain facts relevant to the problem." Literally, the word suggests the factual area that lies, or "turns," around the central inquiry or main problem of the research. The word comes from *uni-*, one, and *vertere,* to turn: that which revolves or turns about one central inquiry.

THE RESEARCH PROCESS IS CYCLICAL

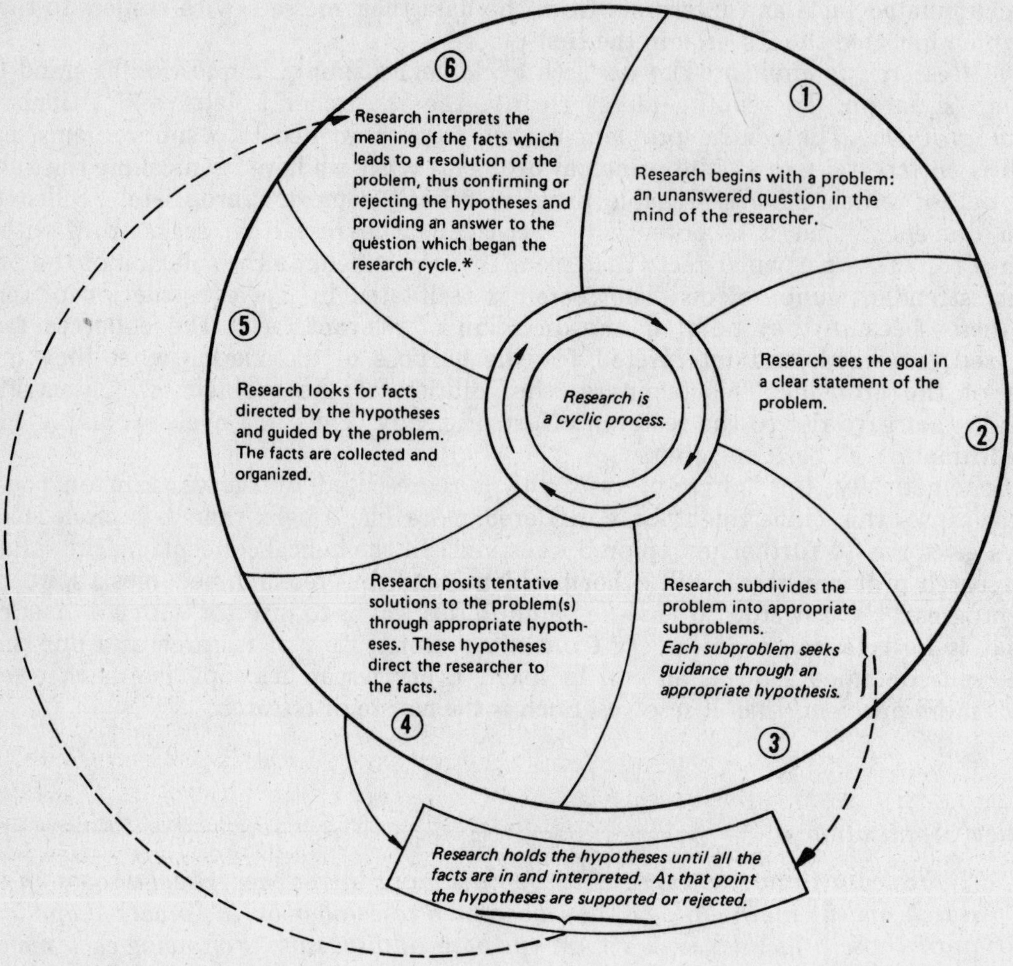

Research is a cyclic process.

(1) Research begins with a problem: an unanswered question in the mind of the researcher.

(2) Research sees the goal in a clear statement of the problem.

(3) Research subdivides the problem into appropriate subproblems. *Each subproblem seeks guidance through an appropriate hypothesis.*

(4) Research posits tentative solutions to the problem(s) through appropriate hypotheses. These hypotheses direct the researcher to the facts.

Research holds the hypotheses until all the facts are in and interpreted. At that point the hypotheses are supported or rejected.

(5) Research looks for facts directed by the hypotheses and guided by the problem. The facts are collected and organized.

(6) Research interprets the meaning of the facts which leads to a resolution of the problem, thus confirming or rejecting the hypotheses and providing an answer to the question which began the research cycle.*

*Frequently the resolution of one research problem gives rise to new questions and further research problems that, for their resolution, demand a repeat of the research cycle. This makes a *helical* concept of the research process perhaps more realistic than a cyclical one.

Perhaps the model we have just presented is an oversimplification of the research process. Some years ago a group of researchers at the Bell Laboratories at Murray Hill, New Jersey, wrote an article, "Computers and Research," which appeared in *Science* and, in connection with which, they presented perhaps a more realistic diagram detailing the complexity characteristic of the modern research process.[3] Here is the diagram. Study it carefully. It shows the human as well as the technological and environmental contributions to the research process.

[3] W. O. Baker, W. S. Brown, M. V. Matthews, S. P. Morgan, H. O. Pollak, R. C. Prim, and S. Sternberg, "Computers and Research," *Science*, 195 (March 18, 1977), 1135.

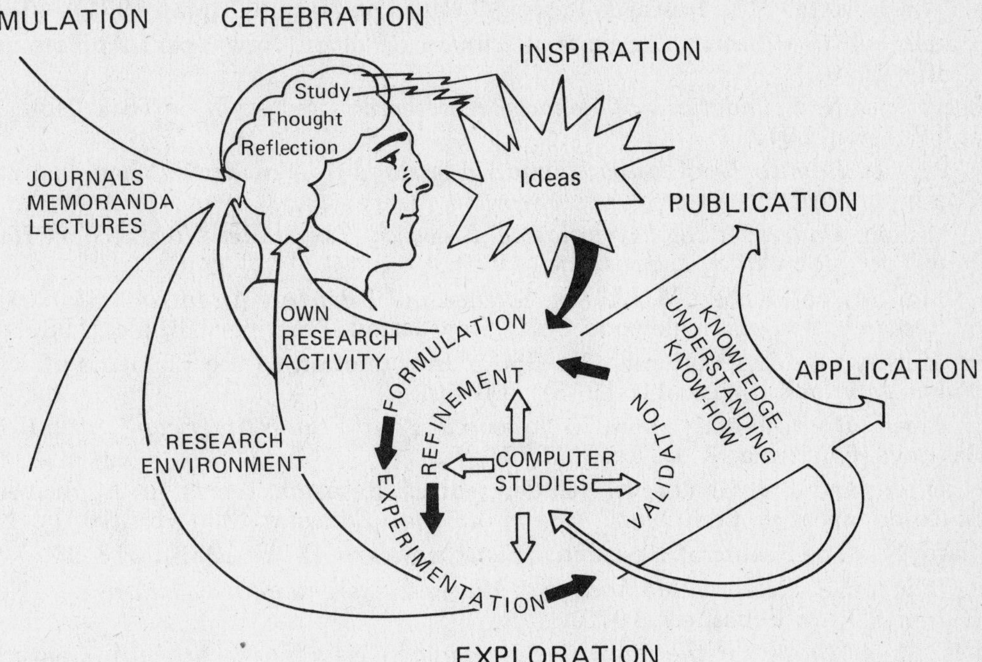

FOR FURTHER READING

The items suggested in these end-of-chapter sections are not, in the strict sense, a bibliography. They are rather a carefully assembled group of "further readings" that relate to topics discussed within each chapter. No text can be all-inclusive; no book so expository but that it leaves some questions unanswered, some topics unexplained. For those who would go further, these references may afford some guidance. They are also selected from a broad spectrum of academic disciplines; for with research, the *principles* of investigational study do not change—each discipline merely *applies those principles* to suit its own particular emphasis.

Barzun, Jacques, and Henry Graff. *The Modern Researcher.* 3rd ed. New York: Harcourt, Brace Jovanovich, Inc., 1977.

Beveredge, I. B. *Seeds of Discovery: A Sequel to the Art of Scientific Investigation.* New York: W. W. Norton & Company. 1980.

Campbell, H. M. "Some Common Sense Suggestions for Nurses New at the Research Game." *Canadian Nurse* 77 (November 1981): 32–33.

Chapanis, Alphonse R. E. *Research Techniques in Human Engineering.* Baltimore, Maryland: The Johns Hopkins University Press, 1959.

Dagsland, H. "Learning to Undertake Research: A Personal View of the Problems Involved." *International Nursing Review* (October 1959): 43–45.

Davitz, Joel R., and Lois Jean Davitz. *A Guide for Evaluating Research Plans in Psychology and Education.* New York: Teachers College Press, Columbia University Teachers College, 1967.

Festinger, Leon, and Daniel Katz, eds. *Research Methods in the Behavioral Sciences.* New York: Holt, Rinehart and Winston, 1966.

Fox, James H. "Criteria of Good Research." *Phi Delta Kappa* 39 (March 1958): 284–86.

Franklin, Billy J., and Harold W. Osborne. *Research Methods: Issues and Insights.* Belmont, California: Wadsworth Publishing Co., Inc., 1971.

Heidgerken, Lovetta. "The Research Process." *Canadian Nurse* 67 (May 1971): 40–43.

Helmstadter, G. C. *Research Concepts in Human Behavior.* New York: Appleton-Century-Crofts, 1970.

Kerlinger, Fred N. *Foundations of Behavioral Research.* 2nd ed. New York: Holt, Rinehart and Winston, 1973.

Leedy, Paul D. *How to Read Research and Understand It.* New York: Macmillan Publishing Co., Inc., 1981.

Lewin, Miriam. *Understanding Psychological Research: The Student Researcher's Handbook.* New York: John Wiley & Sons, Inc., 1979.

Neale, John, M., and Robert M. Liebert. *Science and Behavior: An Introduction to Methods of Research.* 2nd ed. Englewood Cliffs, New Jersey: Prentice-Hall, Inc., 1980.

Nelson, Kathryn J., and Catherine N. Graf. "Introduction to the Elements of Research." *Nursing Outlook* (September 1955): 500–502.

Reed, Robert D. *How and Where to Research Your Ethnic-American Cultural Heritage.* Saratoga, California: R. D. Reed, 1979.

Stacks, D. W., and J. J. Ghalfa, Jr. "Undergraduate Research Team: An Applied Approach to Communication Education." *Communication Education* 30 (April 1981): 180–83.

Uprichard, M. "The Nature of Research." *Canadian Nurse* (April 1959): 318–20.

Walizer, Michael H. *Research Methods and Analysis: Searching for Relationships.* New York: Harper & Row, Publishers, 1978.

Wandelt, M. A. *Guide for the Beginning Researcher.* New York: Appleton-Century-Crofts, 1970.

Wilson, Edgar B. *An Introduction to Scientific Research.* New York: McGraw-Hill Book Company, 1952.

For Your Notes and Comments

READ THIS—BEFORE YOU READ THIS CHAPTER

Just as a carpenter needs a hammer and a saw, a dentist a drill, an architect a T square and a compass, so the research worker needs certain "tools" to accomplish the purpose of a research project. Perhaps what we shall mention as "tools" in this chapter are not generally regarded as such in the conventional sense of the word, but without them the researcher could not accomplish the goal of the research itself. In that sense, whatever is needed to do the job may be considered a tool — an intermediary instrument for facilitating the ultimate goal of the research.

In this chapter, we shall discuss the role of the library, that of statistics, of the computer, and of measurement as tools of research. With all of these instruments the researcher should be familiar. Learn their possibilities and characteristics.

Obviously, in this chapter, we cannot discuss any of these tools except in the most generalized terms. The chapter is but an introduction to the tools needed for research. At the end of the chapter, the bibliography will direct you to more detailed reading for each of them.

2
The Tools of Research

Research, as we have pointed out in the preceding chapter, is simply a *systematic quest for undiscovered truth.* In pursuit of that goal, however, the researcher frequently needs to enlist the aid of ancillary areas. These areas are peripheral to the research endeavor itself, but facility with and a knowledge of the resources available to the researcher expedite the means by which a research endeavor may be conducted. The skills and competencies which the researcher has in such ancillary areas of knowledge are called *tools of research.* These are commonly grouped into five categories: *(1) bibliothecal* or *library tools, (2) measurement as a tool of research, (3) statistical tools, (4) the computer as a tool of research,* and *(5) language as a research tool.* In this chapter we shall discuss the first four of these tools.

Every researcher needs facts, some of which lie in already published documents. Have you, therefore, the independence and the necessary skills to use the library efficiently? Do you know where and how to locate necessary information without wasting time? Do you know the basic references that will aid you in weaving your way expertly through the maze of related literature and important documents in which the resolution of your problem may lie buried?

Many research problems deal with quantitative data. Do you have command of statistics so that you may apply appropriate statistical methods to the analysis of your data as a part of the interpretation of their meaning?

The researcher needs measurement techniques. Measurement is necessary to convert data from the normal state in which it comes to the researcher to a quantified concept so that it may be statistically interpreted. Statistics and measurement are, therefore, closely related as tools of research. In the physical and biological sciences, measurement can be reasonably objective and accurate. In the social sciences, humanities, communication, education, and allied areas, measurement of the data is more difficult, more subjective, more susceptible to varied interpretation. There is a vast difference between a physicist measuring the wavelength of spectral light and a psychometrist attempting to measure the anxiety level of a human being.

We live in an age of computerization. Researchers need to know what computers can and cannot do. They need to be aware of the means of handling and processing data in a world of information explosion.

Do you read with ease and understanding languages in which data indispensable to the prosecution of your research project are found?

Although we have mentioned them separately, the tools of research are intimately interrelated. Unlike a craftsman who finds in a kit the one specific tool that is needed to do the job, the researcher may soon realize that the solution of the research problem depends upon the assistance of one, two, three, or perhaps all of the tools which we have just mentioned.

Obviously, a manual such as this cannot cover in depth a discussion of any one of these tools. There are many appropriate texts which give adequate help in each of the areas. Certain broad guidelines for all researchers can, however, be presented which may clarify for those who need an elementary introduction to some of the essential aspects of tool-of-research areas.

THE LIBRARY : THE FIRST TOOL OF RESEARCH

You should be self-sufficient in the library. You should know its principal resources, understand its classification systems, and be able to find the shortest route to the information that it contains. One rule is basic: *You learn to use the library by using it.* Nothing will take the place of actual hours of exploration spent in the library getting acquainted at first hand with its particular characteristics and the nature of its holdings. Every library is different. Each has its own emphases; its own personality. There are, however, some practical suggestions which will aid you in achieving facility in the use of the library.

Know Your Way Around

The first requirement in using any library is to know its layout. When you go into an unfamiliar library, you should explore it quickly from end to end. This is absolutely essential to a later and more detailed knowledge of its resources.

Some libraries have manuals which will give you this information; and these are available to students upon request, usually at the circulation desk. If there is no such guide, draw your own plan. Learn where the various holdings are located. Indicate on your sketch the location of special collections; the reference section; the location of microfilm and microfiche reels, cards, and readers; the audiovisual materials; the periodicals section; the vertical file; and the areas of the stacks and the reference room where books in the field of your special interest may be found.

Learn to Use the Card Catalog

The card catalog is the heart of the library. It is the principal means of locating its holdings. The catalog is a series of drawers containing 3 X 5-inch index cards on which are found the location and a description of all items that the library contains. As a general index to library resources, the card catalog will alert you to the various kinds of materials available: books, films, film strips, tapes, phonograph records, microfilm, microfiche, microprint, maps, pictures, slides, and similar materials. Frequently, major topics within collected or edited works are indicated in the catalog by special cards, called *author analytical cards* or *title analytical cards.* Thus, if a play by Maxwell Anderson is one of the plays in a collection entitled *Modern American Drama,* it may be indicated by a card cataloged under "Anderson, Maxwell." If a major section of a volume entitled *Great Cathedrals of Western Europe* is given to a discussion of Chartres Cathedral, that fact may be separately indicated by a card in the catalog under "Chartres, Cathedral of," which would refer you to the composite work.

★ *Rules for catalog arrangement.* In most libraries, the cards will be arranged alphabetically by author, subject, and title, but certain rules of precedence within the alphabetical framework are observed by librarians in placing the cards in the catalog. To know the simple rules of precedence is to be able to use the catalog with least loss of time and with greatest efficiency.

Briefly, these rules are: (1) Books *by* a person precede books *about* a person; (2) Collected works usually precede individual works; (3) When the same word is common to (a) a person, (b) a place, or (c) a thing (or the title of a thing), the cards will be arranged in that order; for example:

Lincoln, Abraham (person) precedes cards dealing with
Lincoln, Nebraska (place) which cards precede those relating to
Lincoln Warehouse Corporation (thing)

(4) Saints, popes, kings and others are also arranged in that order of precedence. For example:

John, the Evangelist, Saint, precedes cards relating to
John, Paul II, Pope, which cards precede those relating to

John, King of England, which cards precede those dealing with
John of Gaunt, Duke of Lancaster, whose cards precede those of
John, Henry E. (author) whose cards precede the cards of
John Ericsson Society, The (society, i.e., thing)

(5) When two persons with the same name are listed, the one with the earlier birth date takes precedence over the one with the later birth date:

Girard, Stephen (1750-1831) takes precedence over
Girard, Stephen (1843-1910).

Knowledge of these simple rules of arrangement will save a great deal of time, so that you need not thumb through scores of cards, each of which bears a similar heading. Furthermore, knowing what to look for on a card will save you both time and effort. Rather than taking the trouble to procure the book itself in order to learn its contents, you can find the book and its contents described in the card catalog.

For example: on page 16 is a typical catalog card. It has six separate levels of information. Each of these levels presents certain data that are important for an understanding of the book and for giving a preview of its contents.

Perhaps one of the most important features of the catalog card is the classification symbol, found in the upper left-hand corner of the card. This symbol, known as the *call number*, indicates where the book will be found in the library stacks and the type of material it contains. The call number will belong to one of two systems used in classifying the resources of a library: the *Dewey Decimal Classification System* or the *Library of Congress Classification System*. Each of these will be discussed briefly.

★ *The Dewey Decimal Classification System.* Because the Dewey Decimal Classification System is more widely used than the Library of Congress System, it will be discussed here in greater detail. The Dewey Decimal System is used, for example, in practically all school libraries, in most of the public libraries, and in a considerable number of the college libraries in the United States. [1] Elsewhere in the world, the Dewey Decimal classification is followed by a majority of libraries in the English-speaking world. In addition, it is perhaps the most important single system worldwide and is used in almost every nation of the globe.[2]

The system was conceived in 1873 by young Melvil Dewey, when he was a student at Amherst College. He divided all human knowledge into ten major categories as follows:

000 General works	500 Pure science
100 Philosophy	600 Technology, applied science, useful arts
200 Religion	700 The arts
300 Social sciences	800 Literature, belles lettres
400 Language	900 History, biography

Every student should know these ten categories. They are a part of his basic knowledge as a researcher, and he will use this information every time he enters a library or consults a card catalog using the Dewey Decimal Classification System.

The system progresses from the preceding ten general classification categories to more and more precise subclassifications, based on a decade arrangement. Each of the above ten

---

[1] Thelma Eaton, *Cataloging and Classification: An Introductory Manual.* Third edition (Champaign, Ill.: The Illinois Union Bookstore, 1963), p. 65.

[2] Melvil Dewey, *Dewey Decimal Classification and Relative Index.* Ninth abridged edition (Lake Placid Club, N.Y.: Lake Placid Club Educational Foundation, 1965), p. 7.

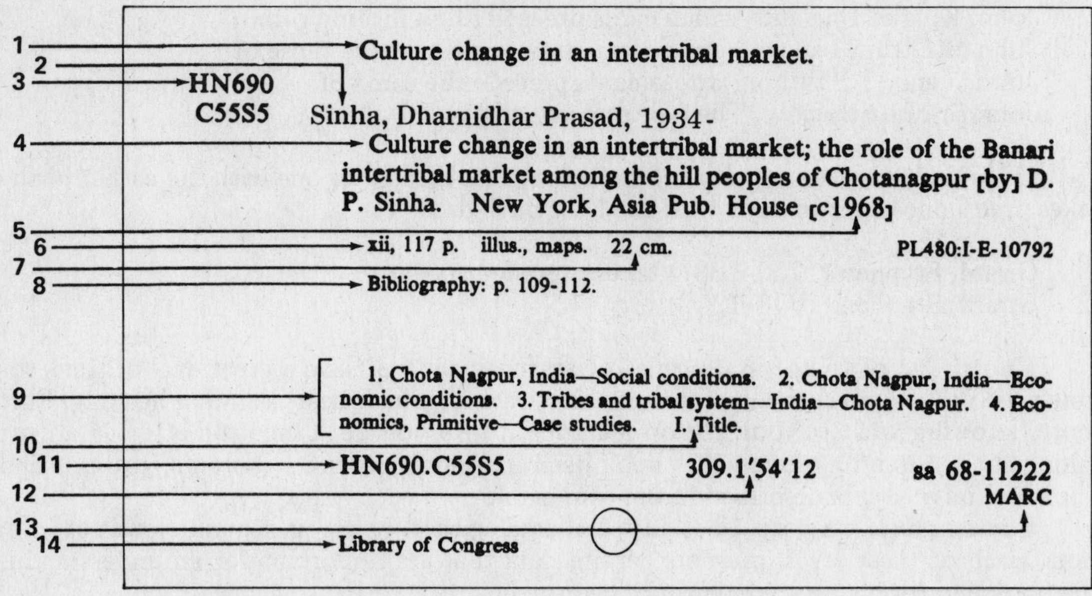

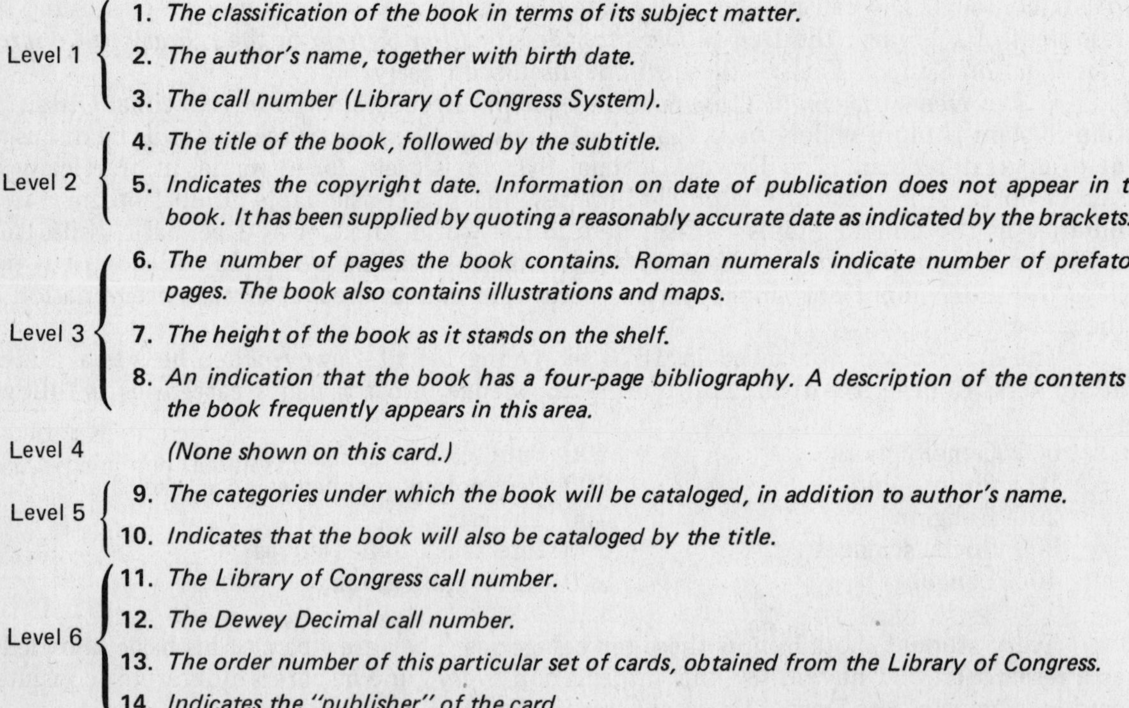
The items which are numbered in the left column are as follows:

Level 1
1. *The classification of the book in terms of its subject matter.*
2. *The author's name, together with birth date.*
3. *The call number (Library of Congress System).*

Level 2
4. *The title of the book, followed by the subtitle.*
5. *Indicates the copyright date. Information on date of publication does not appear in the book. It has been supplied by quoting a reasonably accurate date as indicated by the brackets.*

Level 3
6. *The number of pages the book contains. Roman numerals indicate number of prefatory pages. The book also contains illustrations and maps.*
7. *The height of the book as it stands on the shelf.*
8. *An indication that the book has a four-page bibliography. A description of the contents of the book frequently appears in this area.*

Level 4
(None shown on this card.)

Level 5
9. *The categories under which the book will be cataloged, in addition to author's name.*
10. *Indicates that the book will also be cataloged by the title.*

Level 6
11. *The Library of Congress call number.*
12. *The Dewey Decimal call number.*
13. *The order number of this particular set of cards, obtained from the Library of Congress.*
14. *Indicates the "publisher" of the card.*

categories is again divided into ten subcategories, thus providing 100 slots into which books may be classified. Each of these 100 slots is again divided into ten further classification areas. That makes 1,000 subdivisions. Usually this three-digit thousand category is followed by a decimal point, after which the subdividing continues into tens and hundreds of thousands, and even millions of classes.

★ *The Library of Congress Classification System.* The second classification system which is in general use, particularly in the larger libraries, is the Library of Congress Classification System. Instead of a numerical category classification, the Library of Congress system employs letter designations for the various knowledge areas as follows:

A	General works: polygraphy	L	Education
B	Philosophy, religion	M	Music
C	History: auxiliary sciences	N	Fine arts
D	History: general and Old World; topography	P	Philology and literature
		Q	Science
E-F	History: America	R	Medicine
G	Geography, anthropology, folklore	S	Agriculture
		T	Technology
H	Social sciences	U	Military science
J	Political science	V	Naval science
K	Law	Z	Bibliography and library science

The usual approach to instruction in the use of the library is to overwhelm the student with a multitude of titles in the hope that merely by mentioning them, the student may become aware that such works exist. Merely to list title after title is an exercise in futility. The research student needs to know where to go to discover a master key that will unlock the total resources available in the shortest period of time. Many research students are like the man who died a pauper but who lived in a house in which was hidden a treasure. They have the riches of the informational world at their fingertips but do not know how to uncover that wealth. There is no informational need that cannot be met by some bibliographical tool.

Keys to the Treasury of Printed Knowledge

Eight keys will unlock for you the treasury of printed knowledge. These are master guides to the basic reference literature of the world. Every researcher, though he or she may not have a library, should have a shelf of books with several of these eight books upon it. Go into your library — in the 000–099 category of the Dewey decimal classification system or the Z classification of the Library of Congress system — to explore the eight titles below. Most libraries will have them. You should be intimately acquainted with the format, the content, and the specific purpose of each of the following titles:

Burke, Arvid J., and Mary A. Burke. *Documentation in Education.* New York: Teachers College Press, Columbia University, 1967.

Hillard, James M. *Where to Find What.* Metuchen, N. J.: The Scarecrow Press, Inc., 1975.

Murphey, Robert W. *How and Where to Look It Up.* New York: McGraw-Hill Book Company, 1958.

Prakken, Sarah L., F. J. Sypher, and Jack A. Clark, eds. *The Reader's Adviser: A Layman's Guide to Literature.* 3 vols., 12th ed. New York: R. R. Bowker Company, 1977.

Sheehy, Eugene P., ed. *Guide to Reference Books.* 9th ed. Chicago, Ill.: American Library Association, 1976, and *Supplement*, 1980.

Walford, Albert J. *Guide to Reference Material.* 3 vols, 3rd ed. London: The Library Association, 1981.

Walsh, John J., ed. *Guide to Microforms in Print.* Westport, Conn.: Microform Review, Inc. 1977.

Wynar, Bohdan S., ed. *American Reference Books Annual.* Littleton, Col.: Libraries Limited Inc. Issued annually.

These titles will be a beginning. In the chapter entitled "The Review of the Related Literature," still further resources of a bibliothecal nature are mentioned. Every student of a particular academic discipline should go to the library and, in the reference library, among the reference books relating to the student's particular discipline will be bibliographical titles which will be particularly applicable in locating literature within that discipline.

Practical Application ———————————————————————

Turn to the Practicum in Research Section, Project 2, page 285. There you will be given the opportunity to apply what you have been reading about in these pages.

———————————————————————————

When you began reading this section, you noticed the heading of the section as "The Library: The First Tool of Research." That was a very considered designation because, after researchers select a problem for their research effort, the library is the first place to which they go to clarify the dimensions of the problem. It is in the library that they are able to learn what others have done in the area of the problem or in corollary investigations. It is in the library that they are able to receive ideas which help them to sharpen the focus of their research effort. The library, indeed, is the *first* tool that the researcher uses when a course of research action is decided upon.

After having reviewed briefly the use of the library, we turn to the matter of measurement which is logically the *second* tool which the researcher employs in undertaking the research project.

MEASUREMENT AS A TOOL OF RESEARCH: THE SECOND TOOL OF RESEARCH

An old adage in research and measurement runs to the effect that if it exists, then it is measurable. In fact, if it is to be researchable, then it *must* be measurable. Data must be quantified and evaluated against a standard of one kind or another, or the data are useless to the researcher.

What, then, do we mean by *measurement? Measurement is the quantifying of any phenomenon, substantial or insubstantial, and involves a comparison with a standard.* Let's look at that definition. It may be expressing an idea which is somewhat unconventional and differing in some respects from the familiar process which we exercise in the everyday world under the generic term of *measurement.* We shall take the definition segmentally.

Measurement is the quantifying of any phenomenon. The first word that gives some difficulty is *quantifying.* The word comes from *quantum,* meaning *how much, how many, to what degree.* The researcher thinks of the world around and its manifestations through data observed in terms of adjectives and adverbs. Open to the researcher is a whole range of "how-much, how-many, and to-what-degree" scales. But ultimately these must result in a mathematical value or the equivalent of a mathematical value. Note that we did not say a *numerical* value. Although what is mathematical is frequently numerical, the two terms need fine-tuning discrimination to distinguish one from the other. Mathematical means—from the root of the word—"having to do with more *knowledge* of the thing." Numerical, on the other hand, derives from a base meaning which relates to "expressing a fact in digits"—*numerals.*

The definition continues: "... *substantial or insubstantial.*" Measurements may be of *things*—those objects that are *substantial.* An engineer measures the span of a bridge; a chemist, the weight of a compound both before and after removing a gas or water vapor from it; a Greek philosopher, the length of two shadows cast at the sites of two cities on the identical day of the year to arrive at a figure which indicates the circumference of the earth. These are the quantification of *substantial* phenomena. But, we may also measure those things that are *insubstantial*—that exist only as concepts, as ideas: opinions on national issues, the status of American business, and the evaluation of the quality of an individual's mental processes. These things—if "things" they be—find measurement in such forms as the Gallup Opinion Survey, the Dow Jones Index, and the I.Q. Researchers repeatedly measure life's intangibles, those elusive incorporealities which we cannot capture in substantial form yet which nevertheless exist as truly as a bridge span, a chemical compound, or a shadow upon the earth.

How, for example, do we measure interpersonal likes and dislikes or analyze the attractions or rejections among a given group of individuals? Nothing could be probably more subjective, more insubstantial to "measure." Sociologists evaluate such intragroup and interpersonal dynamics by means of a *sociogram.* A sociogram is a diagram, based upon the choices or expressions of acceptance and rejection which the various members of the group make with respect to each of the other members of the group. Here are a group of nine individuals: Alfred, Bob, Charles, Don, Ernest, Fred, Gordon, Harry and Iz. What are their feelings for each other? If left to gravitate freely toward each other, what constellations of individuals would result? Who would be rejected? Who would be the most popular in such a group; who the least so? Within such a group, personal dynamics of positive and negative feelings are omnipresent. How do we measure these? One way, as we have said, is by means of a *sociogram.*

Below is a sociogram of such a group.[3]

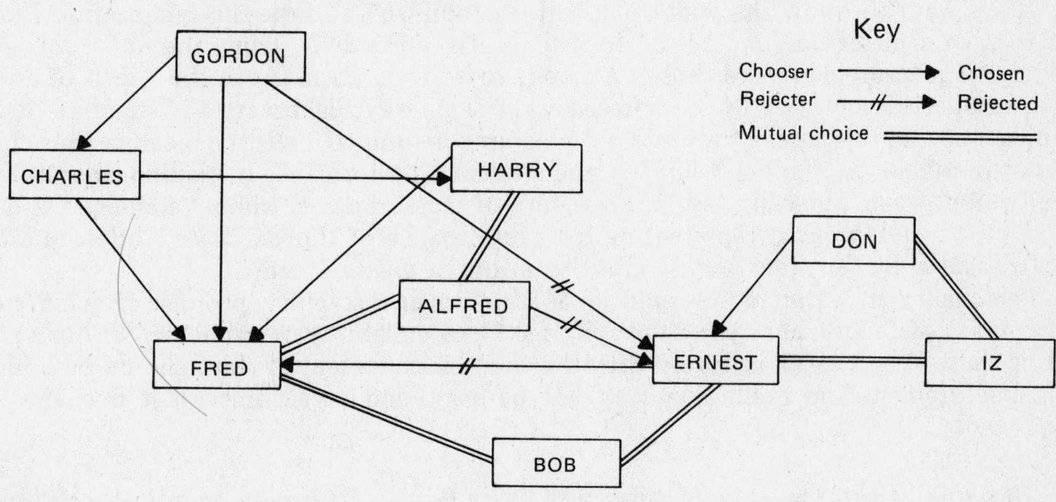

[3] Alvin Gouldner, and Helen P. Gouldner, *Modern Sociology: An Introduction to the Study of Human Interaction* (New York: Harcourt, Brace and World, Inc., 1963), p. 354.

In analyzing the above representation of the group, certain important facts begin to emerge. These, the authors point out as follows:

1. Fred is the informal or popular leader (sometimes called the star) of the group, receiving 5 choices and 1 rejection.
2. There is probably some schism and tension in this group. Note that Ernest, Don, and Iz form a subclique, or "island" which is separated from the larger clique that Fred leads. The "go-between" is Bob, who has mutual choices with both Fred and Ernest.
3. There are a number of friendship pairs which may lend cohesion to the group. Note the mutual choices of Harry and Alfred, Ernest and Bob, Fred and Bob, Don and Iz, Alfred and Fred.
4. Gordon is the isolate of the group. He received no choices; he is neither liked nor disliked. In such a position he is probably the least influential of any member of the group.

Research employing the sociogram as the basis of selection of compatible partners includes the selection of compatible flying partners in the Army Air Force flying school;[4] and in industry, workers have been placed in teams on the basis of sociometric choice with the result of increased job satisfaction and lower turnover.[5]

Thus, we are beginning to see how such abstract realities as public opinion, intelligence, and group dynamics can be "measured." Take one further example. Later in this book, we demonstrate how such an insubstantial abstraction as a personal habit can be "weighed" on an inventory "scale" to reveal the desirability or undesirability of one's reading habits. You may wish, at this point in your reading, to turn to page 145 to study the author's Reading Habit Inventory and to see how such an abstraction as a reading habit can be weighed and analyzed in terms of reading techniques, as well as the visual, and emotional factors in reading.

Now, let us look at the last part of the definition: "*. . . and involves comparison with a standard.*" Measurement, whether with a foot rule or a standardized test involves (1) the thing, the factor, the quality to be measured, and (2) the unit of measurement which is employed to evaluate it.

If we want to know the width of the desk upon which I type this manuscript, I take a foot rule, or a meter bar, and lay it along the edge of the desk. Thing and unit—object and standard of measurement—are thus compared. If we want to measure the width of a wavelength of spectral light, we do it in precisely the same way: light wave and standard of measurement; not, in this case, a foot rule but an angstrom unit. If I wish to measure the achievement of a student in reading, I employ the student's performance in reading (the "thing to be measured") and a reading test (the standard of measurement) whose "standard" is determined by the *test norms,* representing the performance of thousands of student performances measured by the same test. Such is the nature of measurement.

Personality traits, prejudice, emotional stability or instability, promise of achievement or prognosis of failure, ability in exercising a skill, or amiability or animosity within a group unit: if these things exist, as surely they do, then measurement of them should be possible. Such measurement and evaluation may not be easy, and to accomplish it may involve a

---

[4] Leslie D. Zeleny, "Selection of Compatible Flying Partners," *American Journal of Sociology,* LII (1947), pp. 424-431.

[5] Raymond H. Van Zelst, "Validation of a Sociometric Regrouping Procedure," *Journal of Abnormal and Social Psychology,* XLVII (1952), pp. 299-301.

great deal of ingenuity upon the part of the researcher; but if anything exists, it can be measured. A search of the literature in any one problem area may turn up some very ingenious ways in which other researchers, working on related problems to yours, have solved their measurement difficulties. Such studies may provide valuable guidance for you and suggest important means of departure.

How Data Are Measured

In 1946, S. S. Stevens[6] suggested a heirarchy of levels of measurement for data which has been widely adopted by statisticians and researchers as a means of classifying data. Steven's system enlists four types of "measurement" which he calls, severally, *nominal* measurement, *ordinal* measurement, *interval* measurement, and *ratio* measurement.

Basic to all measurement, however, is the essential nature of the data. Data by their very nature, lend themselves to measurement at one level or another according to their characteristics and the manner in which they are considered and classified for analysis. We shall consider each level and its characteristics.

★ *Nominal level of measurement.* The word *nominal* comes from the Latin word, *nomen*, meaning "a name." Hence, we can "measure" data by assigning to them a name. For example, we have a group of children. These we can measure by grouping them into categories or groups (e.g., two groups: girls and boys.) Nominal measurement of the data is elemental—crude and unrefined, to be sure—but it does divide the group into so many girls and so many boys. Every child in the room also has a name and is thus quantified into a class of one. We have Irene and Paul, Kathy and Tom: four individuals of one unit each. Furthermore, the class may meet in Room 12 of the Willowbrook School. By assigning the room a number, we have provided it with a "name" even though that name may, in fact, be a numeral. It should be understood, however, that the number has no quantitive meaning. Room 12, for example, is not bigger, or better, or superior to Room 11, or inferior to Room 13. The numeral is merely a qualitative, or *nominal* (i.e., providing a *name*) designation.

Nominal data may be represented by certain graphic and statistical devices. Bar graphs, for example, are appropriate to represent nominal data.

Class Composition
Sixth Grade, Willowbrook School

Statistically, such a "measurement" of the class will permit us to locate the *mode* to compute the *percentage* of girls and boys with relation to the entire class. The *chi square* can also be computed from nominal data. These concepts we shall discuss later.

★ *Ordinal level of measurement.* In an *ordinal scale of measurement*, we think in terms of the symbols $>$ or $<$. The ordinal scale implies that an object or entity being measured is quantified in terms of being of either a higher or lower, greater or lesser *order* than a comparative entity.

[6] S. S. Stevens, "On the Theory of Scales of Measurement," *Science*, 684 (1946), pp. 677-80.

In measuring on the ordinal scale, there is always an asymmetrical relationship: something is greater than, lesser than, older than, younger than, more desirable than — and we could go on *ad infinitum* — something else. We measure level of education grossly on an ordinal scale by assigning individuals to one of the following categories: unschooled, or having an elementary, high school, college, graduate school, or professional school education. Likewise, we measure a segment of the work force on an ordinal scale by grouping them in one of the following categories: unskilled, semi-skilled, skilled, or master craftsman.

The ordinal scale also expands the range of statistical techniques which may be applied to the data. Using the ordinal scale we may find the mode, the median, determine the percentage or percentile rank, and test by the chi square. We may also indicate relationships by means of rank correlation.

★ *Interval level of measurement.* With interval measurement we introduce for the first time a scale that measures by means of a *basic, standard interval.* An inch, a foot, a mile, a pound, a year — these are all basic, *standard* measures of length, weight, or time. And because it is a standard interval, we can use it as a basis for comparison. One line is two inches longer than another, an object is four pounds heavier, or a person is three years older than another person. Interval data deals with the dimensions of more or less as these situations are determined by applying to the data a standard scale of measurement. For the first time, with interval measurement, we enter the realm of scalar values which are equal to each other and of equal gradation throughout the scale. That is, an inch is an inch wherever it is found on the linear scale.

For the researcher, this opens all kinds of possibilities. If you do not have a scale, construct one. The only requirement is that you keep throughout the entire scale a *basic, standard interval* by which the data are measured.

We have alluded to the common standard measurements utilizing interval units. A common use of interval measurement is in the *rating scale* employed by many businesses, survey groups, and professional organizations. One college uses the following ten-point measurement of teaching effectiveness of the faculty. Students are asked to rate their teachers on specific qualities of effectiveness. One segment of the scale looks like this:

Place an "X" on the scale below at the point where you would rate the availability of your professor for conferences

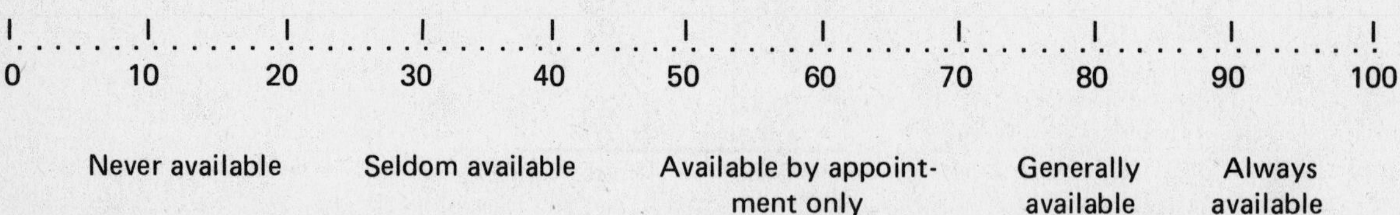

Note that the scale above has ten *equidistant* points. The equidistance creates a standard scalar unit and is, thus, comparable to the inch marks upon a tape measure, or to the second, minute, or hour intervals of time.

Look at the above rating scale a little more closely. On it are ten reference points. It has five judgment categories. The fineness of gradation of the scale might be improved by adding five intermediate points between each of the locations on the ten-point scale. This will create a scale of 50 points for a five-category placement. If, on the other hand, ten points are inserted between each of the above locations, we then have a 100-point scale upon which to make judgments. With indicating availability of a professor, such finesse of discrimination may not be either possible or desirable, but one may conceive situations in which such a degree of discrimination may be required.

A characteristic of the interval scale, however, is that although it has equal units, its zero point is arbitrary.[7]

★ *Ratio level of measurement.* One of the principal differences between the ratio and the interval scale is the nature of the zero point. In the interval scale the zero point is arbitrary, but the interval unit is constant. In the ratio scale, however, the zero point is *absolute* and begins from *true zero.* Fox defines "True zero" as "the total absence of the quantity being measured."[8] Compare the difference between the interval scale purporting to measure a professor's availability with a true ratio scale and the difference between the two scales will be obvious. Obviously, no *ratio* measurement is possible on the professor-availability scale. A professor who is usually available is not *twice* as available as one who is only seldom available, notwithstanding that one may merit a rating of 80 points as against a rating of only 40 points for the other.

Let us consider the above scale in an entirely different orientation. Think of it as a Celsius scale for measuring temperature. We can not say that 80° Celsius is twice as hot as 40° Celsius. Why? Because the zero point of the Celsius scale is not a *true* zero. We can measure in minus values *below* the zero point (and in winter we often do!). With the ratio-scale zero there is nothing to measure below zero because ratio-scale is absolute zero: below it there is nothing to measure. Total darkness is total (zero) darkness: the complete absence of light. You cannot have "more" darkness than that!

Another difference between the ratio scale and all the foregoing scales of measurement is that the ratio scale can express values in terms of multiples and fractional parts. A foot rule is a true ratio scale. We cannot measure length in minus values. The intervals on a foot rule are each equivalent to each other and the data it measures can be expressed as *true ratios.* Two inches is twice one inch; six inches is a half of twelve inches, or a *ratio* of 2:1 or 1:2. We cannot say that a person with an I.Q. of 120 is 5% more intelligent than a person with an I.Q. of 100. We measure I.Q. on the interval scale. But a package weighing 120 pounds *is* 5% heavier than one weighing 100 pounds. An object cannot weigh less than zero. Statistically, all operations are possible with data measured on a ratio scale.

Perhaps Senders[9] has encapsulated this discussion in the following simple test for various types of data measurement:

> If you can say that
> . . .one object is different from another, you have a *nominal scale*;
> . . .one object is bigger or better or more of anything than another, you have an *ordinal scale*;
> . . .one object is so many units (degrees, inches) more than another, you have an *interval scale*;
> . . .one object is so many times as big, or bright, or tall, or heavy as another, you have a *ratio scale.*[18]

The importance of these several scales in measuring data will be appreciated later because the type of statistical analysis to which the data may be subjected will depend entirely upon the type of data the researcher has available or the way in which those data have been chosen or "measured."

---

[7] David Sills, ed., *The Internationsl Encyclopedia of the Social Sciences* (New York: The Macmillan Company and the Free Press), 1968. Vol. 13, p. 97.

[8] David J. Fox, *Fundamentals of Research in Nursing* (New York: Appleton-Century, 1976), p. 73

[9] Virginia L. Senders, *Measurement and Statistics: A Basic Text Emphasizing Behavioral Science* (New York: Oxford University Press, 1958), p. 51.

A SUMMARY OF MEASUREMENT SCALES, THEIR CHARACTERISTICS AND THEIR STATISTICAL IMPLICATIONS

MEASUREMENT SCALE		*CHARACTERISTICS OF THE SCALE*	*STATISTICAL POSSIBILITIES OF THE SCALE*
Non-Interval Scales	Nominal scale	A scale which "measures" in terms of names or designations of discrete units or categories.	Can be used for determining the mode, the percentage values, or the chi square.
	Ordinal scale	A scale which "measures" in terms of such values as "more" or "less," "larger" or "smaller," but without specifying the size of the intervals.	Can be used for determining the mode, percentage, chi square, median, percentile rank, or rank correlation.
Interval Scales	Interval scale	A scale which measures in terms of equal intervals or degrees of difference, but whose zero point, or point of beginning is arbitrarily established.	Can be used for determining the mode, the mean, the standard deviation, the *t*-test, the *F* test, and the product moment correlation.
	Ratio scale	A scale which measures in terms of equal intervals and an absolute zero point of origin.	Can be used for determining the geometric mean, the harmonic mean, the percent variation and all other statistical determinations.

Validity and Reliability

With any type of measurement, two considerations are very important. One of these is *validity*; the other is *reliability*. *Validity* is concerned with the soundness, the effectiveness of the measuring instrument. Take a standardized test, for example. Validity would raise such questions as: "What does the test measure, and how well does it measure it?" We might look at the professor-availability scale above with respect to the validity of its measurement. Note how fuzzy some of the categories are. What does *always* available mean? Twenty-four hours a day? Whenever the professor is on campus? If so, could you call your professor out of a faculty meeting or a conference with the president of the institution? If not, then would this make the professor *generally* available and so reduce the availability factor of such professor by 20 percent, since there are five categories, and *always* does not seem ever to describe accurately the true state of affairs?

Validity is of several types. A summary of the more common types of validity with a brief description of each is shown on the next page.

A SUMMARY OF THE MORE COMMON TYPES OF VALIDITY

Overview statement: Measurement is a tool of research, and *validity* is the attempt to determine whether a type of measurement actually measures what it is presumed to measure. Various disciplines rely upon various types of validity to verify the effectiveness of their measurement procedures. Here are the principal types of validity.

1. **Face validity:** This type of validity relies basically upon the subjective judgment of the researcher. It asks two questions which the researcher must finally answer in accordance with best judgment: (1) Is the instrument measuring what it is supposed to measure? (2) Is the sample being measured adequate to be representative of the behavior or trait being measured?

2. **Criterion validity.** Criterion validity usually employs two measures of validity; the second, as a *criterion*, checks against the accuracy of the first measure. The essential component in criterion validity is a reliable and valid criterion—a standard against which to measure the results of the instrument which is doing the measuring. The data of the measuring instrument should correlate highly with equivalent data of the criterion.

3. **Content validity.** This type of validity is sometimes equated with *face validity*. Content validity is the accuracy with which an instrument measures the factors or situations under study; i.e. the "content" being studied. If, for example, we are interested in the content validity of questions being asked to elicit familiarity with a certain area of knowledge, content validity would be concerned with how accurately the questions asked tend to elicit the information sought.

4. **Construct validity.** A *construct* is any concept, such as *honesty*, which cannot be directly observed or isolated.[1] Construct validation is interested in the degree to which the construct itself is actually measured. To this end a significant procedure has been developed by Campbell and Fiske known as the *Multitrait-Multimethod Matrix Method*. It makes use of the traits of *convergence* and *discriminability*. *Convergence* looks to the focal effect of various methods of measuring a construct. Different methods of measurement of the same construct should "converge" or "focus" in their results. *Discriminability* means that the measuring instrument should be able to discriminate, or differentiate, the construct being studied from other similar constructs.

5. **Internal validity.** This term, and the one following, should not be confused with internal and external criticism, which are tests of validity in historical research and discussed later in this text. *Internal validity* is the freedom from bias in forming conclusions in view of the data. It seeks to ascertain that the changes in the dependent variable are the result of the influence of the independent variable rather than the manner in which the research was designed.

6. **External validity.**[2] This type of validity is concerned with the generalizability of the conclusions reached through observation of a sample to the universe; or, more simply stated: Can the conclusions drawn from a sample be generalized to other cases?

---

[1] Mary G. Kweit and Robert W. Kweit, *Concepts and Methods for Political Analysis* (Englewood Cliffs, N.J.: Prentice-Hall, Inc., 1981), 21, 350.

[2] D. T. Campbell and D. W. Fiske, "Convergent and discriminant validation by the multitrait-multimethod matrix," *Psychological Bulletin*, 56 (1959), 81-105.

Validity looks to the end results of measurement. The principal question that validity asks is: Are we *really* measuring what we *think* we are measuring?

The naive assume that because a test is designed to measure a certain factor or attribute, it does precisely that. Take, for instance, a paper-and-pencil-test of personality factors. By a series of check marks the individual indicates his or her most representative traits or actions in given situations — these traits and behaviors are presumed to reveal the characteristics of personality. The question that validity asks is: Does such a test *in fact* measure the individual's *personality* factors, or does it measure something else, quite removed from pure personality traits? No doubt that the questions are directed toward one's behavioral traits and actions, but the check marks may represent only those by which the student wishes to be represented. Hence, this is not a *valid* evaluation of the student's *real* personality but rather an idealized portrait of the way in which the student hopes that others may regard him or her.

We have now come very close to the second consideration in measurement, and that is *reliability*.

Reliability deals with accuracy. It asks such questions as: How accurate is the instrument that is used in making the measurement? Take the measurement of time, for example. A sundial or a clypsidra may measure time and within certain broad parameters be useful in our knowing whether it is morning, meridian, or afternoon, but as a measure of time, sundials and clypsidrae are not too *reliable.* One would not use them for catching planes or keeping appointments.

Mechanical timepieces are much more reliable. But even these run fast or slow depending upon the degree of their quality, their maintenance, the excellence of their workmanship. They are *fairly reliable* for the exigencies of everyday needs. If, however, we are transiting stars, tracking satellites, and employing time measurements in other ultra-precise research, we need the reliability of the cesium atomic clock of the Naval Observatory or the National Bureau of Standards. Reliability asks one question above all others: with what *accuracy* does the measure (test, instrument, inventory, questionnaire) measure what it is intended to measure?

No research can proceed without data. But merely to collect data in its raw, undisciplined state serves little purpose. We must find some way of corralling data by submitting them to the process of measurement. This measurement consists in seeing facts in orderly fashion and, the common procedure is to measure them by one of the four scales we have already discussed. Measurement, then, is merely the process of taking data in its raw state and arranging them along some scale of comprehensible values. It is to provide some means of "seeing" the data in terms of some specific, manageable unit.

But, having done this, we have done little more than create order from the chaos of unrelated and undisciplined fact. Before the data can be really useful to the researcher, more remains to be done. In many instances, another tool of research must be used to process the data further, so that, by such processing we may still further discern their meaning. This tool is that of *statistics*, and it is the role of statistics to provide the researcher with greater insight into the nature and meaning of the data. Statistics, then, is the third tool of research, and we shall give merely a brief introduction to it in the pages that follow. The presentation can be merely introductory and superficial. The chapter on the analytical method will discuss statistical procedures in some greater depth, but for those who wish to pursue the topic still further the bibliographical references at the end of this chapter will provide sufficient guidance.

STATISTICS: THE THIRD TOOL OF RESEARCH

Statistics represents merely a way of trying to visualize the facts of the real world. These facts reach us in various ways: the size of human aggregations, the intensity of heat, of pressure, of the pull of gravity on physical mass. We are also aware of the concepts of the not-so-real world: the level of one's intelligence, the strength of one's preferences or beliefs, achievement in academic performance, the worth of an employee to an organization, and so on.

All these perceptions we usually express in the form of an *arithmetical* symbol—a *statistical* value: the *number* of people in a group, the *number* of degrees of temperature, the *number* of pounds of pressure, the intelligence *quotient*, the *numerical* grade a student earns, and so on. Thus, many aspects of life are statistical.

It is unfortunate, therefore, that so many students regard statistics as a necessary evil—an ogre lying astride the path of their progress in research. Thousands of students may "love to do research" but shudder at statistics. The strange mathematical symbols, the multistoried and complex equations, the unfamiliar terminology frighten them unnecessarily. Statistics is really a very simple matter. It is a type of language into which the facts of life are constantly translated. When this is done, they are able to speak more clearly and the researcher may see their nature and interrelationships more understandingly. Through statistics, therefore, the researcher is able to conceptualize what otherwise might be incapable of being apprehended. Put very simply, for those who may feel uncomfortable with the thought of statistics, a simple definition of statistics might be: *Statistics is a language which, through its own special symbols and grammar, takes the numerical facts of life and translates them into meaning.* The first and last question of statistics is precisely the same question that the researcher asks of the facts: What do they *mean*? What *message* are they attempting to communicate?

Turning Numerical Facts into Meaning

Let us illustrate what we have just been saying. Take an everyday example. Joe is in high school. During the month of February, he gets the following grades:

92, 69, 91, 70, 90, 89, 72, 87, 73, 86, 85,
75, 84, 76, 83, 83, 77, 81, 78, 79

These are the raw numerical facts—the data, in the researcher's language—directly from a life situation. As they stand in the above array, they do not say very much; other than the fact that Joe's performance seems to be broadly inconsistent.

Now, suppose that we treat these data statistically, employing at first only the very simplest of statistical (or quasi-statistical) processes. We shall begin by arranging Joe's grades in a table, under the respective day of the week, Monday through Friday, on which the grade was earned.

FEBRUARY

	Monday	Tuesday	Wednesday	Thursday	Friday
First week	92	69	91	70	90
Second week	89	72	87	73	86
Third week	85	75	84	76	83
Fourth week	83	77	81	78	79

Remember what we have said: Statistics is a means of taking numerical facts and translating them meaningfully. Joe's grades are *numerical facts.* We have translated them into the most elementary statistical form, a *simple statistical array*, yet even such simple treatment is sufficient to yield a significant amount of information that was not originally apparent.

We now have the scores within a *time sequence*. Formerly we presented the data in *simple linear sequence*. (Is this getting to sound like the language of statistics? If so, do not be concerned. The terms merely describe the status or nature of the data, and that is all that statistical terminology ever does).

Now, we may inspect Joe's grades in a two-dimensional relationship. We may read them horizontally as well as vertically within the time frame of a month. Reading them horizontally, we note that the grades on Monday, Wednesday, and Friday are considerably higher than those on Tuesday and Thursday.

As we read the columns vertically, we note a likewise striking phenomenon. Whereas Joe's grades seemingly deteriorate during each successive week on Monday, Wednesday, and Friday, they steadily improve during successive weeks on Tuesdays and Thursdays. Such behavior of the data should alert the researcher; for such an effect, there must be a cause. To discover the probable cause is the function of research; and in this process, which involves an analysis of the data, the role of statistics is frequently indispensable.

Remember the definition? *Statistics takes the numerical facts of life and translates them meaningfully*. Let's pursue this thought a little further.

We have already read some meaning into Joe's grades. With a little further statistical treatment of the data, subjecting these grades to one or two additional (although extremely elemental) statistical processes, we shall force the data to tell us still more than they have already done. Let us represent Joe's grades in the form of a simple line graph.[10]

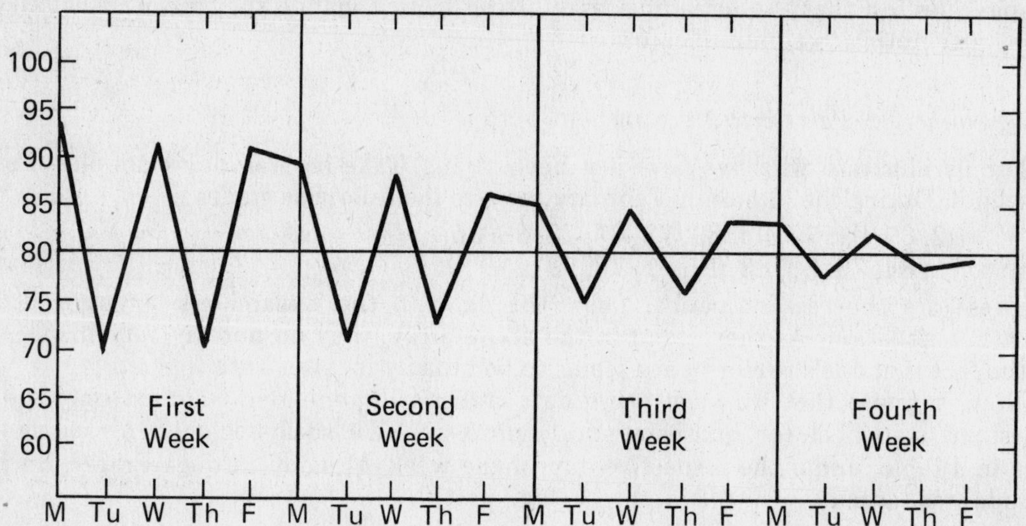

Note the difference between the three presentations of the same set of facts. Each has its own unique characteristic. Each shows certain emphases which no other form of presentation sets forth nearly so well. First, we merely *listed* Joe's grades in the order in which they were earned. The result was a *straight linear sequence.* Of all arrays, this was the simplest and least meaningful. Then, we added the day-month dimension. It placed the data for the first time in a two-dimensional grid setting. The data became more meaningful. Finally, we arranged that same array of data in the form of a line graph. It presented the most dramatic view of all. It revealed certain characteristics of the data not apparent in the first two displays.

---

[10] For a discussion of reading graphic material, see the author's Chapter IV in *Read with Speed and Precision* (New York: McGraw-Hill Book Company, 1963) entitled "Reading Graphic Presentations—The Ability to See Facts in Action," pp. 76–87.

In the line graph presentation, we see some phenomena dramatically set forth that were not apparent in the two previous arrays of the data. No one can miss the wide amplitude of grade disparity in the first and second week of the period. Also quite as apparent is the levelling-out process that seems to be emphasized in the second half of the third week and in the fourth week of Joe's grades. A profile of this sort should raise questions and suggest to the mind of any alert researcher the possibility of underlying causal factors and undiscovered data which may explain the reason for the eccentricity of the graph and its erratic behavior.

Thus far, we have discovered an important fact. *Looking at data in only one way yields but a fractional view of those data and, hence, provides only a small segment of the full meaning that those data contain.* For that reason, we have many statistical techniques. Each technique extracts but *one* aspect of the meaning from the same set of facts. Each time you rephrase the data into different statistical language (i.e., apply a new statistical treatment to the data), you derive new insight and see more clearly the meaning of those data.

We have already looked at Joe's academic performance in three different ways, but all of them have been on only a day-to-day basis. Let us now broaden our viewpoint. In contrast to the nervous fluctuations of peak-and-valley performance as revealed in the graph presentation above, let us by means of statistics take out the jagged irregularities of daily performance, levelling it into a smooth total weekly average. We shall, by means of a simple statistical operation, balance peaks against valleys, week-by-week. The resultant weekly average achievement of Joe's academic performance will be represented by a broken line extending from week-end to week-end. By so doing we shall get a whole new view of Joe's achievement. Whereas the graph originally showed only an erratic zig-zagging between daily extremes whose amplitude became less and less as the weeks went by, the dotted line shows that, week by week, very little change actually occurred in Joe's average *level of achievement.*

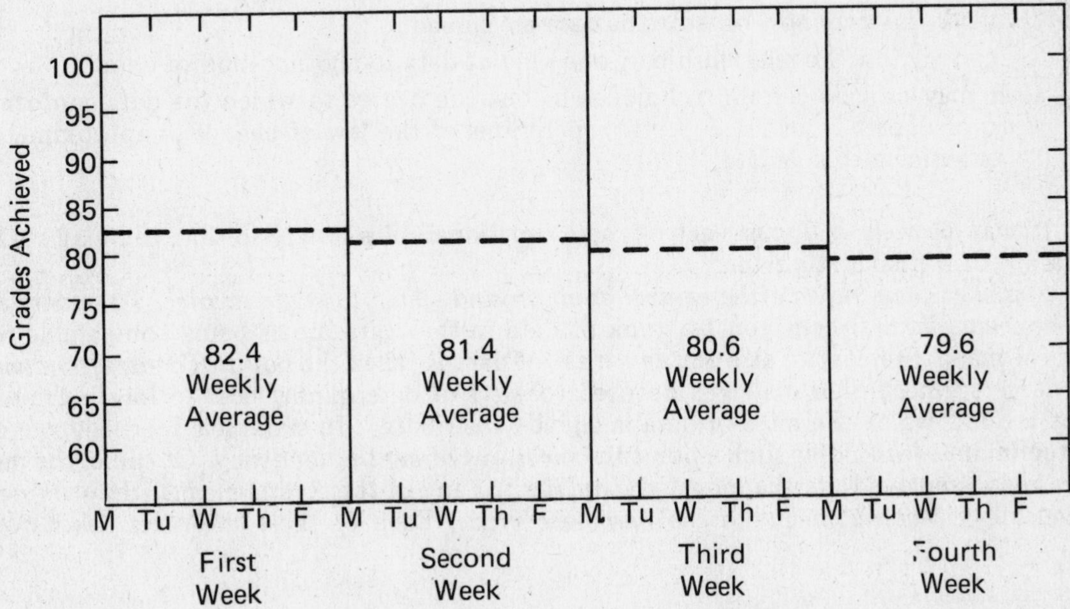

One point should be clearly emphasized: *All presentations of the data are equally important.* Inspecting data is like turning a diamond. With a diamond, each new facet gives forth a different hue. The light from one facet is not *more* beautiful than that of any other;

each is, rather, *unique* in its separate glory. So is the inspection of data. Each statistical manipulation of the data gives forth a new illumination of the facts. One is not *more* significant than the other.

By means of statistics, we have already seen Joe's achievement in four different ways: (1) as a linear set of grades, (2) as a day and weekly set of grades, (3) as a graphic line showing the amplitude of Joe's grades, and (4) as a weekly average of Joe's grades. And we have not exhausted the means by which we might view these same data. We could go on and on, subjecting these data to additional statistical analyses. By so doing, we would learn more and more about Joe's academic performance; but that is not the purpose of this discussion. We have merely cited this situation to illustrate that statistics *as a tool of research* may assist us in seeing what otherwise we may never have known.

The Role of Statistics

Statistics is merely a tool. It is not a be-all and end-all for the researcher. Those who insist that unless research is "statistical research" display a very myopic view of the research process. There are others who are equally adamant that unless research is "experimental research," *it* is not research. One cardinal rule applies: *the nature of the data governs the method that is appropriate to interpret the data and the tool of research that is required to process it.* A historian seeking answers to problems associated with the assassination of President Kennedy or Martin Luther King would be hard-put to produce either a statistical or an experimental study, and yet the research of the historian can be quite as scholarly and scientifically respectable as that of any statistical or experimental study.

If you know what statistics can and, conversely, cannot do, you may appreciate more fully the role of statistics as a tool of research. If the data are expressed as numerical values, then statistics may assist you in four ways:

1. It may indicate the central point around which the data revolve.
2. It may indicate how broadly the data are spread.
3. It may show the relationship of one kind of data to another kind of data.
4. It may provide certain techniques to test the degree to which the data conform to or depart from the expected operations of the law of chance or approximate an anticipated standard.[11]

It may be well to discuss each of these functional roles briefly so that you may see the landscape of statistics at a glance.

Statistics may indicate the central point around which the data revolve. To understand this concept, it may help you to think of data in the aggregate as being comparable to a physical mass. The central axis for any mass of data is called the *point of central tendency.* One large segment of statistics is devoted to ways of determining how to locate the midpoint around which the mass of data is equally distributed. In statistical language, we call the techniques for finding such a point the *measures of central tendency.* Of these, the most commonly employed are the *mode,* the *median,* or any of the several *means*: the *arithmetic mean*, the *geometric mean*, or the *harmonic mean.* Each of these measures has its own

---

[11] The considerations subsumed under items 1, 2, and 3 belong to a branch of statistics known as *descriptive statistics,* because the principal function of the statistical process is to *describe* the data. Item 4 deals with *inferential statistics* because the principal function of the statistical process is to *infer* how closely the data conform to or depart from a hypothetical norm. Hence, we sometimes refer to this statistical area as that which is concerned with testing the *null hypothesis.*

applications and characteristics. As a careful researcher, you will choose the particular indicator of central tendency with full knowledge of its unique capability for indicating accurately the point of central tendency for any particular type of data. Statisticians always *look at the data first*, then choose the statistical technique that is most appropriate to explore those data.

In every statistical situation, one basic rule applies: *The configurational characteristics of the data dictate the statistical treatment that is most appropriate for that particular situation.* If the data assume the distribution approximating the normal curve — as most data do — they call for one type of central tendency determination. If they assume an ogive-curve configuration, characteristic of a growth or developmental situation, they demand another method of statistical management. A polymodal distribution, such as one might find in the fluctuation of the stock market, may call for still a third type of statistical approach to locate the point of central tendency. Every researcher should bear in mind, therefore, that only after careful and informed consideration of the characteristics of the data and the configurational patterns that those data assume, when plotted as a frequency curve, can the researcher select the most appropriate statistical procedure.

Too many students try it the other way around: They attempt to select the statistical technique before they have adequately considered whether that particular treatment is appropriate to the data at hand. They say, "I shall find the mean"—having been conditioned by statistics textbooks and courses in basic statistics to think always in terms of the *arithmetic* mean — when the very nature of the data may dictate that the geometric mean, or the harmonic mean, or perhaps the contraharmonic mean may be *statistically* much better choices. The arithmetic mean may, indeed, be perhaps the *least* desirable. Such sensative discrimination in the choice of a statistical tool is a distinguishing mark of the skilled researcher.

The purpose of this chapter is to discuss statistics merely as one of the tools of research. It makes no pretense at being a résumé of the principles of basic statistics or to teach the student the statistical procedures necessary for most research projects. It will be assumed that the student already has this substantive background. For those who wish to learn the fundamentals of statistics, or who desire to refresh their minds with references to statistical principles, a selected bibliography is given at the conclusion of this chapter.

At this point, a further observation should be made with respect to the nature of a statistic. You should always be aware that what statistically seems very plausible may *in reality* — in the *real* world — have no counterpart whatsoever.

Statistics many times describe a *quasi world* rather than reflect the real world of everyday life. For example, if you add up a series of grades and divide by the number of students in the class, you may get an average grade of 82 for the class. Having done this, you may feel that you have discovered a very substantial fact. If you look down over the class list of individual grades, however, you may be astonished to find that *not one student in the entire class actually received a grade of 82*! What you accepted statistically as solid fact became empirically an illusion in the actual grades earned by the individuals.

Consider the man who read in the paper that the Bureau of Census had just announced that there were 1.75 children in the average American family. With heartfelt gratitude, he exclaimed, "Thank God, I was the *first*born!" What is accepted statistically is sometimes meaningless empirically. All this, however, should not disparage the importance of statistics as *a tool of research*.

Some statistical concepts, even though they have no counterparts in the real world, may assist us in understanding the phenomena of the real world with more appreciation and greater understanding than might otherwise be possible. Many ideas we accept as being substantial have no real substance. Take the North Pole, for example. The North Pole provides a prime reference point for many types of human activity; it is essential in determining linear units of the metric system, and as a basis of commerce between nations. It provides a basic reference point for navigation, for terrestrial latitude, for geodetic measurements, and for many other activities. Yet travel to the Arctic wastes, and you will have to imagine that one particular spot on the ice—which looks precisely like every other spot on the ice which stretches from horizon to horizon—is the North Pole. Just so, a statistic is a valuable benchmark, a reference point, even though in the hard world of fact and reality no such point actually exists. Such is the nature of the point of central tendency.

So much, then, for the first of the four functions of statistics as a tool of research.

★ *Statistics can show you how broadly the data spreads.* Just as it is important to know where the center of a mass of data lies, so it is equally important to know how broadly that mass spreads out on either side of the point of central tendency. Both of these determinations—focal point and dispersion range—help us to see the data with greater clarity and to describe it in terms of a two-dimensional relationship. Such determinations are the fundamental baselines from which we may survey the data and describe its other properties. As a surveyor starts from one or two reference points, so the researcher begins by looking at the data from the viewpoint of certain basic statistical benchmarks.

The usual way of representing data graphically is by means of the familiar bell-shaped curve, although not all data in the world conform to such a bell-shaped configuration.

Much of the natural phenomena, when quantified and expressed in a two-dimensional relationship, does indeed assume the Gaussian (bell-shaped) curve. Such a distribution pattern is often referred to as the *normal curve*. Let us digress from the discussion of grades for a moment to appreciate another statistical concept.

Consider the two distributions of data represented by the following bell graphs:

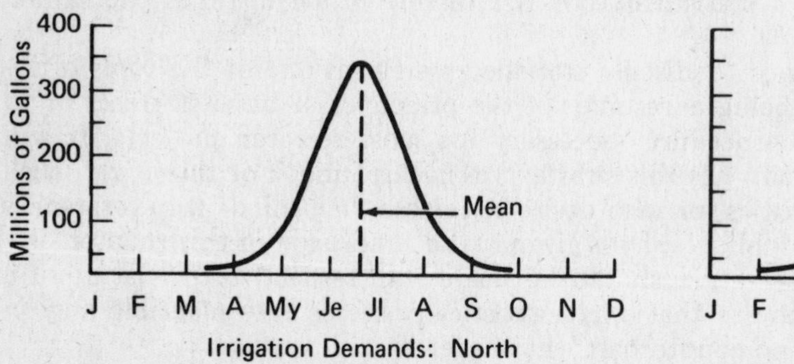

Irrigation Demands: North

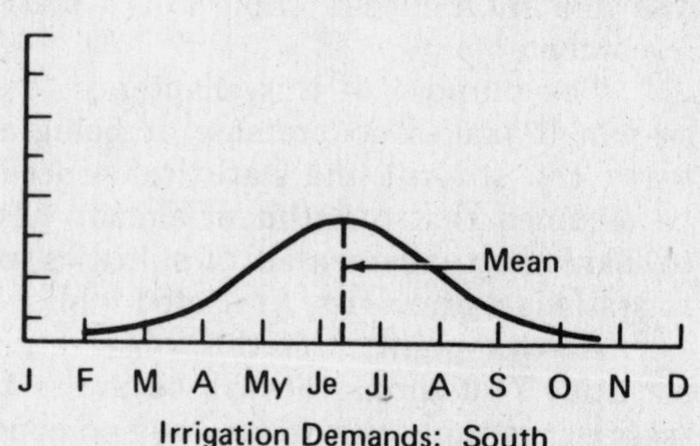

Irrigation Demands: South

These graphs represent the water consumption for irrigation purposes for an entire year in two separate parts of the United States. One graph shows the demand in a northern area which has a short growing season, and which is noted for its hot dry summers, placing an acute seasonal demand on irrigational resources. The other is the water consumption profile for a more southerly region, which has a longer growing season and which is also favored by more rainfall throughout the year. In the northern location the consumption is narrowly spread from mid-March to mid-September, with the greatest demand climaxing severely about mid-June. In the southern location, the demand spreads broadly from the beginning of February to mid-November. There is no sudden heavy demand as in the northern location; the consumption instead is a moderate, gently increasing and decreasing demand that spreads broadly across most of the months of the year. Both situations use approximately the same volume of water; for both distributions the location of the mean is approximately at the same mid-June point.

We measure the spread on either side of the mean. This spread we call the *dispersion* or *deviation*. The most commonly employed dispersion measure is, of course, the *standard deviation*, but other measures include the *range* (the *semi-interquartile range* or *quartile deviation* are both variants of the range), the *mean deviation*, and the *coefficient of variance*.

All these measures attempt to tell us something about the spread of the data. That is their only purpose: to give us another dimension from which to view the facts. With a measure of central tendency and also a measure of dispersion, the researcher can see more intimately the configuration, the characteristics, and the nature of the data with which he is working. What comes straight from the observation of natural phenomena, measured as an aggregation of numerical digits, becomes by means of statistical interpretation manageable and meaningful. With benefit of a few reference points, we can consequently survey statistically the whole mass of the data and plot its dimensional characteristics with more awareness of its essential nature and its mass dynamics.

But let us go back to the discussion of Joe's grades, this time with reference to the statistical dimensions we have been discussing: points of central tendency and measures of dispersion.

Measures of Central Tendency		*Measures of Dispersion*	
Mean	81	Range	23
Median	82	Average deviation	6.0
Mode	83	Standard deviation	6.9

This is the usual way in which these values are reported. But what is the *meaning* of these figures? We have illustrated this in the diagram on page 34.

To see more clearly the concept of central tendency that we have been discussing, think of the median and the mean as the fulcrum points for a mass of data. Both median and mean are points of exact balance. But it is important to understand what each balances. The median is the precise *numerical center* of the array, with exactly as many grades *by number* above the median point as below it. The word *median* comes from the Latin word meaning "middle," and so the median grade is the one precisely in the middle of the series. Joe's record has a total of 20 grades. Ten grades will be above the median; ten grades will be below it.

The mean is also a fulcrum point. It is the precise center of all the amalgamated *values* in the array. The mean balances the *weight* of each grade. Think of 69 as the lightest of all the grades and 92 as the heaviest. The mean indicates the point where the weight of the entire statistical mass is in delicate equilibrium around the center of its own gravity. The median indicates the *distance*, the mid*point*, from one end to the other of an array of figures. The mean indicates the mid*point* where the *weight* of the scores on one side of the mean exactly balance the *weight* of the scores on the other side of the mean. The median is a tape measure; the mean a set of scales.

While we are clarifying the concepts underlying the central tendency, let us now explain the terminology of dispersion. We may say that the *range* is simply the full extent of the data from the lowest value to the highest. Joe's grades from 69 to 92 is a range of 23 grade-points.

If, however, we wish to explore the breadth to which the data are scattered on either side of the mean, we must employ one of two commonly used measures of deviation or dispersion. We may use the less frequently employed *average deviation*. The name describes the process of arriving at the magnitude of the deviation. Each score deviates from the mean score (the *average* score) by a certain amount. If we *sum* all of these amounts of deviation and then *divide* them by the *total number of deviations*, we arrive at the *average* deviation. The more commonly used deviational index, however, is the *standard deviation*, which we will explain later. In the diagram below, we shall indicate both of these deviations as a means of comparison.

Let us now look at Joe's grades with these statistical dimensions indicated. More and more, statistics is giving us greater insight into Joe's academic performance. We are seeing how *statistics takes the numerical facts of life and translates them into meaning.*[12]

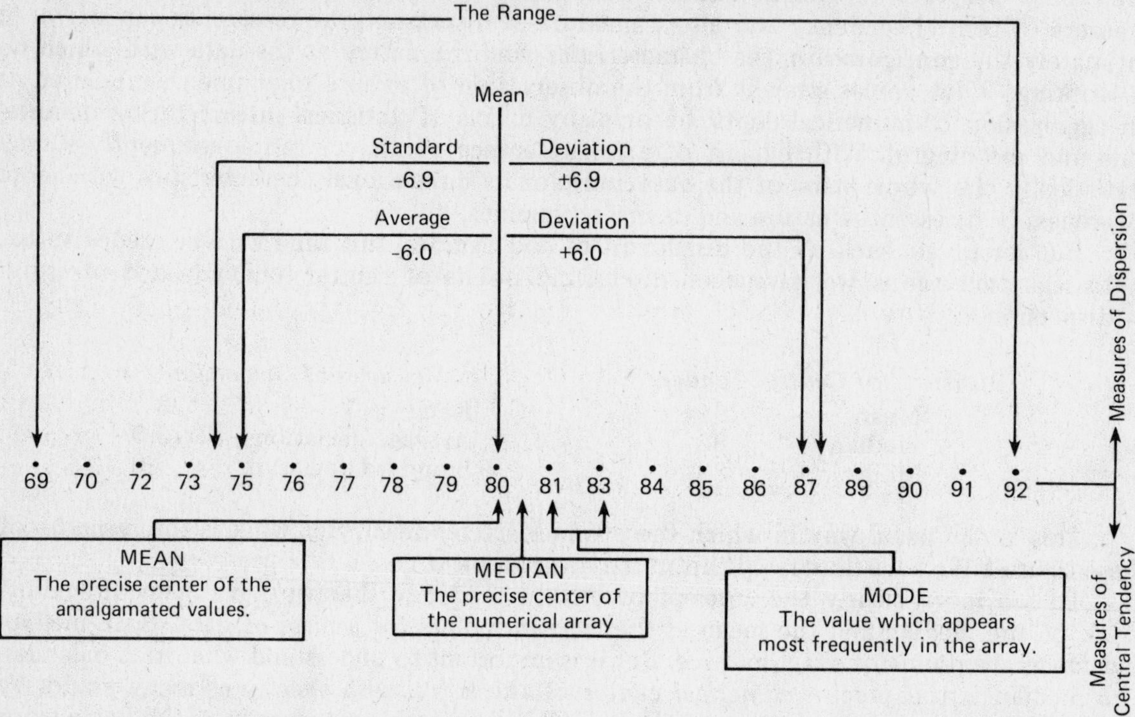

★ *Statistics can show you the existence of relationships.* Up to this point, we have been discussing statistics from only the viewpoint of central tendency and dispersion. These are phenomena that happen with relation to only one parameter of the data: the pivotal axis which we have called the *mean*.

But the facts of life are not always so simple. Nor can life situations be adequately described by a static system where only the central balance point and the amplitude of dispersion account for the world around us. The *raison d' être* of statistics is that it takes the disparate facts of life and translates these into quantitative concepts and formulations that are manageable and meaningful.

In the real world, facts exist, not only in a static linear arrangement, but also in dynamic interrelationships with each other. There is a relationship, for example, between age and mental maturity, the emotional state and the health of the individual, the incidence of rainfall and the price of food in the marketplace. Relationships and interrelationships are all around us. Consider the relationship between temperature and pressure, between the wavelength and intensity of light and the growth of plants, between the administration of a certain drug and the resultant platelet agglutination in the blood. And we could go on and on. Relationships between one kind of data and another kind of data are everywhere. Because life is filled with these interrelationships, one of the functions of statistics is to *describe* or *indicate the intensity and magnitude* of such co-related factors.

To many students, the mere discovery of a relationship between one type of data and another is the prime goal of research. It is nothing of the kind. They have "discovered"

[12] See the definition of statistics at the outset of this discussion, p. 27.

something, so they think. Not so. It is not so much discovery as a description of an already existing status quo which through a statistical technique they have caused to float to the surface. What they have done with a statistical formula, a computer can do better. But computers cannot do research. There is no *interpretation of fact* in what either the student or the computer does. What we are saying does not disparage either the function of statistics or the function of the computer. It merely aims to put both tools into proper prospective with respect to the goals and purposes of basic research.

The statistical process by which we discover the relationship between different types of data is called *correlation.* It is always a decimal fraction, indicating the degree of relatedness between the factors being correlated. Such a fraction is called a *coefficient of correlation.*

Finding a coefficient of correlation is not doing research; it is merely discovering a signpost. That signpost points unerringly to a fact that two things are indeed related. And it also reveals the *nature of the relationship*: whether the facts are closely or distantly related.

So you come up with a coefficient of correlation. This should spark in the mind of the researcher a barrage of questions: what is the *nature* of the relationship; what is the underlying *cause* of the relationship; if two things are related, *how* are they related? Answer these questions and you are *interpreting* what the correlation *means*—you are doing research.

Mention coefficient of correlation and most students will immediately think of only the Pearsonian product moment correlation, commonly called the *Pearsonian r.* Although this probably is the commonest of all correlational techniques, there are nevertheless perhaps a dozen more; and, as in the case of the mean, the nature of the data must always determine the correlational technique that is most appropriate.

Correlations are merely statistical descriptions. They describe the strength of the bond of relationship between one variable and the other. At best, correlations are statistical conclusions of what happens within a correlational matrix, and a correlational matrix is nothing more than a convention for representing graphically facts which, presumably, have some connection with each other.

Data should be thought of as having within them a certain energy potential that reacts within a framework of vertical and horizontal dynamics. Gas, for example, has under normal conditions certain dynamics of pressure and temperature. A child has correspondingly the dynamics of age and reading achievement. These dynamic dimensions are interactive and changeable. Because of their fluctuational nature, we call such dimensions *variables*, so called because their nature is to *vary*. Other data which do not exhibit such variable characteristics, we call *constants*.

In the case of the gas, the pressure varies with the temperature. With the child, the data vary continually. The child is constantly changing with respect to age, to growth, to achievement, to proficiency in reading, and other academic skills.

To represent these variables statistically for the purpose of showing a relationship between one group of data and another set of similar data, we use a grid—a two-dimensional statistical representation called a *correlational matrix. A correlational matrix is a dynamic area within which the forces of the variables interact.*

At the top of page 36 is a correlational matrix on which data variables are represented as interacting: they form a statistically dynamic field of "forces."

Thus, any fact expressed in terms of *one data factor* is also expressed in relation to the *other factor* and is, therefore, located on the grid at some point where the lines extending from the point of magnitude for each variable intersect.

Below is a grid representing the other situation which we mentioned above. On the *ordinate* (the vertical axis), we have represented the chronological age. On the *abscissa*

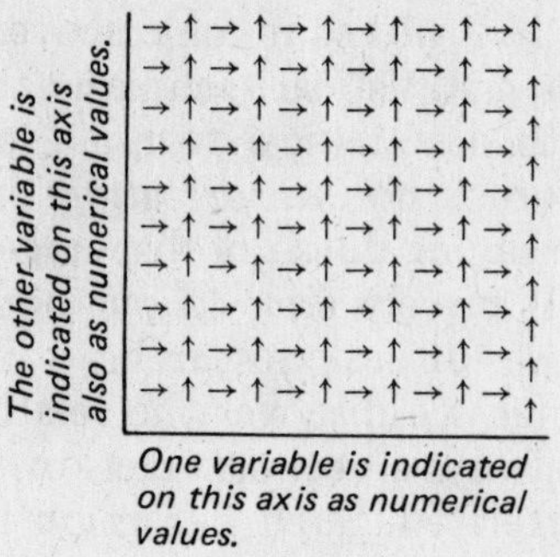

(the horizontal axis) is the reading-grade level expectancy. We shall identify the child that we mentioned above with the symbol △ on the grid. He has made normal progress in reading: at age six, he was reading at the first-grade level; at seven, at the second-grade level; at eight, at the third grade level; and so on. The relationship of age to reading grade expectancy is a perfect one-to-one correspondence: one year of age, one grade of reading achievement. The straight line vector that connects these points is an equilibrium between grade achievement in reading and chronological age. In statistics, such a line is called the *line of regression*, which in this instance represents a perfect, positive correlation of the one factor (age) to the other (reading achievement) in progressive equilibrium. In practice, we represent a coefficient of correlation with the symbol $\underline{r}$ and in this instance we would describe the correlation as $\underline{r} = 1.0$.

In contrast to this instance of perfect linear correlation, we shall plot the ages and reading levels of other children who are classmates of the child we have just been discussing. Some—represented by the symbol ○—are advanced for their age. Others—represented by the symbol ● —are lagging with respect to their reading-grade expectancy. The following is the result of plotting within the correlational matrix the reading-grade placement for each child.

As we inspect this matrix, what can we say about it? We can make statements in two directions. We can (1) merely *describe* the homogeneity or heterogeneity of the data in terms of its statistical dynamics. This description we express merely in the form of an $\underline{r}$, a coefficient of correlation, represented by a decimal fraction: the larger the decimal value, the greater the homogeneity of the data.

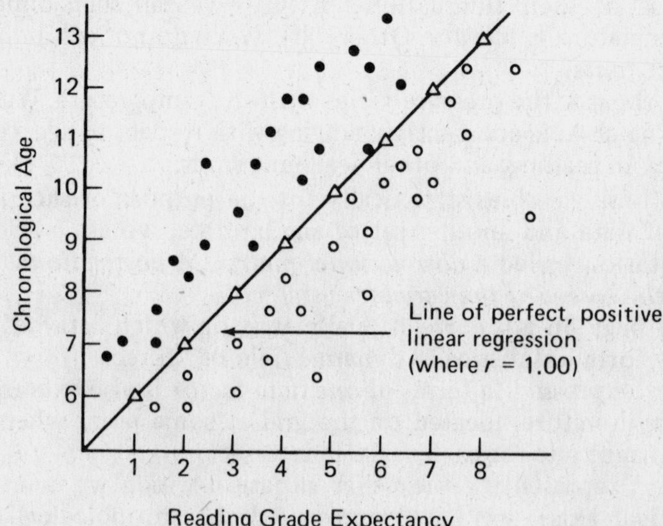

On the other hand, we can (2) *interpret* the meaning of these data within the matrix by investigating the juxtapositions or remotenesses and by considering the data configuration as a whole, which considerations seem to hint at further and more significant meanings than that of a mere decimal fraction.

Research, by its very nature, goes beyond simple statistical description to probe the meaning within the individual instances or significant clusters of data. Its goal is to discover a rationale for the appearance of such data within the matrix itself. We might, for example, *analyze* the placement of those data which represent achievement below the level of reading-grade expectancy. Let us look at each ● in relation to all the other ●s; in relation to contributing factors that have conditioned the placement; in relation to the overall configuration of the ●s; and corresponding cases of the ●s and the ○s with respect to their proximity or remoteness from the norm of expected behavior—the line of perfect, positive, linear regression. When we regard the data in this way, we get *insight* that is not apparent from a correlation coefficient. The matrix has dramatized certain of the events within the data which can now claim our attention.

What we have done with the underachievers, we might do equally with the overachievers. Then, by combining, contrasting, and permuting these two subpopulations, we may probe for further facts. Thus, we are attempting *to dig underneath* the correlational coefficient to see the *reason* for it! What we seek is a knowledge of the internal structure of the entire matrix which may give us further insight into the causes for its being the way it is.

Statistical techniques are thus helpful in providing us with overall views and conclusions about data masses that we could not achieve in any other way. What is important, however, is that the researcher be in command, and know the limitations of each correlational technique employed, and the specific way in which it may assist an entrance into the fuller meaning of the data.

In all relationship studies, however, you should be alert for faulty logic. A tacit assumption is sometimes made that if one factor can be shown to have a statistical relationship to another, then these two factors must necessarily have an influence on each other. In some instances, the influence may indeed by very intimate and direct, as in the case where chronological age seems to have a very direct bearing upon physical and mental development. But to infer that merely because a correlation exists, it therefore implies interaction of the correlational variables, is very questionable reasoning.

Take a logically absurd yet statistically demonstrable instance. Conceivably, we could establish a statistically correct correlation between the number of elephants in Thailand and the size of the Florida orange crop. The facts may be very clear: as the size of the elephant population increases, the Florida orange crop also increases! To reason, however, that because we can show a positive correlation, there must therefore be a causal bond at the root of that relationship, is erroneous. There is no connection whatsoever between the elephant population in Thailand and the production of oranges in Florida. *One variable correlates meaningfully with another only when there is a common causal bond that links the phenomena of both variables in a logical and causal relationship.* And this causal bond always lies below the mere statistical operation.

But where in an extreme situation we recognize the absurdity of the reasoning, as in the elephant–orange crop correlation, in research studies we occasionally find this same kind of questionable reasoning proposed quite seriously. We assume, for instance, that a correlation between low socioeconomic level and poor academic performance implies that one *causes* the other: *because* the family paycheck, the family living conditions, and so forth are inadequate, the achievement of the boys and girls of such families is also deficient. Improve the family economic status and you will improve the learning quality of the children of that family. Does not the coefficient of correlation indicate that's what happens?

And so, we assume on the basis of the correlation coefficient that one situation determines the other. There *may* be some connection between paycheck size and children's grades; again, such an inference may be utter nonsense. Unless we inspect the causal premise very carefully, we may be misled by a statistical statement which, in fact, may have no validity whatever. If we so reason concerning socioeconomic status and academic performance, it may be very difficult for us to account for the world's geniuses and intellectual giants, many of whom have been born of indigent parents and who have lived in constant companionship with poverty.

Figures may not lie, but the casual assumptions that we make with respect to some of our figuring may at times be extremely circumspect and untrustworthy. The genuine researcher is never content to stop at merely finding a correlation. Such a researcher is always aware that *below the correlation* lies a universe of fact and that the interpretation of the data underlying the correlation phenomenon may conceivably lead the researcher to the discovery of new and exciting truth. The coefficient of correlation is, therefore, merely a signpost pointing to further discovery.

Perhaps we have said enough at this point about the correlational techniques and their purpose in research design. We have yet a fourth subarea to discuss, and this is the use of statistics as a tool for testing the expectations of nature.

★ *Statistics may test the conformity of research data to that which is found in the anticipated expectations of nature.* This is a new dimension of our statistical discussion. Up to this point, we have shown all that statistics can do for the researcher is to show an indication of the fulcrum points, to describe the spread and scatter of the data, and to indicate the strength of a relationship—the index of homogeneity or heterogeneity—that exists within a data-mass.

Nature generally behaves according to rule. Karl Friedrich Gauss discovered that fact and formulated his discovery into a mathematical expression of normal distribution. Natural fortuitousness, Gauss discovered, is expressed in the form of a bell-shaped curve. And this curve has ever since become the *sine qua non* of the statistician. The broad implications of Gauss's curve may perhaps best be shown by a well-known presentation demonstrating its properties and applications.

The following illustration of the characteristics and uses of the normal curve is well worth study. The pivotal axis of static equilibrium is indicated as 0 and represents the point of central tendency. On either side of it, in perfect symmetry—because the curve itself represents the perfect balance of nature—the standard deviation areas are shown. The σ is the statistician's symbol for *standard deviation*. The rest of the scales are relative and informative. Here are the yardsticks by which we measure educational achievement, intelligence, social and chance phenomena, sinusidal performance in mechanics and physics, or the behavior of electromagnetic and frequency waves.

Because most of the chance phenomena of life conform to a greater or lesser degree to the Gaussian curve, statistics can assist the researcher in determining how nearly the data conform or depart from the contour of such a curve. The researcher measures data in much the same way that a carpenter measures a piece of lumber. The carpenter uses a foot rule; the researcher employs standards of measurement associated with the normal curve. The principle, however, is the same. In each case, two things are necessary: (1) a standard, and (2) an area for measuring.

In the case of the foot rule, the standard is the foot, the inch, or its integral fractions. With respect to data, the standard is the normal curve. Compared to the units of the foot rule, the mean and the standard deviation are the points of reference for the curve. The Gaussian curve is, in fact, the standard by which phenomena ideally result from pure happenstance. It is the representation of phenomena which take place in a perfect world governed by pure happenstance of nature. The curve is a delicate balance of distributed values pivoted about the mean and spreading out on either side from that mean.

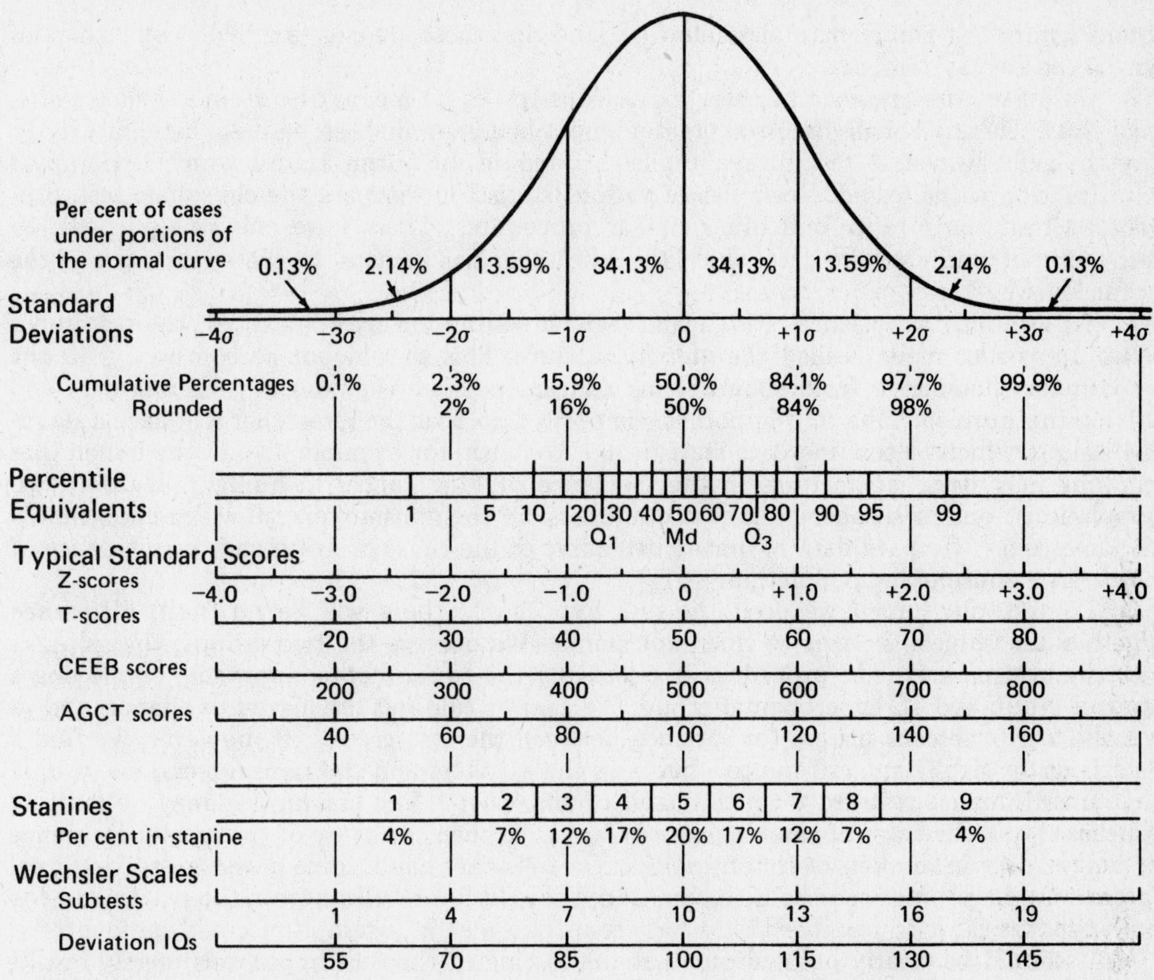

NOTE: This chart cannot be used to equate scores on one test to scores on another test. For example, both 600 on the CEEB and 120 on the AGCT are one standard deviation above their respective means, but they do not represent "equal" standings because the scores were obtained from different groups.

Source: *Test Service Bulletin*, No. 48 (January 1955), The Psychological Corporation.

Within a very slight margin, which we usually think of in terms of 5 percent variation, nature *ideally and uninfluenced* performs her functions within the range of perfectly predestined curvilinear predictions. These predictions are represented in the form of the curve we have just been discussing, known as the Gaussian or bell curve.[13]

Much, however, might happen to upset this delicate balance of natural perfection. Forces, influences, extraneous dynamics of one kind or another may cause the equilibrium of the normal distribution to be altered or destroyed. When this happens, we compare statistically the data that we suspect to have been subjected to some outside influence against the data as they ideally should be, according to the normal distribution pattern, and we sometimes find that the data we have accumulated may be off course from that indicated by the curve by a significant amount. When this happens, we suspect that such aberration is caused by some external force or combination of forces, in addition to those

[13] Gauss, however, did not plot a curve of perfect performance, but of nature's error. It was Sir Francis Galton in his studies of heredity who adapted Gauss's curve to describe life phenomena.

found within the purely natural framework, and that these are exerting their own dynamics within the data system.

We detect the presence of these extraneous forces by means of certain so-called *statistical tests*. These we shall discuss at greater length in a later chapter; enough, here, merely to give the general idea. A test always implies a standard, or norm, against which to compare any situation to be tested. Examples of various statistical tests are the chi square test, Student's t test, the F-ratio, and other similar procedures. These have only one purpose: to test the conformity of the data which the researcher has in hand to the expectancy of the normal curve.

To establish a statistical base against which a situation may be tested, the researcher relies upon a construct called the *null hypothesis.* This should not be confused with the hypotheses that derive from subproblems and are posited as guides in gathering data and solving the problem. The null hypothesis is posited so that the researcher will have a standard against which to test the data statistically. We wish, for example, to test the hunch that smoking may cause an increase in the incidence of lung cancer in humans. We find two populations: one of smokers, one of nonsmokers. Of the nonsmokers, all will, of course, die of some cause. We have data to draw a bell curve of the cause of death and the incidence of cancer in a nonsmoking population.

To test our hunch we posit the null hypothesis: there will be no (null) difference whether the subject smokes or does not smoke. We observe the two groups: the smokers and the nonsmokers. The procedure is essentially the experimental approach, employing a control group and an experimental group. We cannot rule out the matter of chance, and so we allow a 5 percent margin for variance between the two groups. If, however, we find a "statistically significant difference" between the smokers and the nonsmokers, we *assume* that the difference resulted from the habit of smoking.[14] The assumption may be entirely warranted and the habit of smoking may in fact have been the cause of the greater incidence of lung cancer in smokers over nonsmokers. On the other hand, some unrecognized external factor may have produced the difference. In a conclusion resulting from the positing of the null hypothesis, it is possible that what seems like a valid assumption could be incorrect.

It should be clearly pointed out that the testing of the null hypothesis merely results in an indication that points in the direction of a strong probability. Merely to find that one group engaging in a habit develops certain reactions over another group that does not engage in that habit is really not to find out too much. The genuine researcher will seldom be satisfied with such a foggy resolution to the matter. The real researcher will consider this finding only a first step. He will want to know precisely what made the difference and what the difference is from a *qualitative* rather than merely a *quantitative* point of view. Statistics is, therefore, merely the handmaid of the genuine researcher. It is a tool that can reveal that differences do exist. The best research will, however, seldom be satisfied with that fact alone. It will ask more penetrating questions: If the null hypothesis is rejected, then exactly what factors, what influences, what determinants *caused* the statistic to veer out of line from the normal chance occurrence? To discover the fact and degree of divergence from chance expectancy is within the province of statistics; to go beyond this and to read the data in terms of their significance and interpretation—in short, their *meaning*—this is research.

Because the purpose of this chapter is not to teach statistics but merely to give the student some concepts about the minimal knowledge needed in order to appreciate the role of statistics as a *tool of research*, one more area should be discussed before concluding this section: namely, how to read statistical language.

---

[14] *Smoking and Health: A Report of the Surgeon-General of the United States.* Washington, D.C.: Government Printing Office, 1978.

How to Read the Language of Statistics

A statistical formula and a cookbook recipe have essentially the same purpose: to give directions in order to produce an ultimate outcome. Look at the recipe. It has a characteristic format. You read it in a particular way. With a recipe, the reader is usually presented with a list of the ingredients; then he follows directions as to the way in which these ingredients are to be combined and processed. In like manner, you read a statistical formula with equal awareness of its standard format. All too many teachers take for granted that students generally know how to read statistical language. One only needs to know students to recognize the fallacy of that assumption. What is it, then, that a student needs to know to read a statistical expression? Perhaps some elementary matters with respect to symbols and conventions in symbol usuage may merit review.

★ *Conventions in symbol usage*. Greek letters generally are used to denote the characteristics of *population parameters*. Roman letters generally express the characteristics associated with *samples*. For example, we may have the mean of the population or the mean of a sample drawn from the population. If the *population mean* is meant, it is represented by the Greek μ, whereas the *sample mean* is indicated by M. Frequently in statistics, the italic form of the alphabet is used where the Roman letter is appropriate. Likewise, σ denotes the standard deviation of the *population*, whereas s would indicate the standard deviation of the *sample*.

A bar above a symbol, $\overline{X}$, $\overline{Y}$, indicates the *arithmetic mean* of the several items. Generally, the letters x, y, z denote *variables* and observations on individual cases. Constants are represented by letters at the beginning of the alphabet. Small letters from the middle of the alphabet, particularly i and j, used as subscripts, indicate reference to specific individuals or groups.

A few other symbols which you should know are the following:

$>$: $a > b$ means "a is greater than b."
$<$: $a < b$ means "a is less than b."
$\gg$: $a \gg b$ means "a is very much larger than b."
$\ll$: $a \ll b$ means "a is very much less than b."
$\geqslant$: $a \geqslant b$ means "a is greater than or equal to b."
$\leqslant$: $a \leqslant b$ means "a is less than or equal to b."
$=$ means "equal to."
$\neq$ means "not equal to."
$|a|$ means "the absolute value of a without $+$ or $-$ designation."
∞ means "infinity."
$\sqrt{a}$ means "the square root of a."
H_0 means "the null hypothesis."
! means "factorial, or multiply the number by each succeeding number below it to 1." Thus, 4! means $4 \times 3 \times 2 \times 1 = 24$.

★ *Subscripts and exponents*. Common to statistical expressions are small letters or figures written slightly below a quantity. These are called *subscripts*. They function as adjective or qualitative descriptors whose function is to tell *what kind* of quantity is indicated. For example, in the expression M_g, the subscript g tells the kind of M, where M stands for the mean. The symbol stands for "mean geometric" or the geometric mean.

Where a small symbol is written slightly above the quantity, it is called an *exponent*. An exponent is a quantitative descriptor, telling not what kind but *how much*. M^2, for example, is read "*M* squared" meaning, of course, that *M* is multiplied by itself, thus increasing the value of *M*.

★ *Summation.* Another symbol which is frequently seen in equations is the summation symbol. It is an overgrown Greek upper-case sigma, Σ, and it simply means "add." Sometimes it, too, has smaller symbols below and above it to indicate the limits of the additive process. For instance,

$$\sum_{i=1}^{N}$$

which simply means, "add all the items from 1 (i = 1) to *N* (the last item)." Thus, if you had the series 1, 2, 3, 4, 5 and it was expressed as

$$\sum_{i=1}^{5}$$

it would mean: 1 + 2 + 3 + 4 +5 = 15.

★ *Multiplication and division.* Multiplication is indicated in one of two ways: either by two quantities standing in juxtaposition to each other, as XY, or by a quantity in parenthesis juxtaposed to another quantity in parenthesis, or a symbol juxtaposed to a quantity in parenthesis, for example, $(a + b)\ (a + b)$ or $N(N + 1)$.

A horizontal line always means *divide.* Furthermore, the quantity below the line is always divided into the quantity above the line. Thus,

$$\frac{1}{3}$$

means divide 1 by 3, or divide 3 into 1. Likewise,

$$\frac{\Sigma X}{N}$$

means divide *N* into the sum (Σ) of all the *X*s.

How to Read a Statistical Formula

A statistical formula is merely an expression in the shorthand of statistical symbols which gives directions for performing a specific operation, such as finding the arithmetic mean, the standard deviation, or the coefficient of correlation.

A statistical formula always has two major parts: (1) the symbol to the left of the equal sign. This indicates what the (2) statistical operations to the right of the equal sign will produce. Everything to the *right* of the equal sign is *directive* in nature—it tells you what to do. Here are some basic guidelines which may help you to read statistical language:

1. Know what each symbol in the equation means. Following each equation is usually a listing of the symbols employed in the equation with the specific meaning of each, except where these are the common symbols with which every student of statistics should be familiar, e.g., Σ, $\surd$, $<$, $|a|$, and with similar symbols, most of which have been discussed already in this chapter.

2. Begin to read the expression from the extreme *right* and read toward the *left*. This is the *reverse* of normal reading.
3. Where there are quantities in parenthesis, begin *inside* the parenthesis and perform the operations indicated there *first*. Work from *right* to *left*. For example, take this expression: 5(6 + 2) (3 + 4). Add the 4 to the 3 then add the 2 to the 6; you have 7 and 8. Do as you are told, working from *right* to *left*. Here is what you are told: $\overleftarrow{(8)(7)}$ or 7 × 8 = 56; then multiply this by 5 (working always towards the left).
4. Where there is an exponent, do as it directs.
5. Perform all the operations *above* the line first.
6. Then perform the operations *below* the line.
7. Effect the division indicated by the horizontal line. Divide the quantity that is *below* the line *into* the quantity that is *above* the line.
8. Finally, if there is an all-encompassing symbol—a radical, a parenthesis, or any other symbol indicating that the whole expression should be processed in a given manner, or other all encompassing symbol—perform the process indicated by the symbol.

Perhaps a device to help you remember the above procedure may be this jingle:

Right, left!, right, left!
Inside, outside;
Upside, downside;
Do as you are told!

Take, for example, the following formula for finding the standard deviation:

$$s = \sqrt{\frac{\sum_{i=1}^{N} (X_i - \overline{X})^2}{N}}$$

Where $\overline{X}$ = the arithmetic mean
X_i = each individual observation
N = the number of cases
s = the standard deviation of the sample

On p. 44 is that expression with each of the eight directions above numbered accordingly.

The primary purpose of this section has been to give you an overall view and to provide a rationale for thinking statistically. You should know what statistics can and cannot do; and, by having an appreciation of its capabilities, you should be able to appreciate better the way in which statistics may be employed in solving your research problem.

COMPUTERS AS TOOLS OF RESEARCH

As tools of research, computers are relatively new. That fact alone invests them with an aura of mystique. They are sometimes considered the cure-all for any problem that the researcher faces. "Let the computer do it" is the modern equivalent of the older shibboleth, "Let George do it." The purpose of the present discussion is merely to introduce you to

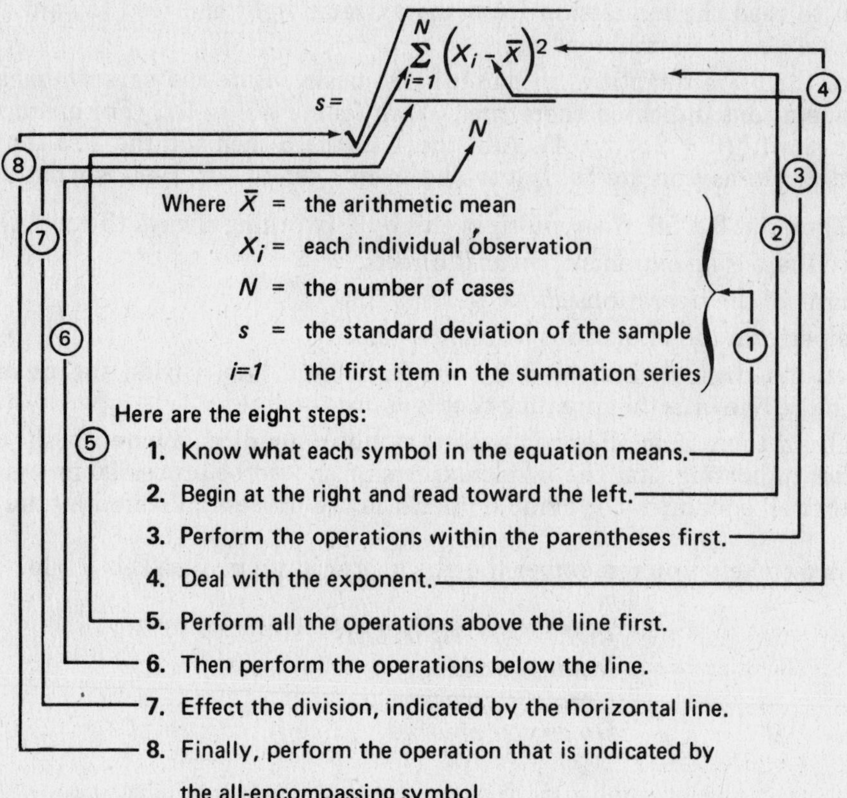

some very fundamental concepts so that you may know what computers can and cannot do, and how they may assist the researcher to complete a problem-solving task.

$s = \sqrt{\dfrac{\sum_{i=1}^{N}(X_i - \bar{X})^2}{N}}$
Where $\bar{X}$ = the arithmetic mean
X_i = each individual observation
N = the number of cases
s = the standard deviation of the sample
$i=1$ the first item in the summation series
Here are the eight steps:
1. Know what each symbol in the equation means.
2. Begin at the right and read toward the left.
3. Perform the operations within the parentheses first.
4. Deal with the exponent.
5. Perform all the operations above the line first.
6. Then perform the operations below the line.
7. Effect the division, indicated by the horizontal line.
8. Finally, perform the operation that is indicated by the all-encompassing symbol.

What Is a Computer?

What is a computer? A computer is a machine that handles information with incredible speed. All of us are familiar with many types of computers: your bathroom scale is a computer. You step on it and in a moment it tells you your total weight. Your telephone: you twirl the dials and in a few seconds another phone rings across a continent. The desk or pocket calculator is perhaps the nearest relative to the big computers. You punch in some numbers, indicate what you want the instrument to do by telling it to multiply (you strike the × key), then you punch in some more numbers and—presto!—you have the answer.

Let us define a computer. IBM, who makes them, defines a computer as a machine that can by following a controlled sequence of instructions perform both logical and arithmetic operations with data. It can also record results for either immediate or future references.[15]

Computers have been called "electronic brains." Let's dispel that myth forthrightly. *Computers cannot think*! They do as they are told. Behind every computer is a mind which has planned every single step which the computer is asked to perform. The plan is known as a computer *program.* All of us have heard of computer programmers. They are the indi-

[15] *Introduction to Computer Systems.* A manual of International Business Machines Corporation, General Systems Division (GR30-0308-1), p. 1–1.

viduals who talk to computers in a language which the computer can understand. This language is a series of electrical impulses fed into the computer by means of punched cards, magnetic tape, or other input source, which carry the information. Sometimes information goes into the computer by means of magnetic ink. The numbers in the lower left-hand corner of your bank checks are printed in this ink, and the computer reads it readily. Other input channels are magnetic tape, punched paper tape, or optical scanners. Optical scanning is familiar to all of us. The strange group of broad and narrow lines found on most merchandise—especially in supermarkets—is programming of this type.

When data enter the computer, they are stored immediately in the memory. This is exactly what you do when you wish to add a column of figures. You *write down* the figures you wish to add. That "stores" them until you can do the actual addition process. Computers work the same way.

In every computer there is a section called a *control unit*. It is here that the instructions for performing the operation, called the *program*, seek out the data and command the arithmetic unit to perform the proper operation. All computer programs—the directives that tell the computer what to do — are called *software*.[16] The actual technology of the whole process is very involved, and we need not discuss it here; but after the arithmetic unit has accomplished the operation, the new data that result — the sum, the various means, the square root, the coefficient of correlation, the analysis of variance, and so forth — are stored again in a memory core awaiting either to be used in a subsequent operation or to be sent to the output equipment for display.

All of us are familiar with the "computer printout" information. Data from the computer need not, however, be recorded in this form. They can be stored on punched cards, punched tape, magnetic tape, and various other media. Sometimes output devices display the data in the form of graphs, or project them upon a screen, similar to a television screen, at a computer *terminal*.

For commonly used research procedures—finding means, standard deviations, correlations, analysis of variance, and the like—most computer centers have standard programs which are generally available for use in connection with the data you have. Suppose you wish to find the standard deviation of a mass of data. The data must be encoded so that the computer can "read" them. This means placing the data on some form for input into the computer, then telling the computer what operations to perform by putting in the directions of the program. The computer then has the information to carry out what it has been told to do. The result will be a printing-out of the standard deviation and other pertinent facts that the computer has determined during the process.

But by no means is the application of computer-assisted research limited only to performing statistical computations. Computers are valuable tools to *all* researchers in every academic area. To scholars, even in such unlikely areas as the humanities — for those investigating problems in literature and linguistics as well as historiography — the computer may serve well their research demands.[17]

The computer can do in a brief time what otherwise may take weeks or months to do by conventional methods. The purpose of the previous discussion has been merely to give you an understanding as to what the computer can and cannot do. *It is not a miracle worker. It cannot do your thinking for you*. The computer is a very fast and faithful servant, but like all servants it must be told precisely what to do and it must be given the data with which to carry out your orders. Used in this way, computers are a researcher's best friend.

---

[16] For probably the most comprehensive directory to computer software, see Ivor Francis, *Statistical Software: A Comparative Review*. New York : Elsevier Science Publishing Company, 1981.

[17] See end-of-chapter references.

Computers are rapidly becoming a *sine qua non* in the total research process. One writer[18] discusses the role of the computer as a tool for the "laboratory scientist":

> The laboratory scientist in a research environment has become increasingly dependent on the computer for carrying out the various facets of his/her investigations. Indeed, over the last 10 years, there has been an evolution (revolution!) of computer capabilities with the net result that no component in the research process is left untouched by the computer—it is being used to design the experiment, to run the experiment, to log the data, to verify, process, analyze, and summarize the data, and to prepare the final research manuscript.

What Dr. Filliben sees in computer-assisted research for the laboratory scientist is equally appropriate for all those who do research. We may thus consider computerization an integral tool for *all* researchers whether they seek to solve problems in the laboratory, to address social issues, to investigate psychological and educational problems, or to undertake the textual criticism of a literary manuscript.

Every university has a data processing center where much of the routine work of record-keeping is turned over to a computer for processing. Such centers frequently make computer time available to students, or will computerize your statistical problems and make the computer printout of the data available to you for a minimal cost. You might inquire about such services, or visit the data processing or computerization center on your campus to discuss your problems with the staff in charge.

A REQUIRED LANGUAGE: THE FOURTH TOOL OF RESEARCH

Little can be said *specifically* about this tool of research because it will vary according to the needs of the individual and the nature of the research project. All graduate programs recognize the need for adequacy in a foreign language, certainly to the level of being able to read it without undue difficulty. A vast body of research literature until very recently was reported in three principal languages: French, German, and English. With the ascendency of research in the Soviet Union, especially in the physical sciences, more and more a reading knowledge of Russian is becoming necessary as a research tool to access the important body of research literature by soviet investigators.

Language as a tool of research may not at first glance seem critical to the needs of the researcher, but this view can be naive and deceptive. The author embarked on a research project which promised to be an investigation of contemporary practices in the modern college but before the problem for the research could be satisfactorily resolved, documents in German as well as records of Harvard University written in the seventeenth century in Latin needed to be reviewed. The need for language adequacy as a research tool should, therefore, never be taken lightly nor its importance underestimated.

Fortunately, the necessity for language competence in the resolution of a research problem may be apparent in the early stages of the investigation. If the researcher, therefore, is not prepared to meet the requirement or unwilling to gain sufficient adequacy with the language for the research needs, a change of course and selection of an alternate problem may be a wise decision.

---

[18] James J. Filliben, "DATAPLOT—An Interactive High-Level Language for Graphics, Non-linear Fitting, Data Analysis, and Mathematics," *Computer Graphics* 15 (August 1981), p. 199.

CONCLUSION

This chapter has had but one purpose: to provide an introductory orientation to some of the tools of research. In none of the sections of the chapter has any attempt been made to present a comprehensive coverage. To do so would be far beyond the province of this book. There are excellent volumes on library research and resources, on measurement and evaluation, on statistics, and on computers and computerization. Should you need additional information in any of these areas, the card catalog of the library or a periodical index will probably point you in the right direction.

Should you desire to read further in the principal areas presented in this chapter, the following list of references may be helpful. The references are merely a beginning exploration of the several areas. For a more in-depth investigation consult the eight titles on pages 17-18 and the card catalog in your library.

FOR FURTHER READING

Further Reading to Assist You in Using the Library

Becker, Joseph, and R. M. Hayes. *Information Storage and Retrieval: Tools, Elements, Theories.* New York: John Wiley & Sons, Inc., 1963.

Berry, Dorothea M. *A Bibliographic Guide to Educational Research.* 2nd ed. Metuchen, New Jersey: Scarecrow Press, 1980.

Cook, Margaret G. *The New Library Key.* 3rd ed. New York: The H. W. Wilson Company, 1975.

Courtney, Winifred F. *The Reader's Adviser.* 2 vols., 11th ed. New York, R. R. Bowker Co., 1969.

Gates, Jean K. *Guide to the Use of Books and Libraries.* 4th ed. NewYork: McGraw-Hill Book Company, 1979.

Goodrum, Charles A. *The Library of Congress.* New York: Praeger Publishers, Inc., 1974.

Katz, William A. *Introduction to Reference Work.* 2nd ed. New York: McGraw-Hill Book Company. 1974.

More, Grant W. *The Concise Guide to Library Research.* New York: Washington Square Press, 1966.

Sheehy, Eugene P. *Guide to Reference Books.* 9th ed. Chicago, Illinois: The American Library Association, 1976.

Further Reading to Assist You in Understanding Statistics

Anderson, Theodore R., and Morris Zelditch, Jr. *Basic Course in Statistics with Sociological Applications.* 2nd ed. New York: Holt, Rinehart and Winston, 1968.

Arkin, Herbert, and R. Colton. *Statistical Methods.* 5th ed. Barnes and Noble Outline Series, New York: Barnes and Noble Books, 1970.

Blalock, Hubert M., Jr. *Social Statistics.* 2nd ed. New York: McGraw-Hill Book Company, 1972.

Hardyck, Curtis D., and Lewis F. Petrinovich. *Statistics for the Behavioral Sciences.* Philadelphia, Pa.: W. B. Saunders Company, 1969.

Keppel, Geoffrey. *Design and Analysis: A Researcher's Handbook.* Englewood Cliffs, N.J.: Prentice-Hall, Inc., 1973.

Key, V. O., Jr. *A Primer of Statistics for Political Scientists.* New York: Thomas Y. Crowell Company, 1954.

McCall, Robert B. *Fundamental Statistics for Psychology.* 2nd ed. New York: Harcourt Brace Jovanovich, Inc., 1975.

Minium, Edward W. *Statistical Reasoning in Psychology and Education.* 2nd ed. New York: John Wiley & Sons, Inc., 1978.

Neyman, J. "Statistics — Servant of All Sciences." *Science* 122 (September 2, 1955): 401.

Novick, Melvin R. *Statistical Methods for Educational and Psychological Research.* New York: McGraw-Hill Book Company, 1974.

Weiss, R. S. *Statistics in Social Research: An Introduction.* New York: John Wiley & Sons, 1968.

Further Reading to Assist You in Understanding Computers and Computerization

Armor, David J., and Arthur S. Couch. *Data Text Primer: An Introduction to Computerized Social Data Analysis.* New York: The Free Press, 1972.

Baker, W.O., *et al.* "Computers and Research." *Science* 195 (March 18, 1977): 1134-39.

Bender, T. K. "Innovations in the Format of Literary Concordances and Indexes." *Linguistics* 194 (July 23, 1977): 53-63.

Borko, Harold, ed. *Computer Applications in the Behavioral Sciences.* Englewood Cliffs, N.J.: Prentice-Hall, Inc., 1962.

Directory of Online Databases. Santa Monica, Calif.: Cuadra Associates, Inc. Published quarterly.

Davis, Gordon B. *Introduction to Computers.* 3rd ed. New York: McGraw-Hill Book Company, 1977.

Francis, Ivor. *Statistical Software: A Comparative Review.* New York: Elsevier Science Publishing Co., 1981.

Gille, Frank H., ed. *Computer Yearbook and Directory* [*of Information on University Computer Systems*]. 2nd ed. Detroit, Mich.: American Data Processing Co., 1968.

Hellwig, Jessica. *Introduction to Computers and Programming.* New York: Columbia University Press, 1969.

Hockey, Susan. *A Guide to Computer Applications in the Humanities.* Baltimore, Md.: The Johns Hopkins University Press, 1980.

Hy, Ronn J. *Using the Computer in the Social Sciences: A Nontechnical Approach.* New York: Elsevier Science Publishing Co., 1977.

Janda, Kenneth. *Data Processing: Applications to Political Research.* Evanston, Ill.: Northwestern University Press, 1965.

Moore, Richard. *Introduction to the Use of Computer Packages for Statistical Analysis.* Englewood Cliffs, N.J.: Prentice-Hall, Inc., 1978.

OSIRIS III: An Integrated Collection of Computer Programs for the Management and Analysis of Social Science Data. Ann Arbor, Mich.: Institute for Social Research, 1973.

Patton, Peter C., and Renee A. Holoien, eds. *Computing in the Humanities.* Lexington Books, Lexington, Mass.: D.C. Heath and Co., 1981.

Rossman, Parker. "Computers and Religious Research." *National Forum* 63 (Spring 1983): 24-26.

Shorter, Edward. *The Historian and the Computer: A Practical Guide.* Englewood Cliffs, N.J.: Prentice-Hall, Inc., 1971.

Singer, B. "Exploratory Strategies and Graphical Displays." *Journal of Interdisciplinary History* 7 (Summer 1976): 57-70.

Stone, P. J., D. C. Dunphy, M. S. Smith, and D. M. Ogilive. *The General Inquirer: A Computer Approach to Content Analysis in the Behavioral Sciences.* Cambridge, Mass.: Massachusetts Institute of Technology Press, 1966.

Williams, Martha E. *Computer-Readable Data Bases: A Directory and Data Sourcebook.* White Plains, N.Y.: Knowledge Industry Publications, 1979.

Wolfart, H. O., and F. Pardo. "Computer Aided Philology and Algorithmic Linguistics." *International Journal of American Linguistics* 45 (April 1979), 107-22.

Computer Journals

The Computer Journal. A publication of the British Computer Society, Spectrum House, London, NW4 2JQ UK (United Kingdom).

Computer Magazine. Published by the IEEE Computer Society, Long Beach, California

Computer Education. A periodical of the Computer Education Group, North Staffordshire Polytechnic Computer Center, Blackheath Lane, Staffordshire, United Kingdom.

Computers and Automation. Berkley Enterprises, Inc., 815 Washington St., R5, Newtonville, Massachusetts 02160.

Computers and the Humanities. Pergamon Press, Inc., Elmsford, New York 10523.

Further Reading to Assist You in Understanding Measurement

Bonjean, Charles M., Richard J. Hill, and S. Dale McLemore. *Sociological Measurements: An Inventory of Scales and Indices.* San Francisco, Calif.: Chandler Publishing Co., 1967.

Cronbach, Lee J., and Lita Furby. "How We Should Measure 'Change'—or Should We?" *Psychological Bulletin* 74 (July 1970): 68-80.

Cutright, P. "National Poetical Development: Measurement and Analysis." *American Sociological Review* 27 (1963): 229-45.

Dellow, E. L. *Methods of Science: An Introduction to Measuring and Testing for Laymen and Students.* New York: Universe Books, 1970.

Guttman, Louis. "A Basis for Scaling Qualitative Data." *American Sociological Review* 9 (1944): 139-50.

Likert, R. "A Techinique for the Measurement of Attitudes." *Archives of Psychology* 21 No. 140.

Lord, Frederic M. "The Measurement of Growth." *Educational and Psychological Measurement* 16 (Winter 1956): 421-27.

Lynch, M. D., H. M. Nettleship, and R. C. Carlson. "The Measurement of Human Interest." *Journalism Quarterly* 45 (1968): 226-34.

Miller, Delbert C. *Handbook of Research Design and Social Measurements.* 3rd ed. New York: David McKay Co., Inc., 1977.

Oppenheim, A. N. *Questionnaire Design and Attitude Measurement.* New York: Basic Book, Inc., Publishers, 1966.

Osgood, C. E., C. J. Suci, and P. H. Tannenbaum. *The Measurement of Meaning.* Urbana, Ill.: The University of Illinois Press, 1957.

Payne, David A., and Robert F. McMorris. *Educational and Psychological Measurements.* 2nd ed. Morristown, N.J.: General Learning Press, 1975.

Payne, James. *Principles of Social Science Measurement.* College Station, Texas: Lytton Publishers, 1975.

Robinson, J. P., and P. R. Shaver. *Measures of Social Psychological Attitudes.* Ann Arbor, Mich.: Institute for Social Research, University of Michigan, 1969.

Shaw, M. E., and J. M. Wright. *Scales for the Measurement of Attitudes.* New York: McGraw-Hill Book Company, 1967.

Stanley, Julian C., and Kenneth D. Hopkins. *Educational and Psychological Measurements and Evaluation.* Englewood Cliffs, N.J.: Prentice-Hall, Inc., 1972.

Stevens, S. S., ed. "Mathematics, Measurement and Psychophysics," in *Handbook of Experimental Psychology.* New York: John Wiley & Sons, Inc., 1951.

Thorndike, Robert L., and Elizabeth Hagen. *Measurement and Evaluation in Psychology and Education.* 3rd ed. New York: John Wiley & Sons, 1969.

Tull, Donald S. *Marketing Research: Meaning, Measurement, and Method.* New York: Macmillan Publishing Co., Inc., 1976.

RESEARCH PLANNING AND DESIGN

READ THIS—BEFORE YOU READ THIS CHAPTER

At the very heart of every research project is the problem.

This chapter will discuss the research problem in all its aspects: where research problems are found, how they are stated, their division into more manageable subproblems, and other matters which make problems intelligible to all who read them and help the researcher in working with them.

The chapter is an especially important one. Study it carefully.

Finally, in the Practicum Section, pages 286-288, you will be given a form with which to evaluate your own research problem.

3

The Problem: Heart of the Research Project

At the very heart of every research project is the problem. It is paramount in importance to the success of the research effort, and it should be so considered by every researcher. The situation is quite simple: no problem, no research. To see the problem with unwavering clarity and to be able to state it in precise and unmistakable terms is the first requirement in the research process.

WHERE ARE RESEARCH PROBLEMS FOUND?

Problems for research are everywhere. Take a good look at the world around you. It teems with researchable problems. Whatever arouses your interest, tweaks your curiosity, and raises questions for which as yet there are no answers, or where answers exist but where dispute arises as to their validity—there is fertile ground for the discovery of a *researchable* problem.

At the outset, it is extremely important that you distinguish between two basic types of problems: *personal* problems and *researchable* problems. When some students think of problems, they lump together all of the perplexities with which they are faced and fail to distinguish between their essential characteristics. *You* may have a problem: how to get along with your mother-in-law, how to ask the boss for a raise, how to make a success of your life. And these problems are real, but they are not *researchable*. Researchable problems fit the requirements of the scientific method which we have outlined on a previous page.[1] And there is no scarcity of them.

The human race does not have the final word on most of the problems that are important to it. Inspect any segment of life, any phenomena happening at this moment, any of the events that swim before your eyes. In all of these situations lie innumerable problems to claim the attention of the researcher.

Where does your interest lie? Is it in agriculture, chemistry, economics, education, electronics, engineering, health sciences, languages and literature, medicine, music, political science, physics, sociology, zoology, or perhaps in any one of dozens of other categories? Go to the library; inspect any volume of *Dissertation Abstracts International* under the general heading of your interest and you will suddenly be aware how intimately the world of research and the world of everyday life have become intertwined. You will see research intimately related to the ever-expanding and exploding universe of knowledge. You may also realize after such an experience that all you need is to see your own area of interest in sharp, clear focus and then enunciate the problems indigenous to it in precise lucid terms, and you will have a problem for your own research efforts. But it is with an unmistakably clear statement of the problem that research begins.

WHAT ARE THE CHARACTERISTICS OF A RESEARCHABLE PROBLEM?

Many students have difficulty in understanding the nature of a problem which qualifies it to be considered as suitable for research. This is partly because they do not understand the nature of research itself. They think that merely "doing something" that termi-

---

[1] See pages 4–7.

nates in a "written paper" is research. They think primarily of activity as the prime ingredient: so long as they are *doing* something: finding a correlation, gathering data, making notes, matching groups, or comparing their achievement, they are thus doing research. None of these activities, in fact, is research; and a problem built *entirely* around activity is not a researchable problem. Research is inseparable from the *thinking*, the *inquiring*, the *insight*—in short, the *cerebration* of the individual engaged in it. One cannot throw the mind out of gear and the body into action and do research! Research requires an inquiring mind which seeks fact and, after finding it, synthesizes the meaning of such fact into an accurate and logical conclusion.

Let us say more about those activities that are often called research but are *not* research. First, we begin with a basic rule: *Where there is no mental struggle on the part of the researcher to force the facts to reveal their meaning, there is no research.* When a machine, a statistical formula, or a computer can arrange and rearrange the data, and present them in neatly categorized or statistically analyzed forms of a terminal product, the process is not research. For this reason, activity which ends in merely finding a coefficient of correlation between two sets of data is not research. A computer can do that! This is not to belittle the correlational technique, but it is merely that—a *technique*—and nothing more.

As we have said earlier, a coefficient of correlation is only a signpost. It points in the direction of meaningful relevancy. And research is not concerned so much with the relevancy as it is with the *meaningfulness* of the relevancy. O.K. We have a correlation of 0.82. That means that two sets of data are somewhat closely related. But to the *inquiring mind* of the researcher, that does not *say* much. The researcher wants to know more: what is the *nature* of that relationship; what is the underlying *cause* of that relationship; and, if these two sets of data are related, *how* are they related? Answer these questions, and you are *interpreting* the data; you are *discovering* what that correlation means. A machine cannot do that, nor can a statistical formula, nor an amanuensis. Only the mind of the researcher can inquire into the meaning of the fact until it reveals its inner significance.

Generally yes-no questions are not research. The are indications that the real researchable problem lies much deeper than does the question being asked.

"Is homework beneficial to children?" That is no problem for research because it does not go deep enough. It misses the central issue. The question is not whether homework is beneficial or whether it is not. If the homework produces good results and a better student, then it is beneficial; if you can discern no good results or it has deleterious effects, than it is not beneficial. The matter is as simple as that and need not involve the complexity of the scientific method for its resolution.

The researchable issue is not *whether* homework is beneficial to children, but *wherein the benefit of homework lies*; or, *if it is not beneficial*, *why* it has no value. Research goes beyond the surface questions to causal and basic considerations. It is interested not merely in observable phenomena *per se*, but it is interested in reasons for, causes of, and *qualitative* —as opposed to quantitative—differences that distinguish one situation from another. When you search for such determinative and basic factors, you are entering an area which may properly be dignified by the term *research*.

Likewise, "comparison" problems are not research. "The purpose of this research is to compare the defections from East Germany during the decade 1950–1959 with those during the decade 1960–1969." All you have to do to "solve" that problem is to make two lists of figures. From what the problem states, there need be no interpretation of data at all, merely the presentation of it—a figure showing the *number* of defections in the one decade in comparison with the *number* of defections in the succeeding decade.

But, you contend, the problem *implied* interpretation. Not at all! Problems must state exactly what the researcher's purpose is. Inexperienced researchers often make the mistake of assuming that problems imply more than they do. They think that because *they* had an assumption in mind but did not state it in their articulation of the problem, that all the world would assume what they had in mind. This points up another basic rule: *State the problem so clearly that the fact of interpretation of the data is plainly evident or that it is so strongly implied in the wording of the problem that it is unmistakably obvious.* Had the preceding problem been stated: "The purpose of this research is to compare *in order to analyze the types of and the reasons for* [the italicized words clearly imply interpretation of the data] defection from East Germany during 1950-1959 in comparison with those defections during 1960-1969," there would have been no question about the intent of the researcher to interpret the data. The italicized words show that the purpose is to get beneath mere comparison to a basic inquiry. The one is a mere *quantitive* comparison of defections versus a *qualitative* identification of the motives for, and the causes of, the defections of one decade as contrasted with those of the following decade.

Comparisons are only mediate steps in arranging data for presentation to the mind of the researcher. Comparisons cause likenesses and differences to float to the surface so that the researcher may be aware of them; but research begins when we seek the *reasons* for the similar or disparate nature of those facts. Simple comparison, of itself, cannot be the end of a research effort.

For a problem to be researchable it must demand an *interpretation of the data* leading to a *discovery of fact.* And that "discovery of fact" must go beyond a mere statistical statement of comparative status or relationship. Inexperienced researchers sometimes become confused in the whole complex process of research, mistaking the *gathering* of data, the *arranging* of the data, or the *processing* of the data with an *interpretation* of the data. The former are vastly different processes from the latter. Interpretation of the data is an *explanation* of what the data that have been gathered, arranged, and processed—whether statistically or by any other means—actually *mean.* The critical and unavoidable question which every researcher facing a corpus of data must ultimately answer is: What is the *meaning* of all these facts?

THE STATEMENT OF THE PROBLEM

There are bad habits in research as there are bad habits in other areas of human behavior. One of the worst of these is to allow yourself to cultivate the habit of fuzzy thinking and forming inchoate concepts evidenced by jotting down meaningless groups of words which are vague verbal fragments. Jotting down a phrase, a clause, a few meaningless words is merely to deceive yourself that you fully comprehend what you are unable to articulate. Problem statement must do better than produce merely a splutter of wordy and meaningless fragments.

If you really know what your problem is, state it clearly. Each word of the problem should be expressive, sharp, indispensable, definitive. *Always state the problem in a complete grammatical sentence.* Your problems should be stated so well, in fact, that anyone, anywhere, (who understands English) could read it, understand it, and react to it without benefit of your presence. If, for any reason, your problem is not stated with such clarity, then you are merely deceiving yourself that you, yourself, know what the problem is. Such self-deception will merely cause you trouble later on.

Here, for instance, are some meaningless half-statements, mere verbal blobs, that only hint at the problem but do not state it.

A student in sociology submitted this:

Welfare on children's attitudes.

A student in music, this:

Palestrina and the motet.

A student in economics proposed this:

Busing of schoolchildren.

Finally, this from a student in a school of social work:

Retirement plans of adults.

All four students have uttered uncommunicative nothings. Generally, fragments such as these demonstrate that the researcher either cannot or will not think in terms of specifics. Although it may be irksome to express your thought accurately and completely—if you are one of those who thinks in terms of scraps and pieces—you had better begin to think in terms of specific researchable goals expressed in complete communicative statements.

We shall take the preceding half-utterances and develop each of them into a complete statement which expresses a fully researchable problem.

Welfare on children's attitudes becomes

What effect does welfare assistance given to parents have on the vocational aspirations of their teenage children?

Palestrina and the motet becomes

This study will analyze the motets of Palestrina to discover their distinctive contrapuntal characteristics in contrast with the same aspects of the motets of Palestrina's contemporary, William Byrd.

Busing of students becomes

What factors must be evaluated and what are the relative weights of those several factors in constructing a formula for cost-estimate busing of children in a Midwestern metropolitan school system?

Retirement plans for adults becomes

The purpose of this study will be to examine the specific relationship which exists between organizational status, sense of professional satisfaction, and organizational identification of a specific group of well-functioning administration and professional men who are in the sixth decade of their lives (ages 50–59) and their attitudes, role expectancies, leisure conception, and actual planning for retirement in order to determine the relative importance of each of these factors in achieving successful retirement.

Note that, in the wording of each of these problems, the groups studied are limited, so that the population is of manageable size. In wording a problem, the parameters of the population should be carefully considered. Students sometimes propose their problems without thinking exactly what their words imply. Take the student who states the problem in this manner: "This study proposes to survey the science programs in the secondary schools in the United States for the purpose of . . ." Let's think about that. There are 26,597 secondary schools in the United States. North to south, they are stretched from Alaska to Florida; east to west, from Maine to Hawaii! How do you plan to contact each of these schools? By personal visit? At most you can probably visit no more than two schools per day. That's 13,298 school days—not counting vacations and weekends. That's almost sixty-six and one-half school years! That's a reasonable lifetime—and you have merely collected the data! It may be that if you are now twenty years old, you are getting started a little late. You will be eighty-six before you are ready to do your study. That says nothing about the rather considerable fortune that you will need for such a project. Counting traveling expenses, lodging, food, and miscellaneous living expenses, $40 a day may be a very conservative estimate. Just for the days when you will be visiting schools—to say nothing of vacations and weekends—you should be prepared to spend on your study $531,920.

But, say you, I will gather the data by questionnaire. Let's explore this approach. At

40 cents per inquiry—for you will want to include a stamped reply envelope for the return of your questionnaire—your initial mailing will come to $10,638.80. Follow-up letters, reminders, additional questionnaires—you can count on one-third of the original cost—will bring your postage alone to $14,185.07, and this does not include the cost of envelopes, stationery, cost of questionnaire duplication, and miscellaneous items. Then, add to this, the processing of some 20,000 questionnaires, programming the data, computer time, and the compilation and typing of a research report, and you will soon realize that the project you have proposed is not an inconsequential effort.

But, you protest, I had no thought of surveying *all* of the secondary schools in the United States! No? That brings up a still further matter of utmost importance.

Say Precisely What You Mean!

Research has no place for evasion, equivocation, or mental reservation. You must mean exactly what you say and assume total responsibility for the thought your words express. You cannot assume clairvoyance on the part of others to know what is in your mind.

A basic rule prevails among those in scholarly pursuit: *Absolute honesty and integrity is assumed in every statement a scholar makes.* You should say only *precisely* what you mean. We assume that what you state in your problem you mean to fulfill in the research effort. In fact, it is upon the intent as stated in the problem and subproblems of a research proposal that largely determines whether a faculty will approve the research project of a graduate student or a foundation award a grant for sponsored research.

Honesty and integrity are absolutely critical. The statement of your problem is a commitment to a solemn obligation, and it should be phrased neither lightly nor irresponsibly. Once you have stated the purpose of the research in the problem, that's it! There can be then no avoidance of your responsibility: no double talk, no pleading ignorance of implications, no avoiding the obligation to perform precisely what you have expressed by your own words.

You cannot, for example, when you come to a realization of the staggering magnitude of your problem, contend that you intended to take only a random sampling of the secondary schools in the United States. Had you intended that, you should have said so plainly: "This study proposes to survey the science programs *in certain selected secondary schools throughout the United States* . . ." Or, perhaps, in a restricted geographical area—the South, east of the Mississippi, or within the boundaries of a single state, Pennsylvania, for example—any of these designations, properly defined, would have given the problem a limitation which the original statement of it lacked. It would have communicated to others precisely what you intended to do.

One further haunting thought lingers with respect to the statement of the problem. If a researcher cannot be completely responsible for the statement of the problem, and its attendant parts, one might question seriously whether such a researcher is likely to be any more responsible in gathering and interpreting the data. And this, indeed, is very serious, for it reflects upon the basic responsibility of the whole effort. It can be a *coup brutal* to one's degree aspirations.

We have discussed two of the three most common difficulties in the statement of the problem: the fragmentary and meaningless splutter, and the irresponsible and extravagant wording. But to these we add a third: the generalized discussion that ends in foggy focus. Occasionally, a researcher will announce an intention to make a statement of the problem. From that point the discussion becomes more and more foggy. Such a researcher talks *about* the problem instead of clearly stating it. Under the excuse that the problem needs an "introduction" or needs to be seen against a "background," the researcher launches into a generalized discussion, continually obscuring the problem, never clearly articulating it.

Take, for example, what one student wrote under the heading of "Statement of the Problem":

> The upsurge of interest in reading and learning disabilities found among both children and adults has focused the attention of educators, psychologists, and linguists on the language syndrome. In order to understand how language is learned, it is necessary to understand what language is. Language acquisition is a normal developmental aspect of every individual, but it has not been studied in sufficient depth. To provide us with the necessary background information to understand the anomaly of language deficiency implies a knowledge of the developmental processes of language as these relate to the individual from infancy to maturity. Grammar, also an aspect of language learning, is acquired through pragmatic language usage. Phonology, syntax, and semantics are all intimately involved in the study of any language disability.

Is there a statement of problem here? If so, where? What is the problem? Where is it explicitly stated? Several problems are suggested. None of them is articulated with sufficient clarity that we might put a finger on it and say, "There, that is the problem."

One need not write an orientational essay in order to state a problem. Earlier in this chapter, we invited you to go to *Dissertation Abstracts International* to see how the world of research and the real world of everyday living are intertwined. Now go back to that same source. Note with what directness the problems are set forth. One comes in direct contact with the problem from the very first words of the abstract: "The purpose of this study is to . . ." No mistaking that; no background build-up necessary—just a straightforward plunge into the depths of the business at hand. With such clarity should research problems be stated.

Edit Your Writing

The difficulties we have been discussing can be avoided by carefully editing your words. Editing is sharpening a thought to a gemlike point and eliminating useless verbiage. Choose your words precisely. To do so will clarify your writing.

The sentences in the paragraph that you have just read began as a mishmash of foggy thought and jumbled verbiage. The original version of the paragraph contained 71 words. These were edited down to 38 words. That is a reduction of 46 percent. Improvement in readability, 100 percent. See the original version and the manner in which it has been edited on the next page.

Editing almost invariably improves your thinking and your prose. Many students think that so long as they have a thought in their own minds, any words that approximate the expression of that thought are adequate to convey that thought to others. 'Tis not so. Approximation is never precision.

You need to be rigorous with the words you write. Punctuation will help you. A colon will announce that what follows is an explanation of the generalized statement that precedes it. Similarly, the semicolon, the dash, quotation marks, parentheses, brackets, and italics are all tools in clarifying your thought. Learn to use the comma correctly.

Any good dictionary will usually have a section dealing with punctuation usage. Most handbooks of English will give you help in writing clear, concise, and effective sentences and help you to combine those sentences into unified and coherent paragraphs.

Clichés, colloquialisms, slang, jargon, and the gibberish of any group or profession usually obscures thought. The evidence of the lazy mind is the irresponsible use of professional jargon. Those who employ it do so usually because they feel that it impresses or that it adds importance to what they are saying.

The thought's the thing. And when it is most clear, it is clothed with simple words,

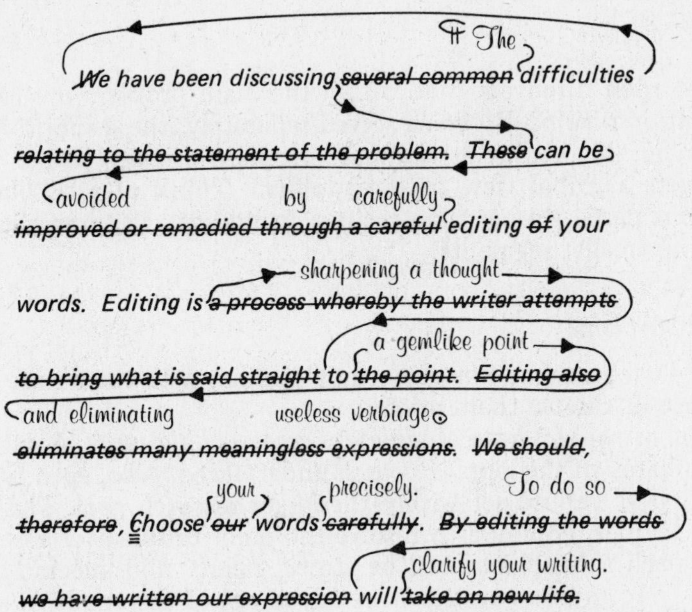

concrete nouns, and expressive verbs. Every student would do well to study how the great writers and poets set their thoughts in words. They have much to say by way of illustration to those who have trouble in putting their own thoughts on paper.

In general, however, some basic guidelines for clear writing may help you to express the problems and the subproblems effectively.

1. Express the thought with the least number of words possible.
2. Use a thesaurus: it will help you find the exact word.
3. Economize on syllables. In straightforward discussion, prefer the one- or two-syllable word to the longer one.
4. Keep the sentence length short. Vary the length, of course, but break up those long contorted sentences into shorter, more succinct ones.
5. Look critically at each thought as it stands on paper. Do the words say exactly what you wish them to say? Read carefully phrase by phrase. See if one word will carry the burden of two or more. Throw out the superfluous and unnecessary words.
6. Be alert to modification. Phrases and clauses misplaced can create havoc with the thought. Here is an example:

   FOR SALE: A piano that has arthritis and cannot play anymore, by a woman with beautifully carved mahogany legs.

   Place the modifiers correctly and all's well that ends well:

   FOR SALE: A piano with beautifully carved mahogany legs by a woman that has arthritis and cannot play anymore.

Practical Application —

Turn now to Appendix B, page 286, Project 3 where you will have an opportunity to state your problem for research and to apply to it several criteria governing an acceptable problem.

— —

THE SUBPROBLEMS

Every researcher soon discovers that within the main problem are logical subcomponents. These we call *subproblems.* By being solved separately, these subproblems resolve the main problem piecemeal. By looking at the main problem through its subproblems, the researcher frequently gets a global view of the problem. Think of a problem, therefore, in terms of its component parts. Rather than make a frontal attack upon the entire problem, divide and conquer it in smaller segments.

Characteristics of Subproblems

Because some researchers may not be entirely familiar with the nature and the purpose of subproblems, we should discuss them briefly.

★ *Each subproblem should be a completely researchable unit.* A subproblem should constitute a logical subarea of the larger research undertaking. Also, each subproblem might be researched as a separate subproject within the larger research goal. The solutions of the subproblems, taken together, combine to resolve the main problem of research. It is necessary, therefore, that each subproblem can be stated clearly and succinctly. Often, a subproblem is stated in the form of a question. The advantage of this mode of statement is that a question tends to focus the attention of the researcher more directly upon the research target of the subproblem than does a mere declarative statement. After all, the interrogative attitude is the normal psychological condition of every true researcher's mind.

★ *Pseudosubproblems are not researchable subproblems.* Every researcher must distinguish clearly between: (1) the true subproblems whose solution will further the resolution of some part of the main problem, and (2) pseudosubproblems, which are, in fact, nothing more than demands arising from the research procedure, requiring arbitrary decisions on the part of the researcher. These pseudosubproblems arise quite logically from the research situation, but they are problems that the researcher must resolve by deciding on a course of action to be followed as a part of the research procedure. Here are some examples of pseudosubproblems:

What is the best way to choose a sample?
What instruments should be used to gather the data?
How can the strength of a person's convictions be measured?
How large should a representative sample be?

These are, without doubt, problems, and they must be resolved before the research project can proceed; but they are problems that have to do more with the procedure that you will follow than with the main problem of the research. They demand for their resolution knowledge on your part and a decision from you as to a course of action. *They are not researchable* in the sense in which we have defined research—as an application of the scientific method to the discovery of truth. They are, rather, knotty impediments that prevent you from coming to grips with the real problems for research. To resolve a pseudosubproblem, make a firm decision on the procedural matter and then get on with the solution of the researchable problem.

★ *Within the subproblems, interpretation of the data must be apparent.* At some point within the statement of the subproblem—as, indeed, within the main problem—the fact that data will be interpreted must be clearly evident. This may be expressed as a part of each subproblem statement, or it may occupy an entire subproblem separately.

★ *The subproblems must add up to the totality of the problem.* After you have stated the subproblems, check them against the statement of the main problem to see (1) that nothing in excess of the coverage of the main problem is included, and (2) that you have no omissions, so that all significant areas of the main problem are covered by the several subproblems taken collectively.

★ *Proliferation of subproblems is circumspect.* If the main problem is carefully stated and properly limited to a feasible researchable effort, the researcher will find that it usually contains in the vicinity of two to six subproblems. Sometimes the inexperienced researcher will come up with as many as ten, fifteen, or twenty subproblems. When this happens it generally means that a careful review of the problem and its attendant subproblems should be undertaken. The researcher should study each subproblem to see whether it is truly a subproblem of the main problem or whether it falls into one or more of the following categories:

1. *The researcher has confused his personal problems with problems for research.* Has the researcher stated as subproblems procedural decisions that need to be made before the research can proceed?
2. *The researcher has fragmented the true subproblems.* Can any of the subproblems be combined into larger researchable units lesser in magnitude than the main problem?
3. *There may be a mixture of the preceding errors.* If so, a careful study of each subproblem is necessary to separate procedural questions from purely researchable goals.

★ *Beware of unrealistic goals.* Be cautious of committing yourself beyond what is possible to achieve. We have discussed this area with respect to the main problem. If it is there controlled, the researcher then will experience little difficulty with it in the subproblems. But it is well to be mindful of this tendency with respect to the subproblems also.

How to Locate the Subproblems

Students sometimes have difficulty in locating the subproblems within the context of the larger problem. Here are some guidelines:

★ *Begin with the problem itself.* If the problem is correctly written, you will be able to detect within it the subproblem areas which may be isolated for separate study. It is axiomatic that the totality of the subproblems must equal the totality of the problem. Therefore, because all the subproblems will add up to the problem, the first step should be to inspect the problem itself with the purpose of seeking the components that compose it.

★ *Write the problem, then "box off" the subproblem areas.* Take a clean sheet of paper and copy the problem. Allow considerable space between the lines. Inspect carefully what

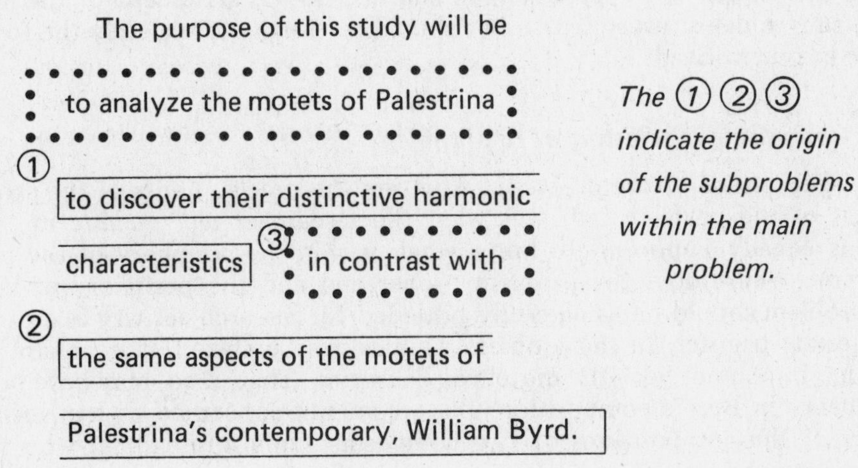

The ① ② ③ indicate the origin of the subproblems within the main problem.

you have written. Look at it to discover the areas that should receive in-depth treatment before the problem can be resolved. Box off these areas. Within these boxes lies the genesis of your subproblems. Enclose within dotted lines those specific words which indicate the necessity to interpret the data. Every researchable problem should contain a word, a group of words *(interpret; analyze; determine; seek the causes of,* or *the reasons for; understand the reason why,* or *the causes of;* and similar expressions that imply that the data must be interpreted) which demand synthesis, analysis, judgment, or decisions by the researcher after the collection of the data.

To illustrate, let us take the problem cited earlier relating to the motets of Palestrina. Let us do with it precisely as we have just described. The problem has been stated on page 56.

Now write the subproblems:

Subproblem 1: What are the distinctive characteristics of the harmonic structure in the motets of Giovanni Pierluigi da Palestrina?

Subproblem 2: What are the distinctive characteristics of the harmonic structure in the motets of William Byrd?

Subproblem 3: What will an analysis of the harmonic characteristics of the motets of Palestrina indicate when these are contrasted with a similar analysis of the harmonic characteristics of the motets of William Byrd?

The procedure for finding the subproblems will work for *any* problem in *any* academic discipline. A problem in musicology was here used merely for the purpose of illustration.

EVERY PROBLEM NEEDS FURTHER DELINEATION

Up to this point, we have been discussing merely the problem and its subparts. The statement of the problem establishes the goal for the research effort. The subproblems suggest avenues of approaching that goal in a practical way. But goal alone is not enough. Certain unresolved areas still remain, if we are to comprehend fully the meaning of the problem. In every research endeavor, it is important that we understand exactly what the researcher intends to do and, conversely, what he does not intend to do. It is also essential to our understanding of the problem that we knew precisely the meaning of the terms employed in stating the problem and the subproblems. What basic assumptions are postulated as underlying substrata upon which the research will rest? What are the hypotheses?

All these are important considerations and together they comprise what is sometimes referred to as *the setting of the problem.* In addition to the statement of the problem and its attendant subproblems, every researcher should set forth quite clearly the four principal areas we have just mentioned.

Components Comprising the Setting of the Problem

★ *The delimitations of the problem.* What are the precise limits of the problem area? The statement of the problem indicates what the researcher *will include* in the research endeavor. It is equally important to know what, within the periphery of the problem, he *will not include.* Where does the problem proper end and the periphery of the problem begin? The problem should be as carefully bounded for research activity as a parcel of land is for a real estate transfer. In the problem we have just analyzed, it is possible that Byrd may have come in contact with the motets of Palestrina. That, if so, may have been a determinative influence in Byrd's composition. But we are not concerned with *influences on* but *characteristics of* the compositions of two composers. Only a researcher who thinks carefully about the problem and the point of its focus will distinguish the difference between these two emphases. The question of influence lies outside the central focus of the problem. It, thus, must be ruled out by a delimitation.

An investigator cannot investigate *all* the aspects of any problem. This does not suggest that these aspects are unimportant; they are simply peripheral to the stated goal of the research. The motto of the researcher is "This *one* thing I do; this *one* area I investigate; this *one* question I attempt to answer; this *one* problem I aim to solve." Peripheral considerations may be very enticing and interesting, but they are *peripheral* and as such cannot be permitted to deter the researcher from pursuing the main quest as stated in the problem.

★ *The definitions of the terms.* What precisely do the terms in the phrasing of the problem and the subproblems mean? For example, when we say that the purpose of the research is to analyze the harmonic characteristics of motets, what are we talking about? What are harmonic characteristics? Without knowing explicitly what a term means, we cannot evaluate the research or determine whether the researcher has carried out what, in the problem, was announced as the principal thrust of the research.

Terms must be defined operatively; that is, the definition must interpret the term *as it is employed in relation to the researcher's project.* Sometimes students rely on "dictionary definitions." Dictionary definitions are seldom either adequate or helpful. In defining a term, the researcher makes that term mean whatever he wishes it to mean within the particular context of the problem or its subproblems. We must know how *the researcher* defines the term. We need not necessarily subscribe to such a definition, but so long as we know precisely what the researcher means when employing a particular term, we are able to understand the research and appraise it objectively.

Formal definitions contain three parts: (1) *the term* to be defined, (2) *the genera,* or the general class to which the concept being defined belongs, and (3) *the differentia,* the specific characteristics or traits which distinguish the concept being defined from all other members of the general classification. For example, *harmonic characteristics* (which is the term to be defined) shall mean *the manner* (the genera) in which tonal values are combined *to produce individualized polyphonic patterns associated with the works of a particular composer* (the differentia: telling what particular "manner" we mean).

A spurious type of definition, commonly called *a circular definition,* or *defining in a circle,* is sometimes encountered. The most classic example of which is perhaps Gertrude Stein's, "a rose, is a rose, is a rose." Defined in a circle, *harmonic characteristics* would be "those *characteristics* which derive from the *harmonic* patterns found in the works of a particular composer." In circular definitions the term to be defined is employed in defining that term. In the above definition *characteristics* and *harmonic* are used to define *harmonic characteristics.*

★ *The assumptions.* We discussed the matter of the assumptions briefly in chapter 1.[2] Here, however, the matter needs further discussion. Assumptions are so basic that without them the research problem itself could not exist. Let us illustrate. For example, we are attempting to determine by means of a pretest-postest whether a particular method of teaching has produced the results hypothesized. A basic assumption in such a situation must be that the test measures what the test is presumed to measure. We must assume also that the teacher can teach. Without these assumptions, we have no problem, no experiment.

Assumptions are what the researcher takes for granted. But taking things for granted may cause much misunderstanding. What I may tacitly assume, you may never have thought of. If I act upon my assumption and in the final result such action makes a vast difference in the outcome, you may face a situation that you are totally unprepared to accept. For

[2] See page 6.

each of us to know, therefore, what is assumed is basic to an understanding of the research results. If we know the assumptions a researcher makes, we are then better prepared to evaluate the conclusions that result from such assumptions. To many students the stating of assumptions may be tantamount to stating the obvious, but because in research we try to leave nothing to chance in the hope of preventing any misunderstanding, all assumptions that have a material bearing upon the problem should be openly and unreservedly set forth. To discover assumptions, ask "What am I *taking for granted* with respect to the problem?" The answer to that question will bring your assumptions into clear view.

★ *The hypotheses.* We also discussed the matter of hypotheses earlier in these pages.[3] There we pointed out that *hypotheses are tentative, intelligent guesses posited for the purpose of assisting the researcher in directing one's thinking toward the solution of the problem.* Hypotheses are necessary because the researcher needs to have some point around which the research may be oriented in searching for relevant data and in establishing a *tentative* goal against which to project the facts.

We should keep in mind that hypotheses are neither proved nor disproved. They are *tentative propositions set forth as a possible explanation for an occurrence or a provisional conjecture to assist in guiding the investigation of a problem.* To set out deliberately to prove a hypothesis would defeat impartiality in research. The researcher would bias the procedure by looking only for those facts which would support the hypothetical position. Difficult as it may be at times, we must let the chips of fact fall where they may. Hypotheses have nothing to do with proof. Rather they are dependent in their *acceptance* or *rejection* upon what the facts—and the facts alone—ultimately reveal.

Hypotheses may originate in the subproblems. A one-to-one correspondence might well exist between the subproblems and their corresponding hypotheses. Generally, we have as many hypotheses as we have subproblems. Each of the hypotheses becomes, in a sense, a target against which the data of each subproblem may be projected. As a point of reference, a hypothesis is to a researcher what a point of triangulation is to a surveyor: it provides a position from which the researcher may begin to initiate an exploration of the problem or subproblem, and also as a checkpoint against which ultimately to test the findings that the data seem to reveal.

If, however, the facts do not ultimately support the hypothesis, you should not let such an outcome disturb you. It merely means that your educated guess as to what the outcome of the investigation should have been was wrong. Frequently unsupported hypotheses are a source of genuine and gratifying surprise for the researcher. When such an outcome occurs, you have truly made an unexpected discovery of truth.

One further type of hypothesis should here be mentioned: the *null hypothesis.* We have also discussed this type of hypothesis earlier.[4] The null hypothesis is an indicator only. It reveals that some influence, some force, some factor either has resulted in a "statistical difference" (other than could be accounted for by mere chance, and within certain arbitrary statistical limits) or it has not resulted in such a difference. Much research stops at this point. This is comparable to getting off at the mezzanine instead of descending to the subbasement where the foundations of the building are located. If the null hypothesis shows the presence of dynamics that have caused a change, then the logical next questions are the following: *what* are these dynamics; *what* is their nature; *how* can they be isolated and studied?

A social worker finds that a particular social program shows statistically that the program is making a great difference in the attitudes of those exposed to it. The hypothesis to the effect that the program will make *no difference* has been rejected. Fine! That's encour-

[3] See pages 5–6, 8.

[4] See pages 30, 40.

aging news. But it's a mezzanine conclusion. What dynamics were at work below the surface that were merely registered on the statistical dial upstairs? What specifically was the factor—or factors—within the program that caused the null hypothesis to be rejected? These are *fundamental* questions, the answers to which will discover facts that may lie very close to the discovery of new substantive knowledge; and that is the purpose of all basic research.

★ *The importance of the study.* Within the dissertation or the research report, the researcher frequently sets forth the reason for undertaking the study. In the proposal, this section may be very important. Some studies seem to go far out into the rarified atmosphere beyond contact with everyday reality and beyond any relationship to the practical world. Of such research efforts one inwardly, if not audibly, asks "Of what *use* is it? What *practical value* does the study have?"

During the space exploration flights to the moon, one of the most frequent questions asked by the average citizen was "Of what good is it? What's the use of it all? How will all this expenditure of money in space flights benefit anyone down here?" Perhaps those engaged in space research did not set forth clearly and succinctly enough the reasons why the missions were undertaken. Only now are we beginning to appreciate the *practical* value of those early missions.

THE RATIONALE OF THE ORDER IN WHICH TOPICS IN THIS TEXT ARE PRESENTED

This text presents topics in a one-to-one correspondence with which the same material will appear in a proposal or a research report. In any proposal, or in any thesis, dissertation, or research report, the first order of business is to present the problem and its setting. Generally the document opens with a statement of the main problem. This is followed by the subproblems. Corresponding to each subproblem, the hypothesis relating to it is stated. Some authors prefer to present all the subproblems as a group and, following them, their corresponding hypotheses in order, as has been done in the sample proposal, pages 255–256. Other researchers insert each hypothesis immediately following the statement of each problem. Either way is equally acceptable.

Once the problem and its component parts have been stated, then the rest of the items comprising the setting of the problem may be presented, usually beginning with the delimitations, the definitions of terms, the assumptions, and a statement with reference to the importance of the study.

In a proposal or research report document, these items usually comprise the first chapter, or the first section, of the report. The report then generally continues with a discussion of the investigations that others have done correlative to your problem. This is frequently referred to as the review of the related literature. We shall discuss this topic in the next chapter.

Practical Application ——————————————————————————

In the Practical Application Section halfway through this chapter, on page 59, you began an exploration of a problem for research. Now turn to the practicum section, project 4, page 288. You will now generate the subproblems and the other corollary items which comprise the setting of the problem.

A sample proposal with comments has also been included in Appendix A. You may wish now to study it to see how the problem and its setting are there presented in proposal form.

——————————————————————————————————

FOR FURTHER READING

Beckingham, Ann C. "Identifying Problems for Nursing Research." *International Nursing Review* 21 (1974): 49-50.

Borg, Walter R., and Meredith D. Gall. *Educational Research: An Introduction.* 3rd edition. New York: Longman, Inc., 1979. In Chapter 2 is a discussion of "The Research Problem."*

Brink, Pamela J., and Marilynn J. Wood. *Basic Steps in Planning Nursing Research.* North Scituate, Mass.: Duxbury Press, 1978. See Chapter 2, "From Question to Problem," and Chapter 3, "The Full and Final Problem."

DeBakey, Selma and Lois DeBakey. "The Title: What's in a Name?" *International Journal of Cardiology* 2 (1983): 401-406.

Diers, Donna. *Research in Nursing Practice.* Philadelphia, Pa.: J. B. Lippincott Company, 1979. See Chapter 1, "Research Problems," and Chapter 2, "Statement of the Problem."

Gephart, William J., and Robert B. Ingle. *Educational Research: Selected Readings.* Columbus, Ohio: Charles E. Merrill Publishing Company, 1969. See Chapter 2, "Problem Identification, Hypothesis Development."

Good, Carter V. *Essentials of Educational Research Methodology.* 2nd ed. New York: Appleton-Century-Crofts, 1972. See Chapter 2, "The Problem and Hypothesis."

Kerlinger, Fred N. *Foundations of Behavioral Research.* New York: Holt, Rinehart and Winston, 1964. See Chapter 2, "Problems and Hypotheses."

——. *Behavioral Research: A Conceptual Approach.* New York: Holt, Rinehart and Winston, 1979. See Chapter 3, "Problems, Hypotheses, and Variables."

Lindeman, C. A. "The Research Question." *Journal of Nursing Administration* 12 (January 1982): 6-10.

Manheim, Henry L., and Bradley A. Simon. *Sociological Research.* Homewood, Ill.: The Dorsey Press, 1977. See Chapter 6, "The Formulation of a Research Problem."

Mouly, George J. *The Science of Educational Research.* New York: Van Nostrand Reinhold Company, 1970. See Chapter 4, "The Research Problem."

Notter, Lucille E. *Essentials of Nursing Research.* 2nd edition. New York: Springer Publishing Co., 1978. See Chapter 3, "Selecting a Problem."

Polit, Denise, and Bernadette Hungler. *Nursing Research: Principles and Methods.* Philadelphia, Pa.: J. B. Lippincott Company, 1978. See Chapter 5, "Selecting and Defining a Nursing Research Problem."

Resta, Paul E., and Robert L. Baker. *Formulating a Research Problem.* Inglewood, Calif.: Southwest Regional Laboratory for Educational Research and Development, 1967.

Sweeney, Mary Ann, and Peter Oliveri. *An Introduction to Nursing Research.* Philadelphia, Pa.: J. B. Lippincott Company, 1981. See Chapter 5, "Starting to Develop the Research Problem."

Travers, Robert M. W. *An Introduction to Educational Research.* New York: Macmillan Publishing Co., Inc., 1978. See Chapter 4, "Methods of Finding a Problem."

Verhonick, Phyllis J., and Catherine C. Seaman. *Research Methods for Undergraduate Students in Nursing.* New York: Appleton-Century-Crofts, 1978. See Chapter 2, "The Research Problem."

Williamson, John B., David A. Karp, and John R. Dalphin. *The Research Craft: An Introduction to Social Science Methods.* Boston, Mass.: Little, Brown and Company, 1977. See Chapter 2, "Generating and Testing Ideas."

*In the periodical and separately published literature, a phenomenal void occurs in the discussion of the research problem. Most of such discussions are found in texts of research methodology. This will explain the predominance of such references in this bibliography.

For Your Notes and Comments

READ THIS—BEFORE YOU READ THIS CHAPTER

You can learn much from others. No one is an island. Around every research endeavor—your own included—is a vast sea of literature: countless reports of what others have done. The knowledgeable researcher will try to learn as much as possible from those who have been engaged with problems ancillary to their own, discoveries they have made, methods they have employed, and conclusions they have reached.

But the exploration of others' efforts cannot be a haphazard undertaking. This chapter will spell out specifically how to begin your search of the research literature related to your own endeavor, how to organize your discussion of that literature, and how to relate that literature directly to the problem of your own research.

Every proposal for a research project always presents that undertaking within the framework of the work of others in collateral or related problems. The study of related research literature is, therefore, extremely important.

The Review of the Related Literature

UNDERSTANDING THE ROLE OF THE REVIEW

As a general rule, students do not understand the purpose of investigating the literature related to their research problem. Its function derives from a fundamental position among researchers that the more one knows about the peripheral investigations germane to one's own study, the more knowledgeably one can approach the problems inherent to one's own area of investigation.

Such exploration and discussion occupies the section in the research proposal or in the completed research report known as the *review* of the *related* literature. The italicized words are emphasized intentionally. They stress what needs stressing. In so doing, they describe precisely what the related literature section does. Its function is to "look again" *(re+view)* at the "literature" (the reports of what others have done) in a *related* area: an area not necessarily identical with, but collateral to, your own area of study.

The Purpose of the Review

What, then, is the purpose of this review? It has several purposes. Primarily, it is to assist you in attacking your problem for research. In any research undertaking, *your own research problem* is always central. Everything that you do, you do because it aids and assists you in attacking your problem. And when you know what others have done, you are better prepared to attack with deeper insight and more complete knowledge the problem you have chosen to investigate. But this is only the principal reason for investigating the literature. Briefly such a review can provide you with many benefits:

1. It can reveal investigations similar to your own, and it can show you how the collateral researcher handled these situations.
2. It can suggest a method or a technique of dealing with a problematic situation which may also suggest avenues of approach to the solution of similar difficulties you may be facing.
3. It can reveal to you sources of data which you may not have known existed.
4. It can introduce you to significant research personalities of whose research efforts and collateral writings you may have had no knowledge.
5. It can help you to see your own study in historical and associational perspective and in relation to earlier and more primitive attacks on the same problem.
6. It can provide you with new ideas and approaches which may not have occurred to you.
7. It can assist you in evaluating your own research efforts by comparing them with related efforts done by others.

For doctoral students, this last advantage is of particular value. Dissertations are generally presumed to be *original* investigations into a hitherto unexplored problem area. Many a doctoral candidate, thinking that a particular problem has a monopoly on an unstudied area, finds, when beginning to review the literature, that what was thought to be unoccupied territory has been so well tilled by others that it is, for all practical purposes, practically "farmed out." It is well to know where others have been before you and in what activities they have been engaged.

How to Begin a Search for Related Literature

★ *Go to the indexes and abstracts.* Refer back to the chapter entitled "The Tools of Research." (Chapter 2). Read again the section dealing with the library. There we discussed the master keys to the library and gave you a list of master reference works which would help you to know how and where to find out the information that you need.

As a general rule, it may be well for you to begin with the indexes and abstracts of the periodicals in your academic area: *Biological Abstracts, Chemical Abstracts, Child Development Abstracts, Dissertation Abstracts International, Psychological Abstracts, Education Index, Index Medicus, Index of Science and Technology, Science Citation Index.* These are simply the more common indexes and abstracts. You will doubtless discover others in your own library. They will provide you with principal current studies and related research projects.

For contemporary events, do not overlook *Facts on File* and *The New York Times Index.* For a guide to the periodical literature of the nineteenth century, such works as *Poole's Guide to Periodical Literature* and the *Nineteenth Century Readers' Guide* are indispensable.

Bibliographies should not be overlooked. Perhaps one of the best current sources is the *Bibliographic Index.* Besterman's *Bibliography of Bibliographies* and similar standard reference sources are helpful. For book location, *Books in Print, Paperback Books in Print,* the *Cumulative Book Index, The Book Review Digest,* and the various catalogs of the Library of Congress, the British Museum, the Bibliothèque Nationale, and other great libraries of the world are found in multi-volume form in many libraries. These sources should not be overlooked.

Also, you should not be unmindful of the wealth of information on microfilm. The informational services, such as MEDLARS, ERIC, and University Microfilms which reduce significant research to microfilm, microfiche, or microprint and make it available to the researcher at a very nominal cost have centers located at strategic points throughout the nation. We have included in the list of master guides to basic reference literature Walsh's *Guide to Microforms in Print* (See page 18).

Do not overlook the wealth of material stored in innumerable databanks throughout the United States. This material is produced by computer and can be had in hard copy through a computer printout. Perhaps the best source of information on what is available through this channel is contained in the *Directory of On-Line Information Resources,* published by Knowledge Industry Publications, Inc. 701 Westchester Avenue, White Plains, New York 10604.

★ *Go to the library armed with data-gathering tools.* You'll need bibliography cards and a container to carry them in. This may be a filing box or an expandable envelope. Bibliography cards are valuable not only for gathering and recording the information but also for locating it again at a future date, should that be necessary, without continual return trips to the library. It is well to have a standard form on which to record every bibliographic item that you inspect. Below we have given a suggested form for such a card. It contains the essential information concerning a bibliographical source. It may be well to duplicate as many of these cards as necessary and always to have a supply with you whenever you go to the library. Sometimes very valuable references are encountered unexpectedly. In the interest of conserving space and aiding in duplication of the bibliographical item, 20-pound bond paper, cut to 3- × 5-inch size, is convenient for card making. It gives the necessary sturdiness for filing, yet it is thin enough to permit making multiple copies of the same note or bibliographic reference.

A sample card might look something like this.

Serial No. ______________

Author(s) ______________

Title of article ______________

Journal title ______________

Vol. _____ No. _____ Month _____ Year _____ Pages ______

Place of publication, publisher, date, edition (books only)

____

Library where info. is located __________ Call No. __________

Source of bibliographic info. ______________

How item relates to research problem ______________

Use reverse side for additional comment. (if used, check here) ☐

★ *Make as many copies of the bibliographic item as necessary.* You should make at least two copies of every bibliographical item and set up two files. One should have the cards arranged by author's last name, alphabetically; the other should have the cards arranged serially, by number. When you make the original notation, carbon paper slipped under the original will make two or more copies at one writing.

In making notes, it is frequently convenient to have a single symbol for a complete source. In the upper right-hand corner of the sample card are the words *Serial No.* If, as you write each item of bibliography, you assign to that bibliographical source a number, upon making notes from that source on your note cards, you will save time and effort merely to indicate the page and serial number of the bibliographical source from which the note was made. A colon may be used to separate the serial number of the source from the page notation. Suppose in a certain work whose bibliographical serial number is 63, we were to extract certain items of information from pages 24, 26, and 29. You would have probably three note cards, each with one item of information from each of the three pages. To identify the source of each reference, therefore, the cards would bear the symbols 63 (the bibliographical serial number) : 24 (the page), and so, 63:26, and 63:29, respectively.

It is important to have, by authors' last names, followed by first names and initial, an *alphabetical file* of bibliography cards, as well as a *numerical* one. Take this, for instance: you are reading other studies, and a work is mentioned which you know you have inspected. You have been working at several libraries. By having the author's last name, you can readily find the information on the work mentioned and the library that owns it, if you consult the alphabetical file under the last name of the author.

Parallel card files thus serve distinctly different purposes; but for an extended research effort, in which you may be inspecting hundreds of items, each file in its own way may be indispensably important and save hours of futile search.

We shall have more to say about note cards and note taking in Chapter 7, where we discuss the historical method.

★ *Be systematic and thorough.* "Make haste slowly" is a sound rule for the researcher. Too many students make careless half-complete jottings that, when consulted later, and after their having consulted scores of other sources in the meantime, are either entirely unintelligible or are lacking in such essential information that they are practically useless. Write legibly, or print clearly. Not being able to distinguish between undotted *i*'s and closed-up *e*'s, carelessly made *a*'s and *o*'s, so that they look alike, and likewise *u*'s and *n*'s, *n*'s and *m*'s will either send you scurrying back to sources to see exactly what is correct or, without confirmation, will fill your document with error.

The original time spent in seeking out the item can be totally wasted. It would have been much better to have taken the required care and given proper attention to doing the job right in the first place. Little is gained by rushing to the extent that one fails to get either adequate or accurate information the first time around and to be able to read it accurately when referring to it some time later.

★ *Relate your bibliography to your problem.* Always keep your research *problem-oriented.* In gathering bibliography, ask yourself: How does this item of literature relate to my problem? Discover a nexus between the problem and the literature. This will be a safeguard against the temptation of merely building a haphazard bibliographic collection. Some students consider that the more sources they are able to cite, the more impressive is the fact that they have made a thorough literature search. Irrelevant literature soon becomes apparent and a little will ruin a lot of conscientious work.

To avoid being accused of irrelevancy, on each bibliographical source card indicate precisely how the particular item that you are recording relates to your problem. The preceding specimen card includes a space for this information. The competent researcher never forgets that everything that is done serves only one purpose: to contribute to the solution of the problem.

How to Write the Section on the Related Literature

After they have amassed an impressive bibliography, many students do not know what to do with it. They have their cards arranged in order, while at the same time they are at a loss to know how to present their findings in the document they are preparing or what to do with the many citations as a result of their reading. A few simple guidelines may help.

★ *Get the proper psychological orientation.* You need to be clear in your own thinking. Know precisely what is it that you are attempting to do. The review of the related literature section is a *discussion* of those others—studies, research reports, scholarly or broad spectrum writings—that bear directly upon your own effort. Consider the review of related literature section in your document as a discussion with a friend (the word *discussion* is purposely italicized above to emphasize its essential nature) about what others have written in relation to what you plan to do. Viewing the literature section in this way will help you develop the proper psychological perspective, and will help you see your own effort in relation to the aggregate efforts of other researchers.

Too many students consider the related literature section as an unnecessary appendage standing in the way of their real goal. They are eager "to get on with the research." To the contrary, a conscientious and thorough review of the literature related to the problem can open up to any researcher possibilities of which one was unaware, can open one's eyes to new ways of looking at the problem which may otherwise be totally missed.

★ *Have a plan.* Too many discussions of related literature are unplanned and disorganized ramblings. The student lists whatever comes first to the attention. Organizational design is lacking. The entire effort lacks structure, unity, and coherence.

Before beginning to write the section on the review of the related literature, the student should outline the discussion that will follow. Perhaps one of the best guides for such an outline is the problem itself. A careful consideration of the problem should suggest relevant areas for discussion and indicate the direction that the discussion of the related literature should take.

First, there are always the "classic" studies, the historically oriented writings which have prepared the way for your research effort as well as those of others. These studies are the efforts of the trailblazers of the discrete area within which your problem lies. They connect your special realm of interest to the broad historical horizon from which you can gain perspective for your own efforts. Those who developed the laser utilized the efforts and writings of those who explored relativistic quantum mechanics, and the theories of matter and light in electromagnetic fields.

Begin your discussion of the related literature from a comprehensive perspective, like an inverted pyramid: broad end first. Then you can deal with more and more specific or more localized studies which focus closer and closer on your specific problem.

As an example of what we are saying in this section, refer to the sample proposal given in Appendix A, page 260. Here the author is interested in constructing a Strong Vocational Interest Blank scale for the identification of potential cartographers. Where does his discussion of the related literature begin? It begins with the writings of the basic educational theorists of the *eighteenth century* who have dealt with the role of human interest and its relation to learning. Note his opening sentence: "The role of interests within the behavioral sciences is not new." That sentence takes you immediately into the eighteenth century and to the beginning of the nineteenth century with a discussion of the writings of Jean-Jacques Rousseau (1712-1778) and Johann Friedrich Herbart (1776-1841).

Note the organizational outline that the author follows in presenting the related literature dealing with his problem. (See Appendix A, pages 260-267.) We have arranged these topics in the form of an inverted pyramid so that you will be able to see how the author of the sample proposal has done precisely what we have already discussed in terms of an overall plan.

Outline of the Review
of the Related Literature

Historical Overview (indicating the studies which underlie the whole problem group)
Interest Measurements as a Vocational Guidance Technique
The Measurement of Interests of Cartographers
The Strong Vocational Interest Approach
The Validity of the Approach
The Construction of a
Scoring Key
Summary

Throughout your discussion of the related literature, the plan of its organization should be clear. Clarity will be enhanced if you use, as has been done in the sample proposal in Appendix A, headings and subheadings to indicate the organization of the discussion.

★ *Emphasize relatedness.* Keep your reader constantly aware of the manner in which the literature you are discussing is related to your problem. Point out precisely what that relationship is. Remember that you are writing a review of the *related* literature.

Too many discussions of the literature are nothing but a chain of pointless isolated summaries of the writings of othe⁻⁻ Jones says. . .; Smith says. . .; Green says. . . . This is the format students generally use. This is also, perhaps, the worst form of a discussion of related literature. There is no discussion, no attempt to demonstrate the *relatedness* of the literature to the problem being researched.

Whenever you cite a study, make yourself account for that particular study in terms of the problem you are researching. Be sure that you specifically point out to the reader in your discussion precisely what the relationship is. Unless you can establish such accountability, you would do well to consider whether you should include the study at all. Use a simple structural device such as a skeleton outline to assist you in establishing the relationship of the literature to the problem.

★ *Review the literature; don't reproduce it!* The review of the literature section of a proposal or a dissertation is perhaps one of the most challenging to write. It requires that you keep a clear focus on just what this section is intended to do. Many students seem to think that here they have the opportunity to quote long passages from the literature, to cite at length the words or ideas of others. More important is what *you* say *about the study* than what the author of the study says *in the study*. A valued colleague[1] gives this advice to his students:

1. Present your own discussion.
2. Paraphrase, (Précis, résumé, give a synopsis, an epitome).
3. Use short direct quotations if necessary.
4. Long quotations are a last resort. Use them only for a *very good reason.*

That is sound advice. Too often students consider the section devoted to the discussion of the related literature as merely conventional "filler" in the document—something that everyone does and, therefore, needs to be done. They fail to see how such a discussion shows the relatedness of the research project to the broad environment of similar research that has been done by others. This is the sole purpose of the literature discussion. In a very real sense, it forms the *raison d'être* for the problem the student is proposing to research.

Showing the Relatedness of the Literature to the Research Project

Since many discussions of the related literate never quite make the nexus between the discussion of the literature others have produced and the research that one is doing, the following procedure is recommended to prevent such a hiatus:

1. Write your problem at the top of the page where you cannot lose sight of it. In this location, you will be constantly reminded of the central axis around which everything else revolves.
2. Dissect the problem by numbering its various subparts.
3. Divide the page into two columns by drawing a vertical line down the middle of the page, starting below the statement of the problem.
4. Cite each specific study in the left-hand column.
5. In the right-hand column, opposite each study, note the particular subdivision of the problem to which the study relates, and note also the rationale for including it in the review of the literature.
6. Gather together all the citations that refer to a particular aspect of the problem, so that you have as many groups as you have subdivisions of your main problem.
7. Study these groups in relation to each other, with the view of planning and organizing the discussion of the related literature.
8. Write the review. Head each section with headings whose wording contains the identical words found in the statement of the problem.

---

[1] Alvin J. Stuart, Department of Education, Indiana University of Pennsylvania, Indiana, Pennsylvania.

By following this procedure, you will avoid mere bibliographical prattle under the guise of reviewing the literature presumably related to your problem.

Summarize What You Have Said

Every discussion of literature and associated research relating to the problem under consideration should end with a brief section in the form of a summary in which the author gathers up all that has been said and sets forth its *significance* in terms of the research problem. Perhaps the most important question that any researcher can ask—and it should be asked continually throughout the whole progress of the research study—is: *Now, what does it all mean?* Too many studies end in a fuzzy blur of verbiage without coming to any focal point. At the end of each section of the discussion of the literature, at the end of the presentation and processing of data in the research report, in the final summary of the disparate subproblems, one question is *always* appropriate: "What does it all *mean?*" One heading is always in order: the heading entitled, "Summary," which epitomizes the discussion and shows its direct relationship to the problem under study.

POINTS OF DEPARTURE

Perhaps one of your most perplexing moments in undertaking a search of the literature will come when you seek a point of departure that will lead you to the significant research studies in your field. It may be well for you to start by inspecting certain general works: abstracts, indexes, accessible on-line computerized data bases, and general works. A brief list of some of the most important of these follows. You will discover many more as you proceed with your search. There has been no attempt at comprehensiveness in the list that follows.

Abstracts

An abstract is a summary of an article or a study. It gives the source of the original study, should a reader wish to refer to it. Here are some of the better-known periodicals publishing abstracts.

African Abstracts
Abstracts of Hospital Management Studies
Abstracts of Reports and Studies in Nursing
Abstracts of Studies in Public Health Nursing
Biological Abstracts
Chemical Abstracts
Child Development Abstracts
Dissertation Abstracts International
Historical Abstracts 1775-1945: Bibliography of the World's Periodical Literature
International Political Science Abstracts
Nursing Abstracts
Pollution Abstracts
Psychological Abstracts
Public Administration Abstracts
Race Relations Abstracts

SAGE Public Administration Abstracts
SAGE Urban Studies Abstracts
Sociological Abstracts
Urban Affairs Abstracts
Women Studies Abstracts

The most comprehensive and relevant abstract *index* for the political scientist is that edited by Alfred de Grazia, *The Universal Reference System: Political Science, Government, and Public Policy Series.* Princeton, N.J.: Princeton Publishing Company, 1967. It consists of ten volumes and is updated through annual supplements.

Indexes

Indexes are compilations listing articles, studies, and research reports in certain specified areas. In using an index, you may do well to look first under the heading of "Research." Indexes are arranged alphabetically. The principal indexes that will provide you with a good starting point are the following.

Agricultural Index
Applied Science and Technology Index
Bibliographic Index: A Cumulative Bibliography of Bibliographies
Biography Index
Book Review Index
British Humanities Index
Business Periodicals Index
Canadian Periodical Index
Comprehensive Dissertation Index: 1861–1972
Current Index to Journals in Education
Education Index
Index of Economic Journals
Index to Foreign Legal Periodicals
Index to Latin American Periodicals
Index to Legal Periodicals
Index Medicus
Index of Publications of Bureaus of Business and Economic Research
Index to Selected Periodicals
International Index: A Guide to Periodical Literature in the Social Sciences and Humanities
Michigan Index to Labor Union Periodicals
National Union Catalog of Manuscript Collections
New York Times Index
Nursing Literature and Allied Health Literature Index
Poole's Index to Periodical Literature, 1802–1889
Serial Bibliographies in the Humanities and Social Sciences
Social Sciences Citation Index
Social Sciences Index
Special Issues and Indexes of Periodicals

United Nations Documents Index
Wall Street Journal Index
Witness Index to United States Congressional Hearings, 1839–

Computerized Information and Data Banks

More and more vast quantities of information are being stored in on-line databanks, many of which can be accessed by telephone connection from a home computer. The proliferation of these data sources is occurring so rapidly that it is impossible to offer anything approximating a current listing. Perhaps the best guide to this material is through directories that contain descriptive listings of the various on-line, computer-retrievable data banks. Two of the principal such directors are given below, followed by a very few of the major banks.

Williams, Martha E. *Computer-Readable Data Bases: A Directory and Data Sourcebook*, 9th ed. White Plains, N.Y.: Knowledge Industry Publications, 1979.

Directory of Online Databases, Santa Monica, Calif. Cuadra Associates, Inc., published quarterly.

Some of the better-known data bases for computerized information search follow.

BIOETHICS. Ethical issues in biology and medicine based on literature acquired and indexed in the Kennedy Center at Georgetown University, Washington, D.C.

CAIN. An agricultural data base.

DIALOG. A service with more than 200 data bases.

ERIC. Information in education and related areas from the United States Office of Education.

EXCERPTA MEDICA. A worldwide coverage of 3,500 biomedical journals.

HISTLINE. Contains 35,000 records relating to history of medicine and related health sciences.

LLBA (Language and Language Behavior Abstracts). World coverage on speech and language pathology. Produced by Sociological Abstracts, Inc.

MEDLINE. Contains *Index Medicus* citations from 1969 to the present; over 2,700 journals are indexed including *International Nursing Index* and *Index to Dental Literature*.

MEDOC. A computerized index to the United States Government documents in medical and health fields.

SCISEARCH. Contains all records printed in *Science Citation Index* and additional records from the *Current Contents* series.

SSIE. Smithsonian Science Information Exchange—research projects supported by over 1,300 government agencies and private organizations.

Practical Application ———————————————————————

You have begun to construct a proposal of your own research problem in Project 4 in the practicum section of this book. Presumably by this time you have your problem stated and the setting outlined. Now turn to the practicum section to go further with the development of your own research proposal.

Turn to Appendix B, Project 5, pages 287-289. You are now ready to plan the Review of the Related Literature section of your proposal. This practicum unit will give you specific directions as to how to proceed.

———————————————————————————————

FOR FURTHER READING

Further Reading to Help You Understand the Review of the Related Literature

Borg, Walter R., and Meredith D. Gall. *Educational Research: An Introduction.* 3rd ed. New York: Longmans, Inc., 1979. See Chapter 4, "Reviewing the Literature."*

Brink, Pamela J., and Marilynn J. Wood. *Basic Steps in Planning Nursing Research.* North Scituate, Mass: Duxbury Press, 1978. See Chapter 5, "Critical Review of the Literature."

Diers, Donna. *Research in Nursing Practice.* Philadelphia, Pa.: J. B. Lippincott Company, 1979. See Chapter 3, "Review of the Literature," pp. 66-69.

Galfo, Armand J. *Interpreting Educational Research.* 3rd ed. Dubuque, Iowa: William C. Brown Company, Publishers, 1975.

Gephart, William J., and Robert B. Ingle. *Educational Research: Selected Readings.* Columbus, Ohio: Charles E. Merrill Publishing Company, 1969. See Chapter 3, "The Review of Related Research."

Good, Carter V. *Essentials of Educational Research Methodology and Design.* 2nd ed. New York: Appleton-Century-Crofts, 1972. See Chapter 3, "Integration of the Related Literature."

Lindvall, Carl M. "The Review of Related Literature." *Phi Delta Kappan* 40 (1959): 179-80.

Manheim, Henry L., and Bradley A. Simon. *Sociological Research.* Homewood, Ill.: The Dorsey Press, 1977. See Chapter 7, "The Library as a Research Tool."

Mouly, George J. *The Science of Educational Research.* New York: Van Nostrand Reinhold Company, 1970. See Chapter 5, "The Library."

Notter, Lucille E. *Essentials of Nursing Research.* 2nd ed. New York: Springer Publishing Co., 1978. See Chapter 4, "The Literature Search."

Polit, Denise, and Bernadette Hungler. *Nursing Research: Principles and Methods.* Philadelphia, Pa.: J. B. Lippincott Company, 1978. See Chapter 6, "Locating and Summarizing Existing Information on a Problem."

Treece, Eleanor W., and James W. Treece. *Elements of Research in Nursing.* 2nd ed. St. Louis, Mo.: The C. V. Mosby Company, 1977. See Chapter 7: "The Library Search."

Verhonick, Phyllis J., and Catherine C. Seaman. *Research Methods for Undergraduate Students in Nursing.* New York: Appleton-Century-Crofts, 1978. See Chapter 4, "Review of the Literature."

*As with references on the statement of the problem, very little has been written in the general literature about the review of the related literature. Most of the discussion appears in standard texts on research methodology. This will explain the citations in this reading list.

For Your Notes and Comments

READ THIS—BEFORE YOU READ THIS CHAPTER

The chapter is divided into three main parts:

1. The Scientific Method and the Sources of Research Problems
2. The Data: Their Nature and Role in Research
3. Research Design and Ethical Standards.

These three matters are closely related in planning any research project. The scientific method is the broad, procedural approach to all research. It is the modern way of discovering knowledge—of seeking the answers to unresolved problems. Next, for any research to take place a problem must be clearly conceived and accurately articulated. For their solution, problems require relevant data. But data are of various kinds and the sole purpose of data is to lead the researcher toward a closer apprehension of the ever-elusive realm of Ultimate Truth.

But even with a clearly conceived problem and adequate data, research cannot proceed without an unambiguous and practical plan. This is the research design. It must clearly spell out what data are needed, where they are located, how they will be secured, and the method of interpreting them.

Finally, all research has certain ethical implications. These we cannot ignore in designing, executing, and reporting the research activity. Thus, all the components of the chapter form a procedural unity.

5

Planning the Research Project

I. THE SCIENTIFIC METHOD AND SOURCES OF RESEARCH PROBLEMS

Successful research is planned research. Much research ends in futility because the researcher has plunged into the research activity—going to the library, making notes, gathering data, making observations, computerizing the data—with only a partially thought-out plan and an inconclusive design.

Research planning and architectural planning have much in common. Each requires a conceptualization of the overall organization and a detailed plan before work on the project can begin. For successful completion, a building requires plans which are clearly conceived and accurately drawn. A research project should be no less totally visualized and precisely detailed.

HOW IS KNOWLEDGE DISCOVERED?

But where does planning begin? It begins with an understanding of the manner in which knowledge is discovered. For that is the sole aim of all research: to discover knowledge.

In all of mankind's long history, we have devised only two ways to seek the unknowable. One of these is by means of *deductive logic,* the other is by means of *inductive reasoning,* or what is familiarly called *the scientific method.*

★ *Deductive logic.* Up to the time of the Renaissance, insight into most problems was sought by means of deductive logic, a methodology identified with Aristotle. It relied upon logical reasoning and began with a *major premise.* This was a statement, similar to an axiom, which seemed to be a self-evident and universally accepted truth: Man is mortal; God is good; the earth is flat.

The terror that gripped Columbus's sailors was a fear supported by deductive logic. To them, the earth *was* flat. That was their major premise. Then they began reasoning. If the earth were flat, then the flat surfaces would have boundaries. The boundaries of flat surfaces would be the edges of those surfaces. If a ship passed across a flat surface, it would come to the edge of it. There, they reasoned, it would fall off. At this point, they posited a second premise. The earth is afloat on Chaos. Those who travel to the edge of the earth will fall into Chaos and be forever lost! Q.E.D.

The logic was sound; the reasoning, accurate; the conclusion, valid. Where the whole proposition went wrong was that the major premise was incorrect. The reasoning began with a preconceived idea that *seemed* to be true.

But such was Aristotelian logic. It provided answers to problems for which no other answer existed: What is the nature of God? Where are angels found? How many of them can dance upon the point of a needle? And similar questions. And it satisfied those who started their quest for knowledge from a dogmatic premise and pursued it to a logical conclusion.

THE ORIGIN OF THE SCIENTIFIC METHOD

But with the Renaissance came a new approach to the discovery of knowledge. The method was the result of an interest in humanism. It represented an entirely new *way* of thinking—an entirely new *approach* to an unsolved problem. It resulted in a different emphasis. The emphasis was upon *this* world and an intense interest in its phenomena. And it gave rise to a method of thinking known as *the scientific method.*

Its basis was a way of thinking known as *inductive reasoning.* Inductive reasoning begins, not with a preconceived conclusion—a major premise—but with an observation. Renaissance man began seeking truth by looking steadfastly at the world around him. He asked questions of Nature. And Nature responded in the form of observable fact.

But fact is fact, and he who seeks it must translate it into meaning. Renaissance man soon found that when facts are assembled and studied dispassionately, they frequently suggest hitherto undiscovered truth. Thus was the scientific method born; and the words mean literally "the method that searches after knowledge" (*scientia* = L. knowledge, from *scire*, L. to know).

The scientific method gained real impetus during the sixteenth century with such men as Paracelsus, Leonardo, Copernicus, Galileo, Vesalius, Vittorino da Feltre and their contemporaries. They introduced scientific methodology to the western world. And it is still the most valid method for problem solving and the resolution of unanswered questions.

WHAT, THEN, IS THE SCIENTIFIC METHOD?

The scientific method is a means whereby insight into an undiscovered truth is sought by (1) identifying the problem that defines the goal of the quest, (2) gathering data with the hope of resolving the problem, (3) positing a tentative hypothesis both as a logical means of locating the data and as an aid to resolving the problem, (4) then empirically testing the hypothesis by processing and interpreting the data to see if the interpretation of such data will resolve the primary question which initiated the research in the first place.

Thus, the diagram which appears on page 8 indicating that research is circular was, in effect, merely a visualization of the scientific method as a basis for research methodology. But, the cycle of research is actually more helical than circular. Each problem begets in the process of inquiry other related problems; and so, what begins as a resolutionary process for one problem actually becomes the initiatory process which creates still further problems.

The true researcher looks at the facts *only,* and as a result of observing *them alone* draws conclusions as to what they apparently say. For, we can never be *exactly* sure of what the facts do indicate. This statement we shall appreciate more fully when we look more intimately at the nature of data in a future chapter. Despite that, the process remains the same. It is a process of *inductive thinking* and may be best represented by this diagram.

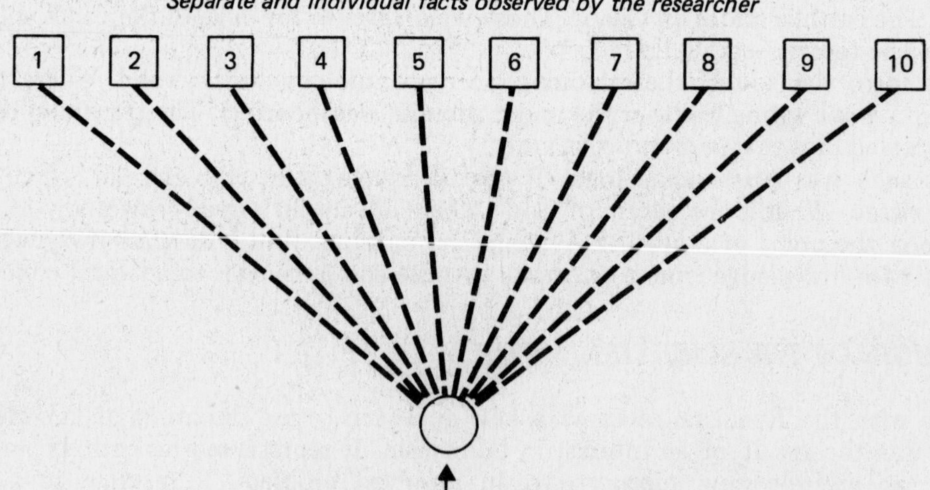
Separate and individual facts observed by the researcher
1
2
3
4
5
6
7
8
9
10
They all seem to lead to a single conclusion.

Let's see how this diagrammatic representation applies to an actual research project. A group of neurologists—Silverman, Schwartz, and others—sought the answer to a problem in medicine: How long can a person have a "flat EEG" (an isoelectric brain tracing indicating cerebral death) and still recover? Silverman and his colleagues observed actual cases—3,000 of them. They noted that in all cases where the flat EEG persisted for 24 hours or more, *not a single recovery occurred.*[1] All the facts pointed to the same conclusion: *It is tragically unlikely that a recovery might take place with those who exhibit flat EEG tracings of 24 hours or more duration.* We cannot, of course, rule out the unexplored cases, but *from the data observed* the conclusion reached was that recovery seems impossible. The line from *each* case led to that *one* conclusion.

ALL RESEARCH HAS A BASIC FORMAT

All research has a basic format. No matter what academic discipline gives rise to the research endeavor, the broad configuration of the research procedure is fundamentally the same. Research is not parochial. And the search for facts to solve a problem seldom fits into the neatly packaged academic disciplines represented by the arrangement of subject areas in a college catalog.

An educator may be compelled to stray far and wide from education or a biologist be led equally afield of biology in the pursuit of a research problem which arises out of each researcher's specialized field. Research which originates in one academic area may more often than not spread across the artificial academic boundaries in pursuit of the factual data needed to resolve the problem. Consider, for example, an educator trying to find the cause of certain behavior syndromes in a learning-disabled child. Such a researcher may be forced to go beyond the bounds of education into psychology, genetics, embryology, neuropathology, endocrinology, or other related fields to understand human behavior. The ramifications of the problem may lead the researcher far afield from that of the original problem.

We perhaps err in thinking too narrowly, in restricting problems for research to one academic area. Instead of thinking according to departmentalized knowledge, the researcher might do much better to think of problems as arising out of broad generic areas within whose boundaries all research falls: *people*, *things*, *records*, *thoughts and ideas*, and *dynamics or energy*.

Briefly, let us consider some problems that may be indigenous to each of these areas.

★ *People*. In this category are found research problems relating to individuals, groups, population, folklore, nationalities, families, sex, community groups and subgroups, employees, management, the disadvantaged, the wealthy, students, ancestors, tribes, mental and physical processes, medical, psychological, educational, social and sociological problems, learning, motivation, adjustment, crime, criminals, rehabilitation, nutrition, language and linguistics, religion.

★ *Things*. In this category are found research problems relating to biological and vegetable life, viruses, bacteria, inanimate objects (rocks, soil, buildings, furniture, and the phenomonology of nature), matter (molecules, atoms, subatomic matter), chemical and pharmacological problems, space, stars, galaxies, the universe, machines, food and clothing.

★ *Records*. In this category are found research problems relating to letters, legal documents, lists, journals, memoranda, books, registers, diaries, memoirs, incunabula, interviews, minutes, speeches, monuments, tablets, recordings, census reports, financial and corporate statements, mementos, artifacts, archeological remains, files, newspapers, sketches, drawings, paintings, music, manuscripts.

[1] *The New England Journal of Medicine*, 283:98, 99. July 9, 1970.

★ *Thoughts and Ideas.* In this category are found research problems relating to opinions, reactions, concepts, theories, viewpoints, philosophical ideas, political theory, religious beliefs, perceptions, observations, issues, language and semantics, judgments, literature, mathematical concepts and theories, confessions, journalistic columns and commentators' viewpoints, cartoons and caricatures.

★ *Dynamics or Energy.* In this category are found research problems relating to human energy and activity, metabolism, bionics, excitation states, radiation, radio and microwave transmission, quantum mechanics, hydrodynamics, hydrologic cycles, atomic and nuclear energy, wave mechanics, thinking, gravity, gravitation, thermodynamics, atmospheric and oceanic energy systems, solar energy, quasars, black holes, and extragalactic radiation.

The purpose of the above suggestions was not to be all-inclusive but merely to suggest the broad ramification of research possibilities in terms of broad categorical classification.

This simplification of the areas from which research problems arise should suggest, however, the folly of attempting to classify research procedures along purely academic and disciplinary lines. The substratum of research principles is all-inclusive and with slight modifications and varying emphases applies to all disciplines.

The physicist exploring subatomic particles and the sociologist exploring social behavior are both employing the same research principles to their respective problems. Their tools of investigation may differ; and their interpretational techniques may have little in common, but their basic research approach is identical. Both employ the tenets of the scientific method. Both begin with a researchable problem. Both hypothesize concerning it. Both collect data relevant to it. Both interpret the data and draw from that interpretation conclusions which support or nullify the hypotheses they have posited.

Such is the nature of research and, in its planning and design, it approaches all problems through certain methodological channels that are particularly appropriate to the nature and type of data which the investigation of the problem requires.

This being so, a critical differentiation must be made in the mind of the researcher between the terms *research design* or *planning*, and *research methodology.*

RESEARCH PLANNING VS. RESEARCH METHODOLOGY

Do not confuse research planning with research methodology. One often hears such statements as: Research in physics is *different from* research in philosophy or history. Such statements reveal that a clear differentiation has not been made between *research as a process* and *the methodology employed* by separate academic disciplines in collecting and processing data within the framework of the research process.

Genuine research follows the broad outline of the scientific method. It also exhibits the seven basic characteristics outlined in chapter 1.[2] Not every academic discipline finds it appropriate, however, to employ the same *methodology* in dealing with the data. This is because data vary so widely. You cannot deal with a blood cell in the same way that you deal with an historical fact, and the problem of finding the sources of Coleridge's *Kubla Khan* are entirely different from the problem of finding the sources of radio signals from extragalactic space. The *method* the one researcher employs is entirely different from that which the other researcher uses. The reason is that the data in the one situation are entirely

[2] See pages 4–7.

different from the data in the other. You cannot investigate chromosomes with a questionnaire.

In planning the research project, therefore, it is extremely important for the researcher not only to choose a viable research problem but also to consider the nature of the data which the investigation of such a problem will demand and the feasible means of collecting and interpreting those data. Many beginning researchers become so entranced with the glamour of the problem that they fail to consider the consequences which the pursuit of that problem entails as to data availability, collection, and interpretation.

To study the brain wave patterns of gifted and normal children may be a most engaging project for research, but unless you have subjects who are willing to cooperate in the study, an electroencephalograph at your command, the technical skill to use it, and the ability to interpret the resultant electroencephalographic tracings, and furthermore, unless you have clearly determined the method that you will employ in interpreting the data and so organizing your findings that you can draw conclusions from them, it probably were better that you give up this project in favor of one in which you have the knowledge, the resources, and the skill to carry it through to completion. Your research should be *practical* research, built upon clear and realistic *planning* and executed within the framework of a clearly conceived and feasible *design*.

Criteria for a Research Project

In the planning of your research project, certain features common to all true research should serve as guidelines. All research is ultimately tested by certain criteria which must, in fact, be built into the research design in the planning stage. Here, briefly, are those standards.

★ *Universality*. The research project should be such that it could be carried out by any competent person other than the researcher himself. The researcher is merely a catalyst. In the presence of the data, the researcher is little more than an agent whose function is to collect, organize and, to the best of his ability, report what the collected data seem to indicate. A surrogate, competent to carry out the research, might take the place of the researcher and bring the project to completion with essentially the same results without prejudice to the project or the validity of the research.

★ *Replication.* The research should be repeatable. Any other competent researcher should be able to take the problem and, collecting data under the same circumstances and within the identical parameters as you have observed, achieve results comparable to those you have been able to secure.

★ *Control.* Parameters are important. All research is conducted within an area sealed off by given parametric limitations. By such control, we isolate those factors which are critical to the research. Control is important for replication. An experiment should be repeated under the identical conditions and in the identical way in which it was first carried out. It is also important for consistency within the research design. In certain areas, control is more easily achieved than in others. In the physical sciences, for example, control of the experimental factors is possible to a very high degree. Such matters as constancy of temperature, pressure, electrical potential, humidity, and the like, are easily regulated and may be exactly replicated. Control is much less possible in research areas concerned with human data and existential variables.

★ *Measurement.* The data should be susceptible to "measurement." This, again, is easily accomplished in the physical sciences. In humanistic and social research, it is much more difficult to quantify, measure, or evaluate the critical factors in the research design. The matter of measurement in these latter areas must rely many times upon comparative judgment (arranging factors in a hierarchy of importance), scaling, scoring (correct vs.

incorrect responses to a given set of questions), and similar procedures. In the humanities and the social sciences, measurement can never be as precise and as accurate as in the natural and physical sciences.

Research Design

Nothing so helps a research effort to be successful as to plan the overall design carefully. You cannot begin too soon to consider the critical matters that we have been discussing. More research effort is wasted by going off half prepared with only a nebulous set of ideas and foggy perceptions than in any other way. To bring all together, a careful early inventory of your resources, your problem, and the sources of the data may be highly desirable to save you time, money, and effort in getting oriented correctly from the beginning.

II. THE DATA: THEIR NATURE AND ROLE IN RESEARCH

DATA: THEIR RELATIONSHIP TO BOTH DESIGN AND METHODOLOGY

The scientific method is a viable approach to any problem only when there are *facts* to support it. Without facts, which within the research community are more properly called *data*, inductive reasoning vanishes and the scientific method collapses. Facts are the life blood of research. Let us, therefore, consider the nature of facts: first, from a philosophical standpoint, and then, from a more practical relation of their role in the research process. We begin with the word *data* and its essential meaning.

The term *data* is plural. We have constantly been referring to data as "they" and "them." In syntactical usage, we employ the word with the plural form of the verb.

The word *data* (singular *datum*) derives from the past participle of the Latin verb *dare*, to give. Data, therefore, are those facts that any particular situation affords or *gives* to an observer. Think of data as synonymous with facts. We often refer to data by saying, "these are the facts of the situation." In that sense, the plural form of the verb seems perfectly appropriate.

What Are Data?

The English word *fact* also comes from the Latin. Its Latin origin is in the word *facere*, meaning "to make"—what the situation "makes" or manifests to the observer.

The etymology provides the first clue as to the nature of data: they are *manifestations* of the truth rather than the truth itself. No one has ever looked upon Truth itself—pure, undisguised, naked Truth: philosophical Truth, the Truth of Plato and the Idealists. In that sense, data are merely representative, intermediate, elusive surrogates of Truth. Data *reflect* Truth as a mirror reflects sunlight. We are like those who live in a dungeon, across the floor of which a beam of sunlight passes. That light gives us an idea of what the sun must be like, but if we are never able to behold the sun, we shall never know the difference between it and the shaft of light upon the dungeon floor.

The researcher is in a factual dungeon. He will never be able to see the *source* of the data. We glibly talk of populations made up of individuals. But the *individual*—the person "inside"—we shall never know!

Research seeks, through data, to discover what is true absolutely. In a sense, research is a constant pursuit after the complete meaning of the data. The experienced researcher is constantly aware that what he most ardently seeks as the ultimate goal of research, namely, Truth, is forever just beyond what is represented by the data and, hence, just beyond human grasp.

The scientist probing the nature of subatomic matter is always conscious of an elusive sub-, sub-, subentity which, like the will-o'-the-wisp, lures the researcher on but at the same time ever evades him. The mind yearns to understand the Ultimate. As a means of access to that goal, we have chosen the pathway of research. But it always ends at the farthest reaches of the data which are at the brink of the canyon in whose depths lies the inaccessible Ultimate Truth.

Data Are Ephemeral and Ever Changing

Whenever we look at data intently and earnestly, we gain new insight; but at the same time we also discern new problems arise which demand still further research. Like the asymptotic curve, the researcher approaches but never quite meets the straight line of the Ultimate Quest.

Data are not only elusive, but also ephemeral. Facts which the researcher is permitted to glimpse exist for only a split second. Consider some realistic research situations. A sociologist is interested in studying conditions within a certain city and among a given population. Social workers plan to make a survey. They start at a given point in the hope of eliciting opinions and reactions from a given population. As they contact family after family, they garner facts and opinions concerning certain matters. Hardly have they surveyed the people of one city block before the data collected are out-of-date. Some people who indicated they held one opinion have now changed their minds and entertain an entirely different opinion. They have seen a television program or heard a discussion which has changed their minds completely. Before the data can be processed, the population has changed: some people have moved out; others, moved in; some deaths have occurred, some have been born. Tomorrow, next week, next year—what we thought we had "discovered" may have no counterpart in reality whatever.

The teacher who presumes to pretest, teach, and posttest the same class may not be testing the "same" class at all. The individuals within that class may be different at posttest than what they were at pretest six weeks earlier. They have been growing, learning, maturing, changing. The pretest-posttest technique seldom takes into account developmental and maturational factors which bias the data.

We plan an attitude survey. It involves asking people about their interests. It sounds fine, but can we be sure that what they tell us is "true?" They may answer our questions honestly and represent the truth as they perceive it at that instant. But their interests may be imperceptibly changing because of many factors: age, maturity, a newscast, an item in a newspaper.

Data are, therefore, extremely ephemeral. We catch merely a fleeting glance of what *seems* to be true about the opinions and reactions of people in a city block, about achievement of students after a teaching experiment, of the attitude positions of a given population.

Researchers should recognize, therefore, that even the most reliable, most refined, most carefully controlled, most trustworthy data may have a very elusive quality about them and that tomorrow or next week or next year they may, in fact, have no counterpart in reality whatsoever. Data are volatile; they evaporate quickly.

What we have been saying about data and their relation to Ultimate Truth as well as a simplification of the entire research process may be best represented by a simple diagram depicting the data in their various states and manifestations.

A careful inspection of the diagram, found on p. 88, reveals certain important facts concerning the nature of data. Lying farthest away—and, hence, most inaccessible—is the

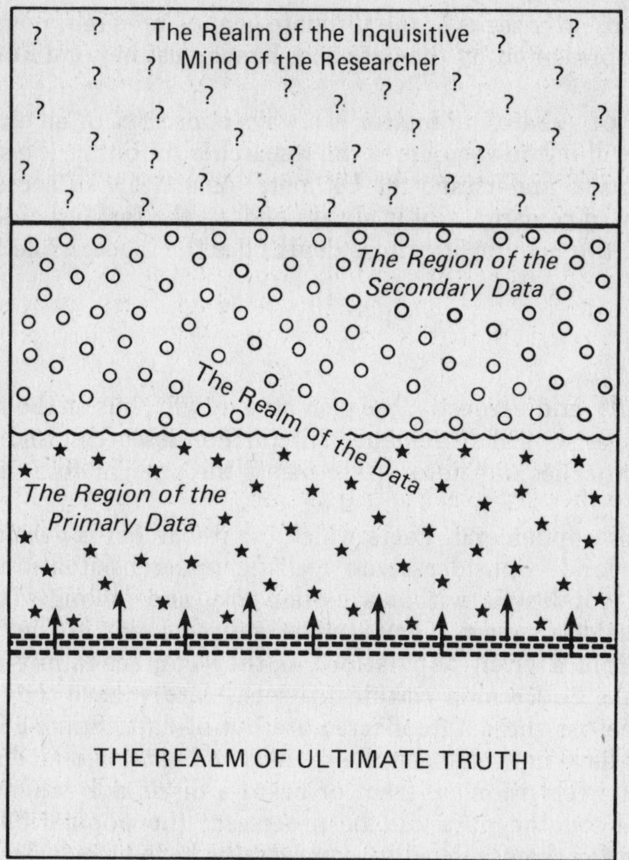

Realm of Ultimate Truth. It can be approached by the researcher only by means of passing through two intermediate areas which, taken together we have labeled The Realm of the Data.

Earlier, we used the example of the researcher as one who sits in a dungeon and attempts to behold the sun only by means of a shaft of sunlight which falls upon the floor. This represents the *primary data*. We may define primary data as *the data which lie closest to the source of the phenomenon.* Primary data reflect Truth more faithfully than any other approach to Truth. Note that in the chart, an impenetrable barrier exists between the Realm of Ultimate Truth and the region of the primary data. Through a shaft of sunlight, we can tell a great deal about the sun, but it does not compare to seeing the sun itself. Consider the following incident to illustrate the point.

I see a car veer off the highway and careen into a ditch. I have witnessed the full occurrence. The driver can afterwards tell me that he had no awareness of the possibility of an accident until the car went out of control. Neither of us will ever be able to fathom the ultimate truth underlying the accident. Did the driver have a momentary seizure of which even he was unaware? Did the mechanism have an imperfection which the accident itself obliterated? Were there other factors that neither of us noticed? The answers lie beyond an impenetrable barrier. The ultimate truth for the cause of the accident may never be known.

The researcher's only perception of truth are the layers of various density of truth-revealing fact. The data that lie in juxtaposition to the Truth are most valid, the most illuminating, the most Truth-manifesting. These data are *primary* in the sense that they lie closest to the truth.

But not all data are primary. Beyond the region of the primary data lies the region of the *secondary data.* Think of the two examples we have just used. The researcher in the dungeon sees the sunlight, not as a direct beam but as a shimmering light upon the wall. It has fallen as primary data upon a mirror and then been reflected—distorted by the imperfections within the mirror—to an image alike yet unlike the original shaft of light.

I am a newspaper reporter. I write an account stating precisely what I have observed of the automobile accident. My account is confirmed by the driver of the car. But when my brother reads the account in the paper next morning he gets, as it were, the sunlight-reflection-upon-the-wall version of the event. The data is of necessity distorted—albeit ever so little—by the channels of communication through which they must pass; my writing skills and my brother's reading skills and the inability of language to reproduce every nuance of detail that a first-hand observation can provide. These all distort what I actually observed, however small that distortion may be.

Another feature of the schematic representation which we have not mentioned is the importance of the barriers. There are, of course, in actuality many more of these than we have here represented: the acuity of the human senses, the sensitivity of instrumentation, the failure of language to communicate thought *exactly*, the inability of two human beings to witness the same event and to report it *precisely* as duplicate accounts. The barriers in the research process are legion.

The precise researcher will never forget the overall idea behind the above diagram. To recall it may prevent the making of exaggerated statements or drawing unwarranted conclusions. It is the remembrance of the philosophical status quo of the several "realms" within the totality of the research process that reminds the researcher, even in the most exuberant moment of discovery, that no one has ever been permitted to glimpse Ultimate Truth, nor can we come to a knowledge of the data that reflect that Truth except through the gross and shadowy channels of our dull and imperfect senses. Such a humiliating awareness helps the researcher to be cautious and adds new respect for such words in the reporting of research findings as *perhaps, it seems, one might conclude,* and *it would appear to be.*

The true researcher is cautious because such a person is wise enough to know that no one can ever be sure that what is beheld is, indeed, even a verisimilitude of what is *actually* the Truth.

Practical Application —

Thus far we have been discussing the nature and the philosophy of data and the role that they play in the research process. At this juncture, therefore, it is important that you learn to think like a researcher with respect to data and their meaning, for researchers regard data differently than do most people. They look at the facts with which they are confronted more open-mindedly, more comprehensively, and they are more careful in drawing unilateral conclusions from the data which they do consider.

Turn to Project 6, Part 1 (pages 291–292). There you will have the opportunity to consider certain situations with respect to the data. You will look at those data as a professional researcher might do.

— —

CRITERIA FOR THE ADMISSIBILITY OF THE DATA

Not all data which come to the attention of the researcher are acceptable for the researcher's use. Data can be defective. If they are, they may affect the validity of the researcher's conclusions.

The imperfections in the data stem from the imperfections and irregularities in nature. If the researcher includes in the mass of data those which are imperfect or irregular in quality, they corrupt the entire corpus of the data. We then have no standard against which to measure any performance.

A researcher is trying to determine the effect of ultraviolet light on growing plants. But *ultraviolet* is a vague term. It may include any light radiation between 500 and 4,000 angstroms.

One of the axioms of research is that any research effort should be *replicable;* that is, it should be able to be repeated by any other researcher at any other time under *precisely the same conditions.* In order to regulate the precision of the conditions, therefore, certain criteria must be adopted, certain limits established, certain standards set up which all data must meet in order to be admitted for study.

By the prescription of such criteria and the insistence upon standards, we can then control the type of data admitted and regulate the conditions under which the research effort is permitted to proceed. Those data not meeting the criteria are excluded from the study. It is, of course, much easier to control data in the physical sciences where we can measure the data in terms of quantitative values, but such control is also possible within the broader disciplines of knowledge—the humanities, the social sciences, the performing arts—to develop standards and requirements to which the data must conform. In these latter and "broader" disciplines, these criteria are usually established by definition, and admissible data must meet the definitive parameters.

But to return to the agronomist studying the effect of ultraviolet rays on growing plants, we must narrow the parameters of the data so that they will fall within certain specified limits. The agronomist must define precisely what he means by ultraviolet light. Within what angstrom range will he accept ultraviolet emission? At what intensity? With what time duration? With plants at what distance from the source of emission? What precisely is meant by the phrase "ultraviolet effect on growing plants?" All plants? A certain genus? A specific species?

We hem the data in on all sides, place upon them the restriction of criterion after criterion so that we are able to isolate only those data which are acceptable for our use. The rest of the data are inadmissible.

When we standardize the data, admitting only those which comply with the criteria, we can more nearly control the research effort and conclude with greater certainty what appears to be true. In order, therefore, to insure the integrity of the research, we must set forth *beforehand* precisely what standards the data must meet; and it is equally important that these criteria be set forth clearly in both the research proposal and the research report. Only in this way can we make the *consumer of the research* a party to the criteria. Only by so doing can both parties to the research effort—researcher and consumer—come to an intelligent understanding of what is being studied.

THE RESEARCH METHODOLOGY

Up to this point in this chapter, we have been discussing the *limitations* of the data: data as a means of communicational linkage between Ultimate Truth at one extreme and the inquiring mind of the researcher at the other; data primary and data secondary—those that are more nearly and more remotely situate with relation to the total truth; data whose value depends upon a refinement process occasioned by being screened through crtieria for their admissibility. After such refinement, we are now ready to discuss the ways in which acceptable data may be processed and utilized so that what truth they hold may be extracted from them.

Data are like ore. They contain desirable aspects of the truth, but to extract from the facts their meaning, we employ certain approaches which are broadly termed among professionals the *research methodology.*

It is particularly important to recognize the fact that data and methodology are inextricably interdependent. For that reason the research methodology to be adopted for a particular problem must always recognize the nature of the data which will be amassed in the resolution of that problem. *Methodology is merely an operational framework within which the facts are placed so that their meaning may be seen more clearly.* A review of any of the standard textbooks on research will reveal a broad spectrum of methodological terminology. In practice, however, these many methodologies resolve into only four approaches by which data may be processed.

Let us take one last look at data from a global viewpoint. Actually, data are of two types only: writings and observations. We shall discuss these two main categories under four subcategories:

1. *Written records and accounts* of past happenings and events (commonly called *historical* data); literary productions (commonly known as *literary* or *critical* data).
2. *Observations for whose transmission description is the best vehicle.* These are observations which a researcher makes directly at the scene of occurrence and then relays as facts (commonly called *normative survey* or *descriptive survey* data).
3. *Observations which are quantified and exist in the form of numerical concepts.* These data are expressed in the language of mathematics and must, consequently, be evaluated and interpreted by means of appropriate mathematical or statistical procedures. (Such data are commonly called *analytical survey* or *statistical* data.)
4. *Observations of certain differences and likenesses which arise from comparison or contrast of one set of observations with another set of similar observations.* Generally, these two sets of data have been derived from observations under differing conditions or effected at subsequent time modules. (These data are usually referred to as *experimental* data.)

These four kinds of data demand four discrete and different research approaches—*methodologies,* we call them. It is impossible, for example, to apply a methodology to data which are inappropriate to the demands of that particular method. Historical data, for example, are facts gleaned from written records. There is no possible way that you can take the writings of a historical record or the similar writings of a literary author and extract from these historical or literary data any meaning by means of an experimental methodology. The method is simply not suited to the nature of the data.

The above discussion suggests a basic rule with respect to the selection of a research methodology: *The data dictate the research methodology.* And, since there are four kinds of data, it is difficult to defend the position of those who claim that unless research fits an arbitrary prejudice for a given methodology, it fails to be research. Such an attitude denies that our understanding of the poetry of Coleridge has been increased because of the scholarly research of John Livingston Lowes[3] or that we have a more insightful appreciation of Western civilization through the historiography of Arnold Toynbee[4] because they have not unveiled their findings under the aegis of the experimental method or shown their conclusions by benefit of statistical analysis. No provincial group of scholars has a monopoly upon

---

[3] John L. Lowes, *Road to Xanadu: A Study in the Ways of the Imagination.* Rev. ed. (Boston: Houghton Mifflin Co., 1955).

[4] Arnold Toynbee, *A Study of History.* 12 vols. London: Oxford University Press (Royal Institute of International Affairs), 1939–1961.

any one highway that leads toward the enlargement of insight into the unknown. All highways are of equal excellence; each, however, traverses a different terrain, but they all converge on the same destination: the enlargement of human knowledge, the discovery of new truth.

The four kinds of data demand four principal research approaches—methodologies—to deal with each type of data appropriately. For simplicity, we shall keep a one-to-one correspondence between the above categories of the preceding types of data and the methodology appropriate for each data type.

1. The *historical method* is appropriate to be applied to those data that are primarily documentary in nature or literary in form.
2. The *descriptive survey method*, or as it is sometimes called, *the normative survey method* is appropriate for those data that are derived from simple observational situations, whether these are actually physically observed or "observed" through benefit of questionnaire or poll techniques.
3. The *analytical survey method* is appropriate for data that are quantitative in nature and that need statistical assistance to extract their meaning.
4. The *experimental method* is appropriate for data derived from an "experimental control" situation or a "pretest-posttest" design in which two separate groups, or one group from which data are derived at two separate intervals, is involved. In the instance of two separate groups, one is conditioned by an extraneous variable while the other group is sealed off from the influence which affects the first group. Thus, the *control* or isolated group may be used as a "yardstick" against which to measure any change that has taken place in the *experimental* group which has been subjected to the extraneous variable. In the "pretest-posttest" design, the same group is measured before and after exposure to an extraneous influence.

Each of these several methods has its discrete characteristics. Each, likewise, makes certain demands upon the data, so that the methodology must be able to reveal the meaning of the particular data with which it presumes to deal.

These are, however, broad methodological categories following, in general, innate characteristics of the several kinds of data with which the researcher works. Other writers have proposed different categories, the most common of which are tabulated in the list on the page following.

Practical Application No. 1 ———————————————————————————

To appreciate the discreteness of methodological approaches to the data as produced by the several academic disciplines, turn to pages 292–293 where you will be directed to a practical application of the material in this part of the chapter which will provide you with an appreciation of each methodological application in research.

———————————————————————————————————

Practical Application No. 2 ———————————————————————————

To determine the feasibility of the research project you may be considering, study the form that follows on pages 94–96. It will also be a practical application of the material presented thus far in this chapter.

———————————————————————————————————

METHOD	CHARACTERISTICS OF THE METHOD AND THE RESEARCH GOALS THE METHOD ATTEMPTS TO ACHIEVE
ACTION RESEARCH	The approach in action research is to do something to see if it works. Will playing video games improve eye-hand coordination in typing? Method: Get a bank of computers, a group of typists; set up a training session. See if typing skills improve.
CASE AND FIELD STUDY RESEARCH	A type of descriptive research in which data is gathered directly from individuals (individual cases) or social or community groups in their natural environment for the purpose of studying interactions, attitudes, or characteristics of individuals or groups. Case study method: AIDS Syndrome is a good example. Case-by-case has been studied until continually recurring facts have suggested certain conclusions. Field study method: Social workers observe certain recurring features indigenous to given social groups. These observations lead to conclusions.
CORRELATIONAL RESEARCH	A statistical investigation of the relationship between one factor and the degree of relationship it seems to have to one or more other factors. Correlational research looks at surface relationships but does not necessarily probe for causal reasons underlying the correlational manifestation. Example: An investigation of the degree of relationship between college grade-point average of freshman students and selected high school achievement scores and personality assessment scores.
DESCRIPTIVE SURVEY or NORMATIVE SURVEY	This research method is fully discussed in Chapter 8 of this text.
DEVELOPMENTAL	This type of research is an observational-descriptive genre of investigation that usually stretches over a period of time and is frequently called "the longitudinal study." The classic Gesell-Ilg studies in child development is an excellent example of this type of research. Trend studies and projections of future trends are sometimes considered as developmental research projects.
EX POST FACTO or CAUSAL-COMPARATIVE	The ex post facto method is discussed in this text as a subtype of the experimental method. (See pages 221-223.) The method observes existing conditions and searches back through the data for plausible causal factors. It is the "detective method" in which the situation of the crime is discovered and then the search for the cause or motivation for the crime is sought.
HISTORICAL	The historical research method is fully discussed in Chapter 7 of this text. It is the attempt to solve certain problems arising out of a historical context through a gathering and examination of relevant data.
QUASI-EXPERIMENTAL	Quasi-experimental research designs are explained as a subsection of Chapter 10 of this text.
TRUE EXPERIMENTAL	This variety of research design is discussed in Chapter 10 of this text.

ESTIMATION OF THE FEASIBILITY OF A RESEARCH PROJECT

Many beginning researchers avoid looking the practical problems of research straight in the eye. The appeal of an exotic investigation, an appealing problem, a consummation-devoutly-to-be-wished project sometimes has the effect of causing the researcher to fail to take a solid account of stock and to make an impartial judgment as to the practicability or impracticability of the project. To keep you solidly related to the world of reality, the following Estimation Inventory may help you to plan wisely and to evaluate accurately the feasibility of your research project.

ESTIMATION SHEET
TO DETERMINE THE FEASIBILITY OF THE RESEARCH PROJECT

The Problem

1. *With what area(s)* * *will the problem deal?*

   ☐ *People*
   ☐ *Things*
   ☐ *Records*
   ☐ *Thoughts and Ideas*
   ☐ *Dynamics or Energy*

   * *Conceivably the problem may involve more than one of these areas. A study of the philosophic viewpoints in the poetry of Robert Frost would deal with the area of people and the concomitant area of thoughts and ideas.*

2. *State the research problem clearly and in the form of a question:*

   ____

3. *Are data, which relate directly to the problem, available from one or more of the categories listed in item 1?* ☐ *Yes* ☐ *No.*

4. *What academic discipline is primarily concerned with the problem?* ____________

   ____

5. *What academic discipline or disciplines are related to the problem secondarily, or in ancillary relationship?* ____________

   ____

ESTIMATION SHEET (Continued)

6. *What special aptitude have you as a researcher for this problem?*
   ☐ *Interest in the problem* ☐ *Education and/or training*
   ☐ *Experience in the problem area* ☐ *Other: Specify* ______

____

The Data

7. *How available to you are the data?* ☐ *Readily available* ☐ *Available, with permission* ☐ *Available with great difficulty or rarely available* ☐ *Unavailable*

8. *How frequently do you personally contact the source of the data?* ☐ *Once a day* ☐ *Once a week* ☐ *Once a month* ☐ *Once a year* ☐ *Never*

9. *Will the data arise directly out of the problem situation?* ☐ *Yes* ☐ *No.*
   * *If no, where or how will you secure the data?*

____

____

10. *How do you plan to gather the data?* ☐ *Observation,* ☐ *Questionnaire,* ☐ *Tests or inventories,* ☐ *Photographic copying of records,* ☐ *Interview and tape recording,* ☐ *Other, Explain:* ______________

____

11. *Is special equipment or special conditions necessary to the gathering or processing of the data?* ☐ *Yes,* ☐ *No. If "yes" specify:* ______________

____

12. *If the answer to question 11 was "yes," have you access to such equipment and the skill to use it?* ☐ *Yes* ☐ *No. If the answer is "no" how do you intend to overcome this difficulty? Explain:* ______________

____

ESTIMATION SHEET (Continued)

Criterional Evaluation

13. Does your research project meet the criteria proposed in the chapter as applicable to all research?

Universality	☐ *Yes*	☐ *No*
Replication	☐ *Yes*	☐ *No*
Control	☐ *Yes*	☐ *No*
Measurement	☐ *Yes*	☐ *No*

14. As you review this estimation evaluation, are there any of the factors considered, or any other factors, which may hinder a successful completion of your research project? ☐ *Yes* ☐ *No*

III. RESEARCH DESIGN AND ETHICAL STANDARDS

RESEARCH DESIGN

What is *research design?* It is planning. It is the visualization of the body of the data and, the problems associated with the employment of those data in the entire research project. Research design is the common sense and the clear thinking that is necessary for the management of the entire research endeavor: the complete strategy of attack upon the central research problem.

The researcher must have some structural concept, some idea of the manner in which the data will be secured and how it will be interpreted so that the principal problem under research will be resolved; and all this must be conceived and formulated in the researcher's own mind before he or she begins to write the research proposal.

Research design is a matter of thinking, imagining, and thinking some more. As DeBakey and DeBakey advise, "Thinking through your project clearly and thoroughly before beginning to write a proposal is crucial."[5] Or, to take a definition from a research text in political science research methodology: "Research design is the strategy, the plan, and the structure of conducting a research project."[6]

A further definition may make the concept and the purpose of design in research methodology more understandable:

---

[5] L. DeBakey and S. DeBakey, "The Art of Persuasion: Logic and Language in Proposal Writing," *Grants Magazine*, 1 (1978), 43-60.

[6] M. G. Kweit and R. W. Kweit, *Concepts and Methods for Political Analysis.* (Englewood Cliffs, N.J.: Prentice-Hall, Inc. 1981), p. 357.

> The design is the plan for the study, providing the overall framework for collecting data. Once the problem has been concretely formulated, a design is developed in order to provide a format for the detailed steps in the study. The design is relatively specific consisting of a series of guidelines for systematic data gathering. The type of design depends upon the statement of the problem.[7]

Some writers seem to consider the design and the proposal as synonymous. But they are, in fact, not the same. The design phase *precedes* the proposal phase, as DeBakey suggests:

> A frequent, and grievous, error among novices is to begin writing too soon. The result is a diffuse, rambling, confused proposal that lays bare the incertitude and chaotic thinking of the applicant. An obscurely defined, vaguely described, sloppily developed project is bound to suggest murky thinking and is likely to portend haphazard research. Before you write the first word of the proposal, make sure that the concept you plan to examine has some point of originality, that it is well defined in your own mind, and that it is worthy of support. To satisfy these three criteria, you must have a good grasp of current knowledge of the subject, which means that your preliminary bibliographic research must have been thorough. If you betray an ignorance of certain vital aspects of the subject, you will be judged poorly qualified to perform the study.
>
> First, write down on paper the *precise question* or problem you plan to study. Make sure it is based on a sound premise. Then, write the possible or *expected answer(s)* or solutions. Seeing these two ends of your research project on paper will fix the limits of your study firmly in mind. Next write the *title*. Make it accurate, clear, succinct, and provocative. . . . An informative title is indispensable; select key words carefully to highlight the essence of the subject.[8]

Basic to design, therefore, are four fundamental questions that must be resolved with respect to the data. And, if the researcher is to avoid serious trouble later on, these questions must be answered specifically, concretely, and without mental evasion or reservation. The forthright answers to these questions will bring any research planning and design into clear focus.

★ *What are the data needed?* This question may seem like an oversimplification; but visualization of the data, an appreciation of their nature, and a clear understanding of the treatment of which they are capable is fundamental to any research effort. At this point, it may be well to take a sheet of paper. Write down the answers to the following questions and to similar ones that demand resolution before the project can be seen in its global dimensions.

To resolve the problem, what data are mandatory? What is their nature? Are they documentary? Statistical? Interview data? Questionnaire replies? Observations? Experimental data, recorded before and after certain processes? Specifically, what data do you need and what are their characteristics?

★ *Where are the data located?* Those of us who have taught research methodology are constantly amazed at students who come with perfectly fascinating problems for research projects. But then, we ask a most basic and obvious question, "Where will you get the data to resolve the problem?" The student either looks bewildered and remains speechless, or stutters out a confused remark, such as, "Well, they must be available *somewhere.*" Or, "Maybe I can go to the library to look in a book. I guess I can find them *somewhere.*" Not *somewhere*, but *precisely where?* If you are doing a documentary study, where are the documents you need? Precisely *what library* and *what collection* do you need to use? What society or what organization has the files that you must see? Where are these organizations

[7] Phyllis J. Verhonick and Catherine C. Seaman, *Research Methods for Undergraduate Students in Nursing* (New York: Appleton-Century-Crofts, 1978), p. 30.

[8] Lois DeBakey, "The Persuasive Proposal," *Journal of Technical Writing and Communication*, 6 (1976), 8–9. (Slight changes with permission of the author.)

located? Specify geographically—by town, street address, and zip code! A nurse or a nutritionist is doing a research report on Walter Olin Atwater, who, probably more than any other one individual, is responsible for establishing the science of human nutrition in the United States. Where are the data on Atwater located? The researcher can go no further until *that* basic question is answered.

★ *How will the data be secured?* To know where the data are is not enough; you need to know how they may be obtained. With invasion-of-privacy laws, protection of individual integrity, confidentiality agreements, and similar hindrances to access of personal data, securing the information you need may not be as easy as it may at first appear. You may indeed know what data you need, and where it is located; but an equally important question is: How will you get it? In designing a research project this question cannot be ignored. In the research proposal, the delineation of this matter may spell the difference between a viable research project and a pipe dream of research.

★ *How will the data be interpreted?* This is perhaps the most important question of all. The three former hurdles have been overcome. You have the data in hand. Now, spell out *precisely* what you intend to do with the data to effect the solution of the research problem or subproblem.

At this point, it may be well for you to go back and to read very carefully the wording of the problem. How *must* you treat the data to resolve the problem? If you process the data as you propose, what will the result be? How do you propose to "measure" the data? (Read again pages 18–26, "Measurement as a Tool of Research.")

If you are proposing to test the null hypothesis, are the statistical procedures appropriate for the characteristics of the data? Are you proposing a statistical technique that requires interval or ratio data when the data you have is nominal or ordinal? Are you suggesting a parametric procedure for nonparametric data?

Probably no part of the design requires more detailed thinking and explicit planning than does this section. In fact, it may be well for you to analyze your procedure for interpreting the data by using the form that follows.

At this point, it may be well also for you to turn to the sample proposal, pages 270–279, to see how the author of that proposal spelled out exactly the data and procedures that we have been discussing the the above paragraphs.

RESEARCH DESIGN:
PROCEDURE FOR INTERPRETING THE DATA[8]

1. Problem and/or subproblem to be resolved: ____________________

____

____

2. Data to be employed in resolving the problem: ____________________

____

[8] Lois DeBakey, "The Persuasive Proposal," *Journal of Technical Writing and Communication*, 6 (1976), 8–9. (Slight changes with permission of the author.)

RESEARCH DESIGN:
PROCEDURE FOR INTERPRETING THE DATA (Continued)

3. What kind of data will you employ? ☐ Documentary? If documentary, will you use ☐ primary data, or ☐ secondary data. If secondary data, justify your reason for not using primary sources: ______

______

☐ Survey? If survey, which of the following modes of data collection will you employ?
☐ Interview ☐ Questionnaire ☐ Observation ☐ Other
If other, explain: ______

☐ Experimental? If experimental data will be collected, describe briefly the type, or organization, of the experiment: ______

______

4. Will the data be processed statistically? ☐ Yes ☐ No. If, yes, what type of data, according to measurement, will they be? ☐ Nominal ☐ Ordinal ☐ Interval ☐ Ratio.

5. What kind of statistical techniques do you plan to employ to interpret the data?[9] ☐ Parametric ☐ Nonparametric

6. Is the technique suited to the type of data? ☐ Yes ☐ No
If no, go back to item 4 to reevaluate your statistical approach.

7. What will you finally have as the result of the statistical technique you plan to use to process the data? ______

8. Will this result resolve the problem? (Compare your answer to item 7 with the statement of the problem, or subproblem, in item 1 and mark the appropriate box.) ☐ Yes ☐ No. If no, what further needs to be done to resolve the problem? ______

______

9. What criteria have you established to control the quality and limit the admissibility of the data? List the criteria. ______

______

______

10. Does your research project meet all of the ethical standards outlined earlier in this chapter? ☐ Yes ☐ No

11. Are you still convinced that your research project is feasible and practical? ☐ Yes ☐ No. If "yes," you are, then, ready to consider writing your proposal. If "no," you may then need to reedit the wording of the problem or select another problem entirely.

[9] The answers to some of these questions may be too advanced for you to respond to at this point in your study of the text. They are, however, pertinent to the research design of your project and should be considered in the final planning and design of your research project.

ETHICAL STANDARDS IN RESEARCH

Within certain disciplines—education, the behavioral sciences, criminology, nursing and the medical sciences, and similar areas of study—the use of human subjects in research is common. This fact raises the question of ethical standards. The ethics involved in the use of human subjects in the research project should not go without careful scrutiny.

Many disciplines have their own codes of ethical standards with respect to involving human subjects. A listing of some of these codes will be found in the bibliography immediately following this chapter.

The principles of ethical propriety lying at the base of most of these guidelines resolve into simple considerations of fairness, honesty, openness of intent, disclosure of methods that will be employed, the ends for which the research is executed, a respect for the integrity of the individual, the obligation of the researcher to guarantee unequivocally individual privacy, and an informed willingness on the part of the subject to participate voluntarily in the research activity.

Certainly no individual should be asked to cooperate in any research that may result in a sense of self-denigration, embarrassment, or a violation of ethical or moral standards or principles.

Every researcher should live up to the fullness of the commitments made to those who assist in the research endeavor. No research should ever be conducted under circumstances in which total disclosure of the aims and purposes of the research cannot be fully set forth—preferably in writing. Nor should any subject be inveigled into cooperating in any research endeavor without knowing fully what participation in the project will involve and what demands may be made upon that subject.

A Résumé of a Professional Code of Ethics

A résumé of the Code of Ethics of the American Sociological Association may be sufficient to indicate the ethical considerations that should govern the activity associated with any research project.

1. Researchers must maintain scientific objectivity.
2. Researchers should recognize the limitations of their competence and not attempt to engage in research beyond such competence.
3. Every person is entitled to the right of privacy and dignity of treatment.
4. All research should avoid causing personal harm to subjects used in the research.
5. Confidential information provided by a research subject must be held in strict confidentiality by the researcher.
6. Research findings should be presented honestly, without distortion.
7. The researcher must not use his prerogative as a researcher to obtain information for other than professional purposes.
8. The researcher must acknowledge all assistance, collaboration of others, or sources from which information was borrowed from others.
9. The researcher must acknowledge financial support in the research report or any personal relationship of the researcher with the sponsor that may conceivably affect the research findings.
10. The researcher must not accept any favors, grants, or other means of assistance which would violate any of ethical principles set forth in the above paragraphs.[10]

---

[10] *American Sociological Association Footnotes,* 10 (March, 1982), 9-10.

Any situation that employs human subjects in a research endeavor may raise questions of propriety, misunderstanding, or solicitation to go beyond one's own expectation of demands consistent with pure research objectivity. A signed statement of willingness to cooperate in the research endeavor and an acknowledgment that the purpose and procedure of the research project has been explained to the subject may well be a safeguard for both researcher and subject. Such a statement should contain a clause indicating that if, at any time during the research procedure, the individual on the basis of ethical, moral, or personal choice should not wish to continue to be associated with the research effort, he or she shall have the right to withdraw. If this situation occurs, the subject should notify the researcher in a written memorandum, in which is set forth the specific reason or reasons for the decision to discontinue cooperation.

But ethical practice goes quite beyond the specific area that we have just been discussing. It concerns the personal behavior of the researcher. Researchers are trustees of truth and, as such, need to be scrupulously aware of the ethics of their own conduct.

In writing a research report—the student's dissertation or thesis—the researcher must be sure that what purports to be the researcher's own work is *indeed* his or her *own* work. Those who aspire to a graduate degree and present a research document in partial fulfillment for the requirements of that degree should at least have fully mastered the common skills and abilities of written communication which are presumed to be part of one's educational achievement at the public school level. These are, of course, the ability to spell correctly, to write a grammatically correct and effective sentence, and to construct a unified and coherent paragraph. These skills are the elemental components of education.

To ask others to check your spelling, correct your grammar, or "ghost" your document is not only unethical but academically dishonest. You are attempting to offer as your own work that which, presumably, you are incompetent to produce. Those who engage in such subterfuge are guilty of fraudulent misrepresentation of their abilities and educational competence.

Any appropriation of writing that belongs to another demands full acknowledgment. Otherwise, it constitutes plagiarism and documentary theft. Full documentation of all material belonging to another person is mandatory. To appropriate the thoughts, the ideas, or the words of another—even though you paraphrase the borrowed ideas in your own words—without acknowledgment is unethical and highly circumspect. Those who are honest will not hesitate to acknowledge their indebtedness to others.

The DeBakeys, writing on "Ethics and Etiquette in Biomedical Communication," summarize the matter succinctly:

> Like other forms of social behavior, ethics and etiquette in . . . communication change with time. Their basis, however, remains the same—honesty, integrity, humanity, courtesy, and consideration. Ethical codes thus depend more on what is morally proper than on what is legally enforceable.
>
> The responsible author makes certain that what he publishes has a sound thesis, that his data are ethically obtainable and scientifically valid, that he writes his report himself, that he documents it properly, and that he makes it intelligible and readable. . . . For everyone involved in communication . . . the Golden Rule is a useful guide to [scholarly] ethics and etiquette.[11]

FOR FURTHER READING

Further Reading in Understanding the Scientific Method

Airaksinen, Timo. "Five Types of Knowledge." *American Philosophical Quarterly* 15 (October 1978): 263-74.

[11] Lois DeBakey and Selma DeBakey, "Ethics and Etiquette in Biomedical Communication," *Perspectives in Biology and Medicine*, 18 (Summer 1975), 538-39.

Beardsley, Monroe C. *Practical Logic.* Englewood Cliffs, N.J.: Prentice-Hall, Inc., 1961.

Fowler, William S. *The Development of Scientific Method.* New York: Pergamon Press, Inc., 1962.

Giere, Ronald H., and Richard S. Westfall, eds. *Foundations of Scientific Method: the Nineteenth Century.* Bloomington, Ind.: University of Indiana Press, 1973.

Goldstein, Martin, and Inge F. Goldstein. *How We Know: An Exploration of the Scientific Process.* New York: Plenum Publishing Corporation, 1978.

Lastrucci, Carlo L. *The Scientific Approach: Basic Principles of the Scientific Method.* Cambridge, Mass: Schenkman Publishing Co., 1963.

Ritchie, Arthur D. *Scientific Method: An Inquiry into the Character and Validity of Natural Laws.* Paterson, N.J.: Littlefield, Adams, Inc., 1960.

Rougement, D. Translated by R. S. Walker. "Information Is Not Knowledge," *Diogenes* 116 (Winter 1981): 1-17.

Wilson, Edgar B. *An Introduction to Scientific Research.* New York: Mc-Graw Hill Book Company, 1952.

The Design and Planning of Research

Campbell, D. T., and J. C. Stanley. *Experimental and Quasi-experimental Designs for Research.* Chicago, Ill.: Rand McNally & Company, 1963.

Davitz, Joel R., and Lois J. Davitz. *A Guide for Evaluating Research Plans in Psychology and Education.* New York: Teachers College Press, Teachers College, Columbia University, 1967.

Ferber, Robert, Sidney Cohen, and David Luck. *The Design of Research Investigations.* Chicago, Ill.: American Marketing Association, 1958.

Isaac, Stephen, and William B. Michael. *Handbook in Research and Evaluation.* San Diego, Calif.: Robert R. Knapp, Publisher, 1971.

Kempthorne, Oscar. *The Design and Analysis of Experiments.* New York: Robert E. Krieger Publishing Company, Inc., 1973.

Kirk, R. E. *Experimental Design: Procedures for the Behavioral Sciences.* Belmont, Calif.: Wadsworth Publishing Co., 1968.

Lakatos, Imre. *The Methodology of Scientific Research Programmes.* Edited by John Worrall and Greg Currie. New York: Cambridge University Press, 1977.

Myers, Lawrence S., and Neal E. Grossen. *Behavioral Research: Theory, Procedure, and Design.* San Francisco, Calif.: W. H. Freeman and Company, 1974.

Miller, Delbert C. *Handbook of Research Design and Social Measurement.* 3rd ed. New York: David McKay Co., Inc., 1977.

Stroud, J. G. "Research Methodology Used in School Library Dissertations." *School Library Media Quarterly* 10 (Winter 1982): 124-34.

The Importance of Ethical Standards in Research

Beauchamp, Tom L., Ruth R. Faden, R. Jay Wallace, Jr., and LeRoy Wallace. *Ethical Issues in Social Science Research.* Baltimore, Md.: The Johns Hopkins University Press, 1982.

Cassell, Joan and Murray L. Wax, "Toward a Moral Science of Human Beings," *Social Problems* 27 (February 1980): 259-64.

DeBakey, Lois, and Selma DeBakey. "Ethics and Etiquette in Biomedical Communication." *Perspectives in Biology and Medicine* 18 (Summer 1975): 522-40.

DeBakey, Lois. "Honesty in Authorship." *Surgery* 75 (May 1974): 802-804.

———. "Rewriting and the By Line: Is the Author the Writer?" *Surgery* 74 (January 1974): 38-48.

Freund, Paul A. *Experimentation with Human Subjects.* New York: George Braziller, Inc., 1970.

Hoffman, R. "Scientific Research and Moral Rectitude." *Philosophy* 50 (October 1975): 475-77.

Kelman, H. "Human Use of Human Subjects: The Problem of Deception in Social Experiments." *Psychological Bulletin* 67 (January 1967): 1-11.

———. *A Time to Speak Out: On Human Values and Social Research.* San Francisco: Jossey-Boss, 1968.

Schuler, Heinz. *Ethical Problems in Psychological Research.* Translated by Margaret S. Woodruff and Robert P. Wicklund. London: Academic Press, 1982.

Sjoberg, Gideon, ed. *Ethics, Politics and Social Research.* Cambridge, Mass: Schenkman Publishing Company, Inc., 1967.

Smith, Harmon L. "Ethical Considerations in Research Involving Human Subjects," *Social Science and Medicine* 14 (October 1980): 453-58.

Codes of Ethics of Various Professional Organizations

American Association for Public Opinion Research. *Code of Professional Ethics and Practices of the American Association for Public Opinion Research* (A.A.P.O.R.). 420 Lexington Avenue, Suite 1733, New York, N.Y. 10017.

American Nurses Association. "The Nurse in Research: Guidelines on Ethical Values." *Nursing Research* 17 (1968): 104.

American Psychological Association. "Ethical Principles of Psychologists." *American Psychologist* 36 (June 1981): 633-38.

American Political Science Association. Committee on Professional Standards and Responsibilities. "Ethical Problems of Academic Political Science." *Political Science* 1 (1968): 3-29.

American Sociological Association. *Revised American Sociological Association.* Washington, D.C.: American Sociological Association, 1980.

Code of Federal Regulations. Title 45, Public Welfare, Department of Health and Human Services, Part 46: "Protection of Human Subjects." Revised as of January 26, 1981.

Office of Science and Technology, Executive Office of the President of the United States. *Privacy and Behavioral Research.* Washington, D.C.: United States Government Printing Office, 1967.

READ THIS—BEFORE YOU READ THIS CHAPTER

Writing the research proposal is perhaps one of the most critical steps in the entire research process. The proposal is you. It lays bare your foresight, your insight, and your ability to plan with hardheaded practicality and steel-edged logic.

Proposals are necessary. Whether you are a graduate student or a researcher seeking research-grant funding, nothing will attest to your competency to conduct a research project more clearly than your ability to present a clear, logical, and convincing proposal.

The chapter you are about to read outlines carefully the steps in writing the research proposal and provides you with a checklist to test the practicality of your thinking and planning a project for research.

6
Writing the Research Proposal

Research is never a solo flight. It is an activity that involves many people and presumes the accession to and the use of resources far beyond one's personal possessions. For that reason, research is not some "do-it-in-a-corner" activity. It must be aired, laid out, inspected, and, in nearly every instance, approved by others.

The graduate student must get approval of an academic committee. A researcher seeking a grant must get approval from the university or the organization for which he or she works, and the project must merit the approval of the grant-awarding agency. These approvals are usually secured through the submission to proper authorities of a document known as a *research proposal.* The proposal discusses openly the problem for research, exactly how the research will be executed, and it will spell out in precise detail the resources—both personal and instrumental—that the researcher has available for producing the proposed results.

A proposal is as essential to successful research as an architect's drawing is to the construction of a building. No one would start building a structure by rushing out to dig a hole in the ground for the foundation without knowing in detail how the house will look when finished. Before one turns a shovelful of earth, many questions must be answered, many decisions made. What kind of building do you propose to construct? A dwelling? Will it be a two-story, a split level, or a ranch type? How will the house be placed on the building lot? Where will the openings be located? What kind of roof will it have? What will be its pitch? What kind of heat will it have? Where will the electrical outlets and switches be placed? We could go on and on. Every one of these questions is extremely important, and each must be answered specifically *before* a pound of dirt can be excavated or a nail driven.

Even then, after you have made all these decisions, do you immediately begin digging? Not at all! Yet another preliminary phase remains. The architect now draws a plan of the entire structure, floor by floor, showing to the fraction of an inch precisely where every detail will be located. Insofar as possible, nothing is left to chance.

A researcher proceeds in exactly the same manner. He draws upon a research proposal in which the problem and its attendant subproblems are stated clearly, all necessary terms are defined, the delimitations are carefully stated, the hypotheses articulated, and the importance of the study practically and succinctly spelled out. The researcher then spells out every detail of acquiring, arranging, processing, and interpreting the data.

Let us return to the architect. His work is not complete with the executing of the floor plans. He, then, draws a series of elevations of the proposed building, showing each side to scale as it will appear when completed. Finally, the architect will draw up a set of specifications for the building indicating exactly what lumber is to be used, how far apart certain members are to be placed, the sizes and types of windows and doors, and all other details. Nothing is left unspecified.

The researcher does likewise. Parallel to the architect's elevations, the researcher produces an Outline of the Proposed Study. Parallel to the specifications, the researcher sets forth the resources at hand for doing the research: his own qualifications (and those of his staff, if any); the availability of the data; the means by which they will be secured; computerization facilities, if these are needed; and any other aspects of the total research process that merit explanation. Nothing is overlooked: all questions that may arise in the minds of those who review the proposal are anticipated and answered. Any unresolved matter is a weakness in the proposal and may seriously affect its approval. The importance of the proposal cannot be overemphasized. It is frequently the magic key that will unlock for the researcher the door that gives free access to the research endeavor. Conversely, if it is not clearly and explicitly delineated, it may cause the whole project to be turned down.

Some students—and others seeking research grants—seem to think that the proposal is merely a necessary formality and do not give it the serious consideration it deserves. They try in a few pages to set forth the project. It usually fails. Those sponsoring a project, whether a graduate committee or a funding agency, realize that in doing research there is too much money, time, and effort invested to rush into it without a clearly conceived design.

Whether you seek funding of a project from a grant foundation or whether you seek to show your professor or your graduate committee that you have the ability to plan and carry out an investigation independently, a clear, well-written proposal is indispensable. Nothing is a substitute for an explicit setting forth of both problem and procedure. Other names for a proposal are *prospectus*, *plan*, *outline*, *statement*, and *draft*. If you are asked to present any of these, you are asked to present a research proposal.

CHARACTERISTICS OF A PROPOSAL

More than any other one factor, research demands that those who undertake it be able to *think* without confusion clearly. The proposal will demonstrate, fortunately or unfortunately, whether you possess that quality. When one reads a proposal that is poorly organized, filled with extraneous details, poorly planned, and foggily focussed, one gets the immediate impression that the mind that produced such a mélange of confusion can never be disciplined to regard facts objectively and construe them logically. Unwelcome as the fact may be, your reputation as a researcher more often than not rests squarely upon the quality of the proposal you submit.

It is well, therefore, to appreciate exactly what characteristics a proposal should have.

★ *A proposal is a straightforward document.* It should not be cluttered with extraneous matter. It begins without introduction with a straightforward statement of the problem to be researched. It stands upon its own feet; it needs no explanatory props. There is no need for introduction, prologue, or statement of reasons why the researcher became interested in the problem or feels a burning need to research it. That may be interesting, but none of it is necessary or appropriate. Those who will review your proposal are not interested in such autobiographical excursions. These, indeed, suggest that you cannot separate essentials from irrelevancies; and *that*, unfortunately, will neither enhance your stature as a researcher nor recommend you as one who can think without irrelevancy and digression.

Whatever does not contribute *directly* to the delineation of the problem and its solution must be eliminated. Anything else only obscures and is diversionary. Remember the architect's drawing: clean, clear, and economical. It contains all that is necessary; not one detail more.

★ *A proposal is not a literary production.* An architect's drawing is not a work of art; a proposal is not a "literary" (in the sense of being consciously a piece of fine writing) production. The mission of neither is to be artistic; the purpose of both is to communicate clearly. As an architect's drawings present an idea of construction with economy of line and precision of measurement, so a proposal indicates how a research project is to be executed to completion, with an economy of words and a precision of expression. It provides no opportunity for fine writing, for literary composition, for verbal extravagance. Quite to the contrary, stylistically it is generally stark and prosaic.

The language must be clear, precise, and sharp. The proposal provides a chance to show with what ultimate clarity and precision the researcher can state a problem, delineate the treatment of the data, and establish the logical validity of a conclusion.

To those who have been nurtured in the idea that writing should be stylistically interesting and artistically creative, the preceding statements may come as a distinct shock. But to write a superb proposal calls for skills of expression quite as demanding as those needed for the forging of an unforgettable sentence.

★ *A proposal is clearly organized.* Proposals are written in conventional prose style and thoughts are expressed in simple paragraph form. The organization of the thought—the outline, as it were—is indicated by the proper use of heading and subheading. The use of the indented outline is neither conventional nor acceptable in the presentation of formal proposals. Those who employ the indented outline form may lay themselves open to criticism on two counts: they may be suspect of never having learned how to express the outline of their thought by the use of headings and subheadings; but more seriously, outlines hint at brevity, brevity hits at superficiality, superficiality suggests a most undesirable quality on the part of the researcher. Such may, of course, not be so; but no proposal should ever result in its author being represented in an unfavorable light.

Nevertheless, organization and outline are absolutely essential. *They* hint at an orderly and disciplined mind—one of the highest tributes to a researcher's qualifications. If you are not conversant with the use of headings to indicate thought organization, refer to Chapter 11, pages 229-230. There you will find a working knowledge of the basics of this stylistic convention. Efficient readers recognize immediately the outline organization of the thought when expressed with appropriate headings. Turn back to Chapter 4. Notice the headings. There you have three levels of importance of material presented and, by merely thumbing through the chapter, you will find that the headings indicate the following organization of the thought.

IV. The Review of the Related Literature
- A. Understanding the role of the review
  - 1. The purpose of the review
  - 2. How to begin a search for related literature
    - a. Go to the indexes and abstracts
    - b. Go to the library armed with data-gathering tools
    - c. Make as many copies of the bibliographic item as necessary
    - d. Be systematic and thorough
    - e. Relate your bibliography to your problem
  - 3. How to write the section on the related literature
    - a. Get the proper psychological orientation
    - b. Have a plan
    - c. Emphasize relatedness
    - d. Review the literature; don't reproduce it
  - 4. Showing the relatedness of the literature to the research project
  - 5. Summarize what you have said
- B. Points of Departure

Were you aware when you read that chapter that *that* was the outline of it? You should have been, and you should impart the outline of your thought to your readers in the same way. It is the professional way in which thought organization is expressed. Examine your textbooks—even current magazine articles—and you will find how prevalent the outline structure expressed by headings really is.

CONTENT AND ORGANIZATION OF A PROPOSAL

Proposals follow a simple logical form of presentation. Although there are many ways to arrange the items within the proposal, the following is the outline of the proposal that we shall follow in this text. A sample proposal for a research project is presented in Appendix A, and the significant features of the proposal are commented upon in the right-hand column. Refer to it.

However, to reduce the major divisions of any proposal to outline form, the following is offered. It may serve as a checklist of items in your writing of a proposal.

I. The problem and its setting
  A. The statement of the problem
  B. The statement of the subproblems
  C. The hypotheses
  D. The delimitations
  E. The definitions of terms
  F. The assumptions
  G. The importance of the study
II. The review of the related literature
III. The data, their treatment, and their interpretation
  A. The data
    1. The primary data
    2. The secondary data
  B. The criteria governing the admissibility of the data
  C. The research methodology
  D. The specific projected treatment of each subproblem
    1. Subproblem 1 *(The subproblem is here restated)*
      a. Data needed
      b. Where the data are located
      c. How the data will be secured
      d. How the data will be treated and interpreted
    2. Subproblem 2 *(Here, again, the subproblem will be restated and the four steps: a, b, c, and d are detailed. Then each succeeding subproblem will be given similar treatment.)*
IV. The qualifications of the researcher (and the qualifications of each one of the researcher's staff if more than the researcher is involved in the project)
V. The outline of the proposed study
VI. A selected bibliography

One rule governs the writing of proposals and final documents: *The arrangement of the material should be so presented that it forms for the reader of the document a clear progressive presentation by keeping items together that belong together* (such as the problem and its resultant subproblems; the subproblems and their corresponding hypotheses).

In suggesting ways to write a convincing proposal, Dr. Lois DeBakey gives some valued directives.[1] Extracts from Dr. DeBakey's article follow:

> Write the first draft [of the proposal] with attention exclusively to orderly sequence and without consideration for grammatical or rhetorical perfection. Stopping to examine each work phrase, or clause will shift your attention from thought to form and will interrupt the rational flow of ideas. You can always refine your compositions later, but if the presentation of your ideas is disorderly, major excision and reconstruction will be required to repair the damage. Use succinct language; and assign to appendices any auxiliary information, to prevent cluttering the text with excessive detail.

---

[1] Lois DeBakey, "The Persuasive Proposal," *Journal of Technical Writing and Communication*, 6:1 (1976), 5–25.

Introduction

In any unit of exposition, be it a sentence, a paragraph, or a full composition, two of the most important positions are the first and the last. The introduction, therefore, should be prepared with special care, for if you fail to engage the reviewer's interest in the beginning, you may lose it altogether. . . .

State the problem and the aims clearly and promptly, rather than make the reader transverse several pages before he finds out what your central point is. . . . Emphasize what is unique about the project. . . .

Your opening paragraph should inspire confidence and convince the reader that what you wish to do warrants careful consideration. *Remember that cold print alone must sell your idea.*

Materials and Methods

The introduction should lead naturally and smoothly to the section on methods, which is probably the most carefully examined section of the [proposal] and, therefore, one of the most important. . . . Describe clearly the method of selection of subjects or materials and the provision of controls for variables that might later be confused with experimental effect. To defend your choice of procedure, you must obviously be familiar with the capabilities and limitations of all available methods. . . .

Be sure that your experimental design is rational, ethical, and defensible and that it can yield answers to your stated problem. . . .

Never assume that the reader knows anything of vital significance that you have omitted from your presentation. Even if he knows it, he will not know that *you* know it too unless you tell him. Make certain that you have at least described the sample, the experimental design and procedure, the method of collection and analysis of data.

Expected Results

Following the section on methods is that on expected results, which should be written honestly and objectively. Overstated claims . . . should be avoided in favor of sober statements based on logic and reason. Try to estimate the potential generality of the results and the basis for your judgment. When tables and graphs summarize data for this section more efficiently than text, they may be used to advantage. Any tests, instruments, publications, films, or other educational material that may be by-products of the project should be noted.

Discussion

In the Discussion, you have an opportunity to show your broad familiarity with the various aspects and implications of the problem and to present the potential significance of the prospective results. Be sure to indicate any distinctive qualities of this research as compared with previous studies. Wild speculation is anathema. This is the place to persuade your reader that your proposed study holds real promise. . . . And you may wish to suggest new directions for subsequent or concurrent projects in related research.

Revision

When you have completed the first draft, lay it aside for a couple of weeks or so—long enough to be able to read it with detachment and objectivity. If you re-read it too soon, you may read what you *thought* you wrote, not what you actually put down on paper. Read first for logical order and coherence, accuracy, clarity of purpose, unity of thesis, and consistency; then for grammatical integrity, punctuation, grace of expression, and mellifluence. Note, too, whether the narrative flows smoothly and logically from one statement to the next and from one paragraph to the next. Reading aloud will uncover defective rhythm or cadence, as well as improper balance and emphasis.

If I had to identify the most important literary requisite for [a proposal], I would choose precision—precision in choice of words and their arrangement to convey the intended meaning.

Conclusion

The applicant should remember that the proposal is a kind of promissory note. It is a mistake to promise mountains and deliver molehills, because the day of reckoning will come—when you will have to write a formal report of your research project. It is through writing, therefore, that both the need for the research and the importance of the results are communicated, and the investigator with literary prowess has a distinct advantage in achieving both of these objectives.

THE GREATEST WEAKNESSES IN PROPOSALS SEEKING FUNDING

The United States government is perhaps the greatest underwriter of research in the country, certainly in funding research projects in the form of grants. Each grant is announced by the division funding it and invitations for proposals are issued. Specific details may be had by writing to the particular division administering the grant awards and issuing the grant contracts.

Competition is keen. Frequently, thousands of proposals are submitted, and these are read and evaluated usually by an award committee. For one reason or another, most of the proposals fail to be funded. The cause for this usually lies in the quality of the proposal itself. Many proposals do not measure up to the excellence that the agency expects and are, thus, eliminated in the winnowing process.

An article in *Science* reported on a study of 605 rejected applications for grants (out of approximately 2,000).[2] In the twelve months that ended June 30, 1959, the National Institutes of Health received and acted upon nearly 6,000 competitive applications for grants to conduct projects in medical and related biological research. Nearly one-third of the proposals submitted were not approved because of obvious research difficulties with the problem, with the research approach, with the researcher himself, or with other miscellaneous matters.

The following table sets forth each of the twenty-six shortcomings in these proposals. The percentages indicate the frequency of each weakness contributing to disapproval. The percentages corresponding to the four main classes add up to more than 100 percent; and those, also, within any one of the four groups, add up to more than the percentage for that group. In both cases, the excess is due to the fact that a given research proposal may have had more than one adverse characteristic.

Proposals submitted by students for academic research projects share these weaknesses. The following list should therefore merit careful study.

[2] Ernest M. Allen, "Why Are Research Grant Applications Disapproved?" *Science*, 132 (November, 1960), 1532-34.

WEAKNESSES FOUND IN A STUDY OF 605 GRANT APPLICATIONS DISAPPROVED BY NATIONAL INSTITUTES OF HEALTH

No.	*Shortcoming*	%
	Class I: Problem (58 percent)	
1	The problem is of insufficient importance or is unlikely to produce any new or useful information.	33.1
2	The proposed research is based on a hypothesis that rests on insufficient evidence, is doubtful, or is unsound.	8.9
3	The problem is more complex than the investigator appears to realize.	8.1
4	The problem has only local significance, or is one of production or control, or otherwise fails to fall sufficiently clearly within the general field of health-related research.	4.8
5	The problem is scientifically premature and warrants, at most, only a pilot study.	3.1
6	The research as proposed is overly involved, with too many elements under simultaneous investigation.	3.0
7	The description of the nature of the research and of its significance leaves the proposal nebulous and diffuse and without clear research aim.	2.6
	Class II: Approach (73 percent)	
8	The proposed tests, or methods, or scientific procedures are unsuited to the stated objective.	34.7
9	The description of the approach is too nebulous, diffuse, and lacking in clarity to permit adequate evaluation.	28.8
10	The over-all design of the study has not been carefully thought out.	14.7
11	The statistical aspects of the approach have not been given sufficient consideration.	8.1
12	The approach lacks scientific imagination.	7.4
13	Controls are either inadequately conceived or inadequately described.	6.8
14	The material the investigator proposes to use is unsuited to the objectives of the study or is difficult to obtain.	3.8
15	The number of observations is unsuitable.	2.5
16	The equipment contemplated is outmoded or otherwise unsuitable.	1.0
	Class III: Man (55 percent)	
17	The investigator does not have adequate experience or training or both, for *this* research.	32.6
18	The investigator appears to be unfamiliar with recent pertinent literature or methods, or both.	13.7
*19	The investigator's previously published work in *this* field does not inspire confidence.	12.6
*20	The investigator proposes to rely too heavily on insufficiently experienced associates.	5.0
21	The investigator is spreading himself too thin; he will be more productive if he concentrates on fewer projects.	3.8
*22	The investigator needs more liaison with colleagues in this field or in collateral fields.	1.7
	Class IV: Other (16 percent)	
23	The requirements for equipment or personnel, or both, are unrealistic.	10.1
24	It appears that other responsibilities would prevent devotion of sufficient time and attention to this research.	3.0
25	The institutional setting is unfavorable.	2.3
*26	Research grants to the investigator, now in force, are adequate in scope and amount to cover the proposed research.	1.5

***The items marked with an asterisk may not be particularly relevant for a student doing academic research.**

The above study is reported with considerable fullness, despite the fact that it was done a quarter of a century ago. It is, perhaps the best analysis in the literature specifically outlining the reasons for proposals being disapproved. Basically, most of the causes cited are related to fundamental shortcomings in the individual writing the proposal (inability to think analytically and clearly, insufficient knowledge of the existing research which has been done, seeming lack of competence to carry out the proposed study, and the inability to see the global concept of the research in terms of its many ramifications and requirements), and these have apparently not significantly changed over the past twenty-five years.

Judith Margolin in an analysis made recently has found essentially the same weaknesses in proposals today that were indigenous to those of the National Institutes of Health study just cited. Here are Margolin's comments and list of shortcomings of many proposals in *The Individual's Guide to Grants* (N.Y.: Plenum Press, 1983, pp. 233-234):

SHORTCOMINGS OF MANY PROPOSALS

Although I dislike stressing the negative, you should be aware that a large proportion of proposals are turned down. Some say as many as 90 out of every 100 applicants are rejected (depending upon the nature of the grant), though it would be very difficult to verify this statistic. You should not be discouraged by the high rejection rate. If you were to examine the rejected proposals carefully, it probably would become evident that most of the applicants simply had not done their homework properly. All too often their proposals were not worthy, inadequately prepared, or thoughtlessly submitted to inappropriate funders.

My research indicates that, like successful proposals, rejected proposals have much in common. Funding executives report the same reasons for rejection time and time again. Note should be taken of the following shortcomings so that you can avoid these pitfalls yourself.

Ten Reasons Proposals Are Turned Down

1. Inadequately presented statement of need—perceived by funder as either not a significant issue or as one of such magnitude that a few grant dollars would barely make a dent in the problem.
2. Objectives are ill defined—put forward as vague goals or as personal aims.
3. Procedures are confused with objectives.
4. Lack of integration within the text among components of the proposal.
5. The funder does not accept proposals from unaffiliated individuals.
6. The funder knows that the proposed idea has already been tried and failed.
7. The funder approves of the concept but believes that the applicant is not the proper individual to conduct the project or that the institution with which the applicant is affiliated is not suitable.
8. The individual has adopted a poor approach and appealed on an emotional or a political rather than a factual basis.
9. The idea costs too much.
10. The funder does not have enough information.

Here is a checklist covering many of the weaknesses in proposal writing cited above. Check your proposal against each item. This is obviously a checklist for *sponsored* research—

for proposals where government, foundation, or other funding is requested. A perfect score results from *no* check mark appearing opposite any item.

CHECKLIST OF FEATURES DETRACTING FROM PROPOSAL EFFECTIVENESS

Check each item to be sure that your proposal exhibits none of the following characteristics

- ☐ 1. *The proposal does not follow directions or conform to the guidelines set forth in the informational literature of the funding or approving agency.*
- ☐ 2. *The statement of the problem is vague, or so obscured by other discussion that it is impossible to find it.*
- ☐ 3. *The problem does not address the research area outlined by the funding agency.*
- ☐ 4. *The methodology is not clearly stated and an explanation of exactly how the research will be conducted is not specifically delineated.*
- ☐ 5. *The proposal is too ambitious for the grant money available.*
- ☐ 6. *Items are included in the budget disallowed by the terms of the grant.*
- ☐ 7. *A clear and explicit budget statement outlining program expenditures is either lacking or the summary of estimated costs is ambiguous and indefinite.*
- ☐ 8. *The deadline for submission has not been met. Late proposals generally do not merit consideration.*
- ☐ 9. *The importance-of-the-study section of the proposal is not clearly enough set forth for the funding agency to see a relationship of the study to the purpose for which the grant is awarded.*
- ☐ 10. *The credentials of the chief investigator (the researcher) and others involved in the study are such that they raise questions of the competence of the researcher and/or members of the research staff to conduct the study.*

CHECKLIST OF FEATURES DETRACTING FROM PROPOSAL EFFECTIVENESS (continued)

☐ *11.* *The application is incomplete; all requested information is either not included or clearly and explicitly stated in the application.*

☐ *12.* *The proposal is not clearly and logically organized. It is rather a rambling discussion without divisions which set forth the various areas of the research project ambiguously: the problem, the subproblems, the related studies, the methodology, the criteria, the data and its availability and interpretation, the importance of the study, and other necessary and related matters.*

☐ *13.* *The outline of the proposed study is missing or so indefinite as to fail to communicate a clear concept of the overall structure of the investigation.*

☐ *14.* *Criteria for the admissibility of the data is weak or nonexistent.*

☐ *15.* *The projected treatment of each subproblem is cursory and is phrased in statements that are too general to convey any clear concept of exactly how each subpart of the entire project will be resolved and the manner in which the data will be interpreted.*

☐ *16.* *The whole proposal is phrased in too general terms, ambiguous and inexact phraseology, to be useful for evaluation. Such phrases as "tests will be given" or "tests will be made" are largely meaningless. The proposal cannot be too specific. Exactly what tests will "be given"? How given? Exactly what "tests" will be made? How made? More proposals are rejected because they are filled with verbal fog than for any other reason.*

This may also be considered an adequate checklist for graduate students preparing a proposal for their academic review committees. The financial factors, of course, in such cases do not apply; but otherwise the student might do well to check the proposal to be submitted against the criteria suggested in this checklist.

A review also of the sample proposal presented in Appendix A may help to clarify exactly what a proposal should contain. The sample proposal is annotated with comments in the margin to indicate its particular strengths and weaknesses. You will find it on pages 255–281.

FOR FURTHER READING

Allen, E. M. "Why Are Research Grant Applications Disapproved?" *Science* 132 (1960): 1532-34.

Berthold, J. S. "Nursing Research Grant Proposals: What Influenced Their Approval or Disapproval in Two National Granting Agencies?" *Nursing Research* 22 (July-August 1973): 292-99.

Brodsky, Jean. *The Proposal Writer's Swipe File II.* Washington, D.C.: Taft Products, Inc., 1000 Vermont Avenue, N.W., 20005 (1976).

DeBakey, Lois. "The Persuasive Proposal." *Journal of Technical Writing and Communication* 6 (1976): 5-25.

DeBakey, Lois, and Selma DeBakey. "The Art of Persuasion: Logic and Language in Proposal Writing." *Grants Magazine* 1 (1978): 43-60.

Dugdale, Kathleen. *A Manual on Writing Research.* 2nd ed. Bloomington, Ind.: Indiana University Bookstore, 1967.

Englebret, David. "Storyboarding—A Better Way of Planning and Writing Proposals." *IEEF Transactions on Professional Communication* 15 (December 1972): 115-118.

Gortner, S. R. "Research Grant Applications: What They Are Not, and Should Be." *Nursing Research* 20 (1971): 292-95.

Hall, Mary. *Developing Skills in Proposal Writing.* Corvallis, Ore.: Office of Federal Relations, Oregon State System of Higher Education, Extension Hall, University Campus, 1971.

Jacquette, Lee F., and Barbara L. Jacquette. "What Makes a Good Proposal?" in *The Foundation Directory, Edition Five.* New York: Columbia University Press, pp. 424-26.

____. "What Makes a Good Proposal?" *Foundation News* (January-February 1973): 18-21.

Kiritz, Norton J. "The Proposal Summary." *Grantsmanship Center News* 1 (1974): 7-10.

____. "The Proposal Introduction." *Grantsmanship Center News* 2 (1975): 37-45.

____. "The Problem Statement for Needs Assessment." *Grantsmanship Center News* 2 (1975): 33-40.

Lindvall, Carl M. "The Review of Related Literature." *Phi Delta Kappan* 40 (1959): 180.

Lisk, D. J. "Why Research Grant Applications Are Turned Down." *BioScience* 21 (1971): 1025-26.

Locke, Lawrence F., and Waneen W. Spirduso. *Proposals That Work.* New York: Teachers College Press, Columbia University, 1976.

Merritt, D. H. "Grantmanship: An Exercise in Lucid Presentation." *Clinical Research* 11 (1963): 375-77.

Plotkin, Harris M. "Preparing a Proposal Step by Step." *Journal of Systems Management* 23 (1972): 36-38.

Stallones, R. A. "Research Grants: Advice to Applicants." *The Yale Journal of Biology and Medicine* 48 (1975): 451-58.

Stolte, Karen. "A Guide to the Process of Preparing a Research Proposal—Strategies for Teaching Nursing Research." *Western Journal Nursing Research* 3 (Fall 1981): 445-50.

White, Virginia, ed. *Grant Proposals That Succeed.* New York: Plenum Publishing Corporation, 1983.

Williams, Cortez. *Grantsmanship and Proposal Writing Manual.* Albuquerque, N.M., Development of Research and Human Services, 1981.

Woodford, F. P. "Writing a Research Project Proposal," in F. P. Woodford, ed. *Scientific Writing for Graduate Students.* New York: The Rockefeller University Press, 1968.

METHODOLOGIES OF RESEARCH DESIGN

READ THIS — BEFORE YOU READ THIS CHAPTER

Every second of every day, a torrential flood of events occurs. These events are the grist — the substance — of history. The detritus they leave behind — artifacts, records, the recollections of those who saw and remember, the photographic record — are the stock-in-trade of the historical researcher. To those who research history, every event is meaningful and important — not in isolation, for then it becomes mere chronology — but in association with other events from the factual matrix of which the *meaning* of the event is discovered.

It is not the fact *that* events happen, but the reason *why* events happen (the *meaning* of the happening of the event) that is important to the research historian.

In this chapter we will explore how those who research history proceed to derive meaning from events. We shall see how researchers discern the fraudulent from the genuine, how they arrange data to speak of significant relationships. Finally, for the specific problems arising from historical research, an extensive bibliography will suggest means of solving special problems or discovering sources that may otherwise elude the historical researcher.

7
The Historical Method

HISTORICAL RESEARCH: THE MEANING OF EVENTS

The historical method is the means by which the researcher deals with the latent *meaning* of history. History is a phenomenon. It is a transcript of the relentless surge of events, the sequential and meaningful record of human activity. The historical method aims to assess the meaning and to read the message of the happenings in which men and women and the events of their lives and the life of the world around them relate meaningfully to each other. The object of the historical method, therefore, is to provide a means through which a researcher may deal with problems that arise from events that happened in times past and to interpret what might otherwise be considered merely as the happenstance of blind fortune.

Events do crystallize into meaningful clusters. As there is cause and effect in the physical world, so cause and effect are equally present in the historical world—the interaction between man and his fellow men, and between man and the environment around him.

In order to appraise accurately the meaning and relationship of events, however, the historical researcher should always seek to get as close to the *original events* as possible in the hope of thus better reconstructing them. To do this, the historical researcher generally relies upon documentary sources, although occasionally artifacts are studied, either alone or in conjunction with documentary evidence. In the search for historical truth, therefore, the researcher relies, if at all possible, upon only *primary* data.[1]

Those who made history and influenced human events may indeed be gone forever—they, and their times with them. In attempting to study them, their activities, and the events which they influenced, and which influenced them, we need to reconstruct as nearly as possible the contemporary scene of their day. To try to do this, however, we must discover primary data sources. And these consist of portraits painted of them, a record of the words which they wrote and those that they are reported to have spoken, the testimony of their friends and acquaintances, the personal records that they have left behind, the objects they used, the houses and towns in which they lived, the places where they worked and effected events important in their times and significant in their lives. Such are the sources of *primary historical data.*

The use of primary data tends to ensure the integrity of the study and to strengthen its reliability. It is, therefore, generally considered to be a *sine qua non* of historical scholarship.

External Evidence and Internal Evidence[2]

The data of historical research are subject to two types of evaluation. We may judge whether the document is authentic or we may decide, if indeed it is authentic, what the document, or the statement within the document, means. The approaches to data which are concerned with these two problems are known as reviewing the data in order to determine their *external evidence* or their *internal evidence*, or subjecting them to *external criticism* or *internal criticism*. The terms *evidence* and *criticism* are interchangeable for all practical purposes. Evidence looks at the problem from the viewpoint of the data; criticism regards the same problem from the psychological attitude of the researcher. Briefly, we shall discuss each of these terms for a fuller appreciation of their use in historical research.

---

[1] See the discussion of primary data in chapter 5, page 88–89.
[2] Sometimes referred to as external and internal *validity*.

External evidence or *external criticism* is primarily concerned with the question: "Is it genuine?" External criticism seeks to determine whether the document that has come to the researcher's hands or the artifact that claims attention is genuinely *valid primary data.* Counterfeits are not uncommon. One needs only to recall Thomas Chatterton and the famous "Rowley Manuscripts" to realize how easy a hoax can be perpetrated upon unsuspecting "scholars." The "Rowley Manuscripts" were famous literary forgeries of the eighteenth century. In the twentieth century appeared a spurious biography of the businessman, motion picture producer, and aviator, Howard Hughes, which fooled one of the world's largest publishing houses and its editors and landed the author in jail!

Frauds are not uncommon, nor is their acceptance by the naive scholar and researcher unusual. Remember how thoroughly archaeologists were taken in by the Piltdown Man, and that Thomas J. Wise issued for years "private editions" of Victorian writings which deceived famous collectors until the fraud was exposed in 1934 by John Carter and Graham Pollard. It is extremely important, therefore, to know whether the document is *genuine.*

External evidence or external criticism of the document is of paramount inportance to the credibility of the research. Establishing authenticity of documents is, of course, a study in itself and involves carbon dating; analysis of handwriting, identification of ink, and paper; vocabulary usage and writing style; and other considerations. This aspect of historical methodology is a study in itself, and we cannot discuss it at length in a text as brief as this one.

Quite apart from the question, "Is it genuine?" is the equally important question having to do with *internal evidence* or *internal criticism.* The question here is not one of authenticity but of *meaning.* In considering a manuscript or a statement, the researcher asks such questions as, "What does it mean?" "What was the author attempting to say?" "What thought was he trying to convey; what inferences or interpretations could be extracted from the words?"

Take a well-known utterance. The time is November 19, 1863. Abraham Lincoln is speaking at the dedication of a national cemetery in Gettysburg, Pennsylvania. In that brief but famous dedicatory address, the President said, "But, in a larger sense, we cannot dedicate—we cannot consecrate—we cannot hallow this ground. The brave men, living and dead, who struggled here, have consecrated it, far above our power to add or detract."

What did Mr. Lincoln *mean* by "the brave men, living and dead?" Did he mean only the brave men of the Union forces? (We must remember that he was dedicating a Union cemetery.) Did he mean the brave Confederate men, as well? Or did he mean brave men, indiscriminately, with no thought of North or South but merely of courage and valor? To a researcher, studying in depth the life of Abraham Lincoln, it is essential to know precisely what the president did mean by those words.

The matter of internal evidence is not so far from us as we might at first surmise. What does the decision of a court mean? What do the words of the decision convey as to the intent and will of the court? The question comes up all the time in legal interpretation. In such instances, the primary question is *what do the words mean?* This is the sole concern of internal evidence.

The Role of Chronology in Historical Research

The student of historical research needs to distinguish very carefully between two concepts that are frequently confused under the general rubric of "the study of history." One of these concepts is *genuine historical research—historiography,* as it is sometimes called. It is with historiography that the historical researcher should be primarily concerned. The other concept is *chronology*; the setting down of occurrences and events in the order of their happening. The *Anglo-Saxon Chronicle* is an example of chronology; Toynbee's

A Study of History is historiography—historical research. Chronology is usually merely a listing of dates and events. It is not research because it does not *interpret the meaning* of those events. It does not point out any significance to the event, as a unit within the larger constellation of events.

The following is chronology:

1492:	Columbus discovered America.
1607:	First permanent English settlement in America at Jamestown, Virginia.
1620:	Pilgrims landed at Plymouth, Mass.
1624:	The Dutch settled New Amsterdam.
1630:	The Puritans established Massachusetts Bay Colony.
1634:	Lord Calvert settled in Maryland.
1682:	William Penn founded the colony of Pennsylvania.
1733:	Georgia founded by James Oglethorpe
1754-1763:	The French and Indian Wars.
1775-1783:	The War of American Independence.
1789:	George Washington was inaugurated the first President of the United States of America.
1792:	The first political parties appeared in America; the Industrial Revolution began in America with the introduction of Eli Whitney's cotton gin.

In this form, the list is merely a succession of twelve dates marking a series of events in the first three centuries of the history of the original thirteen colonies.

Moreover, format does not change genre. The mere recasting of a chronological list into paragraph form with the amenities of prose composition and appropriate documentary footnotes does not change the nature of the process nor transform pedestrian chronicle into historical research. The paragraph still merely reports happenings and recounts the sequence of events—nothing more.

This is not to imply that chronology does not fill a very important place in historical study. It does. It is the grist of the research mill. It provides the first step in the process of data interpretation, and interpretation is—as we have previously stated—the indispensable element of all research. How essential chronology is in historical research may be recognized if you attempt to visualize the disadvantage that would result from attempting to reconstruct without the *Anglo-Saxon Chronicle* the history of early England.

In consequence of what we have just noted, let us now look analytically at the chronology given above. What, in fact, *do* these events say? What do they *mean?* Are they merely isolated happenings or do they have a relationship to each other and to the whole tercentenary time span? These are questions that the historical researcher is always asking of the data. Such questioning represents a basic attitude in historical research. If we are to do historical research, we must seek not only to identify the chain of events of substantive history but also to understand the *meaning* of these events, both as to their relationship to each other and to the problem under study.

History is dimensional. It has the *dimension of historical time.* It has also the *dimension of historical space.* Both of these dimensions are extremely important in interpreting historical data. We will discuss, first, the concept of historical time; then, we shall explore the idea of historical space. Because history is inseparable from the time in which its events occurred, we should examine the preceding chronology in terms of its time orientation and relationships.

Many beginning researchers fail to become familiar with the time dimension; hence, they do not appreciate the significance that the temporal relationship gives to the data.

Earlier,[3] we demonstrated that the more angles from which data were regarded, the more meaningful those data became with each angular viewpoint. Historical data are no exception.

In the chronology that we gave you above, the time span was 300 years: 1492 to 1792. Therefore, let's do a very simple thing: Draw a line 150 millimeters long. For a 300-year span, a line of such length makes each millimeter equal 2 years. So divided the period 1492 to 1792 will look like this:

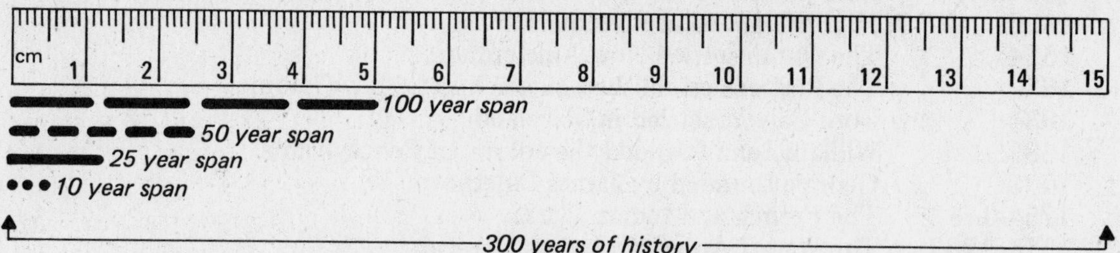

Now, within the preceding time frame, let us insert at the proper points the events listed in the chronological sequence on page 121. The linear chronology now looks like this:

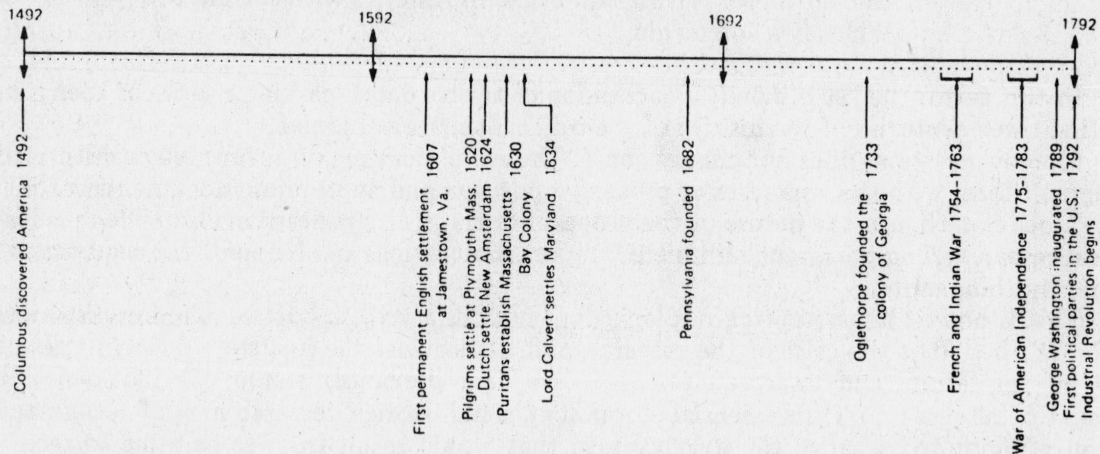

How different the chronology now appears. It is no longer merely a list of items. It has become, rather, a series of events placed along a time continuum at the precise points of their relative occurrence. The *dynamics of history* are now becoming apparent. Note also the *rhythms* along the time line. An event happens: the discovery of America. Then, an apparently sterile 115 years (1492-1607) elapse between that event and the first permanent English settlement at Jamestown, Virginia. But such, of course, was not the case. The *total* stage of history was, of course, crowded with events during that 115-year hiatus. Even, in what is now the United States of America, the Spanish were busy: the Spanish conquistadores and the missionaries in the Southwest and Florida. The French were in the Mississippi valley. But, if we look at the activity in the thirteen original colonies, during that span of years, only silence of the historical record responds.

Then, beginning with 1607, for slightly more than a quarter of a century, events happen in rapid succession: the English in Virginia, in Massachusetts, the Dutch in New

[3] See Chapter 2, pages 27-30.

Amsterdam, and the Calvertists in Maryland. Other events, unmentioned, of course, were taking place: Roger Williams and the Antinomians in Rhode Island; the Swedes in Delaware; John Mason and David Thomson in New Hampshire—this quarter century of American Colonial history teemed with activity! But *for our purposes within the particular chronology we have cited*, we have not cited these other events.

The time line proceeds. Another century, unbroken except for one event—the founding of Pennsylvania. Then the final half of the third century—again a time of renewed activity, of turbulent events: the birth of a nation and the beginning of an industrial revolution.

We need only a little imagination to realize that the device which we have been discussing briefly—and merely for the purpose of presenting a historiographical method—is capable of great potential. It is also capable of numerous variations. The historical researcher who is studying more than one set of chronological data within the same time frame may gain increased insight by arranging multiple time-line scales in slide-rule fashion. We might superimpose above the events which we have plotted on one time line another series of events—for example, the principal events in the history of England which determined the discoveries and settlements in the New World. Similarly, we could plot on a third scale the meaningful events from European history over the same tercentenary period. We would then read the chart as we read a slide rule: one scale against the other.

Sometimes, a realistic way to regard the time-distance dimension in historical perspective is to see it in reverse. As historical data stand in perspective at a distance of centuries or millennia from the researcher, they have a tendency to telescope and to become unrealistically crowded upon each other. Historical time has a subtle way of becoming deceptive unless we are very alert to its realities. A pencil and some simple substraction will reveal a great deal which may otherwise escape our awareness. If we lay a particular historical period *backward* from the *present*, it brings dramatically into focus the slowness or the rapidity with which events moved in times past. Into the block of time that elapsed between the discovery of America and the establishment of the first permanent English settlement at Jamestown, you could pack all of American history from the assassination of Abraham Lincoln to the present moment! To reel time backward frequently puts historical events in vivid and dramatic perspective.

The Concept of Historical Space (Historical Geography)

We have been discussing history as a *time phenomenon*, and we have demonstrated the role of time in seeking the interpretation of historical fact. But events also happen in a particular *place*. They have a *space dimension*.

In trying to understand the significance of historical fact, the *where*, or spatial/dimension is frequently as important as the *when*. Let us now consider the same events that we have plotted above in relations to the *geographical location* where the action took place. Here is the manner in which the events are related to historical geography. Study the map on page 124 carefully. Note how English colonization began at the extremes (Virginia and Massachusetts) with the Dutch settling at New Amsterdam approximately 275 miles north of Jamestown and 225 miles south of the Massachusetts Bay Colony. Calvert founded Maryland. Half a century later, Penn settled Pennsylvania. In the interim, the Swedes had come to Delaware and New Jersey was being negotiated between Dutch and English with the whole situation complicated by conflicting deeds and permissions granted by authorities ignorant of each other's acts. The colonization that began at the fringes was now closing in toward the center. Only a map can reveal this phenomenon. Below, the events on the time-line on page 122 have been transferred to a map and are expressed in terms of historical space facts.

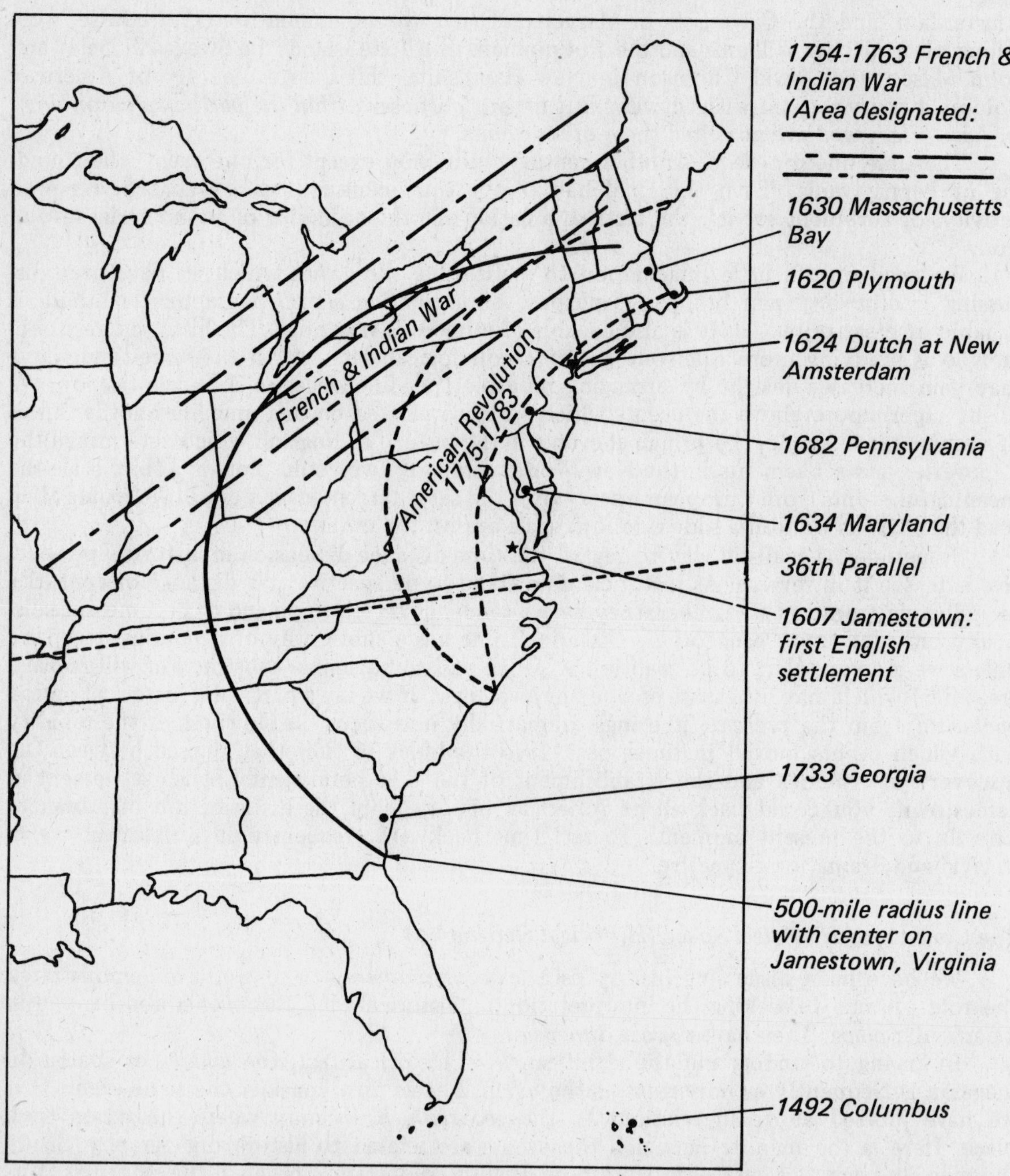

Now, see what we have done with one set of facts. We have arranged the same historical data in three separate presentations: first, as a simple chronological listing; next, along a time-line continuum; and, finally, we shall present them in geographical relationship. Each arrangement provided a different insight into the meaning of the data. In each instance, we more fully answered the basic question every researcher asks of any data: "What do these facts *mean*?" The following geographical placement of the information reveals a number of *new* insights aside from those apparent through the chronological and time-line presentation. These may be tabulated as follows:

1. Colonization, as represented by the time-line chronology, was not equally spread along the Atlantic coast. It clustered north of the 36th parallel of latitude.
2. The first English colony at Jamestown, Virginia, (represented on the map by a star) was pivotally located. It was just about equidistant from the northernmost as well as the southernmost point of colonization activity.
3. An arc, inscribed on the map, using Jamestown as the pivotal point, will include an area in which almost all of the events of the first three hundred years of history of colonial America took place. Compare the radius of the arc to the scale of miles and you will see that it inscribes an area of just about 500 miles equidistant from Jamestown.
4. By referring to the limits of such an arc, we see that the French and Indian War took place in the hatched area lying across the outer and northern limits of such an arc. If we have imagination, we must also realize that such a war must probably have seemed as remote to the colonists of Jamestown, Philadelphia, New York, and Boston as Vietnam and the Middle East seem to the air-age mind of today.
5. The War for American Independence, on the other hand, was a very intimate struggle. It swept through the colonies in a wave of events which traveled in a north-to-south- direction. The only variation to this pattern was the Vincennes exploit of George Rogers Clark (1779). The broad arrows on the map indicate the general direction of events from 1775 to 1781.
6. The landing of Columbus on the Island of San Salvador is perhaps the only event lying outside the area of principal activity as bounded by the 500-mile radial line. Not only is it some 950 miles south of Jamestown but it is also removed from the settlement at Jamestown by 115 years of history. Probably this one event does indeed lie outside the corpus of historical fact which we are studying and is convenient only as a point of chronological reference.

THE SYSTEMATIZING OF HISTORICAL DATA

We have perhaps said quite enough about the several ways in which historical data may be studied. Because, however, most of the data of the historical researcher will be gathered from documents and will finally be studied in terms of hundreds or even thousands of note cards, it is imperative for the researcher to have some means of gathering and controlling the data so that one reaps the greatest return from the innumerable hours spent in archives, document rooms, and libraries. In historical investigations, perhaps more than in any other type of research, the investigator can soon find himself in a morass of notes, note cards, bibliography cards, and memoranda. It is easy to read and to take notes, but it is difficult for many students to organize those notes into useful and meaningful facts for interpretation. Historical data-collecting demands a systematic plan, not only for the collection of the data, but also for data retrieval and analysis. Before beginning historical research, therefore, you should have a specific plan for the acquisition, organization, storage, and retrieval of the data. Some of the following suggestions may assist you in developing that systematic approach.

Note Cards and Bibliography Cards

The planning for the organization of one's note cards and bibliography cards should be done with a thorough understanding of the importance of such foresight. Despite the widespread use of filing cards for note and bibliographical purposes, they have their disadvantages. Quantities of them take up an inordinate amount of file space, and because of the thickness of the filing-card stock, only one copy can be made of any note or bibliographical item. The suggestion was made earlier that you consider using 20-pound paper for notes and bibliographical information.[4] Cut the sheets to 3 × 5-inch size for bibliographical notes. Cut other sheets to 4 × 6, or 5 × 7-inch sheets for substantive notes. For your own convenience, you may well wish to have certain items duplicated on these sheets. Such prepared sheets will save you time and ensure that you do not overlook important information which may be essential at a later date. By mimeographing or duplicating forms and sizes on regular 8½ × 11-inch or 8½ × 14-inch sheets, these can then, before use, be cut to smaller size with an ordinary hand paper cutter. From a regular typewriter size sheet, four 3 × 5-inch bibliography cards or two 4 × 6-inch and two 3 × 5-inch cards can be cut. On page 71 a suggested form for a bibliography card was given. A 4 × 6-inch note card for notes of a substantive nature might look something like this:

Main Heading Classification	Subheading	Card No.____ One of ____ cards

Check here if note is continued on reverse side ☐

Source Information: Author's last name __________ Date of book _____ pp. _____
First significant word of title __________ Bibliog. card No. __________

The importance of the box in the upper right-hand corner of the card is apparent when making an extended note. For example, one knows precisely where the particular card belongs if it reads: "Card 2. One of 3 cards." At the bottom of the note card is a brief but exact short form for bibliographical reference. To find the complete bibliographic reference, all one has to do is to refer to the bibliographical file, which should be alphabetically arranged by the author's last names.[5]

---

[4] See pp. 70–71.
[5] See Chapter 4, page 71.

Multiple Files and Color Coding

All notes should be written in *multiple* copy—probably in triplicate or quadruplicate, depending upon your ultimate analysis of the data. Behind the suggestion of substituting 20-pound paper for filing cards was the thought of making multiple copies. Earlier we discussed the multi-dimensional nature of historical data. A fact may lie simultaneously in the province of time, of space, of personality, and perhaps of subject matter. Take, for example, a note which a researcher might make in studying Edgar Allan Poe's poem "Annabelle Lee." Poe wrote that poem in 1849 while living in a small cottage in the Fordham section of the Bronx (now part of New York City). A student studying this poem may wish to see it from various angles. A note on the poem may have various facets. A student may be interested in studying all of Poe's poems which were written in 1849. He may wish to study Poe's life in Fordham. He may wish to study the poems Poe wrote about his child wife, Virginia Clemm. He may wish to have a quick reference to all the information collected on the poem, "Annabelle Lee." Thus, one item of information conceivably might be studied from *four* separate angles.

By taking four note cards (sheets of paper) and interleaving them with three pieces of carbon paper, cut to size, four copies can be made of the same note instead of one. Other notes can be made similarly. When the sheets are separated after writing the note, the headings can then be added. The headings of the four identical notes might look something like these:

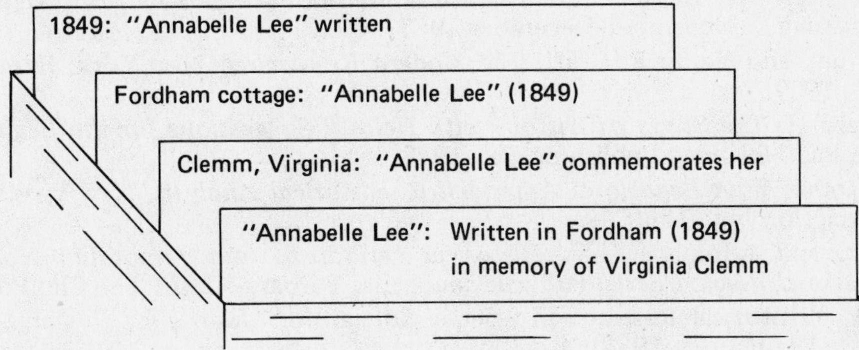

1849: "Annabelle Lee" written
Fordham cottage: "Annabelle Lee" (1849)
Clemm, Virginia: "Annabelle Lee" commemorates her
"Annabelle Lee": Written in Fordham (1849)
in memory of Virginia Clemm

If the researcher continues to produce cards in quadruplicate, then these notes will result in four separate, but parallel files of the same data. Through this method all *chronological data* can be gathered together into a progressive file, day-by-day, month-by-month, year-by-year. *The geographical place data* (in this case, Fordham) can be assembled as one corpus of information. By arranging the geographical data alphabetically according to place locations, quick reference may be had to Poe's activities in every location where he lived: Baltimore, Fordham, Richmond, and so forth. Another file will hold all the information about separate poems. A final file may be devoted to persons important to the life of the subject being studied. These may also be filed alphabetically for rapid reference.

For each of these areas of study, the researcher may wish to use, for ready identification, *color coding. Color coding* is effected by selecting a different color of note card for each category of information: white, yellow, pink, light greeen, and so on. If the dates, for example, are all on white cards and a blue card is used for cross-referencing interrelationships of the information, not only does the card stand out—and blue would be employed then with all the other colors for "See also" cards—among the other cards of the category, but it affords an efficient and rapid means of relating the data of one category to that of another category. When seen thus in a three-, four-, or five-dimensional matrix, interpretation of historical data is greatly facilitated. By such a system, one can readily see meanings and interpretations which, in a one-card system, might have been missed.

Perhaps we have said enough about the historical method for the purposes of the beginning researcher. We now turn to another of the research methodologies, as another avenue to the discovery of truth.

Practical Application —

Look in the practicum section (Appendix B), pages 293–295. There you will find an application of some of the aspects of the historical method as discussed in this chapter.

— —

FOR FURTHER READING

Further Reading in Historical Research Methodology

Austin, Anne L. "The Historical Method in Nursing." *Nursing Research* 7 (February 1958): 4–10.

Aydelotte, William O. "Quantification in History." *American Historical Review* 71 (1966): 803–25.

Barnard, K. "Research Designs: the Historical Method." *American Journal of Maternal Child Nursing* 6 (November-December 1981): 391.

Barzun, Jacques, and Henry F. Graff. *The Modern Researcher.* New York: Harcourt, Brace and Co., 1957.

Bauer, Richard H. *The Study of History with Helpful Suggestions for the Beginner.* Philadelphia, Pa.: McKinley Publishing Co., 1948.

Berkhofer, Robert F. *A Behavioral Approach to Historical Analysis.* New York: Macmillan Publishing Co., Inc., 1969.

Boehm, Eric, and Adolphus Lalit. *Historical Periodicals: An Annotated World List of Historical and Related Serial Publications.* Santa Barbara, Calif.: The Clio Press, 1961.

Bybee, R. W. "Historical Research in Science Education." *Journal of Research in Science Teaching.* 19 (January 1982): 1-13.

Caron, Pierre, and Marc Jaryc. *World List of Historical Periodicals.* New York: The H. W. Wilson Company, 1939.

Christy, Teresa E. "The Methodology of Historical Research: A Brief Introduction." *Nursing Research* 24 (May-June, 1975): 189-92.

Clubb, Jerome M., and Howard Allen. "Computers and Historical Studies." *Journal of American History* 54 (1967): 599-607.

Dollar, Charles M., and Robert J. Jensen. *Historian's Guide to Statistics: Quantitative Analysis and Historical Research.* New York: Holt, Rinehart and Winston, 1971.

Felt, Thomas E. *Researching, Writing, and Publishing Local History.* Nashville, Tenn: American Association for State and Local History, 1981.

Floud, Roderick. *An Introduction to Quantitative Methods for Historians.* Princeton, N. J.: Princeton University Press, 1973.

Fox, William L. *List of Doctoral Dissertations in History in Progress or Completed at Colleges and Universities in the United States since 1958.* Washington, D. C.: The American University, 1961.

Freundlich, Y. "Methodology of Science as Tools for Historical Research." *Studies in the History and Philosophy of Science* 11 (December 1980): 257-266.

Gawronski, Donald V. *History: Meaning and Method.* 3rd ed. Glenview, Ill.: Scott, Foresman and Company, 1975.

Gottschalk, Louis R. *Understanding History.* New York: Alfred A. Knopf, Inc., 1950.

Gray, Wood et al. *Historian's Handbook: A Key to the Study and Writing of History.* 2nd edition. Boston, Mass: Houghton Mifflin Company, 1964.

Greenwood, Val D. *The Researcher's Guide to American Genealogy.* Baltimore, Maryland: Genealogical Publishing Co., 1973.

Hale, Richard W. *Methods of Research for the Amateur Historian.* Technical Leaflet No. 21. Nashville, Tennessee: American Association for State and Local History, 1969.

Hockett, Homer C. *The Critical Method in Historical Research and Writing.* New York: Macmillan Publishing Co., Inc., 1955.

Hoover, Dwight W., ed. *Understanding Negro History.* New York: Quadrangle Books, 1968.

Humphries, R. Steven. "The Historian: His Documents and the Elementary Modes of Historical Thought." *History and Theory* 19 (February 1980): 1-20.

Heller, G. N. and B. D. Wilson. "Historical Research in Music Education." *Bulletin of the Council on Research in Music Education,* No. 69, (Winter 1982): 1-20

Kaplan, Abraham. *The Conduct of Inquiry: Methodology for Behavioral Science.* Scranton, Pa.: Chandler Publishing Co., 1964.

Kent, Sherman. *Writing History.* New York: F. S. Crofts and Co., 1941.

Lichtman, Allan J. and Valerie French. *Historians and the Living Past: The Theory and Practice of Historical Study.* Arlington Heights, Ill.: AHM Publishing Corp., 1978.

Marston, Doris R. *A Guide to Writing History.* Cincinnati, Ohio: The Writer's Digest, 1976.

Maynes, M. J. "Theory and Method in Recent German Historical Studies," *Journal of Interdisciplinary History,* 10 (Autumn, 1979), 311-317.

McCoy, F. N. *Researching and Writing in History.* Berkeley, Calif.: University of California Press, 1974.

McMurtrie, Donald "Locating the Printed Source Materials for United States History, with a Bibliography of Lists of Regional Imprints," *Mississippi Valley Historical Review,* 31 (1944): 369-378.

Milligan, J. D. "Treatment of an Historical Source," *History and Theory,* 18 (No. 2, 1979), 177-196.

Mommsen, W. J. "Social Conditioning and Social Relevance of Historical Judgments," *History and Theory,* 17 (No. 4, 1978): 19-35.

Morison, Samuel Eliot. "Faith of a Historian," *The American Historical Review,* 56 (January, 1951): 261-275.

Murphy, George G. S. "Historical Investigation and Automatic Data Processing Equipment," *Computers and the Humanities,* 3 (1968) 1-13.

Platt, Jennifer. "Evidence and Proof in Documentary Research, I and II (I. Some Specific Problems of Documentary Research; II. Some Shared Problems of Documentary Research), *The Sociological Review,* 29 (February, 1981): 31-52, 53-66.

Poulton, Helen J. *The Historian's Handbook: A Descriptive Guide to Reference Works.* Norman, Oklahoma: University of Oklahoma Press, 1972.

Rowney D. K. and J. Q. Graham, Jr. *Quantitative History: Selected Readings in the Quantitative Analysis of Historical Data.* Homewood, Illinois: Dorsey Press, 1969.

Rubicam, Milton, ed. *Genealogical Research Methods and Sources.* Belcherville, Mass.: American Society of Genealogists, 1966.

Sabin, Joseph, and continued by Wilberforce Eames and R. W. G. Vail. *Dictionary of Books Relating to America from the Discovery to the Present Time.* 29 volumes. New York: J. Sabin, 1868-1936.

Shafer, R. I. *A Guide to Historical Method.* Revised edition. Homewood, Ill.: The Dorsey Press, 1974.

Shorter, Edward. *The Historian and the Computer: A Practical Guide.* Englewood Cliffs, N. J.: Prentice-Hall, Inc., 1971.

Siegel, S. *Nonparametric Statistics for the Behavioral Sciences.* New York: McGraw-Hill Book Company, 1956.

Stevenson, Noel C. *Search and Research: Addresses of Libraries Having Genealogical Collections.* Salt Lake City, Utah: Deseret Book Company, 1959.

Swierenga, Robert P. "Computer and American History: The Impact of the 'New Generation'." *The Journal of American History* 60 (March 1974): 1045-70.

Thernstrom, Stephan. "Quantitative Methods in History: Some Notes." in Lipset, S. M. and Richard Hofstadter, eds. *Sociology and History: Methods.* New York: Basic Books, 1968.

Vincent, John Martin. *Historical Research: An Outline of Theory and Practice.* New York: P. Smith, 1929.

Weitzman, David. *Underfoot: An Everyday Guide to Exploring the American Past.* New York: Charles Scribner's Sons, 1976.

Westmoreland, Guy T. *An Annotated Guide to Basic Reference Books on the Black American Experience.* Washington, D. C.: Scholarly Resources, Inc., 1974.

Wheeler, Helen. *Womanhood Media: Current Resources about Women.* Metuchen, N. J.: The Scarecrow Press, 1972.

Yeomans, K. A. *Statistics for the Social Scientist.* Volume 1: *Introductory Statistics;* Volume 2: *Applied Statistics.* Baltimore, Md.: Penguin Books, 1968.

FOR YOUR NOTES AND COMMENTS

READ THIS – BEFORE YOU READ THIS CHAPTER

Descriptive survey research is merely observation with *insight*.

And observation is much more than visual beholding. We observe in so many ways and through varied channels: we see the happenings in the world around us, we probe through questionnaires, interviews, and inventories. We observe what others do, what they think, what they believe, prefer, or aspire to. And, having assembled all these data, we examine them carefully to discern their real meaning, thereby seeking an insight into them that lies below the act of mere observation.

And we must survey selectively. Obviously, we cannot observe *all* members of a group: *all* the members of a given profession, *all* those comprising a certain social group, *all* those with decided political, ideological or moral convictions. We must, therefore, select a sample of such specific populations. But how do we select the sample? There are many ways, and the chapter will discuss some of them.

The descriptive survey method has its weaknesses. One of the most subtle and ineradicable shortcomings is the presence of bias. It is indigenous and surreptitious, and every researcher must recognize its inevitability. The descriptive survey is a research method that relies upon observation for the acquisition of the data but which demands extreme vigilance in both gathering and interpreting those data.

8

The Descriptive Survey Method

The researcher soon learns that the *nature of the data* dictates the research methodology that must be employed in the processing of those data. For this reason we have the several so-called *research methods.*

The *descriptive survey method*, or what is sometimes called *the normative survey method*, is employed to process the data that come to the researcher through *observation.* These are discrete data, as different from historical type data—which come to the researcher through written records—as the subject matter of chemistry is from that of literature.

SURVEY RESEARCH: OBSERVATION WITH INSIGHT

All truth is not apprehended by means of studying past records. We learn some truth by studying, through observation, the events that are taking place in the world around us. The nature of historical data is static. Records remain records. But the data of events is fleeting. What happens in a public square today may never be exactly repeated in days to come. But there is, within limits, conformity and uniformity in life processes, and we are able to judge from what has happened at any fleeting moment what may happen again. The researcher, by drawing conclusions from one transitory collection of data, may extrapolate what is likely to happen again *under similar circumstances.* At best, this is a conjecture and sometimes a hazardous one at that, but it is our only way to generalize from what we *see.*

The method of research that simply looks with intense accuracy at the phenomena of the moment and then describes precisely what the researcher sees is called the *descriptive survey.* This type of research is also called the *normative survey.* The name implies the assumption that whatever we observe at any one time is *normal* and under the same conditions, could conceivably be observed again in the future. The basic assumption underlying such an approach is that given phenomena usually follow a common pattern, or *norm.*

The Meaning of the Term "Survey"

The word *survey* is composed of two word elements which indicate precisely what happens in the survey process. *Survey* has the basic connotation of "the act of looking over or beyond." It has nothing to do with casual or purposeless observation.

Sur- is a derivative of the Latin *super*, meaning "above," "over," or "beyond." The element *-vey* comes from the Latin verb *videre* "to look" or "to see." Thus, the word *survey* means "to look or to see over or beyond" the casual glance or the superficial observation.

The word *descriptive*, frequently coupled with the word *survey* in describing this method, also gives insight into the nature of the method. The word *descriptive* comes from *de-* meaning "from," and *scribere*, "to write." The term, therefore, describes the essential character of the method. In employing this method, the researcher does two things: first, he observes with close scrutiny the population which is bounded by the research parameters; second, he makes a careful record of what he observes so that when the aggregate record is made, the researcher can then return to the record to study the observations that have been "described" there. In this sense, survey research has a common denominator with historical research: namely, the study of records.

The point should be clearly emphasized that "looking" or "seeing" is not restricted to perception through the physical eye. In research, we have many ways of seeing which have nothing to do with physical vision. The physician "looks" at the patient's heart through a stethoscope and by means of an electrocardiogram. The educator, the psychologist, the guidance and vocational counselor "look" at achievement, intelligence, attitudes, beliefs, or personality structure through tests, inventories, attitude scales, and other tests and evaluation scales. Hundreds of thousands of survey studies have been conducted in which the "looking" has been by means of a questionnaire; and, in interview studies, the "looking" has largely been by the *ear* rather than by the *eye*!

But in each instance, *observation* has been accompanied by the making of a *record*. And the record is always a part of the observation. Look up the word *observe*. Study its etymology. You will discover that it is indissolubly linked with "a record," "a description" of some kind.[1] This preservation of fact—the record—is sometimes narrative, as in the instance of the *case study*. Glance at any medical journal. What you will find are *descriptive survey studies* of patients whose symptomatology is discussed at length in the professional article that follows, together with a discussion of treatment and conclusions and recommendations. These latter are the *interpretation of the data*. A case study lies midway between the descriptive survey method and the experimental method.

Other recording of facts resulting from observations occur in the form of tables, charts, graphs, and other summary and trend-indicating techniques.

What, then, are the practical considerations in conducting a descriptive survey study? Reduced to its basic elements, the method is essentially simple in design. It is a common approach, used with more or less sophistication in many areas of human activity. From the neighbor who canvasses the adjoining property owners to solicit opinions or obtain the signing of a petition on the granting of a variance which permits a violation of the building code, to the Gallup Poll which aims to determine the attitude of the people of the nation toward the popularity of a presidential action or their position with respect to a national issue, surveys are commonplace features of contemporary American life.

This is not to suggest, however, that because of its frequent use, the survey is any less demanding in its design requirements or any easier for the researcher to conduct than any other method of research. Quite to the contrary, the survey design makes certain specific and critical demands upon the researcher which, if not carefully respected, may place the entire research effort in jeopardy.

Characteristics of the Descriptive Survey

We shall begin by outlining the basic structure of the descriptive survey as a method of research, indicating its salient characteristics.

1. The descriptive survey method deals with a situation that demands the *technique of observation* as the *principal* means of collecting the data.
2. The population for the study must be carefully chosen, clearly defined, and specifically delimited in order to set precise parameters for ensuring discreteness to the population.
3. Data in descriptive survey research are particularly susceptible to distortion through the introduction of bias into the research design. Particular attention should be given to safeguard the data from the influence of bias.
4. Although the descriptive survey method relies upon observation for the acquisition of the data, those data must then be organized and presented systematically so that valid and accurate conclusions may be drawn from them.

---

[1] *Ob-*, toward, before, completely + *sevare*, to save, preserve, keep [in written form]. Hence, *observe* suggests a preserving or keeping completely [in the form of a written record].

Each of the preceding four steps will be discussed at greater length in the pages that follow. Each is important because each deals with a critical area in survey research.

With survey studies, observation in one way or another is absolutely essential. We have already discussed briefly the meaning of observation in its wider connotation. It may be considered to be almost synonymous with *perception* in the broad sense of that term, namely *being aware of data through some means of detecting them.* Many times the researcher may never see, in the conventional sense of perceiving with the eyes, the source of the data.

In a very real sense, while the researchers in the physical and biological sciences like to think of their research as purely "experimental," many aspects of research in these disciplines draw on descriptive survey techniques. It is well, therefore, for the physicist, the biologist, the psychologist, and others who consider their research to be purely empirical and experimental, to recognize that they can employ other methodological approaches and, among these, the descriptive survey.

The Questionnaire

Data sometimes lie buried deep within the minds or within the attitudes, feelings, or reactions of men and women. As with oil beneath the sea, the first problem is to devise a tool to probe below the surface. A commonplace instrument for observing data beyond the physical reach of the observer is the *questionnaire*. The questionnaire may be sent to human beings who are thousands of miles away and whom the researcher may never see. In this sense, the social scientist who collects data through the means of a questionnaire and the physicist who determines the presence of radioactivity through the probe of a Geiger counter are in just about the same degree of remoteness from their respective sources of data. Neither sees the source from which the data originate. The questionnaire, like the Geiger counter, is a totally impersonal probe. It is because of this impersonality associated with the questionnaire method of gathering data that we need to be governed by several practical guidelines when employing a questionnaire as a tool in survey research.

★ *The language must be unmistakably clear in soliciting precisely what the researcher wishes to learn.* Communication is a deceptive skill. What may be crystal-clear to you may be so much meaningless jargon to another person. For example, take a very simple question: "How many cigarettes do you smoke each day?" That seems, of course, a very clear and unambiguous question. Especially does it seem so if we accompany the question with certain choices and all the respondent has to do is to check one of them:

How many cigarettes do you smoke each day?
(Check the appropriate box.)

□ *more than 25* □ *25–16* □ *15–11* □ *10–6* □ *5–1* □ *none*

The trouble with the question is, of course, the assumption underlying it. The assumption is that people smoke an identical number of cigarettes each day. But what happens in an actual situation to an assumption of that kind?

A nervous erratic smoker gets that questionnaire. He does not fit the assumption. At the office, when the pressure is on and he is working full speed to keep on top of things, he is a chain smoker. When he gets home, on holidays and weekends, and on his days off, he may smoke one or two cigarettes a day, or go without smoking at all. How is he supposed to answer the question? What box does he check?

What we have just said, points to the vulnerability of the questionnaire as a data-gathering instrument. Life is a complex situation. There are many degrees and gradations of circumstance. For very few of us and at very infrequent moments do the affairs of life fit into neat choices between yes and no or into primly graduated scales. The researcher who constructs a questionnaire with neatly trimmed choices all too often assumes that experience can be precisely categorized, that life has no contingent circumstances, and that men and women are automatons, doing the same thing over and over, day by day.

The first guideline, therefore, for questionnaire construction is: *Inspect the assumptions underlying the question. Do the assumptions fit with the realities of life?*

All questionnaires should be pretested on a small population in what is often referred to as a *pilot study*. Every researcher should give the questionnaire to at least half a dozen friends, or neighbors, to test whether there are any items that they may have difficulty in understanding or in comprehending exactly what the writer of the questionnaire is seeking to determine.

Perhaps we have hinted at one of the principal causes for ambiguity in the questionnaire and the inability of recipients to understand the questions that are asked. One of the major causes for such a situation is that the researcher has not spent enough time and care in *defining the purpose* for each item in the questionnaire, nor have the questions been *edited* so that each question is phrased with that meticulous precision of language necessary to elicit the answer that the researcher is seeking.

★ *Questionnaires should be designed to fulfill a specific research objective.* Many questionnaires are so inexpertly written that they bear the hallmarks of a quick effortless attempt "to gather some data" which "may be helpful" in solving the research problem. Aimless haphazard thinking and careless imprecise expression are the most commonplace faults in questionnaire construction. This lack of design and precision of expression may also account for the small return of questionnaires when these are sent to a given population.

Item by item, a questionnaire should be built and quality-tested again and again for precision of expression, objectivity, relevance, suitability to the problem situation, and probability of favorable reception and return. Have you concentrated upon the recipient of the questionnaire, putting yourself in the place of one who is asked to invest time on your behalf? If *you* received such a questionnaire from a stranger, what would your honest reaction be? These questions are very important and should be answered impartially.

We have hinted at a very important matter. The writer of a questionnaire should never forget that he is asking of his addressee a gift of time and of effort and the favor of a reply. This brings up several important considerations in questionnaire construction.

•••1. *Be courteous.* A request beginning, "Would you please check . . ." will oil the wheels of cooperation and enhance your chances of having your questionnaire receive more kindly attention than one which continually pushes the questions before the respondent with only the commanding imperative that exudes an "it-is-your-duty-to-answer-these-questions-for-me" attitude.

•••2. *Simplify.* Make the instrument as simple to read and to respond to as possible. The questionnaire should demand as little effort and time on the part of the respondent as possible. A check-item questionnaire is generally preferable to the "completion" type or one which asks the respondent to reply with an extended discussion.

•••3. *Think of the other fellow.* Put yourself in the place of the respondent. What would be your reaction if someone you never saw sent you a questionnaire such as you presume to impose upon another? What is the initial impression your questionnaire makes as a stranger draws it from the envelope? Is it inordinately long and time-consuming? Is it cleanly and neatly typed? Does it have adequate margins, giving the impression of relaxation and uncluttered ease? Are the areas for response adequate and clearly indicated? Is the tone courteous and are the demands reasonable? Have your provided *return postage and an addressed envelope* for the return of the questionnaire?

•••4. *Concentrate on the universal.* Try to address your questions to universals rather than to specifics, to general problems and ideas rather than to purely personal matters, local conditions and concerns; unless, of course, you are specifically making a study of local conditions and issues, which fact you have presumably already announced to your addressee.

•••5. *Make it brief.* The questionnaire should be as brief as possible and should solicit only those data essential to the research project. This need not curtail the adequacy of the instrument, but the researcher should test every item by the following two criteria: (a) What do I intend to do with the information I am soliciting? and (b) Is it absolutely essential to have this information to solve any part of the research endeavor?

•••6. *Check for consistency.* In questionnaires dealing with debatable or opinion-sensitive issues or in situations where you may suspect that the respondent may give answers that are deemed prudent in certain cases, rather than what represents the candid truth, you may wish to incorporate a countercheck question into your list of questions at some distance from the first question. This helps to verify the consistency with which the questionnaire was answered. For example, take the following two questions appearing in a questionnaire as item numbers 2 and 30. This placement causes them to be widely enough separated to test their consistency. Note how they have been answered:

2. *Check one of the following choices:*
   ☒ *In my thinking I am a liberal.*
   ☐ *In my thinking I am a conservative.*

30. *Check one of the following choices:*
   ☐ *I find new ideas stimulating and attractive,*
   and I would find it challenging
   to be among the first to try them.
   ☒ *I subscribe to the position of Pope:*
   "Be not the first by whom the new is tried
   Nor yet the last to lay the old aside."

The two responses do not agree with each other. In the first, the respondent indicated that he was a liberal in his thinking, but later, when given the liberal and the conservative positions in another form, he indicated that his position would be more conservative than liberal.

•••7. *Send return postage.* Accompany your questionnaire with a self-addressed stamped envelope for the convenience of your respondent in returning the questionnaire. To impose upon another's time and spirit of cooperation, and then to expect the other person to pay the postage for you to get the data with which to carry out your study is being unreasonable.

•••8. *Offer the results of your study to your respondent.* In return for the investment of time and the courtesy of replying to your questions, offer to send your respondent a summary of the results of your study at its completion, if your respondent wishes it. You might provide a check space, either at the beginning or at the end of your instrument, where your respondent might indicate the desire to have such summary, together with space for name and address. Do not fail to ask for zip code in connection with the address. In questionnaires where anonymity is desirable, a separate post card may be included to indicate the desire for a summary. It also should request name, address, and zip code, and be accompanied with the request that it be mailed separately from the questionnaire.

•••9. *Think ahead.* The researcher should have clearly in mind, even before constructing the questionnaire, precisely how the data will be processed after the results are received. Data-processing procedures will determine the form the questionnaire should take.

If, for example, the data are to be card-punched and computerized, the questionnaire needs to be structured quite differently than if the data are to be handled in more conventional ways.

★ *Questionnaires succeed as their success is planned.* One researcher who conducted a particularly successful questionnaire study handled it this way:

After selecting her population, she sent to each of them a letter describing the potential value of the study. The letter emphasized the importance of the study *to the addressee*, and it invited the addressee to cooperate by answering the questionnaire. Here is a copy of the researcher's letter of inquiry with marginal comments on some of its features.

THE AMERICAN UNIVERSITY
Massachusetts and Nebraska Aves., N.W.
Washington, D.C. 20016

The School of Nursing

August 15, 1980

Dear Alumna,

Your School of Nursing is appealing to you for help. We are not asking for funds - all we ask is a few minutes of your time.

It is to your advantage to be recognized as a graduate of a school which has an excellent reputation for the education and training of nurses to meet the realities of nursing practice. You can assist us to maintain - and to improve this reputation - by cooperating in the evaluation of the program of Nursing Education at The American University. What we would like to ask you is to give us your candid, honest opinion of the nursing program in effect when you were a student nurse in training at The American University. We have a questionnaire which we would like to send you, with your permission, and which will take no more than fifteen minutes of your time to answer.

The Lucy Webb Hayes School of Nursing at The American University is growing. With your help it can grow in professional stature and educational excellence. We are sure you will be willing to cooperate with us toward those desired goals.

As an enclosure with this letter, you will find a return post-card on which you may indicate your willingness to cooperate with us by answering the questionnaire. Thank you for the courtesy of your assistance.

Very sincerely yours,

Ruth G. Thomas

Ruth G. Thomas, R.N.

This letter was sent out by a student who was doing an evaluative study entitled: "A Study to Evaluate the Academic Program of the Lucy Webb Hayes School of Nursing at The American University."

The questionnaire was designed to gather information on one of the subproblems of the study: "How adequately do the graduates consider the program to have been in preparing them for a professional nursing career?"

Note the direct "other-fellow" appeal. The author quickly indicates this is not an appeal for money—only a few minutes of time.

The fact is strongly made that it is to the advantage of the addressee to answer the questionnaire.

Note: "with your permission!" Also, an estimate of time required helps to convince.

The positive is emphasized: we are growing; we want to grow in excellence—but we need you!

This is a splendid device for getting a commitment. The card will be reproduced later.

Note the tone. No "yours truly" here. The courteous tone is carried out to the very end of the letter.

Compare the preceding letter with the following brief note which, unfortunately, is all too typical of the hundreds of similar ones that the author has seen proposed by his students in their first attempts at drafting such a letter:

X Y Z UNIVERSITY
Campus Station

April 1, 1980

Dear Sir:

I am a graduate student at X Y Z University, and the enclosed questionnaire is sent to you in the hope that you will assist me in obtaining information for my Master's thesis.

I should appreciate your early reply since I am attempting to get my degree this June.

Yours truly,
John Doe
John Doe

This letter represents a flagrant foisting, without benefit of common courtesy of one's own selfish demands as an imposition upon others. In letters of this sort may lie another reason for the poor return of questionnaires when beginning researchers attempt to employ the survey method.

How does the person react who receives such a letter? Perhaps with a "So what?" "Who cares?" "Why should I do you a favor; your degree means nothing to me!" "Get it the best way you can!"

And these reactions are not without some degree of justification.

★ *The initial letter is all-important*. It should be carefully and thoughtfully structured and its emphasis should stress the concerns of the person receiving the letter rather than the selfish interests of the sender. Some students forget this; and, in so doing betray their own self-centeredness without perhaps intending to do so.

Let us return to the first letter. Mention was made there of a card which was enclosed and which gave the recipient an opportunity to express a willingness to answer the questionnaire. The card was simple and straightforward, containing the following wording. It was addressed and stamped and required only a check mark and a signature on the part of the recipient.

Dear Mrs. Thomas:

☐ Please send the questionnaire; I will be happy to cooperate.

☐ I am sorry but I do not wish to answer the questionnaire.

Comments:

Date:__________ ________________
Name

Upon receipt of the card indicating a willingness to cooperate the researcher mailed the questionnaire immediately. A log was kept of questionnaires mailed, to whom, their addresses, and the date of mailing. In a desk memo date book, precisely three weeks after the mailing of each questionnaire, the respondent's name was entered so that if a reply was not received until that date, a reminder letter would be sent.

The reminder was in the same vein as the initial letter. The wording of it, with comments, is at the top of p. 141.

The letter brought results. In the *entire* approach of the student, much persuasion was built into the correspondence; but it was done so deftly and tactfully that a fine human relations situation was created and kept throughout the entire procedure. Courtesy, understanding, and respect for others pay large dividends and in no place more than in a situation where a researcher needs the cooperation of others. This is especially necessary in questionnaire survey studies.

The Interview

Closely allied to the questionnaire is the *structured interview.* The interview, as a data-gathering technique, is frequently misunderstood. Most students think of it as "simply asking a person some questions"; and, of course, it is that. But it is not asking just *any* questions in *any* way. The questions for the interview should be as carefully planned and as accurately worded as the items in a questionnaire. Interviews should be considered as strictly professional situations which demand equally professional planning and conduct on the part of the interviewer. We have seen how the questionnaire demands considerable thought and planning for its effective administration. Equally careful planning is no less necessary for the interview.

We have described in detail the approach of a researcher who employed the questionnaire technique in a professional and scholarly way. Perhaps an equally effective way to illustrate the use of the interview technique may be to cite its use by another researcher who employed it with equal effectiveness.

The student's problem concerned the field of international relations. It was desirable that he interview certain United Nations personnel in order to get their respective opinions concerning issues within the province of his study. He hoped to gather his data quickly, but systematically, and he planned his approach toward that end. He planned to go to New York for a series of interviews and wished to schedule them as tightly as possible to conserve both time and expense. His procedure was organized and logical.

★ *How to proceed to arrange an interview.* Approximately six weeks before going for the interviews, the student wrote the several United Nations representatives with whom he wished to confer indicating that he would be in New York on certain specific days and requested the courtesy of an interview lasting not more than half an hour. He asked each prospective interviewee for an indication of several time slots when the interview might be scheduled. In his letter, he explained clearly what information he was seeking and his reasons for seeking it. (*Not* among his reasons was the fact that he was writing a thesis!) Rather, his reasons were mature and meaningful, and were so phrased that they held some interest for those he was to interview. If you must reveal that you are collecting the data for a thesis, use the word *study* in lieu of *thesis*. Look at the world realistically. Aside from the student and the graduate adviser, theses hold very little glamour in the everyday world. Studies are much more acceptable.

Enclosed with the letter referred to above was a separate sheet containing the questions that the student intended to ask during the interview, arranged in the order that he would ask them. Also, in the letter he suggested that if the interviewee had no objections, taping the conference would facilitate matters considerably. To do so, it was suggested, would conserve time and lessen the distraction of handwritten notes. He provided a check box on a return postcard for the interviewee to indicate whether there was any objection to recording the interview.

THE AMERICAN UNIVERSITY
Massachusetts and Nebraska Aves., N.W.
Washington, D.C. 20016

School of Nursing

September 5, 1980

Dear Alumna,

All of us are busier these days than we should be, and most of us have a hard time keeping abreast of those obligations which are essential and required. We know how the little extras sometimes receive our best intentions, but we also know that in reality none of us have the time which we would desire to fulfill those intentions.

From the questionnaire which reached you --we hope-- about three weeks ago, we have had no reply. Perhaps you mislaid the questionnaire, or it may have miscarried in the mail-- any one of dozens of contingencies could have happened.

In any event, we are enclosing another copy of the questionnaire. We are sure you will try to find fifteen minutes somewhere in your busy schedule to check its several items and drop it in the nearest postal box. Most of them have been returned. We'd like to get them all back. Will you help us?

Thanks. We shall appreciate your kindness.

Very sincerely yours,

Ruth G. Thomas

Ruth G. Thomas, R.N.

This letter applies tactfulness, diplomacy, psychology, and human relations techniques at their very best.

Note the universal and appreciative tone of the letter from the first three words: "All of us. . .". The first letter began with a "you" approach. This one is much more understanding. It takes any trace of guilt or failure-to-reply out of the sutuation.

No need for the recipient of this letter to make excuses; the writer has disarmed the situation by offering two and suggesting that there may be dozens more.

By enclosing a second questionnaire, come what may, the recipient has now no excuse for not returning the questionnaire—and she indicated on a card previously that she would carry through.

Note how gently the suggestion is made that she is one of the few delinquent ones.

The faith in this letter is boundless. It would be difficult indeed not to respond in the face of such belief that you will do so.

When he received his replies, he set up a master chart of appointments and places and confirmed immediately, by letter, the appointment time, thanking the interviewee for his cooperation. Where there was a time conflict, he sought to resolve it by suggesting alternate times which were still open.

Ten days before the interview, he mailed a reminder, together with another copy of the interview questions, just in case the interviewee had misplaced the copy previously sent. He also enclosed his full interview schedule so that his interviewee might appreciate the time exigencies under which he was working.

On the day of the interview, he arrived promptly. When taken in to see the person to be interviewed, he introduced himself, stated briefly that he had come in accordance with previously made arrangements, asked whether his interviewee wished a copy of the questions he had previously sent, and began with the first question. He tried to guide the interview, keeping always to his agenda of questions and seeking to preserve an easy, friendly, yet professional atmosphere.

As the interview drew to a close, he thanked his interviewee for his courtesy in giving his time and went off to his next appointment.

In three and a half days, he had interviewed 35 United Nations representatives and had over four-fifths of his data on tape. Subsequently, he transcribed from the tape the substance of the interview and submitted within ten days following his visit a typed transcript to each interviewee, together with a letter thanking him for granting the interview. He asked each official interviewed to read the typescript carefully and, if it was correct, to sign at the end of the copy a statement that the typescript was a correct record of the interview. If the official found it inexact or incorrect in any place, the interviewee was requested to correct the script or to edit it as he desired. As in all manuscript, the typescript was wide-margined and double-spaced, which permitted ample room for corrections.

In the statement acknowledging the typescript to be correct, the researcher also incorporated a "permission" clause in which he requested permission to use whatever part of the interview that might provide data for his study with the full understanding that before the study was released, the interview material would again be submitted to the interviewee for his complete approval. This was done, of course, prior to submitting the report as a final document for the degree. In the final document, all acknowledgments were made, and the researchers noted the fact that the authors had inspected and approved all their quoted statements. This is the only way that a researcher or an author can find protection against the accusations of falsification of the facts, libel suits, and other legal entanglements.

★ *Summary*. The steps, then, for successfully handling the interview as a technique for gathering data for one's research study are simple, but very important:

1. Set up the interview well in advance.
2. Send the agenda of questions you will ask the interviewee.
3. Ask for permission to tape the conference.
4. Confirm the date immediately in writing.
5. Send a reminder together with another agenda of questions ten days before you expect to arrive.
6. Be prompt; follow the agenda; have a copy of your questions for your interviewee in case he or she has mislaid his or her copy.
7. Following the interview, submit a typescript of the interview and get either a written acknowledgment of its accuracy or a corrected copy from the interviewee.
8. After you have incorporated the material into your research report, send section of report to interviewee for final approval and written permission to use the data in your report.

Tape Recording of the Data

We have been discussing two specific techniques of gathering the data within the descriptive survey methodology: by means of the questionnaire, and by means of the interview. In the study we are about to discuss, the student gathered the data not by either of these two methods but through the use of a tape recorder.

We made the point earlier that observation need not always be a visual experience. We "observe" through the ear as well as through the eye. Below is a description of "ear observation" as described by a student who used an audio-observational approach in gathering data for her dissertation.[2]

The student's problem for research was to categorize and to describe the classroom interaction of certain music teachers at two grade levels, and also to analyze and to interpret the variation in the classroom-interaction patterns of these music teachers in the same grades.

Here is her procedure for the collection of the data by using a tape recorder, as described in the introductory chapter of her dissertation:

---

[2]Alicia Leonard Pagano, "A Study of the Classroom-Interaction Patterns of Selected Music Teachers in First-Grade and Sixth-Grade General Music Classes (unpublished doctoral dissertation, The American University, 1972), pp. 52–55.

The primary data, or raw data, for this study were secured by audio-tape recording the necessary class sessions of the ten teachers in the sample. The recording machine was a Wollensak Magnetic Tape-Recorder, Model 7-7500.

Each teacher in the sample prepared a schedule of her first-grade and sixth-grade music classes and agreed to permit the researcher to enter unannounced into the specified classrooms prior to the beginning of each class that was to be recorded. The reason for not pre-arranging the taping sessions was to prevent any special preparation, conscious or unconscious, on the part of the teachers.

The researcher entered the classroom prior to the beginning of the music class, started the tape-recording machine, and left the classroom before the commencement of the music class. At the end of the class session, the music teacher deactivated the tape-recorder and the researcher returned to collect the tape and the equipment. This procedure was followed in order to eliminate bias in analyzing the tapes. The researcher first heard all of the tapes after having witnessed neither the teacher teaching nor the class in progress. Because of this procedure, there was unnecessary information recorded at the beginning of each tape. The analysis of the class session began with the start of instruction.

Each session was identified by the date, the time, the grade level, and the code letter of the teacher being recorded.

The classroom in which music teachers taught their students varied from school to school and often varied from day to day within the same school. Sometimes the teacher entered the regular classroom of the students; and at other times, the students came to a music room or to a room designated for music on a particular day. This flexible scheduling procedure made it impossible to conceal the tape-recorder from the students. Since this was true, and since students were accustomed to seeing and using audio hardware in their music classes, a decision was made to inform all of the students that their teacher and their class were being taped as a part of an educational project.

If the schedule of a music teacher was changed without notice, if a music teacher was absent when the researcher came to tape, or if other circumstances prevented the recording or the coding of the tape, the researcher returned to record other sessions until a sufficient number of acceptable tapes had been collected.

First-grade classes in several school systems were scheduled for a much shorter time than the sixth-grade classes. Therefore, the first-grade classes in these schools were taped during six class sessions in order to increase the total number of tallies at the first-grade level.

The tape-recording of the music classes with the teachers in the sample began in February and continued for a time period of eight weeks. Prior to the collection of the data, tape-recordings of several music classes were obtained to provide the researcher sufficient time and materials with which to achieve observer accuracy and reliability. These tapes were not included in the data of the study.

The Flanders' System of Interaction Analysis[3] was used as the basis for the categorization and analysis of the material on the tapes. The Flanders' System contains ten categories, divided into three major divisions; these are concerned with teacher talk, student talk, and silence or confusion.

Thus, we have seen in detail how a tape-recording approach was devised and managed. What was structured for the tape-recording approach might have been used, with slight modification, with video tape and with a one-way viewing panel.

[3]Edmund J. Amidon and Ned A. Flanders, *The Role of the Teacher in the Classroom: A Manual for Understanding and Improving Teachers' Classroom Behavior.* (Minneapolis, Minnesota: Paul S. Amidon and Associates, Incorporated, 1963).

The Checklist and the Sliding Scale Inventory

We shall discuss one further type of observational technique: the *differential sliding scale checklist or inventory.*

When looking at a situation, a researcher needs to look purposefully, to have an agenda of objectives or behavioral goals toward which to direct one's attention.

In its simplest form, such a list of observational goals is perhaps the ordinary *checklist*. A *checklist* is simply a list of items after each of which a check mark is made in one of two columns: either in the column "observed" or in the column "not observed." Such a simple observational checklist is found in connection with the survey which you made earlier in this text with respect to research studies and the presence or absence of critical aspects of basic research.[4]

Often, however, instead of a simple either-or choice, the researcher wishes to record varying degrees of intensity or range of frequency in the happening of certain events. A scale on which such ranges can be recorded is a checklist, with the checking being done on a variable scale—hence its name: *a differential sliding-scale checklist.* Sometimes this type of observational instrument is known as a *rating scale*.

On page 145 is an example of this type of scale. The author constructed it so that the reader could evaluate himself in terms of the development of certain specific habits that are critical to effective reading. The various aspects of the reading act are evaluated in terms of the techniques of effective reading, visual factors, and emotional factors. The inventory explores exactly twenty-five items. By so doing, an evaluation system having five choices for each item results in a full-scale performance of 100 percent and, similarly, by weighting each of the categories with an assigned value, we can then express any degree of intensity within the entire range of values in terms of percentage strength.

We have discussed at sufficient length the various observational tools and techniques generally employed in the descriptive survey study. In the last analysis, every researcher must devise the particular observational approach most appropriate to the demands of the particular problem and the data which the investigation of the problem will demand.

SELECTING THE POPULATION

We must now turn to another aspect of the descriptive survey method, namely *the choosing of the population for the study*, which earlier we indicated to be the second of the four essential factors of the descriptive survey method.[5]

A basic rule governs the descriptive survey: Nothing comes out at the end of a long and involved study which is any better than the care, the precision, the consideration, the thought that went into the basic planning of the research design and the careful selection of the population. *The results of a survey are no more trustworthy than the quality of the population or the representativeness of the sample*. Population parameters and sampling procedures are of paramount importance and become critical as factors in the success of they study.

Many students in phrasing their problems forget what we have just been saying. They announce, for example, that their goal is to "survey the legal philosophies of the attorneys of the United States and to analyze the relationship of these several philosophical positions with respect to the recent decisions of the Supreme Court of the United States."

A student who words a problem in this way has simply not thought through the

---

[4] See pages 284–285 in the practicum section.
[5] See page 134.

Reading Habit Inventory

For each of the following statements, check under Never, Rarely, Sometimes, Usually, or Always. Do not omit any of the items. Be truthful and utterly realistic. Represent your reading habits as they actually are.

	Never	*Rarely*	*Sometimes*	*Usually*	*Always*
1. When I pick up a page of print, I notice the paragraphs specifically.					
2. I read as I drive, with varying rates of speed, depending upon varying reading conditions.					
3. While reading, I find it easy to keep my mind on the material before me.					
4. After I have been reading for a while, I stop reading for a few moments and rest my eyes by looking at some distant object.					
5. I am alert to the role which punctuation plays in aiding me to get the meaning.					
6. When I pick up a piece of reading matter for the first time, I look for certain specific items which will aid me in reading the piece more efficiently.					
7. I read groups of words at one glance.					
8. I notice a distinctive style, or flavor, of the author.					
9. I enjoy reading.					
10. I can read for long periods of time without a feeling of eye fatigue or tiredness.					
11. After I read a paragraph, if required to do so, I could sum up the main idea clearly and briefly in my own words.					
12. I make a practice of skimming articles frequently.					
13. In reading a paragraph I usually try to see the organization of its thought content: I look for the main idea, and the details which support it.					
14. I do not lose my place, or skip words or lines, while reading.					
15. I am mildly conscious of grammatical structure while reading.					
16. I feel comfortable and perfectly at ease while reading.					
17. In reading larger units of writing (articles, chapters, etc.) I try to see the outline and total structure of the author's thought.					
18. I have little difficulty in remembering what I read.					
19. When I read, especially for any length of time, I make sure that the page before me is adequately illuminated.					
20. When I read, I am reading for some definite purpose, and I try to keep that purpose clearly in mind as I read.					
21. I read the preface of a book.					
22. In reading more difficult material, after reading a paragraph or a section, I pause to summarize in a momentary flashback the material I have just covered.					
23. While reading, I am aware of questions which arise in my own thinking about the material being read.					
24. While reading, I hold the page 15 to 20 inches from my eyes.					
25. I am aware that with practice a person can improve his reading skills, and I make a conscious effort generally toward that end.					

Count the checks in each column to obtain:	(A)					
Multiply by:	(B)	0	1	2	3	4
to obtain:	(C)		%	%	%	%

Now add the figures in row C for your final score: ____ %

Analysis of Your Reading Habits

Now, analyze your reading habits. What does the above Inventory mean? If you have marked it carefully and conscientiously, it should prove a helpful guide in aiding you to develop more effective reading habits than those you now have. This means that ultimately you will be a more efficient reader.

To analyze your reading habits, carefully check on the chart below, under the number of the item of the Inventory statement, the category (Always, Usually, Sometimes, Rarely, Never) as you marked it in the Inventory above. Out of the 25 items that you marked, certain of them attempted to appraise your habits associated with certain specific reading techniques. Other items attempted to evaluate the more important matters associated with ocular hygiene and visual efficiency. Finally, a few items sought to probe some of the emotional factors which may aid or hinder your total reading efficiency.

Note the line in the forms below marked, "Danger Line." As you transcribe your check marks from the Inventory above, you will find that you have checked either above or below this danger line. The check marks *below* the danger line indicate that in these matters you need to give attention to your reading habits and practices. Try to put into practice each time you read, the procedures suggested by the Inventory statements of those items which you have checked below the danger line.

1. What does the Inventory indicate as to my reading techniques? To find out, transcribe a check mark from the Inventory to the proper box in the chart following:

Item No.	*1*	*2*	*5*	*6*	*8*	*11*	*12*	*13*	*15*	*17*	*18*	*20*	*21*	*22*	*23*	*Total*
Always																
Usually																
DANGER LINE																
Sometimes																
Rarely																
Never																

Total number of check marks below the danger line: ______

2. What does the Inventory indicate about my visual factors in reading? Check the following chart to find out:

Item No.	*4*	*7*	*10*	*14*	*19*	*24*	*Total*
Always							
Usually							
DANGER LINE							
Sometimes							
Rarely							
Never							

Total number of check marks below the danger line: ______

(Inventory continued on next page.)

Reading Habit Inventory (concluded)

3. What does the Inventory indicate about my emotional factors in reading? Check the following chart to find out:

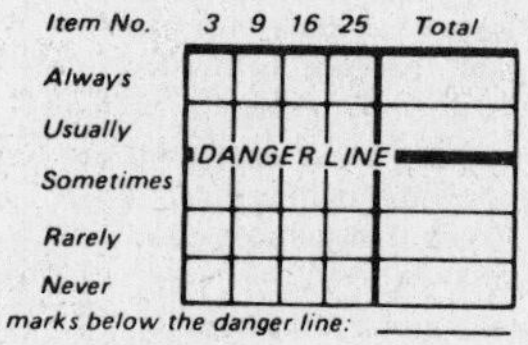

Item No.	*3*	*9*	*16*	*25*	*Total*
Always					
Usually					
DANGER LINE					
Sometimes					
Rarely					
Never					

Total number of check marks below the danger line: ________

Total number of check marks in all three charts *above* the danger line: ________

Divide 25 into the *total* number of check marks you have *above* the danger line. This will give you your percentage score of *desirable* reading habits: ____%

[15] Paul D. Leedy, *Improve Your Reading: A Guide to Greater Speed, Understanding and Enjoyment* (New York: McGraw-Hill Book Co., 1956). A McGraw-Hill Paperback, pp. 40-44. Reprinted by permission of the publisher.

meaning of his own words. "The attorneys of the United States"! The American Bar Association consists of over 147,000 attorneys, distributed over 3,536,855 square miles in the fifty states. But these are merely first hurdles. As we look at the problem more closely, we begin to discern other, more serious difficulties. What are "philosophical attitudes"? How does one isolate these attitudes in order to study them? How can you show a "relationship of philosophical positions" with "recent decisions of the Supreme Court"? How will this relationship be expressed? Will it be expressed statistically? If so, how will you quantify "philosophical positions" and "decisions"? If not, then what will it be?

Earlier in these pages, we discussed the necessity for considering carefully the size, the selection, and the parameters of the survey population.[6] The failure of the researcher to recognize population parameters and their demands upon research procedures and research design as well as upon the resources available is generally indicative of inexperiences in the area of practical research planning and design.

With survey studies particularly, the researcher needs to calculate all costs of both time and money. The age of automation and computerization has given a roseate, but false sense of ease to the solution of many knotty problems associated with survey research. Inexperienced researchers frequently think that the computer is the magic and perfect answer to all their research difficulties. If anything poses a problem, so they reason, all you have to do is to "feed the data into a computer" and out will come the resolution of all your research worries and the meaning of the data as well. Unfortunately, 'tis not so. What amateur researchers sometimes fail to realize is that computers merely rearrange the data and perform mathematical and statistical operations strictly in accord with their programmed instructions. They solve no design difficulties, nor do they *interpret* any data. In addition, their use may be both time-consuming and expensive. There is a basic rule for computers. It is known as the *GIGO* Law: Garbage in; garbage out! Computers are not *thinking* machines; they are *robots*. They do precisely what they are told to do. Their function is to rearrange existing data into new and potentially meaningful patterns, much as a kaleidoscope rearranges the existing bits of colored glass that were originally sealed into it and presents them to the eye of the observer in varied and fascinating designs.

But to get back to our more than 147,000 attorneys and their thoughts, it is not necessary, of course, to poll each and every one of them to get some indication of their composite thought. It may be well for us to refer back to page 7 and to review the concept of *universe*. There, we defined it as "the factual area that lies or 'turns' around the central inquiry or main problem of the research." Here we shall define it in basically the same way but with particular reference to the data: *A universe of data consists of the totality of those data within certain specified parameters*. Here the "specified parameters" were that those individuals who were to be studied were "the attorneys of [*in*] the United

[6] See pages 56-57.

States." But a universe of data is usually too large to be studied *in toto*. Where such is the case, we have devised a process that is both logically and statistically sound, namely the *process of sampling*.

Referring back to the attorneys once more, we should point out that the difficulty basically arises out of the statement of the problem. If the researcher has said what he means, then he has indicated that he is proposing to survey "the attorneys"—all of them! If, on the other hand, he intends to survey only a certain cross section of the attorneys, then the statement of his problem should have accurately represented that fact through appropriate wording within the problem itself by the insertion of such qualifying—and accurately descriptive—words as *selected, representative, typical, certain, a random sampling of*, and so on. Careful researchers say precisely what they mean. Note the difference in the meaning between the wording which says, "The purpose of this research is to survey the representative legal philosophies of a random sample of attorneys. . ." and the wording as it stands in the student's phrasing: "The purpose of this research is to survey the legal philosophies of the attorneys of the United States. . . ."

How, then, is sampling done? The answer is, "In a number of ways." Perhaps at the outset, the method of sampling is not nearly so important as the purpose of sampling and a careful consideration of the parameters of the population.

Look through the wrong end of a telescope. You will see the broad world in miniature. This is precisely what the sampling procedure chosen for any particular project should seek to achieve. *The sample should be so carefully chosen that through it the researcher is able to see all the characteristics of the total population in the same relationship that he would see them were he actually to inspect the totality of the population in fact.*

That may indeed be a consummation devoutly to be wished, and, ideally, samples are population microcosms. In optics, unless lenses are precision-made and accurately ground, one is likely to get distortion through the spyglass. Similarly, unless the sampling is carefully planned and statistically tested, distortion is likely to be present in the conclusions that the researcher draws from the data. Such distortion we call *bias*. We shall discuss this subject further in the next section. For the moment, however, we shall concern ourselves with the types, methods, and procedures of sampling.

Types, Methods, and Procedures of Sampling

One basic rule holds whenever a researcher is considering methodology in relation to data—it matters not whether this methodology concerns sampling, a statistical procedure, or any other type of operation. The general rule is: *Look carefully at the nature of, the characteristics of, and the quality of the data.* After the researcher sees this clearly, he can then more intelligently select the proper methodology for the treatment of those data. Not all data lend themselves to sampling. Wherever large populations are present, instances that have an outward semblance of homogeneity of structure that evidence common characteristics,—with such situations, sampling is appropriate.

The composition of the sample is derived by selecting units from those of a much larger population. In survey studies, the *manner* in which the sample units are selected is very important. Generally, the components of the sample are chosen from the population universe by a process known as *randomization*. Such a sample is known as a *random sample.* The two elements that are more important than any others in survey research are *randomization* and *bias*.

Randomization means *selecting a sample from the whole population in such a way that the characteristics of each of the units of the sample approximates the broad characteristics inherent in the total population.*

Let's explain that. I have a beaker which contains 100 cc. of water. I have another container that has a concentrated solution of 10 cc. of acid. I combine water and acid in proportions 10 to 1. After thoroughly mixing the water and acid, I should be able to extract 1 cc. from *any* part of the solution and find that in that 1-cc. sample, a mixture of water and acid is in precisely a 10:1 proportion. Just so, if we have a conglomerate population with variables such as differences of race, status, wealth, education, and other factors, and *if we have a perfectly selected random sample* (a situation which is usually more theoretical than practical), we will find in the sample those same characteristics that exist in the larger population universe, and in the same ratio.

A sample is no more representative of the total population, therefore, than the validity of the method of randomization employed in selecting it. There are, of course, many methods of random selection. We shall look at merely a few of the more common ones.

★ *The Roulette Wheel Method.* If the population is small—50-75 individuals—each individual may be assigned a number in some orderly sequence: alphabetically by surname, by birth date (youngest to oldest or the reverse), by respective total weight of each individual, or by any other systematic arrangement. Corresponding numbers are on a roulette wheel. A spin of the wheel and its fortuitous stopping at a particular number selects the individual assigned to that number as a unit within the sample. The process of spinning the wheel and selecting the sample goes on until all the individuals needed to compose the sample have been chosen.

★ *The Lottery Method.* In the lottery method the population again is arranged sequentially and assigned a numerical identification. Corresponding numbers are marked on separate tabs and put into a revolving drum or closed container. The numbers are tossed so that they are thoroughly intermixed. Then one tab bearing a number is selected from the total number of tabs in the container, without the selector seeing the pool. The number which has been selected is recorded and then *the tab is tossed back into the pool again.* This is an important feature of the lottery method. It ensures that every individual has the same chance of being chosen as every other individual. If, for example, we are selecting 50 units out of a population of 100 and we do not cast each tab back after it has been selected, we will have an ever-diminishing population from which to make choices. And, whereas the first choice would have been one in 100 chances of being selected, the last unit chosen would have one in 50 chances of being selected, or, in other words, the chances of being selected would be twice as great for the last individual as those for the first one chosen.

In the event of the same number being drawn twice, the second drawing is ignored; the number is returned to the pool; the entire mass of numbers is tumbled again, and another drawing is made. Drawing and tumbling go on until 50 tabs have been selected purely by chance.

★ *The Table of Random Numbers Method.* The table of random numbers method is perhaps the most frequently used method for the random selection of a sample. Following is a part of a table of random numbers. We may employ this table in any manner in which we choose to use it. Generally the researcher enters the table according to some predetermined method.

Entrance into the table may, in fact, be accomplished in many ways. One fundamental principle must be kept in mind, however: *the purpose of randomness is to permit blind chance to determine the outcomes of the selection process to as great a degree as possible.* Hence, in determining a starting point for the selection of random numbers, *pure chance* must always initiate the process.

Consider the table of random numbers on the next page. There are ten blocks of random numbers in horizontal arrangement. From top to bottom of the table, in vertical arrangement, there are ten blocks of numbers. Tables of random numbers may be found in most statistics textbooks. On page 151 we have presented a partial table and numbered each of the columns horizontally from 1-5 and vertically also 1-0. The horizontal and vertical

	1	2	3	4	5	6	7	8	9	0
1	03 47 43 73 86 97 74 24 67 62 16 76 62 27 66 12 56 85 99 26 55 59 56 35 64	36 96 47 36 61 42 81 14 57 20 56 50 26 71 07 96 96 68 27 31 38 54 82 46 22	46 98 63 71 62 42 53 32 37 32 32 90 79 78 53 05 03 72 93 15 31 62 43 09 90	33 26 16 80 45 27 07 36 07 51 13 55 38 58 59 57 12 10 14 21 06 18 44 32 53	60 11 14 10 95 24 51 79 89 73 88 97 54 14 10 88 26 49 81 76 23 83 01 30 30	53 74 23 99 67 63 38 06 86 54 35 30 58 21 46 63 43 36 82 69 98 25 37 55 26	61 32 28 69 84 99 00 65 26 94 06 72 17 10 94 65 51 18 37 88 01 91 82 81 46	94 62 67 86 24 09 82 90 23 07 25 21 31 75 96 61 38 44 12 45 74 71 12 94 97	98 33 41 19 95 79 62 67 80 60 49 28 24 00 49 32 92 85 88 65 24 02 71 37 07	47 53 53 38 09 75 91 12 81 19 55 65 79 78 07 54 34 81 85 35 03 92 18 66 75
2	16 22 77 94 39 84 42 17 53 31 63 01 63 78 59 33 21 12 34 29 57 60 86 32 44	49 54 43 54 82 57 24 55 06 88 16 95 55 67 19 78 64 56 07 82 09 47 27 96 54	17 37 93 23 78 77 04 74 47 67 98 10 50 71 75 52 42 07 44 38 49 17 46 09 62	87 35 20 96 43 21 76 33 50 25 12 86 73 58 07 15 51 00 13 42 90 52 84 77 27	84 26 34 91 64 83 92 12 06 76 44 39 52 38 79 99 66 02 79 54 08 02 73 43 28	02 63 21 17 69 64 55 22 21 82 85 07 26 13 89 58 54 16 24 15 34 85 27 84 87	71 50 80 89 56 48 22 28 06 00 01 10 07 82 04 51 54 44 82 00 61 48 64 56 26	38 15 70 11 48 61 54 13 43 91 59 63 69 36 03 62 61 65 04 69 90 18 48 13 26	43 40 45 86 98 82 78 12 23 29 69 11 15 83 80 38 18 65 18 97 37 70 15 42 57	00 83 26 91 03 06 66 24 12 27 13 29 54 19 28 85 72 13 49 21 65 65 80 39 07
3	18 18 07 92 46 26 62 38 97 75 23 42 40 64 74 62 36 28 19 95 37 85 94 35 12	44 17 16 58 09 84 16 07 44 99 82 97 77 77 81 50 92 26 11 97 83 39 50 08 30	79 83 86 19 62 83 11 46 32 24 07 45 32 14 08 00 56 76 31 38 42 34 07 96 88	06 76 50 03 10 20 14 85 88 45 32 98 94 07 72 80 22 02 53 53 54 42 06 87 98	55 23 64 05 05 10 93 72 88 71 93 85 79 10 75 86 60 42 04 53 35 85 29 48 39	03 92 18 27 46 62 95 30 27 59 08 45 93 15 22 07 08 55 18 40 01 85 89 95 66	57 99 16 96 56 37 75 41 66 48 60 21 75 46 91 45 44 75 13 90 51 10 19 34 88	30 33 72 85 22 86 97 80 61 45 98 77 27 85 42 24 94 96 61 02 15 84 97 19 75	84 64 38 56 98 23 53 04 01 63 28 88 61 08 84 57 55 66 83 15 12 76 39 43 78	99 01 30 98 64 45 76 08 64 27 69 62 03 42 73 73 42 37 11 61 64 63 91 08 25
4	70 29 17 12 13 56 62 18 37 35 99 49 57 22 77 16 08 15 04 72 31 16 93 32 43	40 33 20 38 26 96 83 50 87 75 88 42 95 45 72 33 27 14 34 09 50 27 89 87 19	13 89 51 03 74 97 12 25 93 47 16 64 36 16 00 45 59 34 68 49 20 15 37 00 49	17 76 37 13 04 70 33 24 03 54 04 43 18 66 79 12 72 07 34 45 52 85 66 60 44	07 74 21 19 30 97 77 46 44 80 94 77 24 21 90 99 27 72 95 14 38 68 88 11 80	72 84 71 14 35 88 78 28 16 84 45 17 75 65 57 96 76 28 12 54 43 31 67 72 30	19 11 58 49 26 13 52 53 94 53 28 40 19 72 12 22 01 11 94 25 24 02 94 08 63	50 11 17 17 76 75 45 69 30 96 25 12 74 75 67 71 96 16 16 88 38 32 36 66 02	86 31 57 20 18 73 89 65 70 31 60 40 60 81 19 68 64 36 74 45 69 36 38 25 39	95 60 78 46 75 99 17 43 48 76 24 62 01 61 16 19 59 50 88 92 48 03 45 15 22
5	68 34 30 13 70 74 57 25 65 76 27 42 37 86 53 00 39 68 29 61 29 94 98 94 24	55 74 30 77 40 59 29 97 68 60 48 55 90 65 72 66 37 32 20 30 68 49 69 10 82	44 22 78 84 26 71 91 38 67 54 96 57 69 36 10 77 84 57 03 29 53 75 91 93 30	04 33 46 09 52 13 58 18 24 76 96 46 92 42 45 10 45 66 04 26 34 25 20 57 27	68 07 97 06 57 15 54 55 95 52 97 60 49 04 91 11 04 96 67 24 40 48 73 51 92	50 44 66 44 21 22 66 22 15 86 96 24 40 14 51 31 73 91 61 19 78 60 73 99 84	66 06 58 05 62 26 63 75 41 99 23 22 30 88 57 60 20 72 93 48 43 89 94 36 45	68 15 54 35 02 58 42 36 72 24 95 67 47 29 83 98 57 07 23 69 56 69 47 07 41	42 35 48 96 32 58 37 52 18 51 94 69 40 06 07 65 95 39 69 58 90 22 91 07 12	14 52 41 52 48 03 37 18 39 11 18 16 36 78 86 56 80 30 19 44 78 35 34 08 72
6	16 90 82 66 59 11 27 94 75 06 35 24 10 16 20 38 23 16 86 38 31 96 25 91 47	83 62 64 11 12 06 09 19 74 66 33 32 51 26 38 42 38 97 01 50 96 44 33 49 13	67 19 00 71 74 02 94 37 34 02 79 78 45 04 91 87 75 66 81 41 34 86 82 53 91	60 47 21 29 68 76 70 90 30 86 16 92 53 56 16 40 01 74 91 62 00 52 43 48 85	02 02 37 03 31 38 45 94 30 38 02 75 50 95 98 48 51 84 08 32 27 55 26 89 62	84 37 90 61 56 36 67 10 08 23 07 28 59 07 48 10 15 83 87 60 55 19 68 97 65	70 10 23 98 05 98 93 35 08 86 89 64 58 89 75 79 24 31 66 56 03 73 52 16 56	85 11 34 76 60 99 29 76 29 81 83 85 62 27 89 21 48 24 06 93 00 53 55 90 27	76 48 45 34 60 33 34 91 58 93 30 14 78 56 27 91 98 94 05 49 33 42 29 38 87	01 64 18 39 96 63 14 52 32 52 86 63 59 80 02 01 47 59 38 00 22 13 88 83 34
7	66 67 40 67 14 14 90 84 45 11 68 05 51 18 00 20 46 78 73 90 64 19 58 97 79	64 05 71 95 86 75 73 88 05 90 33 96 02 75 19 97 51 40 14 02 15 06 15 93 20	11 05 65 09 68 52 27 41 14 86 07 60 62 93 55 04 02 33 31 08 01 90 10 75 06	76 83 20 37 90 22 98 12 22 08 59 33 82 43 90 39 54 16 49 36 40 78 78 89 62	57 16 00 11 66 07 52 74 95 80 49 37 38 44 59 47 95 93 13 30 02 67 74 17 33	53 81 29 13 39 51 86 32 68 92 35 91 70 29 13 37 71 67 95 13 93 66 13 83 27	35 01 20 71 34 33 98 74 66 99 80 03 54 07 27 20 02 44 95 94 92 79 64 64 72	62 33 74 82 14 40 14 71 94 58 96 94 78 32 66 64 85 04 05 72 28 54 96 53 84	53 73 19 09 03 45 94 19 38 81 50 95 52 74 33 01 32 90 76 14 48 14 52 98 94	56 54 29 56 93 14 44 99 81 07 13 80 55 62 54 53 89 74 60 41 56 07 93 89 30
8	05 26 93 70 60 07 97 10 88 23 68 71 86 85 85 26 99 61 65 53 14 65 52 68 75	22 35 85 15 13 09 98 42 99 64 54 87 66 47 54 58 37 78 80 70 87 59 36 22 41	92 03 51 59 77 61 71 62 99 15 73 32 08 11 12 42 10 50 67 42 26 78 63 06 55	59 56 78 06 83 06 51 29 16 93 44 95 92 63 16 32 17 55 85 74 13 08 27 01 50	52 91 05 70 74 58 05 77 09 51 29 56 24 29 48 94 44 67 16 94 15 29 39 39 43	02 96 08 45 65 49 83 43 48 35 84 60 71 62 46 18 17 30 88 71 79 69 10 61 78	13 05 00 41 84 82 88 33 69 96 40 80 81 30 37 44 91 14 88 47 71 32 76 95 62	93 07 54 72 59 72 36 04 19 96 34 39 23 05 38 89 23 30 63 15 87 00 22 58 62	21 45 57 09 77 47 45 15 18 60 25 15 35 71 30 56 34 20 47 89 92 54 01 75 25	19 48 56 27 44 82 11 08 95 97 88 12 57 21 77 99 82 93 24 98 43 11 71 99 31
9	17 53 77 58 71 90 26 59 21 19 41 23 52 55 99 60 20 50 81 69 91 25 38 05 90	71 41 61 50 72 23 52 23 33 12 31 04 49 69 96 31 99 73 68 68 94 58 28 41 36	12 41 94 96 26 96 93 02 18 39 10 47 48 45 88 35 81 33 03 76 45 37 59 03 09	44 95 27 36 99 07 02 18 36 07 13 41 43 89 20 24 30 12 48 60 90 35 57 29 12	02 96 74 30 83 25 99 32 70 23 97 17 14 49 17 18 99 10 72 34 82 62 54 65 60	75 93 36 57 83 38 30 92 29 03 51 29 50 10 34 21 31 38 86 24 29 01 23 87 88	56 20 14 82 11 06 28 81 39 38 31 57 75 95 80 37 79 38 86 24 58 02 39 37 67	74 21 97 90 65 62 25 06 84 63 51 97 02 74 77 37 79 81 53 74 42 10 14 20 92	96 42 68 63 86 61 29 08 93 67 76 15 48 49 44 73 24 16 10 33 16 55 23 42 45	74 54 13 26 94 04 32 92 08 09 18 55 63 77 09 70 47 14 54 36 54 96 09 11 06
0	34 50 57 74 37 85 22 04 39 43 09 79 13 77 48 88 75 80 18 14 90 96 23 70 00	98 80 33 00 91 73 81 53 94 79 73 82 97 22 21 22 95 75 42 49 39 00 03 06 90	09 77 93 19 82 33 62 46 86 28 05 03 27 24 83 39 32 82 22 49 55 85 78 38 36	74 94 80 04 04 08 31 54 46 31 72 89 44 05 60 02 48 07 70 37 94 37 30 69 32	45 07 31 66 49 53 94 13 38 47 35 80 39 94 88 16 04 61 67 87 90 89 00 76 33	16 90 82 66 59 11 27 94 75 06 35 24 10 16 20 38 23 16 86 38 31 96 25 91 47	83 62 64 11 12 06 09 19 74 66 33 32 51 26 38 42 38 97 01 50 96 44 33 49 13	67 19 00 71 74 02 94 37 34 02 79 78 45 04 91 87 75 66 81 41 34 86 82 53 91	60 47 21 29 68 76 70 90 30 86 16 92 53 56 16 40 01 74 91 62 00 52 43 48 85	02 02 37 03 31 38 45 94 30 38 02 75 50 95 98 48 51 84 08 32 27 55 26 89 62

From Ronald A. Fisher and Frank Yates, *Statistical Tables for Biological, Agricultural, and Medical Research* (New York: Hafner, 1963).

numbering of the columns has been done merely for purposes of convenience in locating a starting point for entering the table. Thus, any block within the table will be at the intersection of two guide numbers. Therefore, to enter the table you need an "entry number" of two digits—one which will be the guide number, designating a location on the horizontal column and the other a guide number designating in like manner a location on the vertical column. But how do we find an entry number?

To find an entry number, pull a dollar bill from your wallet. The one which we have just pulled has the serial number C 45 391827A. We shall choose the first two digits of the serial number, which makes the entry number 45. But which is the vertical and which the horizontal digit? We flip a coin. If it comes down *h*eads, the first digit will be that of the *h*orizontal series. The coin comes down "heads." This places the 4 in the horizontal series and the 5 in the vertical series. The block where these two digital columns intersect is the location where we begin within the table. On page 151 we have presented a partial reprint of the table of random numbers, showing the manner in which we enter the table.

But, what other ways are there to find an entry number? Let your ingenuity have free rein. Only one rule governs the selection: *pure chance* should dictate the choice. We shall begin with the technique we have just used.

•••*Look at a dollar bill.* Note the first two digits of the serial number in the lower left- or upper right-hand corner. These will be your "Entry digits."

•••*Check the stock quotations.* Take any newspaper. Turn to the stock quotation page. Take the first letter of your surname. The first stock listed which begins with that letter will be your predetermined stock. Note its quotation for high and low. Disregard the fractional quotations. Take the two digits in either the high or low quotation column; or, if only one digit appears in each column, take the two digits together.

•••*Ask a friend for his social security number.* Select one of your friends at random. Ask for his social security number. Take the first two or the last two digits of that number. It will give you an "entry number" to locate a beginning block within the table of random numbers.

•••*Consult the World Almanac.* Look up any state within the United States. Take the figure representing the area. Select any one of three two-digit numbers: (a) the first two digits of the area, (b) the last two digits of the area, or (c) if it is a six-digit number, the middle two digits of the area. These will be your entry digits to the table.

•••*Use a telephone directory.* Open a telephone directory at random. Take the last two digits of the first number in the first column on either the left-hand or the right-hand page. Toss a coin again to decide. "Tails" decide the page will be the left-hand one (Tai*l*-*l*eft).

•••*Note a vehicle registration tag.* Step outside. Observe the first vehicle which passes. Note the last (or first) two digits on the registration tag. The digits will serve as an "entry number" to the table of random numbers.

Having arrived at the digital block location, the next step is to determine the size of the proposed sample. If it is to be less than 100 individuals, we shall select only two-digit numbers; if it is to be less than 1,000, we shall need three digits to accommodate the sample size.

Let us go back to the total population for a moment to consider the total group from which the sample is to be drawn. It will be necessary to designate these individuals in some specific manner. It is, therefore, advantageous to arrange the individuals within the population in some systematic order (alphabetically, for example, by surname) and to assign to each a serial number for identification purposes.

Now, we are ready for the random selection. We shall start with the upper left-hand digits in the designated block and work first downward in the column; if there are not enough digits for the demand of the total sample in that direction, we will return to the starting digits and proceed upward. Having exhausted all 50 digits in any one column, move to the adjoining columns and proceed as before until the sample requirement is filled. As each digit designation comes up, select the individual in the population who has been assigned that number. Keep so selecting until the entire sample total is reached.

The illustration above recapitulates what we have been describing. You will recall that our random number from the dollar bill was 45. This we selected as the entering number to find the random block within the table. For purposes of illustration, we shall assume that the total population consists of 90 individuals from which we shall select a sample of 40. We will need random numbers of two digits each.

Beginning in the upper left-hand corner of the designated block, and remembering

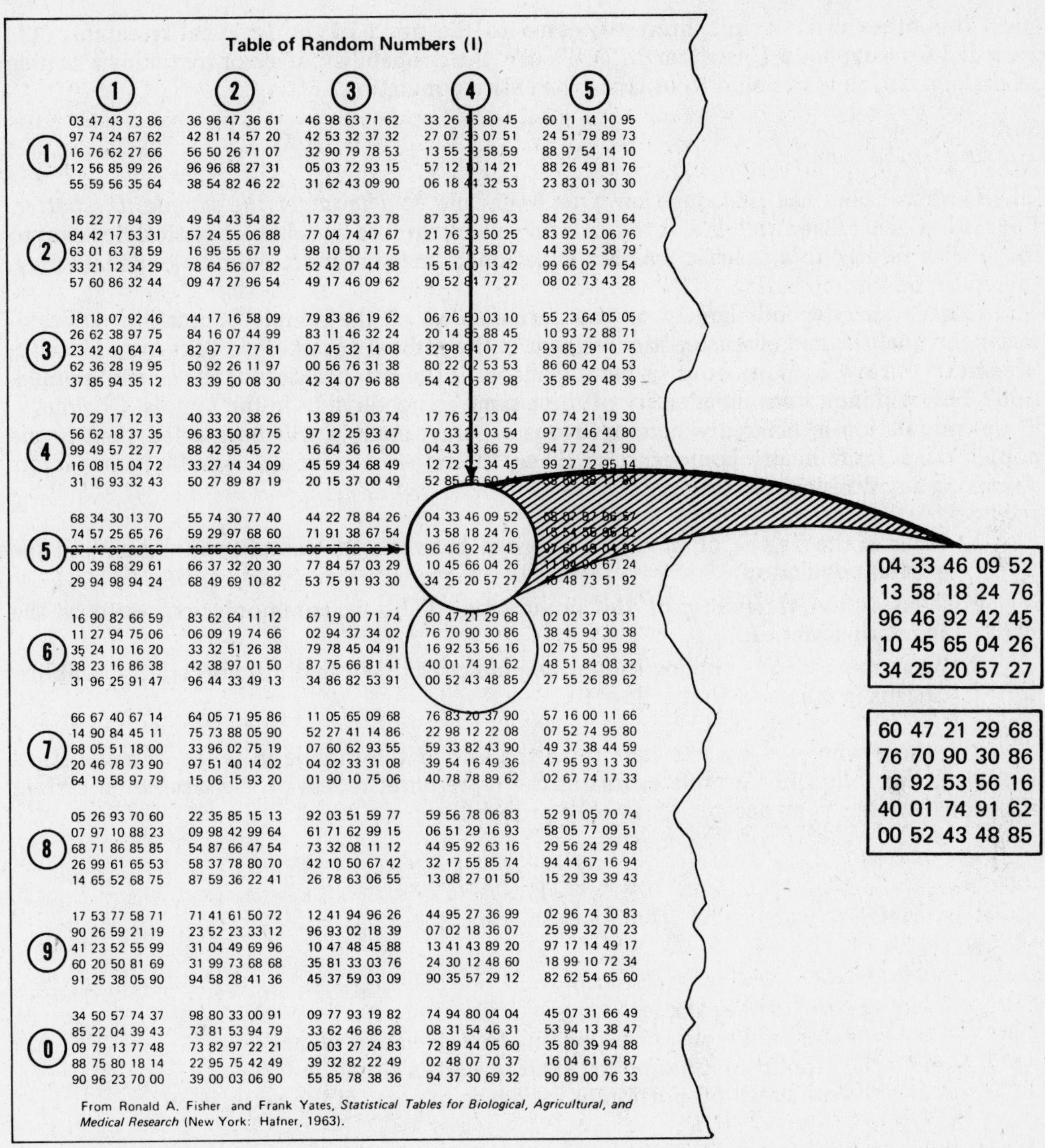

Table of Random Numbers (I)

	1	2	3	4	5
	03 47 43 73 86	36 96 47 36 61	46 98 63 71 62	33 26 16 80 45	60 11 14 10 95
	97 74 24 67 62	42 81 14 57 20	42 53 32 37 32	27 07 36 07 51	24 51 79 89 73
1	16 76 62 27 66	56 50 26 71 07	32 90 79 78 53	13 55 38 58 59	88 97 54 14 10
	12 56 85 99 26	96 96 68 27 31	05 03 72 93 15	57 12 10 14 21	88 26 49 81 76
	55 59 56 35 64	38 54 82 46 22	31 62 43 09 90	06 18 44 32 53	23 83 01 30 30
	16 22 77 94 39	49 54 43 54 82	17 37 93 23 78	87 35 20 96 43	84 26 34 91 64
	84 42 17 53 31	57 24 55 06 88	77 04 74 47 67	21 76 33 50 25	83 92 12 06 76
2	63 01 63 78 59	16 95 55 67 19	98 10 50 71 75	12 86 73 58 07	44 39 52 38 79
	33 21 12 34 29	78 64 56 07 82	52 42 07 44 38	15 51 00 13 42	99 66 02 79 54
	57 60 86 32 44	09 47 27 96 54	49 17 46 09 62	90 52 84 77 27	08 02 73 43 28
	18 18 07 92 46	44 17 16 58 09	79 83 86 19 62	06 76 50 03 10	55 23 64 05 05
	26 62 38 97 75	84 16 07 44 99	83 11 46 32 24	20 14 85 88 45	10 93 72 88 71
3	23 42 40 64 74	82 97 77 77 81	07 45 32 14 08	32 98 94 07 72	93 85 79 10 75
	62 36 28 19 95	50 92 26 11 97	00 56 76 31 38	80 22 02 53 53	86 60 42 04 53
	37 85 94 35 12	83 39 50 08 30	42 34 07 96 88	54 42 06 87 98	35 85 29 48 39
	70 29 17 12 13	40 33 20 38 26	13 89 51 03 74	17 76 37 13 04	07 74 21 19 30
	56 62 18 37 35	96 83 50 87 75	97 12 25 93 47	70 33 24 03 54	97 77 46 44 80
4	99 49 57 22 77	88 42 95 45 72	16 64 36 16 00	04 43 18 66 79	94 77 24 21 90
	16 08 15 04 72	33 27 14 34 09	45 59 34 68 49	12 72 07 34 45	99 27 72 95 14
	31 16 93 32 43	50 27 89 87 19	20 15 37 00 49	52 85 66 60 44	38 68 88 11 80
	68 34 30 13 70	55 74 30 77 40	44 22 78 84 26	04 33 46 09 52	68 07 97 06 57
	74 57 25 65 76	59 29 97 68 60	71 91 38 67 54	13 58 18 24 76	15 54 55 95 52
5	27 42 37 86 53	48 55 90 65 72	96 57 69 36 10	96 46 92 42 45	97 60 49 04 91
	00 39 68 29 61	66 37 32 20 30	77 84 57 03 29	10 45 66 04 26	11 04 96 67 24
	29 94 98 94 24	68 49 69 10 82	53 75 91 93 30	34 25 20 57 27	40 48 73 51 92
	16 90 82 66 59	83 62 64 11 12	67 19 00 71 74	60 47 21 29 68	02 02 37 03 31
	11 27 94 75 06	06 09 19 74 66	02 94 37 34 02	76 70 90 30 86	38 45 94 30 38
6	35 24 10 16 20	33 32 51 26 38	79 78 45 04 91	16 92 53 56 16	02 75 50 95 98
	38 23 16 86 38	42 38 97 01 50	87 75 66 81 41	40 01 74 91 62	48 51 84 08 32
	31 96 25 91 47	96 44 33 49 13	34 86 82 53 91	00 52 43 48 85	27 55 26 89 62
	66 67 40 67 14	64 05 71 95 86	11 05 65 09 68	76 83 20 37 90	57 16 00 11 66
	14 90 84 45 11	75 73 88 05 90	52 27 41 14 86	22 98 12 22 08	07 52 74 95 80
7	68 05 51 18 00	33 96 02 75 19	07 60 62 93 55	59 33 82 43 90	49 37 38 44 59
	20 46 78 73 90	97 51 40 14 02	04 02 33 31 08	39 54 16 49 36	47 95 93 13 30
	64 19 58 97 79	15 06 15 93 20	01 90 10 75 06	40 78 78 89 62	02 67 74 17 33
	05 26 93 70 60	22 35 85 15 13	92 03 51 59 77	59 56 78 06 83	52 91 05 70 74
	07 97 10 88 23	09 98 42 99 64	61 71 62 99 15	06 51 29 16 93	58 05 77 09 51
8	68 71 86 85 85	54 87 66 47 54	73 32 08 11 12	44 95 92 63 16	29 56 24 29 48
	26 99 61 65 53	58 37 78 80 70	42 10 50 67 42	32 17 55 85 74	94 44 67 16 94
	14 65 52 68 75	87 59 36 22 41	26 78 63 06 55	13 08 27 01 50	15 29 39 39 43
	17 53 77 58 71	71 41 61 50 72	12 41 94 96 26	44 95 27 36 99	02 96 74 30 83
	90 26 59 21 19	23 52 23 33 12	96 93 02 18 39	07 02 18 36 07	25 99 32 70 23
9	41 23 52 55 99	31 04 49 69 96	10 47 48 45 88	13 41 43 89 20	97 17 14 49 17
	60 20 50 81 69	31 99 73 68 68	35 81 33 03 76	24 30 12 48 60	18 99 10 72 34
	91 25 38 05 90	94 58 28 41 36	45 37 59 03 09	90 35 57 29 12	82 62 54 65 60
	34 50 57 74 37	98 80 33 00 91	09 77 93 19 82	74 94 80 04 04	45 07 31 66 49
	85 22 04 39 43	73 81 53 94 79	33 62 46 86 28	08 31 54 46 31	53 94 13 38 47
0	09 79 13 77 48	73 82 97 22 21	05 03 27 24 83	72 89 44 05 60	35 80 39 94 88
	88 75 80 18 14	22 95 75 42 49	39 32 82 22 49	02 48 07 70 37	16 04 61 67 87
	90 96 23 70 00	39 00 03 06 90	55 85 78 38 36	94 37 30 69 32	90 89 00 76 33

From Ronald A. Fisher and Frank Yates, *Statistical Tables for Biological, Agricultural, and Medical Research* (New York: Hafner, 1963).

04	33	46	09	52
13	58	18	24	76
96	46	92	42	45
10	45	65	04	26
34	25	20	57	27

60	47	21	29	68
76	70	90	30	86
16	92	53	56	16
40	01	74	91	62
00	52	43	48	85

that there are only 90 individuals in the total population, we see that by going down the leftmost column of numbers, we will begin by choosing from the total population individual number 4, and then individual number 13. The next number does not apply (since we have only 90 persons in the population and this is 96). Our next choices will be 10, 34, 60, 76, 16, 40, and again we ignore the 00, as well as the next number, 76, which has already been chosen.

We have perhaps said enough with respect to the use of a table of random numbers; but because randomization is so often effected by the use of just such a table, the foregoing discussion is probably justified.

Two other matters will, however, come to the mind of the practical researcher: (1) How large a sample do I need? and (2) What is the probability of error by taking a sample of the population as opposed to utilizing the entire population?

The Size of the Sample

Let's consider the first question. One basic rule is: *The larger the sample, the better.* But such a generalized rule is not too helpful to a researcher who has a practical decision to make with respect to a specific research situation. Somewhat more definite guidelines may, therefore, be formulated.

Sample size depends largely on the degree to which the sample population approximates the qualities and characteristics resident in the general population. Take homogeneity, for instance. How homogeneous or heterogeneous is the composition of the general population? This will indicate some identity of these same characteristics in the sample. Obviously, if the population is markedly heterogeneous, a larger sample will be needed than if the population is more nearly homogeneous. Thus, the researcher should consider three factors in making any decision as to sample size:

1. What is the degree of precision required between the sample population and the general population?
2. What is the variability of the population? (This is commonly expressed as the standard deviation.)
3. What method of sampling should be employed? (We shall discuss briefly sampling designs in the pages that follow.)

For those who may wish to determine the size of the sample in terms of a statistical approach, the following formula estimates the representativeness of the sample on certain critical parameters at an acceptance level of probability:

$$N = \left(\frac{z}{e}\right)^2 (p)\,(1-p)$$

Where

N = the size of the sample
z = the standard score corresponding to a given confidence level
e = the proportion of sampling error in a given situation
p = the estimated proportion or incidence of cases in the population

In considering the second question, namely, the probability of error by taking a sample of the population as opposed to utilizing the total population, we must consider how far the sample mean deviates from the mean for the total population. This is usually determined statistically through a determination of the *standard error of the mean.* This is determined as follows:

$$SE_{\overline{x}} = \frac{s}{\sqrt{N}}$$

$SE_{\overline{x}}$ = the standard error of the mean
s = the standard deviation of the sample
N = the number of units in the sample

This method of determining the standard error of the mean is true for both large and small samples. The sampling distribution of means is very nearly normal for $N > 30$ even when the population may be nonnormal.

Sampling Designs

We should discuss the most common types of sampling designs that are found in normative survey studies. Many times have we commented that all sound research data begins with a careful consideration of the data. What is the nature of the data? Methodology depends upon a careful answer to this question. That fact is equally true in sampling. You do not just go out to sample. No researcher is so naive to think that all you have to do in normative design research is merely "to pick a sample." Careful consideration of the total population is *most* important. This fact will become ever more important as we review the several types of sampling designs that are available for descriptive survey research.

The descriptive survey method demands that the researcher select from the general population a sample population which will be both logically and statistically defensible. The first step in selecting any sampling design is to analyze carefully the *integral characteristics of the total population.* In view of these, then, the researcher may select the sampling technique most appropriate for the population type.

The following comments have been taken from the Interviewer's Manual of the Survey Research Center of the Institute for Social Research of the University of Michigan.

> Survey sampling is the process of choosing, from a much larger population, a group about which we wish to make generalized statements so that the selected part will represent the total group. Such a sample must be very carefully selected so that it will faithfully represent the particular group being studied. No matter how good the gathering of data is, from such a group, the survey cannot be accurate if the people in the sample are improperly selected.
>
> The sampling procedures the Center uses are based on the same principles that would be used if a choice were made by listing each member of the group to be sampled on identical slips of paper, mixing the slips in a giant hopper, and drawing again and again until a large number of selections had been made. Obviously, it would take an inordinate amount of time and money to list all of the dwellings in the United States on slips of paper and then draw the required number of addresses from some enormous hopper. We can, however, save expense and trouble by *multi-stage sampling of areas.* This is accomplished in various steps:
>
> *Step 1: Primary Sampling Unit Selection.* We divide the entire geographical area of the United States into small areas which we call Primary Sampling Units. These units are usually counties or metropolitan areas because they are convenient units within which the interviewer can operate.
>
> *Step 2: Sample Place Selection.* Each of the Primary Sampling Units is further subdivided into smaller areas. For purposes of illustration, we shall consider the Primary Sampling Unit to be a county. Since there is only one large urban unit within the county no random selection will need to be made. Among the smaller towns selection would be made by randomization.
>
> *Step 3: Chunk Selection.* Each sample place, whether New York City or a rural township in Iowa, is divided into *chunks.* A chunk is an area having identifiable (but not necessarily visible) boundaries: a city block, a rural area bounded by roads, streams, or civil boundaries such as county lines. Chunks usually have an average of 20 to 30 dwelling units, although in large cities a chunk may have many more dwellings.
>
> *Step 4: Dividing Chunks into Segments.* Chunks are subdivided into smaller areas containing about 4 to 12 dwelling units. Always all decisions are made by means of pure random selection.

Step 5: Dwelling Unit Selection. About four dwellings are chosen from a given sample segment. If the original address does not produce an interview, the interviewer must not substitute one address for another. An unanswered doorbell does not entitle the interviewer to step next door. Substitutions would quickly destroy the representativeness of the sample.[7]

Reduced to a graphic presentation the Survey Research Center sampling method is as follows:

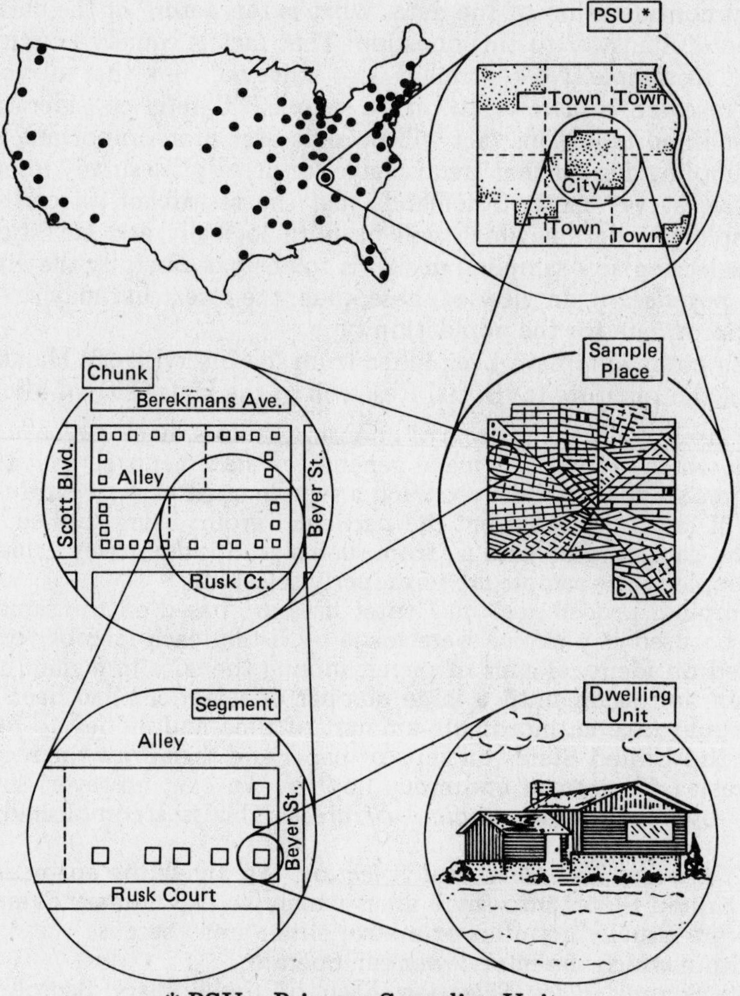

* PSU = Primary Sampling Unit

One further observation should be made concerning the methodology of the Survey Research Center in selecting the Primary Sampling Units. Each of these units is selected by chance. Chance, however, does not mean that they are selected haphazardly. They are chosen by a mathematical procedure so that the selection is random and purely the result of blind chance. The sampling technique employs a process known as *stratification* or *simple stratified sampling.* Stratification helps to select the proper proportion of different types of areas: for example, in selecting Primary Sampling Units the total population is stratified

---

[7] *Interviewer's Manual.* Survey Research Center, Institute for Social Research, Ann Arbor, Michigan: University of Michigan (1969), pp. 8-1 - 8-3. Some slight liberties have been taken with the wording of the *Interviewer's Manual* to adapt the thought to this textbook.

to select the proper number of urban areas and rural areas, eastern and western areas, and so on. This provides a balanced heterogeneity to the entire sample, and as great a homogeneity within each stratum as possible.

At this point, we may appropriately consider some of the characteristics of populations in general.

1. The population may be generally homogeneous. The separate units may be similar in observable characteristics.
2. The population may contain definite strata of discretely different units.
3. The population may contain definite strata but *each strata may differ from every other stratum* by a proportionate ratio of its separate stratified units.
4. The population may consist of clusters whose *cluster* characteristics are similar, but whose *unit* characteristics are as heterogeneous as possible.

If this is somewhat confusing to you, a study of the chart that follows will present the same information in a different format.

Population Characteristics and Sampling Techniques Appropriate for Each Population Type

Population Characteristic	Example of Population Type	Appropriate Sampling Technique
I Population is generally a homogeneous mass of individual units.	A quantity of flower seeds of a particular variety from which random samples are selected for testing as to their germination quality.	Simple random sampling
II Population consists of definite strata, each of which is distinctly different, but the units within the stratum as homogeneous as possible.	A particular town whose total population consists of three types (strata) of citizens: white, European-background type; black, African-background type; and Mexicano-Indian-background type.	Simple stratified sampling
III Population contains definite strata with differing characteristics and each strata has a proportionate ratio in terms of numbers of members to every other strata.	A community in which the total population consisted of individuals whose religious affiliations were found to be Catholic, 25 per cent; Protestant, 50 per cent; Jewish, 15 per cent; nonaffiliated, 10 per cent.	Proportional stratified sampling
IV Population consists of clusters whose cluster characteristics are similar yet whose unit characteristics are as heterogeneous as possible.	A survey of the nation's twenty leading air terminals by soliciting reactions from travelers who use them. (All air terminals are similar in atmosphere, purpose, design, etc., yet the passengers who use them differ widely in individual characteristics: age, sex, national origin, philosophies and beliefs, socioeconomic status, and so forth.)	Cluster sampling

All sampling procedures demand certain levels of "processing" of the sample. In all sampling, the following three processes are indigenous to the selection of the sample:

1. The population must be identified, an analysis made of its structure, and an assessment made of its characteristics.
2. The process of randomization must be outlined and the selection of the sample from the total population must be made in accordance with a method of the randomization.
3. The data must be extracted from the sample population.

The charts that follow on the next several pages show graphically the structuralization of each of the several methods of sampling.

Certain populations, particularly where their composition consists of disparate elements in proportional ratios, require an equalization process in addition to the three processes indicated above. The equalization process ensures proper balance among all the elements of the population in proportion to their relative strength or significance.

Schematically we may represent each of the sampling procedures as follows:

★ *Simple random sampling.* Simple randomized sampling is the least sophisticated of all sampling procedures. It consists of having a population whose texture is either homogeneous or homogeneously conglomerate. The derivation of the sample is by means of a simple randomization process. Schematically, the process of simple random sampling would look something like the flow chart following.

SIMPLE RANDOM SAMPLING DESIGN

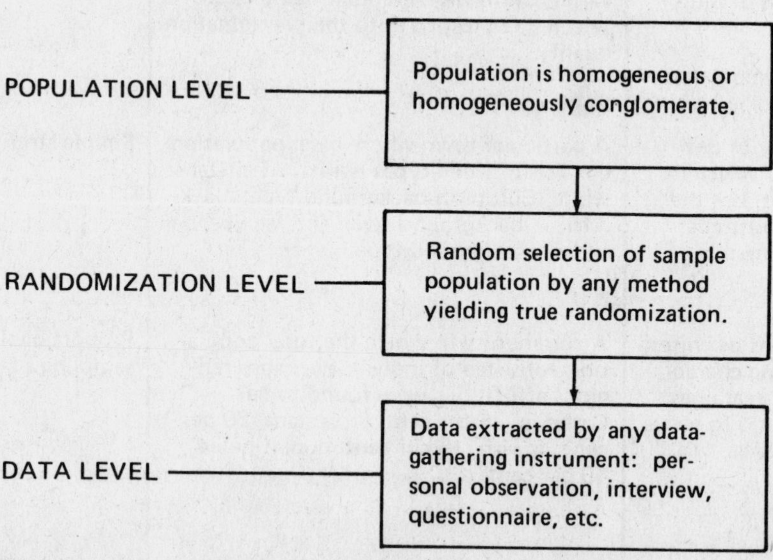
POPULATION LEVEL
Population is homogeneous or homogeneously conglomerate.
RANDOMIZATION LEVEL
Random selection of sample population by any method yielding true randomization.
DATA LEVEL
Data extracted by any data-gathering instrument: personal observation, interview, questionnaire, etc.

★ *Stratified random sampling.* In the stratified random-sampling design, certain differences between this process and the simpler method are at once apparent. The population, instead of a homogeneous mass, is composed of layers (strata) of discretely different types of individual units.

Think of grades 4, 5, and 6 in a public school. This is a *stratified population.* Generally, the stratification layers are somewhat equal—a schoolroom has just so much seating capacity. If we were to sample a population of fourth-, fifth-, and sixth-grade children in a particular school, we should probably take equal samples from each of the three grades. Our sampling design would look, then, like the following diagram, with the addition of one more level, the *equalization level*, at which point we would be careful to see that the sample was indeed representative of the entire population.

In the equalization process, we attempt to get three sub-populations of approximately the same size. To do so preserves equalization in one dimension, and the fact that all students within that particular sub-populational cell are all of the same grade level seeks to assure equalization in a second dimension. In this way, we can be reasonably assured that the population is not skewed or biased because of inequality in any of the cells.

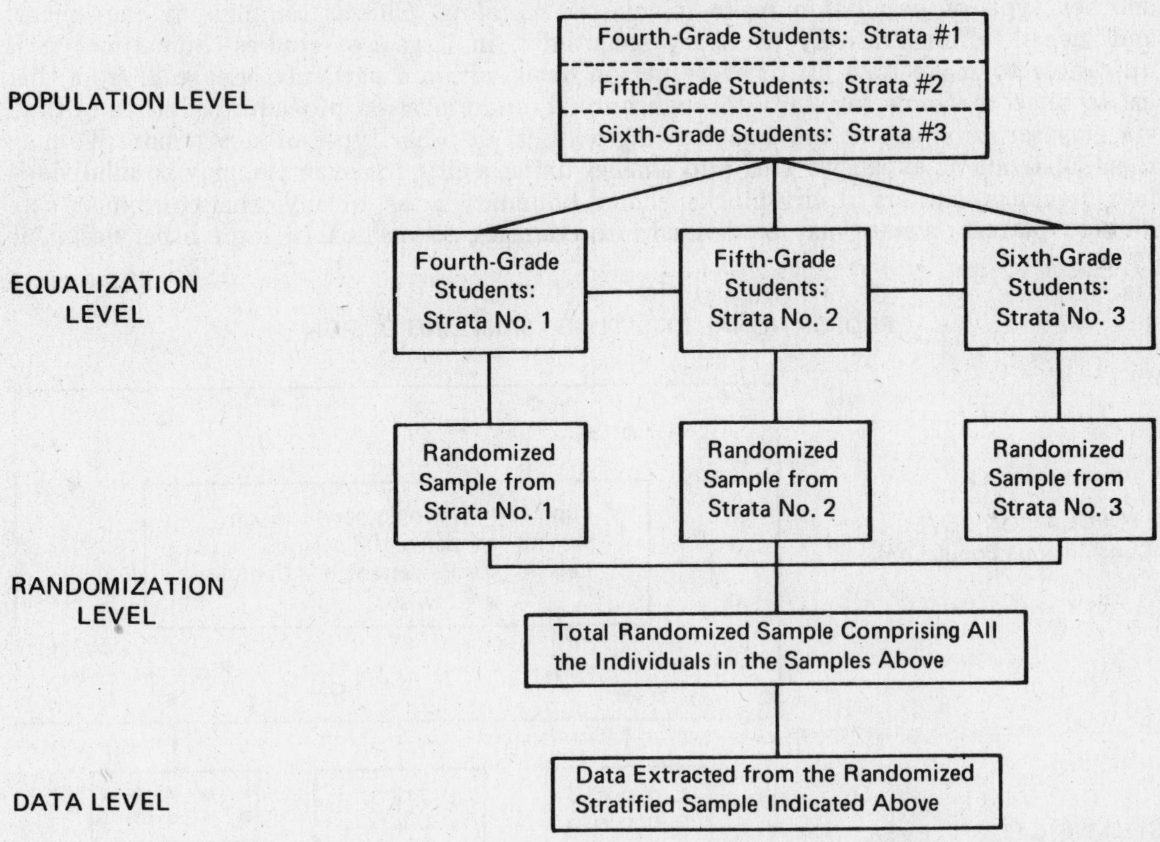

★ *Proportional stratified sampling.* We have just looked at the simple stratified random-sampling design. In it, all the strata of the population were essentially equal in size. But now we come to a population situation which is markedly different. Consider how different are the strata of religious groups within a community which has, for example, 3,000 Protestants, 2,000 Catholics, and 1,000 Jews. Let us postulate a survey situation. We have a local newspaper which publishes a religious section dealing with interfaith church news, religious events, and syndicated articles of interest to the religious community in general. The editor wishes to determine certain facts from his readership.

It is now obvious that, instead of an orderly stratification, as in the previous population, here the population is a conglomerate, religiously heterogeneous, proportional mixture in the ratio strength of 3 to 2 to 1. Unlike the three public school grades in which the separate homogeneous strata were arranged one above the other, in this population an *integral mixture of separate disparate units in conglomerate relationship* exists.

The first problem, therefore, is to effect a separation of the several discrete elements in the total population and from each of the individual groups, then, to select a random sample proportionately representative of the numerical strength of each of the components within the entire conglomerate structure.

The proportional stratified design may, therefore, be the answer to the problem. We have represented schematically the organizational structure of this type of sampling in the flow-chart below.

★ *Cluster or area sampling.* But we have not exhausted all of the population variants that exist in real life. Up to this point, the population structure has been either homogeneous, composed of layers of different units, or conglomerate; but now we come to still another type of population make-up, *cluster sampling.* Cluster sampling is convenient, and indeed administratively necessary sometimes, in large-area studies. Sometimes it is unfeasible to make up a list of every person living within a particular area and, from that list to select a sample for study through normal randomization procedures. In lieu of that, we may secure a map of the area showing political or other types of subdivision. We may then subdivide an expansive area into smaller units: a city, for example, may be subdivided into precincts, clusters of city blocks, school boundary areas, or any other convenient subdivision pattern; a state may be divided into counties, townships, or some other definable

PROPORTIONAL STRATIFIED SAMPLING DESIGN

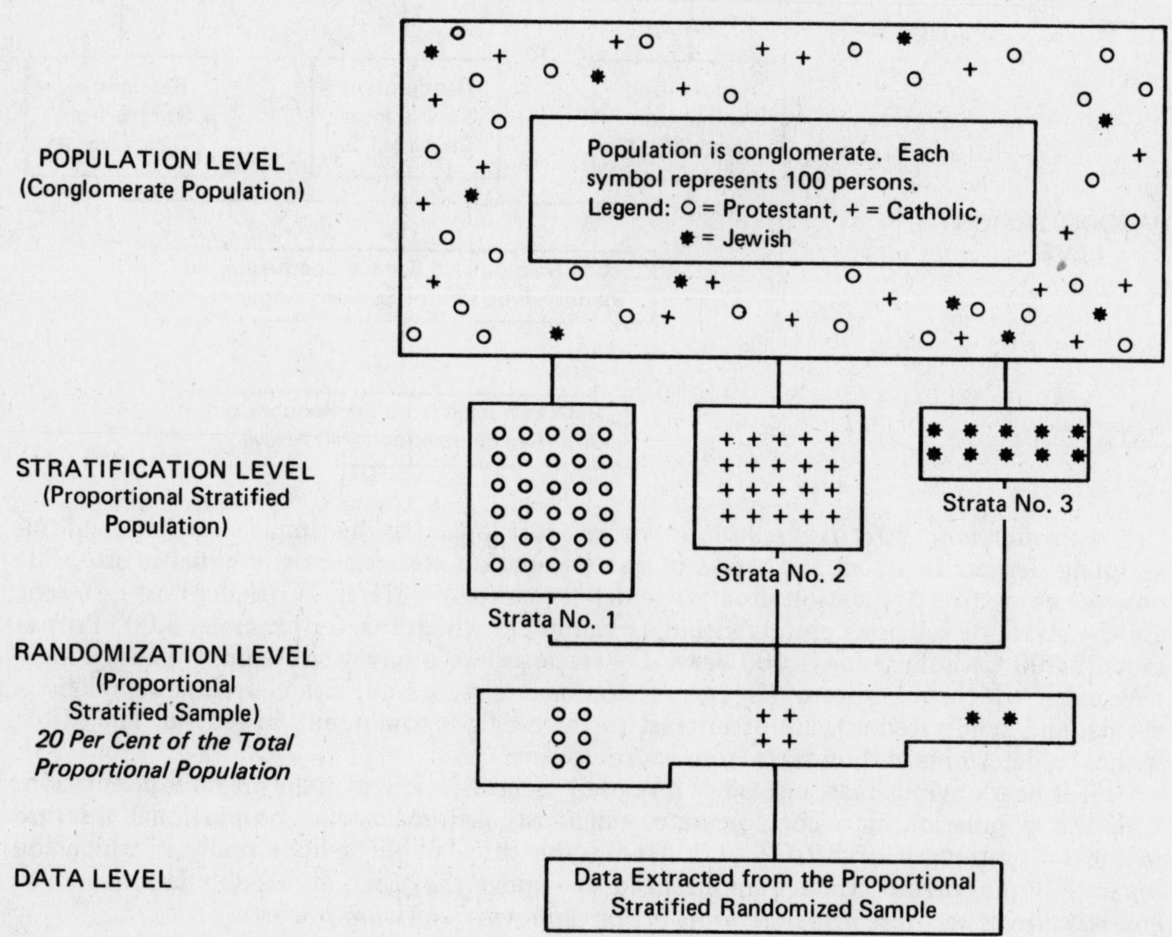

subdivision. In cluster sampling, it is important that each cluster be as similar to the other clusters as possible and yet that within the clusters the individuals be heterogeneous.

From all the clusters a random selection of specific clusters is made as the nucleus from which the sample population is ultimately derived, again by random selection. Let us take the previous situation with respect to the religious groups within a community. This we used to illustrate proportional stratified sampling. Let us assume that the community is a large city that we have divided into twelve areas or clusters. The design, schematically represented, is shown on this page.

★ *Systematic sampling.* Systematic sampling is the final major type of sampling design we will discuss in this chapter. Obviously, there are other ways of sampling, and variants of the basic designs that we have discussed. Any good text devoted to survey design or sampling

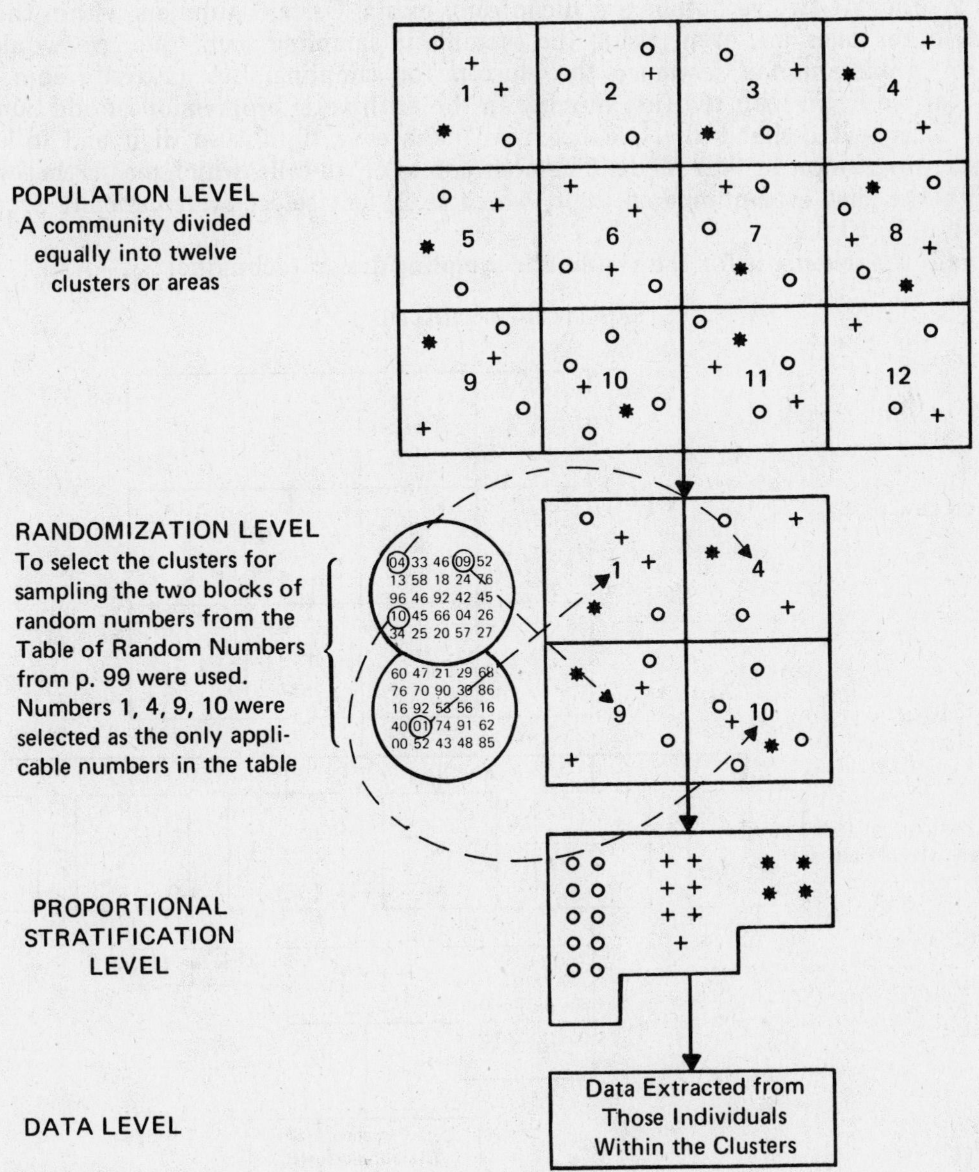

theory will discuss them all. The reason for the elaboration which has been here given in terms of the basic types is that in research planning and design where one is doing a descriptive survey study, the weak links in the chain are usually found in the techniques and procedures of sampling and in the unwitting admission of bias into the study. The subject of bias will be our next consideration. But bias can be minimized if the researcher has an intelligent and knowledgeable grasp of sampling procedures.

Systematic sampling is precisely what the name implies: the selection of certain items in a series according to a predetermined sequence. The origin of the sequence must be controlled by chance. Let us take the cluster diagram that we have just presented. Randomization was achieved in the discussion of the cluster sampling section by resorting to the table of random numbers. But there are other approaches that might have been employed.

There are twelve cells, or clusters, of the population as suggested by the schematic. We might have chosen through the technique of systematic sampling a group of clusters quite as much by chance as was done by benefit of the table of random numbers.

In a series of twelve numbers a dichotomy exists. Certain numbers within the series are odd, other ones are even. Using the systematic sampling technique, we would have chosen by *predetermined sequence* the clusters for sampling. Let us toss a coin. Heads dictate that we begin with the first number in the arithmetic progression of odd numbered clusters. Tails will demand that we begin with the even numbered digit and follow the arithmetic progression in that mode. The coin comes down tails, which means that we shall start with the first even-numbered digit, which is 2, and select *systematically sequential* clusters 4, 6, 8, 10, 12.

Here is the schematic for the systematic sampling design technique:

SYSTEMATIC SAMPLING DESIGN

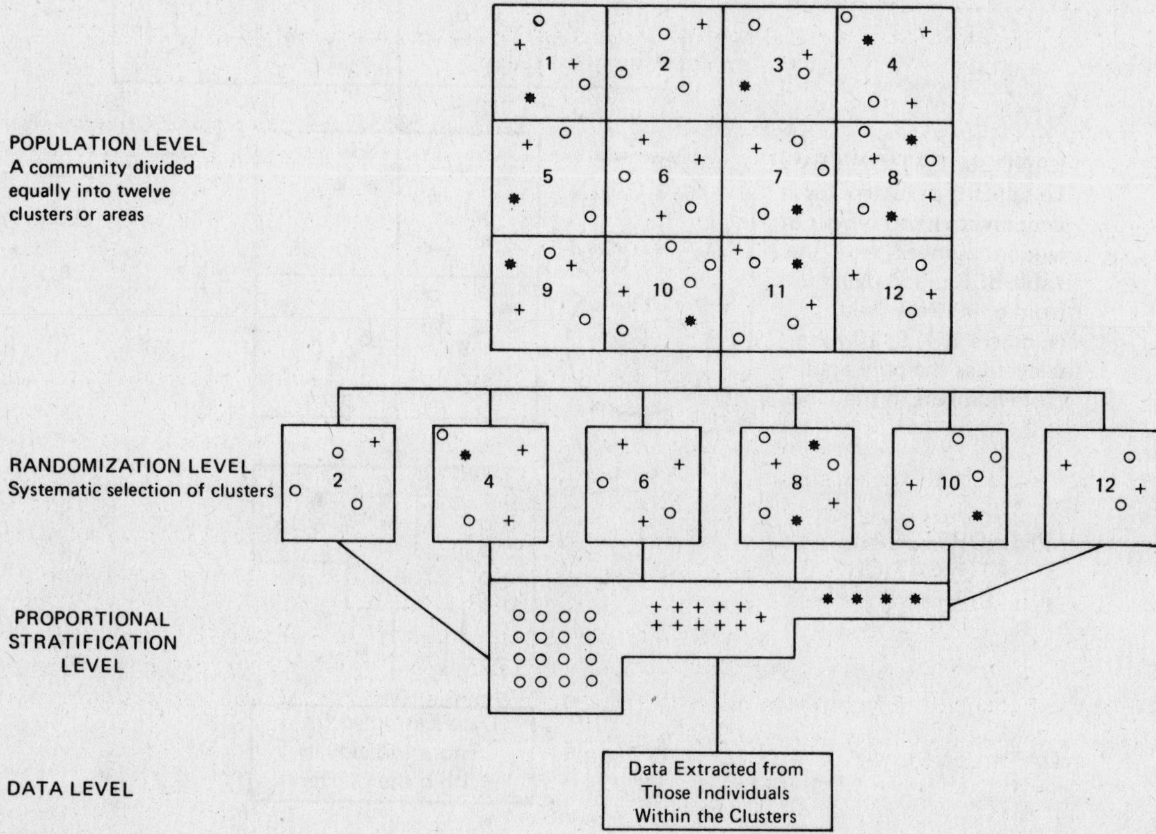

Before leaving this discussion of sampling design, the fact should be underscored that the design diagrams as presented on previous pages emphasize graphically the fact that each design is uniquely suited for the particular characteristics resident within various population situations. In choosing a sampling design, therefore, you should not choose blindly nor willy-nilly. The design should be considered, in a sense, as a *tool of research*, and this tool should be chosen with a full recognition of the task at hand and its discrete demands on the sampling procedure. A careful study of the diagrams and a consideration of the characteristics of the research population will aid in selecting the sampling design that is best suited to the parameters of that population.

BIAS IN THE RESEARCH DESIGN

We turn now to the matter of bias in the research design. In enumerating the basic characteristics of the descriptive survey method, we indicated that the researcher needed to be particularly alert for the presence of bias in descriptive or normative survey studies. *Data in descriptive survey research are particularly susceptible to distortion through the introduction of bias into the research design. Particular attention should be given, therefore, to safeguard the data from the influence of bias.*[8]

Bias is, of course, inherent in all research; but because it can infect the descriptive survey more easily than most other methodological genres and because it is sometimes difficult for the researcher to detect, we have chosen to discuss it here. We may define *bias as any influence, condition, or set of conditions, which, singly or together, cause distortion or aberration of the data from those which may have been obtained under the conditions of pure chance; furthermore, bias is any influence which may have disturbed the randomness by which the choice of a sample population has been selected.*

Data are, in many respects, delicate and sensitive to extraneous influences. We talk about the solid truth, the hard fact, and yet every researcher soon learns that data are neither so hard nor so solid as the hackneyed phrase might suggest. Data are highly susceptible to distortion.

Bias is frequently minute and imperceptible in its infiltration into the research design and may be easily overlooked by even the most sensitive and careful researcher. Bias attacks the integrity of the fact. It is particularly vicious when it enters surreptitiously into the research system and its presence and influence go undetected. It will render suspect even the most carefully planned research effort.

How Bias Enters the Research Design

The best way to appreciate bias is to see it at work. To understand precisely how bias does influence the data, let us take several instances and inspect them carefully. A researcher decides to use a city telephone directory as a source for selecting a random sample. He will open the page at random, close his eyes, put the point of his pencil down on the page, and the name that comes closest to the pencil point will be selected. You can't get much more random than that, he reasons. But the demon of bias is there. The selection made in the way it has been done does not represent the entire spectrum of the general population. The lower economic strata of the population will not be adequately represented because many of them are unable to afford a telephone and, hence, will not be represented in the book. The affluent also will not be adequately numbered among the general population because many of them have unlisted telephones. Hence the sample will be biased in the direction of middle-strata population.

---

[8] See page 134.

Questionnaire-type studies frequently also fall victim to bias, often without the awareness of the researcher. In questionnaire studies, the researcher is frequently more concerned about the percentage of the return of the questionnaire than about the bias influence which may be exerted by those subjects who do not return the questionnaire.

Let us take a very simple situation. A questionnaire is sent to 100 citizens, asking, "Have you ever been summoned by the Internal Revenue Service to justify your income tax return?" Seventy out of the 100 questionnaires are returned: Thirty-five of these reply that they have been summoned; thirty-five indicate that they have never been summoned. The researcher might conclude, therefore, that 50 percent of the respondents had never been summoned, and that 50 percent had received summonses. He may even make generalizations on this basis concerning the whole population. But this may be a very misleading conclusion. He is basing his assumption on the fact that he considers a 70 percent return of his questionnaire to be a "reasonably" good return and "that there are always some people who do not return questionnaires anyway" and so he writes off the 30 percent as "normal attritional loss" in any questionnaire study. What he may have overlooked is the inward motivation that may have influenced the 30 percent of the respondents not to return their questionnaires.

Being summoned to defend one's income tax return can be considered by many to be a reflection on one's integrity. For that reason, the nonrespondents may not have wanted to indicate that they had been summoned, and hence they may have ignored the whole matter. The bias growing out of an attempt to reserve one's integrity may have operated to distort truth of the situation. Instead of seemingly equally divided on a 50-50 basis, a 35 and 65 percent proportion may be more realistic figures.

Bias may also creep into the research in other innocuous ways. In interviewing, one's personality may affect the responses of the interviewee. In asking questions, the tone of one's voice, the inflection or accent within the sentence may influence the manner in which a respondent replies.

Two teachers, having been trained exactly alike, teaching classes whose composition is as nearly alike as it is possible to make it may, in a comparable study of their teaching—in which they apply the same methods, use the same texts, appear like mirror images of each other— be grossly influenced by bias which has seeped into the system from a number of sources:

1. The personality of each teacher is different.
2. Each class, no matter how carefully paired, is composed of individuals each of whom is different.
3. The inner group dynamics are different with each group.
4. Surroundings, modulated by such delicate influences as gradations of light, temperature, noise level, and other imperceptible factors alter individual reactions to the situation.
5. The preconditioning factors of the home environment of each student may reach into the classroom situation and affect that student's behavior and reactions within the class situation.

In each of the preceding situations, typical of the normal classroom—and we might go on to cite many more similar conditioning factors—we have influences, conditions, or sets of conditions which may cause distortion of the data.[9] When this happens, bias has affected the data arising out of the research situation.

[9] See definition of *bias*, page 161.

Acknowledgment of the Presence of Bias

It is almost impossible for man to live in this world without contacting microorganisms. Likewise, in the research environment, the researcher cannot avoid having his data contaminated by bias of one sort or another. What is inexcusable, however, is for the researcher not to acknowledge the likelihood of biased data or to fail to recognize the possibility of bias in the study. To interpret the data and to formulate conclusions without acknowledging the effect that bias may have had either in causing distortion of the data or in conditioning the outcome of the research is to demonstrate naiveté and an immature approach to serious research.

Those with greatest maturity in research skill demonstrate their integrity by admitting without reserve that bias is omnipresent and may very well have influenced their study. The most fearless among them will point out precisely how bias may have infiltrated the research design. With this knowledge, we may then appraise the research realistically and judge its merits honestly. Nothing is gained by ignoring what all of us know exists. Bias for the researcher, like the presence of germs for the surgeon, is next to impossible to avoid. As researchers, we must learn to live with bias, but at the same time to guard against its infective destruction.

Some students, however, strive so hard to make the data support their hypotheses that in so doing they deny the realities inherent in the research situation. Nothing is thereby gained. In research, we cannot force the facts to support anything. The facts should be, as much as possible, immune to influence of any kind, and should speak for themselves. If they are tainted with bias, we must accept that as an inevitable condition in most research, particularly in descriptive survey studies, and we should not be unduly upset by its presence.[10]

The Presentation and Interpretation of the Data in the Descriptive Survey Study

Data are of no value merely as data. In this discussion of descriptive research methodology, we have been discussing principally the acquisition of fact: how to winnow the data from the general population by appropriate techniques: questionnaires, interviews, sampling; how to protect those data against infection by distortion of bias. We have been thinking of the process of accumulation only; and, while amassing data is certainly a necessary aspect of research and one of the cardinal tenets of the scientific method, it is not the end for which the process of research was instituted. The purpose of research is to solve problems. It is to accomplish that purpose that we amass data.

In order to see the descriptive survey method in its proper perspective let us review some fundamental principles.

Survey Research Is More than Activity

At this juncture, it may be well to review what has already been said in Chapters 1 and 4 of this book. In these chapters, you were constantly reminded of two basic principles of research:

1. The purpose of research is to seek the answer to a problem in the light of the facts that relate to that problem.

[10]Note on page 143 the openness with which the researcher recognizes the likelihood of bias entering the study and not only acknowledges the fact but provides a technique for minimizing its effect: "This procedure was followed in order to eliminate bias in analyzing the tapes."

2. Although facts relative to the problem must be assembled for study and inspection, *the extraction of meaning from the accumulated data*—what we have called the *interpretation of the data—is all important.*

The descriptive survey method is a very "busy" research method from the standpoint of the researcher. Therein lies an element of danger. It demands more activity than perhaps other methodologies. It is also probably the most complex of all the research methodologies. In the light of the problem, the researcher must decide upon a population, study it, choose a technique for sampling it, determine how randomness will be guaranteed, minimize the entrance of bias into the study, send questionnaires or conduct interviews, or observe the data directly, record and systematize the facts gleaned through the survey, and perhaps do more that we have failed to mention. All this is enough to keep any researcher busy. The activity connected with descriptive research is complex, time-consuming, and distracting. With all this motion going on around him, it would not seem unreasonable if the researcher lost sight of the nuances of the problem and the subproblems. But it is precisely the problem and the subproblems that are the reason for all the rest of the activity.

All the activity is subordinate to the research itself. Sooner or later, all this activity must come to rest in an interpretation of the data and a setting forth of conclusions, drawn from the data, in order to resolve the problem being investigated.

Inexperienced researchers forget this. Activity for activity's sake is seductive. It gives them a sense of well-being to have amassed great quantities of data. Like Midas, looking at his hoard of gold, they lose sight of the ultimate demands that the problem itself makes upon those data. They feel that now all they need to do is to present the data in a series of displays and summaries: graphs, charts, tables. Unfortunately, these do nothing more than demonstrate the researcher's acquisitive skills and consummate ability to present the same facts in different settings.

Success Begins with the Initial Proposal

It is a frustrating and defeating experience for a researcher to have gone through all the activity of data gathering and processing and then to have a graduate committe turn down the effort because the data have not been interpreted, the hypotheses have not been resolved, or any one of many reasons such committees may give for not approving the student's efforts.

Success begins long before the tumult of activity begins. All research begins with a proposal. The proposal is a clear statement of the problem and the subproblems, the data and how these will be processed; and, most important of all, how they will be interpreted. It is at this critical juncture where most students fail to make the nexus that takes the research out of a mere activity occupation and transfers it to a research endeavor.

In planning research, in preparing the proposal, or in writing the research report, researchers come to the point where it is necessary to answer the life-and-death question: "How will the data be interpreted?" Here is where the success of the research effort hangs upon a thread.

Let us take a typical situation to see how many students attempt to answer that most important of all questions. We shall take a page from one student's proposal. It attempts to spell out how the student will interpret the data for the purpose of resolving a subproblem in a dissertation in economics dealing with labor relations. The general problem was to "analyze the attitudes of professional employees toward certain aspects of management policy and to evaluate the relationship between these attitudes and the responsibility of management to articulate such policy for its employees."

The student is spelling out the manner in which he expects to resolve a particular

Treatment of Each Specific Subproblem

Restatement of Subproblem 1. The first subproblem is to determine through an analysis of employee responses the attitudes of employees toward certain aspects of management policy for salary increases and merit pay.

The Data Needed

The data needed to resolve this subproblem are those employee responses to questions concerning salary increases and merit pay.

Where the Data Are Located

The data are located in the employee responses to questions 3, 7, and 13 of the questionnaire, "Survey of Employee Attitudes Toward Management."

How the Data Will Be Secured

The data will be secured by accurately tabulating all of the responses of employees to the above questions on the questionnaire.

How the Data Will Be Interpreted

From the responses of the questions a table will be constructed similar to the following structural model. It will indicate the employee attitudes, their frequency, and the percentage of these attitudes to the total attitude response to each question.

Attitude	Frequency	Percentage
Totals		

A graph will then be constructed to show which attitudes have received the greatest number of reactions and those which have had the least number of reactions. The median and the mean will also be found for the total group as a basis for comparison.

subproblem. The subproblem is: "What does an analysis of the attitudes of employees toward management policy for salary increases and merit pay reveal?" On page 000 is a page from the student's proposal, indicating how he intended to resolve this question.

Now, let us look at that page. First, consider the working of the subproblem:

> The first subproblem is to determine *through an analysis of employee responses* the attitudes of employees toward certain aspects of management policy for salary increases and merit pay.

Now read the section "How the Data Will Be Interpreted." What has the researcher really done? Has he *interpreted* (shown what the data mean) any of the data? Has he "determined" anything *through an analysis of employee responses?*

No! He has merely *tabulated* and *graphed* the data. He has rearranged it and presented it in another form. It, thus, remains as "raw" as it originally was in the questionnaire. Finally, the researcher informs us that he intends to find two points of central tendency for the data—the median and the mean. Why? What do these tell us about "attitudes of employees toward certain aspects of management policy. . ."? Median and mean of what?

The frequencies or percentages? Which? And for what purpose? What will these measures tell us about the "attitudes of employees"? What is the rationale of the statistical operation? These are primary questions that should be answered *in the proposal* as well as *in the student's own mind.*

If, at this juncture, the researcher returns to the subproblem and reads it carefully, he should see immediately that what he has suggested doing will never produce an *analysis* of employee responses, but merely an *amassing, a tabulating, a conversion, a statistical manipulation* of employee responses into another form. Granted, what he proposes to do may be the first step in preparing the data for analysis, but if he does what he affirms he intends to do, no analysis will be affected.

If, after codification of the data, the researcher had then considered it *analytically*, he would have resolved the responses into various gradational categories, he would have classified the responses into those supportive of and those opposed to managerial policies. He would have carefully reviewed each of the categories to discern the characteristics of each. Were those who supported management lukewarm in their support? What key words were used in their responses? What did the overall category response indicate about the group psychology behind the *attitudes of the employees* (Read the subproblem!)? What the student intended to do as expressed by the excerpt from the proposal would never have resulted in any indication of employee *attitude.*

Guidelines with Respect to Interpretation of the Data in the Descriptive Survey Study

We have said enough about the example. But from the foregoing discussion some basic guidelines for handling the data may be helpful.

★ *Be systematic in describing the treatment of the data.* In the proposal especially, indicate a logical systematic sequence of the steps necessary to solve *each* subproblem *separately.* Refer to Appendix A. Note how the author of the proposal there presented has taken each subproblem and clearly presented four steps in the resolution of it: what data were needed, where these data were located, how these data would be secured—many students know where the data are, but they have no idea how they will gain access to them—and, most importantly, how the data will be interpreted. Perhaps you would do well to repeat the subproblem immediately before explaining how the data will be interpreted. This restatement will keep in the forethought of the researcher precisely what goal the subproblem is aiming to achieve. Then *read* the subproblem *carefully.* Are there critically important "key" words: "to *determine* through employee responses the *attitudes* of employees"?

★ *State clearly the data you need to resolve the subproblem.* Under a heading, "The Data Needed," indicate specifically the data you will need for the resolution of the subproblem being investigated. Do not engage in generalities. The sample page just presented was excellent with respect to specifying the precise data needed. It indicated that the researcher needed responses to questions 3, 7, and 13 of the questionnaire.

★ *State precisely where the data are located.* With respect to the sample page presented, this section was largely a repetition of the preceding statement. Nothing is wrong with this. In research, better to repeat than to leave a hiatus that raises unresolved questions in the mind of the consumer of your research.

In some studies, however, where a student may need a certain kind of records—and this is particularly true with respect to historical research—the student should know precisely the exact location of these records. Too many students begin research projects assuming that records are available only to learn too late that either no records exist or that, if they do exist, they are in an inaccessible location or under such heavy restriction that they are not available. To face the question frankly, "Where are the data located?" and to answer such a question in writing by giving a specific address or a definite location for the repository for such records may clear the air at the beginning of one's research effort.

★ *State without equivocation how the data will be secured.* Again, with the sample page given above, little difficulty is presented at this point. The student already had the data! But suppose the data are letters of a famous person in possession of his family. You may know precisely where the letters are located; the next question is, how do you intend to get them for your research purposes? Perhaps in cases like this—or with any records under the control of others—the name and address should be given of the individual by whom the data are preserved. A statement should be included to the effect that this custodian of the data has consented for you to use them for research purposes. This should be clearly stated in the proposal so that your sponsor, your academic committee, the funding agency, or whoever may be interested in reading your proposal before the research is begun may see clearly that you have provided for all contingencies against failure to secure the data, which is a very common situation with many students who dream great dreams and upon the airy substance of them alone undertake research projects without sufficient preliminary groundwork.

★ *State fully and unequivocally precisely how you intend to interpret the data.* This is often the weakest link in any research endeavor. It is also the most difficult aspect of any research project. Truth, hope, faith are all fine in their place; but they cannot be substituted for clear thinking and hardheaded planning.

Some students, and others, who purport to do research, sometimes skirt this requirement by the subterfuge of employing vague and generalized language—so vague, so generalized that their statements are worthless from a practical research planning and design standpoint. A basic test for the adequacy of your statement of the treatment of the data is the following: *The plan for the treatment of the data should be so unequivocal and so specific that any other qualified person seeing only your proposal could carry out your research project without benefit of your presence and by means of your proposal alone.*

Every contingency should be anticipated; every methodological problem should be resolved. The degree to which you delineate how the data will be interpreted will auger the success or failure of your research endeavor. It is the key to research success, and it should be presented with utmost care and precision.

★ *Every step in the interpretation of the data should be fully spelled out.* Too many students assume this is unnecessary. They prefer to cut corners. They assume that others know what they mean and so they avoid taking the trouble to express it. All these assumptions are false. Too many students attempt to do in a tenth of a page what they should take ten pages to do. We may add that those who apply for funding for their projects frequently suffer from the same deficiency.

Spelling out the treatment and the interpretation of the data is a tedious, time-consuming, lengthy process. To attempt to relegate it to the broad sweep, the quick and easy statement, the careless approach is almost invariably to court disaster. Certain procedural guidelines may, therefore, be given.

•••*Ask yourself continually just what it is that you are doing.* Research is euphoric. Make a clear distinction between *arraying* the data and *interpreting* the data. Tables, charts, graphs, maps—all these contrivances—are merely ways of arraying the data. The process is repackaging. All these intermediate modalities for data may be highly important to its ultimate interpretation. This is not to disparage or discredit their function; it is merely to see without confusion clearly.

•••*Insist that your statistics have a defensible rationale.* It is pointless to tell us you will derive the mean and/or standard deviation and stop there. Why do you need these statistical values? How will they help you derive meaning from the data? Is this statistical manipulation of the data indispensable to the understanding of it? What are your formulas?

Why did you choose these formulas? Where did you get them? (Footnote your source, and give the symbol equivalents.)

•••*At what specific point does the manipulation of the data cease and your own thinking begin?* There is a point in every project where fumbling with the facts ceases and research begins. Unless you can indicate the precise point where you assume control of the data—where the ministrations of computers, graphics, tabulations, and so forth cease—and unless you can describe what role *you* will play in processing the data, you should be very circumspect in calling whatever you have done *interpretation* of the data. Only the genius of human insight can cause dead facts to speak. There is no other way.

★ *The research process is cyclical.* That the entire research process is cyclical was one of the basic propositions with which this book began. Because we have been considering a subunit of the total research design—namely, the treatment of the data with respect to a subproblem—we find that the principle of circularity applies here equally as well as it does with the overall design. The difference is, however, that here it is only a shrunken orbit of the greater circular process.

To test the circularity and, likewise, the validity of your research design use the "If-Test" technique. It goes like this:

The If-Test Technique

1. The point of beginning is the subproblem. State it completely. Then answer the following seven questions.
2. If I have this subproblem, what data do I need to resolve it?
3. If I need these data, where are they located?
4. If they are located there, how can I obtain them?
5. If I can obtain them, what do I intend to do with them?
6. If I do that with the data, will the result of doing it resolve my subproblem?
7. If my subproblem is resolved, then what hypothesis was I testing based on that subproblem?
8. If that was my hypothesis, what do the facts show with respect to the support or rejection of it?
9. If my hypothesis is supported, I hypothesized correctly.
10. If my hypothesis is not supported, then I have discovered something that I did not suspect to be so.

★ *Be sure the data support your conclusions.* Unfounded enthusiasm is one of the hazards you will need to guard against. One of the marks of the immature researcher is that, bewildered by the many data he must handle or dazzled by a newly emerging concept, he makes extravagant claims or reaches enthusiastic conclusions that are not warranted by the data. Research indeed is an exciting quest, but the researcher must learn—particularly the one who is doing a descriptive survey study—that though his data frequently lie close to the vibrant pulse of life, he cannot permit this to influence his objective judgment of their message. Archimedes running through the streets of Athens screaming, "I have found it." is perfectly justified to make his claim after he is sure that he has found it. It was only after the Athenian bathtub ran over that he reached his conclusion. Much research contains unfounded conclusions unsupported by the data and based upon shaky statistical procedures or unwarranted extrapolation of the facts. Research, particularly the descriptive survey study, should rest solidly and completely upon its own factual foundation.

Look the facts steadfastly in the face. Report honestly what those facts reveal to you. That is good research; that is also excellent descriptive survey reporting.

Practical Application —

Turn to Appendix B, pages 295–297 where you will find a practical application of some of the matters discussed in this chapter. (Projects 7 and 8.)

— —

FOR FURTHER READING

Further Reading in the General Area of the Descriptive Survey Method

Babbie, Earl R. *Survey Research Methods.* Belmont, Calif.: Wadsworth Publishing Co., Inc., 1973.

Cartwright, D. P. "Analysis of Qualitative Material," in *Research Methods in the Behavioral Sciences.* Edited by L. Festinger and D. Katz. New York: Holt, Rinehart and Winston, 1953.

Deming, W. E. *Sample Design in Business Research.* New York: John Wiley and Sons, 1960.

Dillman, Don A. *Mail and Telephone Surveys: The Total Design Method.* New York: John Wiley & Sons, 1978.

Goldstein, H., and B. H. Kroll. "Methods of Increasing Mail Response." *Journal of Marketing* 22 (1957): 55-57.

Holley, F. S. and L. L. Barker. "Assessing Effect Size in Communication Research: A Case Study." *Communication Quarterly* 56 (September 1979): 269–76.

Miller, Delbert C. *Handbook of Research Design and Social Measurement.* New York: David McKay Co., Inc., 1970.

Namias, Jean. *Handbook of Selected Sample Surveys in the Federal Government.* New York: St. John's University Press, 1969.

Niles, A. G. "Using Survey Research Methodology: An Examination of One Project." *Journal of Continuing Education in Nursing* 12 (November -December 1981): 28–34.

Partan, Mildred. *Surveys, Polls, and Samples.* New York: Harper and Brothers, 1950.

Selvin, Hanan C. "A Critique of Tests of Significance in Survey Research." *American Sociological Review* 22 (October 1957), 519-27.

Sinquist, John A., and William C. Dunkelberg. *Survey and Opinion Research: Procedures for Processing and Analysis.* Englewood Cliffs, N.J.: Prentice-Hall, Inc., 1977.

Warwick, Donald P., and Charles A. Lininger. *The Sample Survey: Theory and Practice.* New York: McGraw-Hill Book Company, 1975.

Weisberg, Herbert F., and Bruce D. Bowen *An Introduction to Survey Research and Data Analysis.* San Francisco, Calif: W. H. Freeman and Company, Publishers, 1977.

Williams, Thomas R. "A Critique of the Assumptions of Survey Research." *Public Opinion Quarterly* 23 (Spring 1959): 55–62.

Further Reading in the Use of the Questionnaire

Berdie, Douglas R., and John F. Anderson. *Questionnaires: Design and Use.* Metuchen, N.J.: The Scarecrow Press, 1974.

Bradburn, Norman M., and Seymour Sudman. *Improving Interview Method and Questionnaire Design.* San Francisco, Calif. Jossey-Bass Publishing Co., 1979.

Brandt, K. "The Usefulness of a Postcard Technique in a Mail Questionnaire Study." *Public Opinion Quarterly* 19 (1955): 218-22.

Clausen, J. A., and R. N. Ford. "Controlling Bias in Mail Questionnaires." *Journal of the American Statistical Association* 42 (1947): 497-511.

Colley, R. H. "Don't Look Down Your Nose at Mail Questionnaires." *Printer's Ink* (March 16, 1945): 21-108.

Flitter, H. "How to Develop a Questionnaire." *Nursing Outlook* 8 (October 1960): 566–69.

Frazier, G., and Bird, K. "Increasing the Response to a Mail Questionnaire." *Journal of Marketing* 23 (1958): 186-87.

Futrell, Charles M., and Charles W. Lamb, Jr. "Effect on Mail Survey Return Rates of Including Questionnaires with Follow-up Letters." *Perceptual and Motor Skills* 52 (February 1981): 11-15.

Herzog, A. Regula, and Jerald G. Bachman. "Effects of Questionnaire Length on Response Quality." *The Public Opinion Quarterly* 45, (Winter 1981): 549-59.

Kahn, R. L. "A Comparison of Two Methods of Collecting Data for Social Research: The Fixed-alternative Questionnaire Method and the Open-ended Interview." Unpublished Ph.D. Dissertation, Ann Arbor, Mich.: University of Michigan, 1962.

Kendall, Patricia L. *Conflict and Mood Factors Affecting Stability of Response.* Glencoe, Ill.: The Free Press, 1954.

Kornhauser, A., and P. B. Sheatsley. "Questionnaire Construction and Interview Procedure," in C. Selltiz, L. S. Wrightman, and S. W. Cook, *Research Methods in Social Relations*, 3rd ed. New York: Holt, Rinehart and Winston, 1976, Appendix B.

Oppenheim, Abraham N. *Questionnaire Design and Measurement.* New York: Basic Books, 1966.

Wiasanen, F. B. "A Note on the Response to a Mailed Questionnaire," *Public Opinion Quarterly* 18 (1954): 210-12.

Further Reading in the Use of the Interview

Brady, John. *The Craft of Interviewing.* Cincinnati, Ohio: Writer's Digest, 1976.

Benney, Mark, David Riesman, and Shirley Star. "Age and Sex in the Interview," *American Journal of Sociology* 62 (1956): 143-52.

Carp, Frances M. "Position Effects on Interview Responses," *Journal of Gerontology* 29 (1974): 581-87.

Dexter, Lewis A. *Elite and Specialized Interviewing.* Evanston, Ill: Northwestern University Press, 1970.

Garrett, Annette. *Interviewing: Its Principles and Methods.* 3rd rev. ed., Edited by Margaret Mangold and Eleanor Zaki. New York: Family Service Association of America, 1982.

Gordon, R. L. *Interviewing: Strategy, Techniques and Tactics.* Rev. ed. Homewood, Ill.: Dorsey Press, 1975.

Hyman, Herbert H. and William J. Cobb. *Interviewing in Social Research.* Chicago, Ill.: University of Chicago Press, 1954.

Katz, Daniel. "Do Interviewers Bias Polls?" *Public Opinion Quarterly.* 6 (1942): 248-68.

Maccoby, Eleanor E., and Nathan Maccoby. "The Interview: A Tool of Social Science," In *Handbook of Social Psychology*, edited by Gardner Lindzey. Reading, Mass.: Addison-Wesley Publishing Co., 1954.

Richetto, Gary M., and Joseph P. Zima: *Interviewing.* Chicago, Ill: Science Research Associates, 1981.

Stewart Charles J., and William B. Cash, Jr. *Interviewing: Principles and Practices.* 3rd edition. Dubuque, Iowa: William C. Brown Company, Publishers, 1982.

Survey Research Center Staff, Institute of Social Research. *Interviewer's Manual.* Ann Arbor, Mich.: Institute of Social Research, University of Michigan, 1976.

Further Reading in the Area of Sampling

Arnold, David O. "Dimensional Sampling: An Approach for Studying a Small Number of Cases," *American Sociologist* 5 (May 1970): 147-50.

Assael, H., and J. Keen. "Nonsampling *vs.* Sampling Errors in Survey Research." *Journal of Marketing* 46 (Spring 1982): 114-23.

Brown, Roscoe C., Jr. "Is There an Optimal Sample Size for Research Involving Human Subjects? Is There a Rule-of-Thumb That Might Be Used in Determining Sample Size?" *Nursing Research* 25 (January–February 1976): 62.

Cochran, William G. *Sampling Techniques.* 3rd edition. New York: John Wiley and Sons, 1977.

Davis, Kingsley, and Wilbert E. Moore. "Some Principles of Stratification," *American Sociological Review* 10 (April 1945): 242–49.

Deming, William E. *Sample Design in Business Research.* New York: John Wiley & Sons, 1960.

Green, Roger H. *Sampling Design and Statistical Methods for Experimental Biologists.* New York: John Wiley & Sons, 1979.

Hansen, M. H., William N. Hurwitz and William G. Meadow. *Sample Survey Methods and Theory.* 2 vols. New York: John Wiley & Sons, 1953.

Kish, Leslie. *Survey Sampling.* New York: John Wiley & Sons, Inc., 1965.

McCall, Chester H., Jr. *Sampling and Statistics Handbook for Research in Education.* Ames, Iowa: Iowa State University Press, 1982.

Slonim, Morris J. "Sampling in a Nut Shell." *Journal of the American Statistical Association* 52 (June 1957): 143–61. Also issued as a paperback in the Fireside series by Simon and Schuster, New York, 1960.

Som, R. K. *A Manual of Sampling Techniques.* London: Wm. Heinemann Limited, 1973.

Sudman, Seymour. *Applied Sampling.* New York: Academic Press, Inc., 1976.

Tumin, Melvin M. "Some Principles of Stratification: A Critical Analysis." *American Sociological Review* 18 (August 1953): 387–94.

Warwick, Donald P., and Chester A. Lininger. *Sample Survey: Theory and Practice.* New York: McGraw-Hill Book Company, 1975.

Miscellaneous References

Edwards, Allen L. *Techniques of Attitude Scale Construction.* New York: Appleton-Century-Crofts, 1957.

The RAND Corporation. *A Million Random Digits.* New York: The Free Press, 1955.

Selby, Samuel M. *Standard Mathematical Tables.* 21st edition. Cleveland, Ohio: The Chemical Rubber Co., 1973.

Summers, Gene F., ed. *Attitude Measurement.* Chicago, Ill: Rand McNally & Company, 1970.

Tull, Donald S., and Gerald S. Albaum. "Bias in Random Digit Dialed Surveys." *Public Opinion Quarterly* 41 (1977): 389–95.

READ THIS—BEFORE YOU READ THIS CHAPTER

The nature of the data alone dictates the research methodology. The historical method relies upon data in the form of records and accounts of past events. The descriptive survey method—which we have just examined in Chapter 8—is best served by data which come to the researcher in the form of observations of one kind or another. In this chapter the data is of still a different type.

In the analytical survey methodology, the data are quantified: they reach the researcher as mathematical or statistical concepts. We describe them in the language of numbers and numerical values.

This chapter, then, will discuss the management of data by statistical means. Our discussion will provide an avenue of insight that has been denied us by the other methodologies. This chapter does not purport to give an in-depth understanding of statistical analysis but merely will indicate how data may be interpreted by using the statistical assistance available to the researcher.

For those who need further help in meeting specific research situations, the chapter closes with an extensive bibliography on statistical approaches particularly suited to discrete research areas.

9
The Analytical Survey Method

The previous chapter has been devoted to a discussion of observational type studies. The researcher describes what he has seen. If he employs statistics in the purely descriptive survey, his techniques are probably those of first-layer older-order statistics which reveal the points of central tendency, variation, and the degree of interrelationship between the variables in the data—that branch of statistics commonly called *descriptive statistics.*

In descriptive surveys, the data have more of a tendency to be verbal because descriptive studies deal with inquiries—questionnaires and interviews—and simple observational information.

THE NATURE OF THE DATA IN ANALYTICAL STUDIES

We come now to a research methodology in which the data are of an entirely different type. The analytical survey study takes data that are essentially *quantitative* in nature and analyzes these data by means of appropriate statistical tools. The purpose is to probe those data by means of statistics so that we may infer certain meanings which lie hidden within the data or, if not that, to discern the presence of certain potentials and dynamic forces which may be a clue to areas that warrant further investigation. In the analytical survey, we are concerned primarily with *problems of estimation* and the *testing of statistically based hypotheses.* The methods employed are those techniques that are generally referred to as belonging to the domain of *inferential statistics.*

We have stressed earlier the necessity of considering the data in terms of their basic qualities and essential nature, of seeing their distinguishing characteristics before adopting a particular methodological approach. Here, as elsewhere, the general rule is that *the data determine the research method.*

Let us now look briefly at the essential nature of *quantitative data.* First, they are *measurable.* Measurement of data is expressed by means of various scales of value. We generally recognize four basic scalar categories for classifying analytical-survey data:

1. *The nominal scale* is the grossest of the differentiational scales. It merely expresses categorical classifications—e.g., boys, girls.
2. *The ordinal scale* is the scale next in refinement, indicating a measurement of *degree* of difference—e.g., more boys, more girls; twice as many boys as girls.
3. *The interval scale* for which a *unit of measurement* has been established—e.g., Tom is *3 inches* [indicating three standard measurement *units*] taller than Kathy.
4. *The ratio scale* in which the values are measured from an absolute or arbitrary designated zero point. The ratio scale measures multiples of one value over another. Examples: This solution of H_2SO_4 has *twice* the acid content of that one. The temperature measures *25°* Celsius.

It is important to keep these four qualitative aspects of the data firmly in mind because later in the discussion of this chapter, we shall show that it is on the basis of the measurement characteristics of the data that we select the most appropriate statistical treatment for those data.

Data have also two other characteristics. Data may be either *discrete* or *continuous. Discrete* data are those which arise from *the process of counting.* The *number* of apples in a bushel, the *number* of eggs in a dozen, the *number* of people in a city are all examples of discrete data. *Continuous* data arise from the measurement of a process which is a *part of a continuum*. Length, width, time, and age values are all continuous data. These data merge into an unbroken flow of units, into a continuum of values.

So much, then, for the characteristics of data. Let us now review certain considerations with respect to statistics.

STATISTICS

Statistics as a part of the science of mathematics goes back to earliest times. The word comes from the word for *state*, and it was as a function of the business of the state that statistics first arose. Originally, statistics was a system of counting employed by the early states and kingdoms to account for their resources. It was used to count people. Moses was commanded to account for the children of Israel and, in fact, the Book of Numbers in the Bible is precisely that, a census of the Israelites. Ancient Egypt, as early as 3050 B.C., Babylonia, and Rome all used statistical data for levying taxes and assessing their military strength. Perhaps the earliest and most famous statistical compilation among English-speaking peoples is the famous Domesday Book, dating from A.D. 1086, in which William the Conqueror directed that a complete record be made of the lands, resources, and population of early England.

The *Oxford Universal Dictionary* indicates the old as well as the more recent meaning of the word *statistics:*

> *In early use, that branch of political science dealing with the collection, classification, and discussion of facts bearing on the condition of the state or the community.*
>
> *In recent use, the department of study that has for its object the collection or arrangement of numerical facts or data, whether relating to human affairs or to natural phenomena.*[1]

The Organization of Statistics

Statistics as an academic discipline has made great advances within recent years. At this point, we should indicate broadly the divisions of statistics and the purpose and function of each division, particularly the role of inferential statistics in dealing with the problems inherent to analytical survey studies. The map of the statistical landscape looks something like this:

The following organizational chart of the realm of statistics should be viewed with some tolerance. The more one knows about research (which is another way of saying that the more one knows about life and the nature of its factual matrix), the less one is sure that anything as closely associated with life processes—such as statistics is—can be neatly isolated and boxed into discrete cubicles. Although the determination of the mean is generally thought of as lying in the domain of descriptive statistics, the testing of an assumption with respect to the population mean as postulated from the sample is conceded to be a problem in the area of statistical inference.

Researchers, especially those whose mathematical backgrounds are somewhat weak, regard statisticians in much the same way as the general public once regarded the alchemists

---

[1] *The Oxford Universal Dictionary on Historical Principles*, 3rd edition, edited by C. T. Onions (Oxford: The Clarendon Press, 1955), p. 2007.

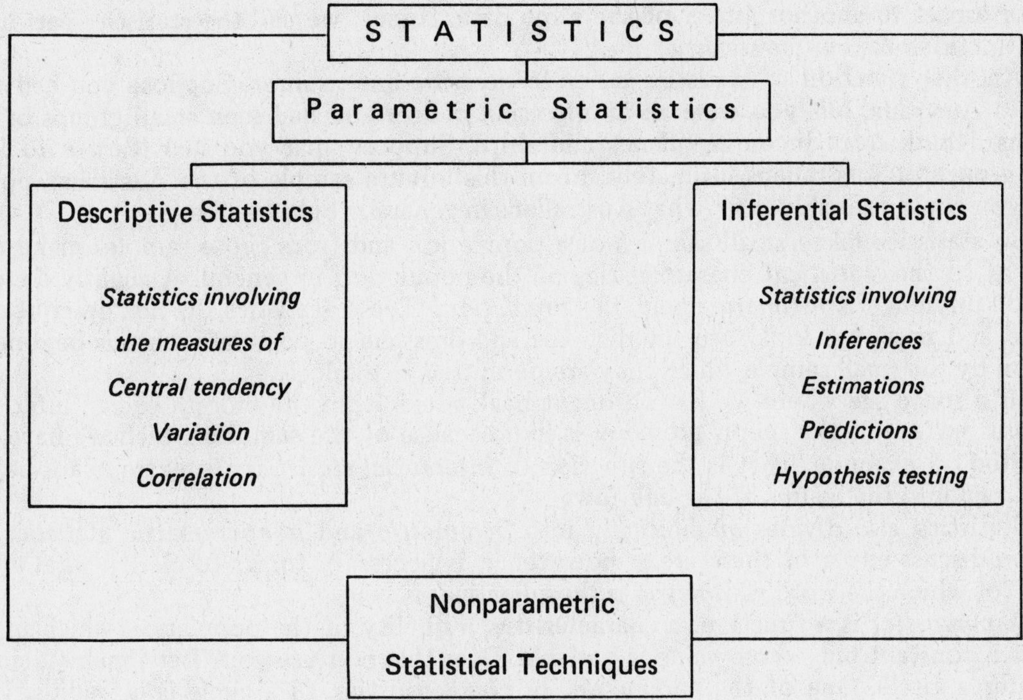

of medieval times: wizards who wield their unnatural powers by means of a strange mystique enshrouded in statistical jargon and expressed as a bizarre statistical formula. The researcher who neither understands the logic nor appreciates the expressive power of statistics is awed by it.

Statistics is a language through whose expressive power those concepts and relationships can be expressed which cannot be communicated in any other way. When one sees statistics in the proper perspective, one sees it as a language—eloquent and adequate—that is capable of expressing facts—frequently hidden from the mind as well as from the eye—which through no other channel of communication can be articulated or made manifest to our comprehension and understanding.

As we have said in an earlier chapter, we do not presume in this text to make any attempt at teaching statistics for research purposes. Any library will furnish adequate volumes to this end. What we shall attempt to do here is to try to clear away some of the underbrush that so often confuses and impedes the progress of research students because they become bewildered in an area whose overall plan they do not comprehend and whose potential for solving their research problems they do not appreciate. We shall try, therefore, to clarify only a few basic concepts and principles with respect to the application of statistics to the demands of the analytical survey method. We shall attempt to create some awareness of the role of statistics in terms of function, possibilities, and limitations in dealing with those problems inherent to analytic survey research.

The Divisions of Statistics

Statistics divides in two ways: first in terms of its *functional* aspects—namely, statistics whose function is to *describe the data*. This branch of statistics describes what the data look like: where their center is, how broadly they spread, and how they are related in terms of one aspect to another aspect of the same data. Hence, we call the statistics performing such functions *descriptive statistics*.

Another function of statistics is not to describe but to *infer*. Suppose you had never been to Australia, but you were an immigration officer and had seen small groups of Australians debark from incoming planes and ships. Suppose that you had learned to know small groups of Australians intimately. From this minute sample of the Australian population, you could probably *infer* what Australians in general would be like.

So statistics takes small samples of a population and from those samples make inferences as to the *statistical* characteristics of the population in general. A slightly different type of inference is *estimation* and the *prediction*. These statistics do not describe what is here and now, but look into the distance and presume to postulate what is beyond the horizon by the small sample which they are permitted to explore.

In a space age where we have brought back rocks from the moon, we can infer what the total surface of the moon probably is like because of the samples which we have been permitted to examine. That is the function of *inferential statistics*: to extrapolate beyond the known into the realms of the unknown.

Statistics also divides *qualitatively* into *parametric* and *nonparametric statistics*. Before we discuss either of these areas, however, it is necessary for us to clarify what a *parameter* (of which the word *parametric* is the adjective) is.

A *parameter* is a function, a characteristic, a quality of the population which in *concept* is a constant but whose *value* is variable. Does that confuse you? Let's make it simple. Consider a circle. One of the parameters, or characteristics, of a circle is its radius. It has a functional relationship to the circle. In *concept* it is a constant: it is always the same for every circle—the distance from the center of the circle to the perimeter. In *value*, it constantly varies, depending upon the size of the circle. Large circles have long radii; small circles, short radii. The *value*—that is, the length of the radius as expressed in so many linear units (centimeters, inches, feet)—is variable. It is different for each circle size.

Thinking of a parameter in this way, we see that each circle has a number of parammeters: circumference, area, diameter. We define these parameters in terms of concepts which are *constants*: the diameter is always twice the radius, the circumference is always $2r\pi$ the area always πr^2.

Parameters are always characteristics of a *population*, a *universe* as it is sometimes called. When we have a similar characteristic of a sample, we call the "sample parameter" a *statistic*. A statistic is not to be confused with *statistics* which is the science that deals with the collection, classification, description, mathematical analysis, and testing of facts, usually for research purposes. In fact, there is a difference in the symbol representing the same characteristic which is common to both the population and to the sample or samples drawn from it.

A table on page 177 shows the conventional symbols employed in statistical notation in each instance.

And so, it is important for us to distinguish between *statistics* and *a* statistic. It is, likewise, important to distinguish between the terms *parametric* and *nonparametric* statistics. *Parametric statistics* assumes that most populations have at least *one* parameter. The parameter that is perhaps the most persuasive and generally encountered in all of nature's manifestations is the great *Gaussian curve of normal frequency distribution.*[2] That seems to be as universal as any phenomenon that man has observed. The *normal curve* is a "hump-backed" curve. In reality, however, each "normal" curve describes an actual life situation and so departs in varying degrees from the *ideal* Gaussian curve.

---

[2]See discussion and illustration, page 38-40.

CONVENTIONAL STATISTICAL NOTATION FOR VARIOUS PARAMETERS

The Factor Being Designated	The Symbol Employed for Designating the Factor: In the Case of a Population	The Symbol Employed for Designating the Factor: In the Case of a Statistic†
The Mean	μ	$\overline{X}$ M_g M_h*
The Standard Deviation	σ	s
Proportion or Probability	P	p
Uncertainty in	H	H
Number or Total	N	n

*M_g = Geometric Mean, M_h = Harmonic Mean

† Notice the wording: *a* statistic.

The Normal Curve

Take any fortuitous happening and analyze its distribution pattern: the corn production of the state of Iowa in any given year. If we could survey the per acre yield of every single farmer in Iowa (literally, the total population, the universe of the corn fields and corn farmers in Iowa), we would find that probably a few farmers had a remarkably poor yield of corn per acre, for no discernable reason except that "that's the way it happened." Quite to the contrary, a few other farmers for an equally unaccountable reason had excessively heavy yields from their fields. Generally, however, most farmers will have had a middle-of-the road yield, sloping gradually in either direction of the greater or the lesser yield categories. And the normal curve will describe the Iowa corn production. No one planned it that way; it is simply the way Nature behaves.

Walk into any clothing store. Take an inventory of men's suit sizes or women's dress sizes. Again the normal curve phenomenon will be confirmed. Test all the children in a given school system. The I.Q. scores will describe a Gaussian curve—as will their heights, their weights, their various abilities to spell correctly.

Look at blind impersonal Nature. Watch an approaching thunderstorm. An occasional flash of lightning will herald the coming of the storm. Soon the flashes will occur more frequently; at the height of the storm they will reach a peak of the number of flashes per minute; gradually, with the passing of the storm, they will subside; and the normal curve is again confirmed. Dip into Nature again and again and you will find the parameter of the Gaussian curve occurring repeatedly.

We could think of thousands of situations, only to find that Nature behaves generally according to the rule of the normal frequency curve. The curve is a *constant*. It is always bell-shaped. In any one situation, the *values* within it vary. The mean is not always at the same place; the shape is overall more broadly spread or more compressed, depending upon the situation being represented.

Because the curve is such a seemingly universal representation of the general distributional pattern inherent to populations generally, statisticians consider it a *basic parameter* which fits *most* life situations and, hence, which may be used as a norm against which to measure population data generally.

Curves Determine Means

We emphasize *most* life situations to call attention to the fact that it is not the *universal* curve of life. Some phenomena do not fit its curvaceous contour. Growth, for example, is one. Growth follows an ogive curve and flattens into a plateau. Speed, for example, is another. Driving to work, I accelerate, decelerate, cruise along for a few moments at maximum speed, then stop for a traffic signal and my speed drops to zero. No normal curve here. For this reason we have various ways of determining the *mean.* Each type of mean is statistically designed to measure with greatest accuracy the particular phenomena with which the researcher is dealing.

If I am recording the growth of bean stalks in an agronomy laboratory, I do not find the average growth by means of the normal curve, or *arithmetic mean.* The statistical technique does not fit the natural fact. For growth phenomena, we use the *geometric mean*—for a very simple reason: *that* is the way things grow, that is the way cells divide—*geometrically*.

If, in driving my car, I could see my acceleration and deceleration curves as they might appear on a cathode tube in an oscilloscope, I would find not one bell-shaped curve but a series of oscillations and harmonics such as the tone from an organ pipe produces. To find my average speed, I must employ a mean that measures such a situation—in this case the *harmonic mean.* Thus, we come to the first rule for the researcher who anticipates the employment of statistics in his research: *The data—the facts of life—govern the statistical technique, not the other way around*. Statistics is the maidservant of reality, and statisticians labor to produce a statistical tool for every life contingency. As the physician must know what drugs are available for specific diseases, so the researcher must know what statistical techniques are suited to his specific research demands.

Let us pick up the matter of means, and curves, and population samples. We shall think of total populations and the samples drawn from them for a moment to discover a very important fact, what statisticians call *the standard error of the mean*.

Random samples from populations display *in general* the same characteristics as the parent population from which they were selected. There are, of course, slight deviations in every sample: samples are not *facsimiles* of the parent population. But the deviations, if the sample has been selected with adequate randomicity so that it is truly a representative sample, are presumably not of such magnitude as to be *significantly* different from the population from which the sample was drawn. The several means of the various samples, however, do form a normal frequency distribution of their own, and that frequency distribution has its own mean. In other words, the mean of each sample is slightly at variance from the mean of the general population from which the sample was drawn. It is axiomatic, however, that the larger the sample, the more the sample mean approximates the population mean. But the distribution of the several sample means gives us a variance phenomenon known as the *standard error of the mean*, which statistically is represented as

$$SE_{\overline{x}} = \frac{\sigma}{\sqrt{N}}$$

But we are here faced at once with a difficulty. This formula involves using the *population* standard deviation (σ), and the purpose of using the sample was that, since we cannot use the population as a whole because of its size, we must then work *backward* through an *estimation*[3] technique which statisticians have devised to estimate the standard deviation of the total population with reasonable accuracy. This formula is as follows.[4]

[3] Note that on page 175 in the organizational chart of statistics, we indicated that one of the subdivisions of inferential statistics was estimation.

[4] Virginia L. Senders, *Measurement and Statistics* (New York: Oxford University Press), p. 467.

$$\tilde{\sigma} = \frac{s}{\sqrt{N-1}}$$

Although statistics may indeed assist in the estimation of parameters in the population when the size of the population prohibits complete surveying of every individual, two important considerations must be recognized:

1. Statistical prediction and estimates are no more accurate than the fidelity with which the parameters of the sample mirror those of the total population.
2. Statistical procedures must be those that are appropriate to the character of the data being analyzed. Nothing substitutes for a careful and intelligent appraisal of the characteristics of the data and a matching of statistical procedures to those characteristics.

Data and Their Characteristics

Not only do all data have certain clearly recognized characteristics, which we shall discuss in a moment, but every statistical approach has its own specific requirements in terms of the type of data appropriate to the demands of that particular statistical procedure. A glance at the classification of statistical techniques on page 182, which charts the domain of statistical methodology, will show the necessity of knowing something about the nature of the data before one considers statistical treatment of it.

Data may assume characteristics according to four varieties of circumstances and may be classified in four separate ways as follows:

1. The kind of data.

   Discrete data: those data existing independently of each other. Examples: Individuals, bacteria, apples, nationalities.

   Continuous data: those data which together form a continuum. Examples: millibars, degrees of temperature, chronological age.
2. The scale of measurement of the data.

   Nominal data: those data which have been distinguished from all other data by assigning them a name. Examples: Pine tree (*Pinus*), Sirius, inner-city children, farmers.

   Ordinal data: those data which have been assigned an order of sequence. Examples: days of the week, faculty rank in a university, rank of a percentile scale.

   Interval data: those data which are measured in terms of difference in standard units between one object and another. Examples: A board 3 feet longer than another, an I.Q. of 30 points higher than the next child in the alphabetical list, a course of alteration of 27°.

   Ratio data: those data which indicate that one item is so many times as large as, as bright as, more powerful than another. Some statisticians indicate that the ratio scale must originate from the zero point of value. Examples: degrees of a circular compass, a percentage scale, measurement of a vacuum in terms of torrs, voltage, or amperage of electrical current.
3. The number of groups from which the data arise.

   One-group data: those data which arise from a single group of subjects. This type of data is often encountered in pretest or posttest investigations of variables in one group of individuals.

Two-group data: those data which arise from a study of two groups or populations such as is typical in experimental studies involving a control-group and an experimental-group design.

Many-groups data: those data which arise from multigroup populations in which contrasting variables are studied against several varying group contexts.

4. Variables.

Univariate data: those data which involve merely one variable within a population. Such studies are of the simplest type and belong to the older order of research. All variables are held constant except the one being studied.

Bivariate data: those data which, as the name suggests, contain two variables. Studies such as those which measure the relative achievement in two areas, such as English and mathematics, for each individual within a certain population are of this type.

Multivariate data: those data which contain within them a number of variables which are usually isolated and then studied by the multivariate analysis technique.

Confusion—and the Way Out

Not only may the terminology of statistics be somewhat confusing, but statisticians do not always agree on the uniform use of either terms or symbols, and often variant formulas are given for identical operations. Consider, for example, the following. These are all formulas whose aim is to accomplish one statistical goal: to find the standard deviation.

$$SD_x = \sqrt{\frac{\sum_{i=1}^{n} x_i^2}{n}}$$

From Sheldon G. Levy, *Inferential Statistics in the Behavioral Sciences* (New York: Holt, Rinehart and Winston, Inc., 1968), p. 22.

$$S_x = \sqrt{\frac{\Sigma f(X - \bar{X})^2}{n - 1}}$$

From Allen L. Edwards, *Statistical Methods*, Second edition (New York: Holt, Rinehart and Winston, Inc., 1967), p. 33.

$$s = \sqrt{\frac{\Sigma x^2}{N}}$$

From Virginia L. Senders, *Measurement and Statistics* (New York: Oxford University Press, 1958), p. 168.

$$S_x = \sqrt{\frac{N\Sigma X^2 - (\Sigma X)^2}{N(N - 1)}}$$

From Max D. Englehart, *Methods of Educational Research* (Chicago: Rand McNally and Company, 1972), p. 213.

These four formulas are apparently different. To the eyes of the statistician, they all say the same thing. To the bewildered mind of the student, each variant form merely adds to the confusion. Among the symbols which indicated the standard deviation, in a brief sampling of textbooks, we came up with the following six variant forms from six different texts:

$$s_x, s, S, SD, SD_x, S_x.$$

If, therefore, you are not too adept at mathematical reasoning nor too familiar with the overall statistical terrain, it may be better for you to meet your quantitative problems with a more functional approach.

In considering the employment of any methodological techniques, but particularly with respect to managing data by means of the analytical methods afforded by statistics, it is always important to look first at the nature and characteristics of the data, and secondly at the ability of the statistical technique to handle the particular type of data under consideration. Any comprehensive statistical textbook will give you direction in this second matter. It is not within the province of this text to discuss the merits or the demerits of any one particular statistical approach.

The field of statistics is a broad and varied one and is developing new techniques and procedures continually to meet the exigencies of various academic disciplines and fields of endeavor. At the close of this chapter we provide a list of texts in statistics particularly appropriate for special areas of research. The list may assist you in discovering a title particularly suited to the requirements of your special field of interest.

The Overall View

To help you choose the statistical approach most logical for the particular data you have in hand, the following chart, which shows the overall view of statistics, may be helpful.

After having had a course in statistics, many a student has faced the predicament of not knowing precisely "where to begin" or what statistical techniques are most appropriate for a particular research situation. Such a student needs a global view of the statistical landscape. It is the problem of not being able to see the statistical "forest" for the myopia that has been acquired by studying the individual "trees." Some terms and approaches are recalled as having been discussed in class, but the student is lost when it comes to applying what has been learned in a course in statistics to his or her own research needs. Such terms as *one-tailed test*, *chi square test*, *phi coefficient*, *geometric mean*, *harmonic mean*, and *goodness of fit* are all vaguely familiar. Precisely where they are appropriate in a statistical analysis is unclear and confusing.

Perhaps the following classification of statistical techniques may assist in bridging the statistical tool-research procedure gap.

The Role of Statistics in Research

Statistics is not a cure-all. It is a tool. And it is no substitute whatever for thinking. But in research, statistics has an ancillary role and the function of statistics may be reduced simply to four basic roles:

1. *Statistics may point you to the center of the mass of data.* It may help you find the balance point, the fulcrum, defining the point at which, on either side, the data are equally divided. In this capacity it may assist you in answering the question: "What is the best prediction? Where do the best bets lie?"
2. *Statistics may suggest to you how diversified the data are.* It may tell you how broadly or how narrowly the facts cluster about the point of central focus. It may reveal how disparate and scattered are the data. It may assist you in answering the question: "How bad may a prediction be based upon these facts?" The wider the scatter the less likelihood are the facts to point to *one* expected outcome.
3. *Statistics may reveal to you how closely or how distantly certain features within the mass of data are related.* It can tell you how the features of the data in one aspect (age, for example, as it relates to height) relate to the features of the same data in another aspect. It can also suggest to you the degree of closeness of one feature as predicted by a knowledge of the proximity or remoteness of the relationship of the other feature of the data.

CLASSIFICATION OF STATISTICAL TECHNIQUES
AND GUIDE TO THEIR USE

Number of Groups	Type of Analysis	Purpose	Type of Data		
			Categorical *	Rank-order †	Measured ††
ONE	Univariate	Description	(1) One-way tables; bar, pie diagrams; modal class; conversion to proportions	(7) Array; ranking; cumulative frequencies and proportions	(13) Frequency distribution; histogram frequency polygon; ogive; percentiles; averages; measures of variability, skewness, and kurtosis
		Inference	(2) Binomial test; chi-square goodness-of-fit test	(8) Kolmogorov-Smirnov goodness-of-fit test	(14) Normal curve theory; z and t tests; chi-square variance test
	Bivariate	Description	(3) Two-way tables; comparative diagrams; conditional and marginal proportions	(9) Bivariate arrays; rank-order correlation coefficient	(15) Scatter diagrams; prediction equations; Pearson correlation coefficient; standard error of estimate
		Inference	(4) Chi-square tests of independence and experimental homogeneity	(10) Testing significance of rank-order correlation coefficient	(16) Bivariate normal distribution; testing significance of Pearson coefficient
TWO OR MORE	Univariate	Description	(5) See cell 3	(11) Comparative tables and cumulative proportions	(17) See cell 13
		Inference	(6) See cell 4	(12) Kolmogorov-Smirnov two-sample test; Mann-Whitney U test	(18) F test of homogeneity of variance; analysis of variance

* Data that result from the application of a *nominal* scale of measurement.
† Data that result from the application of an *ordinal* scale of measurement.
†† Data deriving from either an *interval or ratio* scale of measurement.
Reprinted by permission from C. M. Dayton and C. L. Stunkard, *Statistics for Problem Solving* (New York: McGraw-Hill Book Co., 1971), p. 10.

4. *Statistics may indicate to you the degree to which the facts might have occurred by mere chance or whether there is a probability of their having been influenced by some force other than pure happenstance.* Statistics can help you detect whether the phenomenon you observe or the facts you have chanced upon are there by the pure fortuitousness of chance or whether they have had, in all probability, some external force operating upon them. It can also assist you in groping in a world *beyond* your facts in order to locate certain parameter landmarks; for example, the mean and also the variability of a universe of data which is impossible for you to survey either because of its remoteness or its size.

Look Closely at the Data

Nothing takes the place of looking carefully, inquiringly, critically—even naively—at the data. Data are the raw materials of your research. Inspect them carefully. Do not ignore any data configuration, no matter how elusive or remote it may be from the central axis of your research effort. Think of data as you might think of chessmen on a board: how many positions can they occupy; what does any shifting of position, rearrangement of sequence, or change of observational orientation make? Are the data nominal, ordinal, interval, or ratio? From how many viewpoints can you contemplate them?

Before considering any further statistical treatment, every researcher needs to develop the skill of looking closely at the data only. All too few researchers do so. It is more "exciting" to run off into a "statistical treatment" of the data; to process raw fact before we know what we are dealing with. Eyes, sometimes, are much better interpreters of the data than statistics. Look! Think! Look again!

You need to doodle with data. Try them out in every conceivable arrangement. See what various arrangement patterns the data will fit before beginning to think in terms of means, deviations, correlations, and tests of hypotheses.

Data in a table look different from the way they do in a graph. Arrange them both ways. Data further assume an added dimension when arranged in some configurational order: ascending, descending, categorical, alphabetical, and so on.

Nowhere in the whole research process is inexperience so evident as when researchers are so impatient to get involved in some statistical treatment of the data that they rush into statistical sophistication before they have played with the data long enough to get acquainted with them in their most elemental organization. The complexity of the Law of Universal Gravitation began in a very simple way. An apple hit Isaac Newton on the head!

Primitive simplicity, an open mind, the ingenuity of imagination to see as much as can be seen without benefit of computational complexity—this is the genesis of true research.

Now, with all this exhortation, let's take a very simple example to illustrate the point. Here are the reading achievement scores of eleven children: Ruth, 96; Robert, 60; Chuck, 68; Margaret, 88; Tom, 56; Mary, 92; Ralph, 64; Bill, 72; Alice, 80; Adam, 76; Jennie, 84.

Now, let's try as many arrangements of those scores as possible to see just how much information we can extract from them before subjecting them to what is generally considered statistical treatment. Some of the information may not be of any use to us in terms of our research problem. No matter. What we are after is to see what we can see by the process of looking. The professional researcher discovers everything possible about the data, whether it is immediately useful or not. They leave no stone unturned. They overlook no lurking significances because their investigations do not seem to be uncovering golden revelations or big yields of meaningful information.

We shall start simply. What will an alphabetical arrangement of those students' names reveal. Let's see. Remember, we are merely on the lookout for *any* meaning of whatever kind or type, no matter how *seemingly* trivial or imposingly important.

Adam	76	Mary	92
Alice	80	Ralph	64
Bill	72	Robert	60
Chuck	68	Ruth	96
Jennie	84	Tom	56
Margaret	88		

In columnar form, the array may not be too much more meaningful, but we have isolated individuals and grades more clearly. If nothing else, it is somewhat easier to inspect them in this form. We have, of course, listed the data *nominally*. But does it show anything? Yes. It shows that the highest grade was earned by a girl and the lowest grade belongs to a boy, and, in the list as we have arranged them, they are side-by-side. Silly, you say—and meaningless. Perhaps. But it's an observable fact, and that *is* important.

Let's keep the nominal arrangement, now, but view it in another way. We shall see these eleven boys and girls lined up in a straight row, still arranged in alphabetical order according to their given names.

Look! Now we can discern a *ratio* pattern in these eleven children that was not apparent before. We have a *symmetrical pattern*. Starting from either end the ratios are as follows:

EXPRESSED VERBALLY	EXPRESSED MATHEMATICALLY
one boy—one girl	1 : 1
one girl—two boys	1 : 2
two boys—three girls	2 : 3
three girls—two boys	3 : 2
two boys—one girl	2 : 1
one girl—one boy	1 : 1

Now, let us do another very simple arrangement. We shall separate girls from boys, arranging the group according to sex difference. The data will then appear as follows:

GIRLS		BOYS	
Alice	80	Adam	76
Jennie	84	Bill	72
Margaret	88	Chuck	68
Mary	92	Ralph	64
Ruth	96	Robert	60
		Tom	56

Represented graphically this diverse trend is even more dramatic:

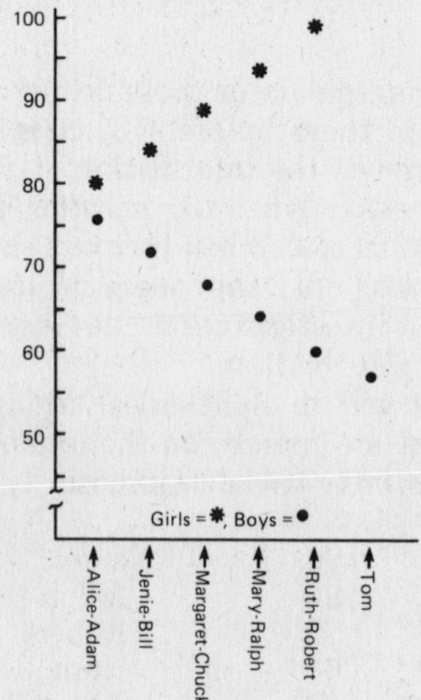

What have we seen? Well, what we have seen may have no importance whatsoever for any project, but because it represents *dynamics within the data*, it is important that we see it. That is the precise point we are making: the researcher should be aware of the dynamics, the phenomena, that are active within the data, whether those phenomena are important to the purpose of the research as he sees it at the moment or not. The astute researcher overlooks *nothing*.

As we originally presented the data in a garbled form, we should never have guessed that when names were arranged in an alphabetical order and the group divided by sex differentiation, that the scores of the girls formed an *ascending* series of values, with the first girl on the list getting the lowest score among the girls, the last girl, the highest score.

With the boys, the situation is precisely reversed. When they are arranged alphabetically, their scores form a constantly *descending* series of values.

Not only is there a divergence of trends, but now we are aware of a very obvious fact that may up to this point have escaped our attention: the intervals between the scores are *equidistant in scalar value*. Each score is four points either above or below the preceding one.

But we have spent enough time on mere manipulation of data. With children and reading scores this may have been an excercise in futility, but for the researcher working in an area of impersonal science, observations of a similar genre may reveal very important new knowledge. Take the case of a paleontologist and an astronomer who noticed data recorded in the form of growth marks on the shells of the chambered nautilus.[5] They noticed that each chamber had an average of thirty growth lines and deduced that the growth lines had appeared at the rate of one-a-day and that one chamber was laid down every lunar month—29.53 days. They also concluded that, if their interpretation of the data were correct, then it might be possible to determine from fossil shells the length of the ancient lunar months. And since the distance of the moon from the earth can be calculated from the length of the lunar month, the scientists examined nautilus fossils—some of them as old as 420 million years. A gradual decrease in the number of growth lines in each chamber as the fossils receded farther and farther into prehistoric time indicated that formerly the moon was apparently closer to the earth and revolved around it more rapidly than it now does—a fact consistent with generally accepted scientific fact.

The fact that the data that we have examined above and that the various constellations of data were spurious is quite beside the point. Certain basic principles with regard to the observation of data begin to emerge. These we should probably note at this point.

For example, where *two* facts are concerned (grades and names; growth rings and lunar month cycles), *one of them becomes dominant* and governs the meaning which emerges from the other. In the data that we have been inspecting with respect to the children, the meaning that was derived from the last arrangement of data emerged primarily because we used an alphabetized list of given names of the students. By arranging the data in other ways, different meanings would probably have been obvious. This suggests a fundamental guideline for looking at the data: *Whatever the researcher does with the data to prepare it for further inspection or interpretation will affect the meaning that those data will reveal, so that every researcher should be able to defend his procedure of the interpretation of the data with a clear and logical rationale.*

In the preceding procedure, we had no rationale whatever for arranging the data according to the given names of the children. Had we used the last names—which would

[5] Peter G. K. Kahn and Stephen Pompea, "Nautiloid growth rhythms and dynamical evolution of the Earth-Moon system," *Nature*, 275 (October 19, 1978), 606-11.

have been equally logical—the entire boy-girl ratio would have gone to the wind. Had we done that, we would have had a simple one-to-one ratio because, alphabetized, the surnames of the children would have arranged themselves in a boy-girl sequence and the list would have looked like this:

Angel, Ralph	George, Ruth	Oglethorpe, Chuck	Thomas, Margaret
Brown, Jennie	Murray, Bill	Smith, Alice	Vaughn, Adam
Daniels, Tom	Nichols, Mary	Street, Robert	

As we have remarked, from a *research standpoint* there is no defensible rationale for using the given name over the surname or the reverse. The *nominal data* were, therefore, not critical to the research purpose. The *ordinal data* may have been. So, also, and probably with more likelihood, may have been the *interval* and even more so, the *ratio data*.

With so-called scientific data, the problem is less complex. Data comes to the scientist generally "prepackaged" and prearranged. The growth rings on the nautilus shell are there. They cannot be altered. What such data need for interpretation is a pair of keen eyes and a curious and inquiring mind. From the standpoint of dealing with the data, therefore, the researcher working in the physical or biological sciences may not have the problems of data arrangement prior to interpretation that may face a colleague researcher who may be seeking to interpret data generated by the social sciences, education, or the humanities.

But irrespective of arrangement, there is enough in both situations above to pique our curiosity. For example:

1. Why were all the scores of the girls higher than those of the boys?
2. Why were all the scores of the boys lower than the lowest score for the girls?
3. Why were the intervals between each of the scores for both boys and girls equidistant?
4. What causes the nautilus to record a growth mark each day of the lunar month?
5. What is the relationship between the forming of the partitions and the lunar month cycle?

Beware of Snap Judgments

It is from questions like these that research springs.

Looking at these situations, we may be inclined to draw hasty and unwarranted conclusions, such as *girls read better than boys.* Again, we are not looking at the data; we are not thinking accurately.

Much research goes wrong at this juncture. Reading ability is a complex skill. The data do not say that girls read better than boys. What the data do say is that *on a particular test* given *on a particular day* to eleven children—five girls and six boys—the scores of the girls were *for this particular testing situation* higher than those of the boys and that each score was precisely equidistant in terms of a point scale from every other score *for both boys and girls.* Furthermore, the apparent excellence of the girls over the boys was limited to test performance in those skills and aptitudes in reading measured specifically by this test.

Honesty and precision dictate that all the conditions in the total situation be considered and that we may make generalizations only as these are in strict accordance with the facts that represent the situation as it actually is. The time-operant-condition relationship is a very unstable one. The same test given to another eleven children, as similar to the first

	QUESTION
SCALE	1. What general picture do the data convey? Answer: Frequency Distributions.
NOMINAL	*Bar graphs:* only the relative heights of the bars have mathematical significance.
ORDINAL	Discrete data: *Bar graphs:* order and heights of bars have mathematical significance. Continuous data: *Histograms:* order and heights of bars have mathematical significance, and adjacent bars must be contiguous. *Frequency polygons:* horizontal distances between points are arbitrary. *Cumulative frequency and cumulative percentage graphs:* horizontal distances between points are arbitrary.
INTERVAL	Discrete data: *Bar graphs:* heights, order, widths, and spacing of bars have mathematical significance. Area inside bars is proportional to number of cases. Continuous data: *Histograms:* as for bar graphs; adjacent bars must be contiguous. *Frequency polygons:* horizontal spacing of points has mathematical significance, and area under curve is proportional to number of cases. *Cumulative frequency and cumulative percentage graphs:* horizontal spacing of points has mathematical significance. The shape of the distribution is meaningful. *Skewness* and *kurtosis* can be described. Theoretical distributions (e.g., normal) can be approximated by obtained data.
RATIO	*Bar graphs* *Histograms* *Frequency polygons* *Cum. freq. and cum. percentage graphs* *Skewness and kurtosis* *Theoretical distributions* } as for interval scale. *Transformed measurements* can be used to approximate a theoretical distribution from obtained data.

From *Measurement and Statistics: A Basic Text Emphasizing Behavioral Science*, by Virginia L. Senders. Copyright © 1958 by Oxford University Press, Inc. Reprinted by permission.

group as we can possibly pair them, the next day—or the next four, for that matter—may produce vastly different data.

The chart above may suggest some ways in which the various categories of data may be studied.

A Matter of Means

We have elsewhere in this text discussed briefly the measures of central tendency and their meaning.[6] Senders, however, regards the matter of central tendency from a somewhat different standpoint. She considers it from the angle of optimal chance: What is the best prediction?[7]

In the normal curve, the greatest mound of data always occurs at the point of central tendency. Take an example. You are driving down the street. Suddenly you come upon a crowd of people forming in contour a human normal-curve configuration. Where is the best prediction that you will find the cause for the crowd forming? The answer is simple. Where the crowd is deepest, where the crest of the curve and the greatest mass of people are, that is probably where the cause lies for the massing of the crowd. It may be a street fight, an accident, a man giving away wooden nickels, but whatever the occasion, your best

[6] See Chapter 2, pages 31-32.

[7] Senders, op. cit., page 181, 191.

guess lies at the point where the human mass—the statistical median, the mean, or the mode of the crowd—is at its "peak."

Similarly, wherever the point of convergence of data is located, that is the most likely point to find what most probably is the best prediction of the meaning of those data. We speak of "the average American" "the average student," "the average wage earner" when we refer to those Americans, those students, those wage earners that we are most likely to find huddled around the point of central tendency in any random sampling of Americans, or students, or workers that we may take. In the broad spectrum of possibilities, we are betting on the average as being the best guess as to what is most characteristic.

You will notice that the points of central tendency—the mean, the median, and the mode, a discussion of which is found in every textbook on research or statistics,—are mentioned in the chart on p. 191. You will find also other points of central tendency that are seldom mentioned in textbooks but that competent researchers should know about if they are to fit the statistical tool to the contour and characteristics of the data. These are the *geometric mean*, the *harmonic mean*, and the *contraharmonic mean*. We shall discuss each of these briefly.

The *geometric mean*, as we have suggested earlier, is employed when the researcher wishes to find the point of central tendency of a growth phenomenon. We must again look at the data configuration. When the data are in the configurational pattern of a normal or "humped" curve, then the *arithmetic mean* is appropriate. The curve of growth is quite different, however. If growth were represented by the normal curve, an individual who begins from two cells might grow to a point of maximum development and then wither away until he returns to a two-celled state again. But, as we all know, growth does not behave like that. Individuals do not grow like that, nor towns, nor cities, nor any other kind of growth phenomena. The growth curve for these events is the normal ogive, or "S" or its variants: the Gompertz curve, the modified exponential curve, or the logistic curve.

Growth is a function of geometric progression. One may recall a certain Thomas Robert Malthus, an English clergyman and economist, who was the first to warn the human race of the fact of population explosion and the possibility of world-wide famine. Malthus's *An Essay on the Principle of Population as It Affects the Future Improvement of Society. . .* was the first serious discussion of the effects of growth mathematics. He contended that population, when unchecked, increases in a *geometric ratio*: 2, 4, 8, 16, 32, 64, 128 . . ., whereas subsistence increases only in *arithmetic ratio*: 2, 4, 6, 8, 10, 12, 14 . . . And Malthus also saw that the eventual flattening of the growth curve was determined by the arithmetic progression factor, subsistence.

Hence, the growth curve appears as follows:

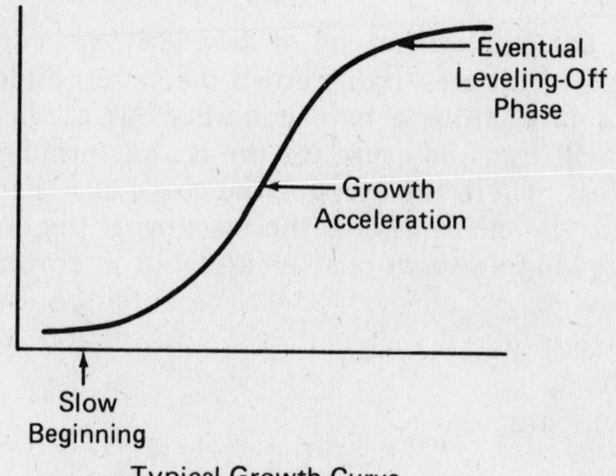

Typical Growth Curve

Biologists, physicists, ecologists, economists—all encounter the growth and decay phenomena in one form or another. They all witness the same typical aspects of growth: a slow beginning—a few settlers in an uninhabited region, a few bacteria on a culture; then after a period of time, rapid expansion—the "boom" period of city growth, the rapid multiplication of microorganisms; the leveling-off period—the land becomes scarce, the city sprawl is contained by geographic and economic factors; the bacteria have populated the entire culture.

Examples of situations where the application of the geometric mean is appropriate are the following:

1. In biological growth situations.
2. In population growth situations.
3. In increment of money at compound interest.
4. In averaging ratios or percentages.
5. In decay or simple decelerative situations.

We usually calculate the geometric mean in practice by the use of logarithms.

$$\text{G.M.} = \sqrt[n]{X_1 \cdot X_2 \cdot X_3 \cdot X_4 \cdot\cdot X_5 \ldots X_n} =$$

$$\log \text{G.M.} = \frac{\log X_1 + \log X_2 + \log X_3 + \log X_4 \ldots \log X_n}{N} =$$

$$\text{G.M.} = \frac{\Sigma \log X}{N}$$

The *harmonic mean* is employed for data derived from fluctuating situations. You drive a car from one point to another. If you had a graphical record of your speed, it would resemble the profile of a series of major and minor peaks in a mountain range. Leaving the point of origin, you accelerate to a speed of 20 miles per hour for a given time; then you climb to 35 miles per hour; then, being impeded by a truck in a no-passing zone, you drop to 10 miles per hour and follow the truck. With a chance to pass it, you accelerate to 50 miles per hour. And so, fluctuating in speed, you finally reach your destination. You want to find your *average* speed. The harmonic mean will help you. Any fluctuating phenomenon may call for the employment of the harmonic mean. A good elementary discussion of both the geometric mean and the harmonic mean can be found in Wert,[8] and an article by Ferger[9] gives advice as to conditions which may call for the use of the harmonic mean.

The harmonic mean is computed as follows:

$$\text{H.M.} = \frac{1}{\frac{1}{N}\left(\frac{1}{X_1} + \frac{1}{X_2} + \frac{1}{X_3} + \frac{1}{X_4} \cdots \frac{1}{X_n}\right)} = \frac{1}{\frac{1}{N}\Sigma\frac{1}{X}} = \frac{N}{\Sigma\frac{1}{X}}$$

One further statistic of the mean, very useful in certain instances, is the *contraharmonic mean*. It is a statistic that approximates a more realistic mean in situations where a few

[8] J. E. Wert, *Educational Statistics* (New York: McGraw-Hill Book Company, 1938), pp. 63-80.

[9] Wirth F. Ferger, *Journal of the American Statistical Association*, 26 (March 1931), 36-40.

individuals contribute disproportionately to the total number of contributions. Take the instance of a college which attempts to show that the average income of its graduates, twenty years after graduation, is about $50,000 per year per graduate. It cites the average income (the *arithmetic average* income!) of the graduates in its twentieth anniversary class. The figures look fine. They do not reveal, however, that one of the members of the class is an oil tycoon with an income of $1.75 million a year. Another graduate is a corporation president whose total income from salary, stocks, and other sources totals $875,000 per year; another is president of a land speculation and realty firm with an income upward of $500,000 per year. A fourth is a corporation lawyer with earnings of $375,000 per year. The rest of the graduates are "white-collar" professionals whose incomes range between $20,000 and $40,000 per year. There are 478 of these out of a class of 493. A few graduates earn between $40,000 and $100,000 a year. If plotted, badly skewed curves should alert us to consider in such instances the possibility that the contraharmonic mean may be more appropriate in determining the point of central tendency.

We can employ the contraharmonic mean in only those instances where each X in the following formula is itself expressed in terms of a *number* of this or that: the *number* of dollars, the *number* of arrests, the *number* of accidents, and so forth.

The formula for deriving the contraharmonic mean is as follows:

$$\text{C.M.} = \frac{\Sigma fX^2}{\Sigma fX}$$

Perhaps the table below[10] will summarize the measures of central tendency and their several uses, together with the various categories of data with which each measure is appropriate.

The Message of Curves and Deviations

We have just been discussing basically the question of "What is the best guess?" Now we turn to the opposite question, "What are the worst odds?" Both questions are important. Some of us would like to look at the first question and forget the second. To react thus means merely that we need to cultivate a more objective and unemotional response to cold fact.

If, as we have just been discussing, the probability index of the correct guess rises with the tendency of the data to cluster about the point of central tendency, then it is, conversely, true that the farther the data are dispersed from the central pivotal axis, the greater the margin of predictive error becomes. Consider, for example, these two curves:

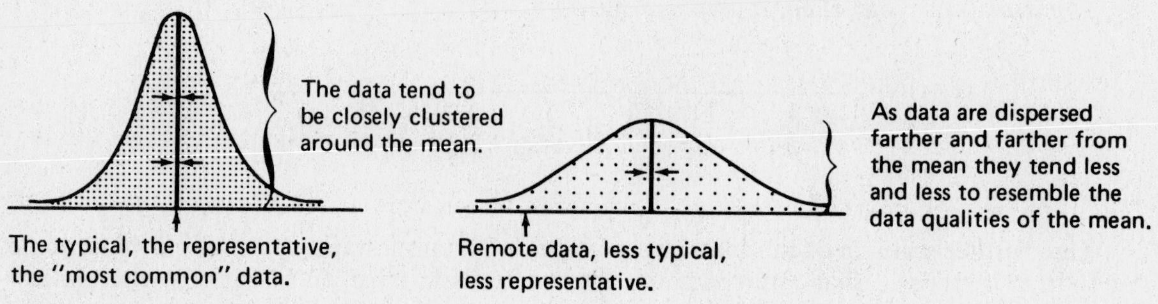
The data tend to
be closely clustered
around the mean.
The typical, the representative,
the "most common" data.
As data are dispersed
farther and farther from
the mean they tend less
and less to resemble the
data qualities of the mean.
Remote data, less typical,
less representative.

[10] Senders, op. cit., p. 330.

SCALE	QUESTION
	What is the best prediction? Answer: Measures of central tendency.
NOMINAL	*Mode:* the mode is the numeral representing the category with the highest frequency of occurrence. It is the prediction most likely to be right.
ORDINAL	*Mode:* as for nominal scale. Appropriate for discrete data only. *Median:* the point above and below which lie 50 per cent of the cases. It is the prediction that is just as likely to be too high as too low. It is more stable than the mode.
INTERVAL	*Mode:* } as for ordinal scale. *Median:* } as for ordinal scale. The prediction that minimizes average error. *Mean:* $\bar{X} = \frac{\Sigma X}{N}$: The prediction that makes the sum of the errors zero, and makes the sum of the squares of the errors a minimum. More stable than the median.
RATIO	*Mode:* *Median:* as for interval scale. *Mean:* *Geometric mean:* $GM = \sqrt[N]{X_1 \cdot X_2 \ldots \cdot X_N}$ *Harmonic mean:* $HM = \frac{N}{\sum \frac{1}{X}}$ *Contraharmonic mean:* $CM = \frac{\Sigma fX^2}{\Sigma fX}$ } Statistics for special situations.

From *Measurement and Statistics: A Basic Text Emphasizing Behavioral Science,* by Virginia L. Senders. Copyright © 1958 by Oxford University Press, Inc. Reprinted by permission.

The data are more uniform when they cluster about the mean. Scatter them, and they lose some of their uniformity. They, then, become more diverse, more heterogeneous. As they recede from the mean, they lose more and more of the quality which makes them "average." It is easy for us to talk about one, two, three standard deviations from the mean. That type of language keeps everything impersonal, faceless. But as there is a difference in atmosphere of living, of culture, of life itself as one goes farther and farther from a metropolitan center, so data change in character as they recede into the second and third standard deviations from the mean.

Also, a high, peaked curve—*leptokurtic*, as it is called—is an indication of a data accumulation which evidences more homogeneity than a low, flat, spreading curve—*platykurtic*, as this type is called—which hints at greater *heterogeneity* within the data.

Statistics and surveying are somewhat similar. Each needs a point of origin from which to make further measurements. With surveying, the origin of measurement is a triangulation point; with statistics, it is one of the parameters of the data, usually the mean, which establishes a measurement point for the mass of data. If we can establish a mean, then from it we can initiate further measurements. In this way, we can learn more about the data, discern their characteristics, and identify their quality.

It is important to see two parameters of the data to make a sound judgment. We need to discern not only their centrality but also their spread. And we need to see these characteristics in terms of quantitative values. Only by seeing the data quantitatively, in terms of *number values*, can the researcher know anything about those data. Researchers are like a cartographer charting an unknown land, the researcher must "chart" the data, appreciate the meaning of the "peaks and valleys" and evaluate the effect of the expansiveness or narrowness of the spread. Such information aids greatly in the later process of interpretation of the data.

How Great Is the Spread?

Whereas we touched upon these matters earlier in a brief survey of statistics as a tool of research, it is important to review the measures of spread, or dispersion, or variability here. We have several statistical measures that assist us in describing the dispersion of the data from the mean or from the median.

Perhaps the most unrefined of the measures of dispersion is the *range*. The range merely measures the overall spread of the data from their lowest to their highest value. This is the entire data-value spectrum. (Reference to page 34 will illustrate the range.) The range has, however, limited usefulness as a measure of dispersion and may even be misleading if the extreme upper or lower limits are inordinately atypical to the other values of the series. Take an example. The following is the range of the number of children in six families: 15, 6, 5, 4, 3, 0. Now we might say that the families range from a childless couple to a family of 15 children. But drop off the extremes and the situation is much more realistic when we say that two-thirds of the families surveyed had from three to six children.

The next measure of dispersion is the *quartile deviation*. The quartile deviation divides the data into four equal parts. Quartile 1 will lie at a point where 25 percent of the items are below it. Quartile 2 will divide the items into two equal parts, and will be identical with the median. Quartile 3 will lie at a point where 75 percent of the values are below it.

If, instead of dividing the data into four equal parts, we divide it into ten equal parts, then each part will be a *decile*; if into 100 equal parts, each part will be a *percentile*.

The *quartile range* is important in several ways, one of which is to provide a means of measuring *skewness*, and because the quartiles are associated with the median, any statistical approach employing the median as a measure of central tendency should also consider the quartile deviation as an appropriate statistical measure for variability. Furthermore, the interquartile range includes within its limits the middle 50 percent of the cases in the distribution. The *interquartile range* is a combination of quartile measurement and range measurement and includes those data that lie from the first to the third quartile.

A test for the symmetry of the distribution is, therefore, the equidistance of Quartile 1 and Quartile 3 from the median. A *skewed distribution* will not present such equidistant symmetry.

A *measure of skewness* takes advantage of this asymmetry. The measure gives a value of zero when Quartile 1 and Quartile 3 are equidistant from the median. The equation, with a lower limit of 0 and an upper limit of 1, may be stated as follows:[11]

---

[11] William A. Neiswanger, *Elementary Statistical Methods.* Rev. ed. (New York: Macmillan Publishing Co., Inc. 1956).

$$Sk_q = \frac{Q_3 + Q_1 - 2Md}{Q_3 - Q_1}$$

We shall have more to say about measures of skewness when we discuss standard deviation. For all practical purposes, one may consider this index of skewness as comparable to a percentage index.

If we measure the dispersion of the data to the right and to the left of the mean and sum the deviations, disregarding the algebraic signs, dividing the summed differences by the number of cases, we get the *average deviation*. The equation for the average deviation is

$$AD = \frac{\Sigma\, |x|}{N}$$

where $|x| = X - \overline{X}$, disregarding algebraic signs.

We can, of course, take the average deviation around any point of central tendency. When calculated from the *median*, the average deviation is *less* than when taken from any other point of central tendency. The equation is

$$AD_{mdn} = \frac{\Sigma\,(x - M_{dn})}{N}$$

The average deviation is very readily understood and, for that reason, has some merit. It is acceptable when no further statistical procedure is contemplated. It is a little-used value, however, and the measures of standard deviation and variance have largely supplanted it in practical research projects.

The *standard deviation* is the standard measure of variability in most statistical operations. It is an expression of variability from the arithmetic mean, and it is the accepted measure of dispersion in modern statistical practice. We have discussed the several forms of its equation on page 180.

To understand the reason for using the *standard* deviation, we must recall what happens numerically when we find the *average* deviation, which we have just been discussing. In finding the average deviation, as we subtract all the deviations of lesser value than the mean, which lie on the normal curve distribution to the left of the mean, all of them become *negative* values. Thus, the values to the left of the mean (which are all negative) and those to the right of the mean (which are all positive) tend in summation to cancel out each other. This is because these values are linear. In practice, we can change this situation by ignoring the algebraic signs, which we suggested that you do in finding the average deviation. But this is rather dubious mathematical ethics. It is neither sound mathematics nor sound statistics to ignore what you do not like. We can, however, change negatives to positives in a perfectly acceptable mathematical manner. In algebra, if we multiply a negative value by itself, it becomes positive. Thus, by squaring all negative derivations, they become positive:

$$-2^2 = (-2)(-2) = +4.$$

Then,

$$\sqrt{+4} = +2$$

Thus, we have changed linear numbers to square numbers and then we take the square root of the square number. By changing all the linear numbers to square numbers and then summing the squared values and dividing this summation by the *number of deviation values* and, finally, taking the square root of the quotient, we have gone full circle mathematically and are back again to an average of the deviations from the mean in which all the values, regardless of what sign they bore originally, have been transformed to positive integers. It is important to note that we divide the *summed squared deviations* (not the summed deviations, squared!) by the total number of deviations from the mean. Finally, we take the square root of the resultant quotient, which, in turn, will give us the standard deviation. In terms of an equation, the standard deviation is

$$s = \sqrt{\frac{\Sigma x^2}{N}}$$

For analyzing data, we shall probably need another measure of dispersion based upon the standard deviation. This statistic is known as the *variance*. The variance is merely the standard deviation squared.

$$s^2 = \frac{\Sigma x^2}{N}$$

In discussing the quartile deviation, we presented a method of determining skewness in the normal distribution.[12] We suggested at that point that another method of determining the degree of skewness in the population would be presented after we had discussed the standard deviation. In this latter method, devised by Karl Pearson, we make use of the major parameters of the normal distribution: the mean, the median, and the standard deviation. It is sometimes referred to as the *Pearsonian measure of skewness.*

The formula for the Pearsonian coefficient is

$$Sk = \frac{3(\overline{X} - Md)}{s}$$

where $\overline{X}$ = the arithmetic mean
Md = the median
s = the standard deviation

For normal distributions the coefficient value is 0. It varies ±3, but a coefficient in excess of ±1 is rather unusual.

These measures—central tendency, dispersion, and skewness—should provide us with sufficient means of *analyzing the data.* Because we call on the aid of statistics to this end, this methodology has been termed *the analytical survey method.* It is a composite approach to the data, first by surveying the data to note its configuration and fundamental characteristics, and then through statistical means to "analyze" those data—seeing, through the eyes of statistical procedures, what the mass of data appears to be.

Up to this point, we have been considering data *en masse* by looking at the parameters which are inherent to that mass. We have attempted to analyze the mass by seeking to determine where the center of it lies, how far it spreads, whether the spread shows distortion or skewness. We have piled up, as it were, all the data and attempted to find the exact point where all those data are exactly balanced. We have also viewed the spreading out on either side of this delicate equilibratory point to see how the mass of data was distributed. We come now to a closer look at those data and their innate characteristics. But, before proceeding, let us summarize in the following table what we have been discussing with respect to the measures of dispersion.

---

[12] See page 193.

SCALE	QUESTION
	What are the worst odds? Answer: Measures of dispersion.
NOMINAL	Except for verbal descriptions ("longer than") this category is inappropriate for indicating measures of dispersion.
ORDINAL	Range: $X_{max} - X_{min} + 1$. Unstable. Interquartile range: 75th percentile − 25th percentile. Semi-quartile range, Q. Half of interquartile range. Other interpercentile ranges.
INTERVAL	Range, quartile ranges, as for ordinal scale *Average deviation: AD:* $AD = \frac{\sum \lvert x \rvert}{N}$ *Standard deviation,* s, *and variance,* s^2: $s = \sqrt{\frac{\sum x^2}{N}}$ $s^2 = \frac{\sum x^2}{N}$ More useful in later computations than *AD.*
RATIO	Various ranges, *AD*, s *and* s^2 — as for interval scale. *Coefficient of variation, V:* $V = \frac{100s}{\bar{X}}$ Expresses variability in terms of absolute size of measured objects.

From *Measurement and Statistics: A Basic Text Emphasizing Behavioral Science,* by Virginia L. Senders. Copyright © 1958 by Oxford University Press, Inc. Reprinted by permission.

So that we do not lose perspective, we should remind ourselves at midpoint in discussing the analytical survey method that this is all merely statistical manipulation of the data. It is not research, for research goes one step further and demands *interpretation* of the data. In finding means, medians, quartiles, standard deviations, and the like, we have not interpreted the data; we have not extracted any *meaning* from the data. We have merely *described* the center of the data mass and its spread. We have attempted only to *see what the data looked like.* After we know what the data are, and what their basic nature is, then we can attempt to say what those data mean. Then we can descry whether there are forces, which are the real culprits in forcing the data to behave as they do, acting upon those data. For example, apropos of skewness, if we toss a die 100 times and the die comes up "5" 53 times out of the 100, we will find a very skewed distribution. It may give us a hint as to the *meaning behind the skewness.* It may *mean* that we are playing with a loaded die!

But, let us consider other ways of analyzing the data.

Measuring Relationships

So far, we have been discussing unilateral factors: points of convergence of data dynamics, the "center of gravity" within the mass of data. We have also been discussing data dispersion. These characteristics are all one-dimensional.

Think of a datum as you think of an atom. Within the atom lies a whole organization of forces: the central proton, the kinetic electrons, the mesons, the neutrons, the neutrinos. All of these forces, each dynamic within itself, each interacting within the structure, causes each atom to be a structure of complex forces.

The same is true of data. Within the data are forces, dynamics, measurable trends which, when discovered and expressed as one data "force" in relation to another data "force," make the entire data mass more meaningful and significant.

Take, for example, growth force. This dynamic which is inherent in all living things may be expressed, in the instance of human beings, in so many units of linear measure at some particular point in time. Jane is six years old and is 3 feet 10 inches tall. The feet and inches are the linear values which express one aspect of the growth force. But there are other dimensions of that same growth force for that same girl. Another "dimension" is the corporeal mass pulled by the force of gravity for the same girl at the same point in time. The two forces are discrete and separate and yet they act simultaneously. Jane weighs so much at the particular time when she is so tall. Thus, the growth force is a complex of dynamics usually expressed in a two-dimensional matrix: height vs. weight.

Now these facts are data; and, with them, we can construct a graph with the one axis representing height and the other axis representing weight, and we shall represent these in terms of standard units: inches, and pounds, or meters, centimeters, and kilograms. On such a grid, we can plot Jane's height and weight, and represent *both* forces by a *single* point. Suppose, now, that we had one hundred Janes. Some of them would be taller; some shorter; some would weigh more; some, less. Nevertheless, each one could be assigned a single point which would represent her composite height-weight relationship.

The process we have been describing is, of course, the process of co-relating two variables in terms of each other. In statistics, we call this process *correlation.*

We should remember, however, that correlational data are generally plotted on a grid. Convention suggests that the independent variable be plotted along the horizontal axis; the dependent variable, along the vertical axis. The independent variable is the one upon which the variations of the dependent variable seem to depend. When neither factor can be said to be the cause of or dependent upon the other, then the *variable to be predicted* should be plotted along the Y, or vertical axis.

On pages 34-38 we have discussed the subject of correlation. We will not, therefore, repeat here any of that discussion. We shall present, rather, a digest of the various correlational procedures which are broad enough to cover most of the needs of the normal researcher. You will appreciate immediately, upon studying the accompanying tabular digest, that invariably *the nature of the data governs the correlational procedure that is appropriate to those data.*

All too many would-be researchers begin by deciding, for instance, that they will use a Pearsonian coefficient of correlation for showing a relationship between two factors when, in fact, that technique may be entirely inappropriate to the nature of the data being correlated.

The cardinal rule is, therefore: *Look at the data! Determine their nature; scrutinize their quality; then select the appropriate correlational technique suited to the type of data with which you are working.*

In the following table we have characterized the several techniques by the type of data required for each variable. Having taken you thus far, the rest is merely a matter of some further searching among the broad range of statistical texts for appropriate formulas and relevant discussions as to the specific application and the discrete characteristics of each statistical approach. We shall not attempt to go any further into the statistical realm of correlational concerns.

DIGEST OF CORRELATIONAL TECHNIQUES

Correlational Technique	*Symbol*	*Variable Characteristic* *X*	*Y*	*Comment*
		Parametric Correlational Techniques		
Pearson product moment correlation	r	Continuous	Continuous	The most commonly used coefficient.
Biserial correlation	r_b	Continuous	Continuous, but forced into an artificial dichotomy	Much used in item analysis. An array of grades in which some are "pass," others "fail" is an artificial dichotomy.
Point biserial correlation	r_{pb}	Continuous	True dichotomy	Example: heights and weights of boys and girls.
Tetrachoric correlation	r_t	Artificial dichotomy	Artificial dichotomy	Less reliable than Pearson r. Do not use with nominal or ordinal data.
The phi coefficient (fourfold coefficient)	ϕ	True dichotomy	True dichotomy	Statistic is related to χ^2. Assumes variable can have values of only +1 or -1.
Widespread biserial correlation	r_{wbis}	Widespread artificial dichotomy	Continuous	Used when interested in cases at extremes of dichotomized variable.
The triserial correlation	r_{tri}	Continuous	Trichotomy	Developed by N. Jaspen. See *Psychometrika*, 1946, 11, 23-30.
Correlational ratio	η	Continuous	Continuous	Nonlinear relationship between variables. Scattergram necessary to determine linearity.
		Nonparametric Correlational Techniques		
Spearman rank-order correlation (Rank difference correlation)	ρ	Ranks	Ranks	Similar to the Pearson r. Particularly well suited to situations of 25-30 cases.
Kendall's coefficient of concordance	W	Used with three or more sets of ranks		Value of W varies between 0 = no agreement to 1 = perfect agreement.

Correlational Technique	Symbol	Variable Characteristic X	Y	Comment
Kendall's tau-correlation between ranks	τ	Ranks	Ranks	Can be used wherever ρ is appropriate but preferable to ρ when number is less than 10.
Contingency coefficient	C	Two or more categories	Two or more categories	Similar to r_t. Closely related to χ^2. Correlations similar to Pearson r with large sample and at least five categories for each variable.
Partial correlation	$r_{12.3}$	Correlational method involving more than two variables.		The partial r is used when the relationship between two variables is influenced by a third variable.
Multiple correlation	$R_{1.234}$	One variable (criterion) vs. many variables		Employed where two or more variables are used to predict a single variable. In the symbol subscript $R_{1.234} \ldots n$ the subscript 1 stands for the criterion variable; the 234 for the predictor variables.

INFERENTIAL STATISTICS

Refer to the chart on page 175 showing the divisions of statistics—the map of the statistical landscape. We are still in the realm of parametric statistics, but we now leave descriptive statistics to discuss inferential statistics.

Inferential statistics has two principal functions:

1. To predict or estimate a population parameter from a random sample.
2. To test *statistically based* hypotheses.

Prediction: One of the Roles of Inferential Statistics

Prediction is division of statistics that have many ramifications. In this text, we cannot venture too far into this area. Again, statistical texts will provide you with this information. We shall, however, comment briefly concerning some general underlying concepts and principles.

Earlier, we discussed prediction or estimation of values in terms of measures of central tendency. We then balanced our estimate of "goodness of guess" with "badness of guess" as indicated by the degree of dispersion or variation. We also considered the predictive implications of the line of regression. These estimating techniques are not, however, those that we usually consider within the realm of inferential statistics.

Inferential statistics is more concerned with estimating *population parameters from sample statistics.*[13] The population estimates that we commonly attempt to make are estimates of *parameters* with respect to frequency distributions or parts thereof, estimates with respect to the population μ (central tendency of the population), the σ (variability of the population), or the proportion or probability, the P. These values in the population compare with the $\bar{X}$, the s, and the p of the sample.

To understand exactly what we mean by estimation, let us take a simple illustration. Joe is a production manager of a manufacturing corporation. He has a sample lot of connecting-rod pins. These pins fit snugly into assembly units, permitting the units to swivel within a given arc. The diameter of the pins is critical. If the diameter is too small, the assembly will wobble in turning; if too large, the assembly will stick and refuse to move. Joe has received a number of complaints from customers that the pins are faulty. He wishes to estimate, on the basis of a sample, how many of the units may have to be recalled for replacement. The sample is presumably random and representative. From this sample, Joe wishes to know three facts relative to the hundreds of thousands of pins that have been manufactured and sold on the market.

1. How many of them are within acceptable tolerance limits?
2. How widely do they vary in diameter measurement: what is the deviation, the variance?
3. What proportion of the pins produced will be acceptable in the assemblies already marketed?

The problem is to judge population parameters on the basis of the sample statistics. From the sample, he can estimate the mean, the variation, and the probability of acceptable pins within the population universe. There are the values represented by the μ, σ, and the P.

Certain basic assumptions underlie all prediction procedures: (1) Estimates of whatever kind assume that the sample is random and representative of the total population. Only by its being so can we have any congruity between the sample and the population universe from which the sample was chosen and, conversely, toward which the prediction will be made; and (2) the sample ideally should be a microcosm of the greater universe of the population. The closer this correspondence, the greater is the predictive accuracy of the sample. When such a situation exists, we then have statistical techniques to effect a projection from the statistic of the sample to the corresponding parameter of the population. Whatever we can determine with respect to a *statistic* of the sample, we can estimate with respect to a *parameter* of the population.

Point vs Interval Estimates

In making estimates of population parameters from sample statistics, we can make estimates of two types: (1) *point estimates* and (2) *interval estimates.*

A *point estimate* is a single statistic which is taken as the best indication of the corresponding population parameter. We have discussed (on pages 178-179) the variability within

[13] The student should review carefully the distinction between a *parameter* and a *statistic.* See page 176.

samples—the error of the means of random samples from the true mean of the total population. This variability we must recognize and take into account when making any kind of estimate, particularly point estimates, where we are shooting for a statistical "bull's-eye."

Point estimates afford us very little freedom. We seek the parallel population parameter value with the sample statistic value. Although point estimates have the virtue of being precise, precision has its own price; and the price for precision is that the point estimate will generally not exactly correspond with the true population equivalent.

An estimate is a statistical flight into the unknown. The prediction of population parameters is at best a matter of dead reckoning. It takes its sightings from a randomly selected sample and, taking into account the other conditioning factors, makes its predictions on the basis of these contingencies. We have seen earlier (page 152) that the accuracy estimating the population mean depends upon (1) the size of the sample, and (2) the degree of its variability.

In the example of the connecting-rod pins, had we been told that the company had produced 500,000 pins, of which Joe had a sample of 1,000 with a given mean diameter and a standard deviation of .005 inch, we then would have been able to have made a parametric estimate. And, although the values we had predicted may not have been precisely accurate for the total production of connecting pins, they would certainly have been better than nothing.

So much for point estimation. A much more comfortable procedure is the *interval estimate* of parameters. In this type of prediction, we specify a band within whose limits we estimate that practically all the values will lie. Such a band is commonly called the *confidence interval* because we have confidence that between the delimitation values we have set, 95 percent of all the data values will be found. At times, depending upon the research refinement that we seek, we may set the limit at 99 percent of confidence. Statisticians usually consider these two values as standard for confidence levels. Sometimes, however, we phrase the same concept in terms of *level of significance.* This is looking at the concept of the confidence interval precisely in reverse.

Any factor which causes *more* than a 1 percent variability in 99 percent of the data or, in the case of a 95 percent confidence limit, a 5 percent variability in the data values is considered to be the result of some influence other than the fortuitous vagaries of mere chance.[14] We speak, thus, of a factor as being *statistically significant* at the 5 percent level or at the 1 percent level of significance. In brief, what this means is that we permit a certain narrow margin of variance, which we deem to be natural and the result of pure chance. Any variation *within* this statistically permissible band is not considered to be important enough to claim our attention. Whatever *exceeds these limits*, however, is considered to be the result of some determinative factor other than that of natural fortuitousness, and so the influence is considered to be a significant one. The term *significant*, in the statistical sense in which we have been using it, is very close to its pure etymological meaning, namely, "giving a signal" that something is operating below the surface of the statistic that merits further attention and investigation. Thus, is new research born. In investigating one problem, we discover a force, a dynamic that we had not anticipated to be present—and a new investigation is facing us. And this is only one of the places in the entire research structure that we may come upon such unexpected events. Wherever they appear, there is the opening of a new avenue leading toward Truth.

We have said enough about estimation for you to appreciate its importance. To venture further would get us involved in a statistical methodology and specific operational pro-

[14] See comment with reference to the die on page 195.

A SUMMARY TABLE OF POINT AND INTERVAL ESTIMATES OF PARAMETERS

SCALE	KIND OF MEASURE			
	Frequency distributions or parts thereof	Central Tendency	Variability	Correlation
NOMINAL	$\tilde{P} = p$ $\quad \sigma_p = \sqrt{PQ/N}$ $\frac{p - P}{\sigma_p}$ is normally distributed when $NP \geqslant 5$. Confidence bands for estimating P from p. Chi-square test for correspondence of obtained and expected frequency distributions.		$\tilde{H} = \hat{H} + 1.3863N$	$\tilde{T} = \hat{T} - \frac{(r - 1)(k - 1)}{1.3863N}$
ORDINAL	Confidence interval for any population percentile made in terms of sample percentiles. Kolmogorov-Smirnov confidence band for entire cumulative percentage histogram.	$\widetilde{\text{Mdn}}_{pop} = \text{Mdn}$ Confidence intervals in terms of sample percentiles.	Confidence intervals for Q_1 and Q_3 in terms of sample percentiles.	
INTERVAL AND RATIO	Chi-square and Kolmogorov-Smirnov tests can be used to determine goodness of fit of any theoretical distribution —e.g., normal.	$\tilde{\mu} = \bar{X}$, $\tilde{\sigma}_{\bar{X}} = s/\sqrt{N - 1}$ $\frac{\bar{X} - \mu}{\tilde{\sigma}_{\bar{X}}}$ has t-distribution for samples from normal populations. For small samples from nonnormal populations, use Tchebychev's Inequality. Same principles for Mdn., but $\tilde{\sigma}_{Mdn} = 1.253\tilde{\sigma}_{\bar{X}}$.	$\tilde{\sigma}^2 = s^2\left(\frac{N}{N - 1}\right)$ For samples from normal populations, Ns^2 has chi-square distribution with $N - 1$ degrees of freedom.	Confidence bands for estimating ρ from r. $z_r = 1.1513 \log_{10} \frac{1 + r}{1 - r}$ $(z_r - z_\rho)(\sqrt{N - 3})$ has unit normal distribution if population is normal bivariate.

From *Measurement and Statistics: A Basic Text Emphasizing Behavioral Science*, by Virginia L. Senders. (Modified at the direction of the author.)

cedures which are not the province of this text. For those who wish a guide to such procedures, we present in the table above a Summary of Point and Interval Estimates of Parameters. The student must consult the textbooks in statistics for these matters.

There still remains the last of the functions of inferential statistics in the analytical survey method, namely, the *testing of hypotheses*, to which we now turn.

The Testing of Hypotheses

At the very outset, we should clarify the matter of terminology. The term *hypothesis* can bewilder you hopelessly unless you understand that it has two entirely different meanings in the literature of research.

The first of these two meanings restricts the word *hypothesis* to a *research problem-oriented hypothesis.* On the other hand, the second usage of the term is limited to a *statistically oriented hypothesis*. In the first meaning of the word, a hypothesis exists because the research problem, or the subproblems issuing from it, arouses a curiosity in the researcher's mind, which, in turn, results in the positing of a *tentative guess* relative to the resolution of the problematic situation. This type of hypothesis we discussed earlier in connection with the discussion of the nature of research.[15] It concerned the perplexed motorist who had trouble in starting this car. The hypothesis is, therefore, in one sense a reasonable and logical conjecture, an educated guess. Its purpose is a very practical one: it provides a tentative objective, an operational bull's-eye, a logical construct which helps the researcher look for the data.

Based on conclusions to which the data force him, the researcher must either confirm or deny the hypothesis which he has posited. In a sense, a problem-oriented hypothesis in research is comparable to a scaffold in construction engineering. Each has its purpose as a function of an ongoing operation: in the case of the hypothesis, it is the pursuit of the data which, when inspected and interpreted, will help in the solution of the problem being researched; in the case of the scaffold, it is the erection of an architectural structure. The completion of the project makes both the hypothesis and the scaffold of no further use. Both are vitally necessary, though intermediary functionaries, whose sole purpose is to facilitate the achievement of the ultimate goal.

When, however, one comes across the phrase *tests of hypotheses*, the matter is entirely different. Here the word *hypothesis* refers to a *statistically based hypothesis*, commonly known as a *null hypothesis*. The null hypothesis postulates that there is no statistically significant difference between phenomena which occur by pure chance and the statistically evaluated behavior of the data as they have been observed by the researcher in a survey or an experimental research design.

If a difference *does* occur, and the magnitude of that difference is such as to exceed the possibility of its having been caused by random error or pure chance, then we conclude that some intervening variable aside from the fortuitousness of nature is energizing the data and, in consequence, we reject the null hypothesis. It is this comparison of observed data with expected results of normative values that we call testing the hypothesis, or—perhaps more accurately—testing the *null hypothesis*.

What is frequently confusing to the uninitiated researcher is that to test the null hypothesis is nothing more than a statistical comparison of the data from two situations: one of these, we consider mathematically "ideal" because it conforms to the parameters of the normal distribution; the other situation we derive from life. To these latter data, we apply certain statistical processes to determine whether their calculated values diverge from the statistical ideal sufficiently to reject the fact that there is "no difference" (*null* difference) between the two sets of data. It is important to keep clearly in mind, therefore, the difference between the two general kinds of hypotheses. You cannot "test" the first type statistically as you can the second type. In the literature, the null hypothesis is generally represented by the symbol H_0.

We should also look at hypothesis testing from another point of view. From the interpretation that we have given to the word *research* early in these pages[16], namely, "a systematic quest for undiscovered truth," through techniques of the scientific method, the testing of the null hypothesis does not contribute much to the fulfillment of this basic aim of pure research. Also, we have indicated that statistics is merely a "tool of research," whose function in the entire research process is merely to take the data, quantify them, and inspect them in their quantified form so that, having been converted into the language of mathematics, they may reply to the researcher in terms of quantitative values and, by so doing, give some indication of the characteristics of the data and the dynamics which affect them.

Statistics has its function, but that function is medial: to inspect the data by means of a tool whose facility is that of revealing aspects of the data of which we might not otherwise be aware. Statistics—the testing of the null hypothesis—leaves us frequently

---

[15] See pages 5–6.

[16] See page 13.

with merely an indication that factors or forces either are or are not present which may influence the data.

In the last analysis, the testing of the null hypothesis merely confirms or denies the deeper presence of "something" that is working within the data. It is this all-important *something* that the genuine researcher seeks to identify and evaluate. To stop with a mere indication that "something" is there which accounts for a significant difference between one set of data and another set of data is to settle for a ghost, and research is not a systematic quest for ghosts. It is a systematic search for Truth.

Statistical hypothesis-testing is an important component in the decision theory and, as such, it has value for those who must make decisions on the basis of statistical characteristics of samples. Every researcher must ultimately develop an intellectual acuity that looks with honest unprejudiced candor at his procedures and his results. If those results reveal *facts* newly discovered and those facts result in new insight, then the data have been interpreted. That is quite a different matter from running those data through a statistical formula and coming out with a numerical value. The one process ends in a decimal fraction; the other, in a deeper understanding of the meaning of the data. The latter includes the former, but they should never be confused as to which is which.

NONPARAMETRIC STATISTICS

Before we leave the discussion of the analytical survey method, we should present briefly the nonparametric methods of dealing statistically with certain types of data. Thus far, we have been subscribing to an assumption: *that all populations and the samples drawn from them demonstrate certain parameters.* We have assumed that the mean and the standard deviation were the common attributes of all data. This is not universally so. Not all data are parametric. Nature does not invariably behave as a Gaussian curve. Consider a page of print. It presents a binary world. No normal distribution there. Any given point on the page is either black or white. Human beings are either male or female, alive or dead. As we have a world of the bell-shaped curve, so also do we have the world of the sharp dichotomy: the world of either/or.

Sometimes also, the data world looks more like a stairway than a bell-shaped curve: the data occur at graduated elevations—data ranked above or below data in a well-escalated arrangement. Take a graduating class. When each student is ranked in academic subjects, John ranks first in English, fifteenth in mathematics. Other students have individual rankings up and down the academic staircase. To study a ranked situation of this kind, a statistical system based upon the assumption of normal distributions, of means, and of standard deviations is simply not applicable.

Data with the characteristics such as we have just been describing demand a statistical methodology which will recognize the particular characteristics of non-normal curve data and provide specialized approaches which will take the singular characteristics of such data into account. Such a methodology is found in *nonparametric statistics*.

The system of nonparametric statistics is less powerful than the parametric techniques. By less powerful we mean that, in general, they require larger samples in order to yield the same level of significance. They also are less likely to reject the null hypothesis when it should be rejected, or to differentiate between groups as sensitively as do the parametric methods.

The Principal Nonparametric Techniques

★ *The Chi Square Test.* Perhaps the most commonly used nonparametric test is the *chi square* (χ^2) *test.* It is generally used in causal comparative studies. We also employ χ^2 in instances where we have a comparison between observed and theoretical frequencies or in testing the mathematical fit of a frequency curve to an observed frequency distribution. Chi square is applicable when we have two variables from independent samples, each of which is categorized in two ways. Chi square is likewise valuable in analyzing data that are expressed as frequencies rather than as measurements. In electronics, for example, a sine wave has a certain amplitude in wavelength. This can be measured in standard measurement lengths. It also has a certain number of frequencies per second. For frequency evaluation in certain research instances, χ^2 is probably the most appropriate statistical technique. Of all the nonparametric tools, χ^2 is probably the most important.

There are, however, other nonparametric approaches which have specialized application; and, although we cannot go into a discussion of these in detail, we can list the principal ones with brief comments as to their significances and usual applications. Any text dealing with nonparametric statistics will discuss these in full and indicate their application to the data.

★ *The Mann-Whitney U-test.* The Mann-Whitney U-test is the counterpart of the *t*-test in parametric measurements. It may be used in determining whether the medians of two independent samples differ from each other to a significant degree.

★ *The Wilcoxon Matched Pairs, Signed-Rank Test.* The Wilcoxon matched pairs, signed-rank test is employed to determine whether two samples differ from each other to a significant degree when there is a relationship between the samples.

★ *The Wilcoxon Rank Sum Test.* The Wilcoxon rank sum test may be used in those situations where measures are expressed as ranked data in order to test the hypothesis that the samples are from a common population whose distribution of the measures is the same as that of the samples.

★ *The Kolmogorov-Smirnov Test.* The Kolmogorov-Smirnov test fulfills the function of χ^2 in testing goodness of fit and the Wilcoxon rank sum test in determining whether random samples are from the same population.

★ *The Sign Test.* The sign test is important in determining the significance of the differences between two correlated samples. The "signs" of the sign test are the algebraic plus and minus values of the difference of the paired scores. Where the difference between the paired scores favors the X variable a plus sign is given; those favoring the Y variable are assigned the minus designation. The null hypothesis postulates a O value with the pluses equaling the minuses. To test for significance between the plus and minus signs, χ^2 can be used.

★ *The Median Test.* The median test is a sign test for two independent samples in contradistinction to two correlated samples, as is the case with the sign test.

★ *The Spearman Rank Order Correlation.* The Spearman rank order correlation, sometimes called Spearman's rho (ρ) or Spearman's rank difference correlation, is a nonparametric statistic that has its counterpart in parametric calculations in the Pearson product moment correlation.

★ *The Kruskal-Wallis Test.* The Kruskal-Wallis test is sometimes known as the Kruskal-Wallace H test of ranks for k independent samples. The H in the title of the test stands for null hypothesis; and the k (from the German *klasse*, "class") for the classes or samples. The test looks for the significance of differences among three or more groups, and it has been developed along the same general lines as the Mann-Whitney U test. The Kruskal-Wallis test is a one-way analysis of variance and is the nonparametric correspondent to the analysis of variance in parametric statistics. Its purpose is to determine whether k independent samples have been drawn from the same population.

★ *The Kendall Coefficient of Concordance.* The Kendall coefficient of concordance is also variously known as Kendall's concordance coefficient W or the concordance coefficient W. It is a technique which can be used with advantage in studies involving rankings made by independent judges. To analyze the rankings the Kendall coefficient will indicate the degree to which such judges agree in their assignment of ranks. The Kendall coefficient W is based on the deviation of the total of each ranking. To test the significance of W, we simply employ the null hypothesis and test it by employing the χ^2 technique.

★ *The Corner Test*. A little-known test is the corner test, whose function is to test the hypothesis that two continuous variables are independent. The test is a graphical one. The data are plotted as for a conventional correlation study. When all the data have been plotted in a matrix plot arrangement, medians are drawn for the X variable, which median will be parallel to the X axis. A Y median is also drawn through the plotted data to divide them equally in a horizontal direction. The four quadrants are then assigned the conventional plus and minus signs and, consequently, the plotted data falling within each quadrant thus become either positive or negative. Now, inspect the data in the four quadrants. Draw a line to the left and a line to the right, also similar lines above and below the median lines at the extremity of the lesser of each of the respective groups of data. The test of significance will be based upon the count of the number of points lying outside the lines marking the boundaries of the lesser groups of data. If a point lies beyond one of the demarcation lines, it is given a value of 1; if it lies beyond two of these lines, it rates a value of 2. The algebraic sum of all the outlying points is the test statistic. From it is computed the degree of association and the nature of that association.[17]

The following is a summary table of both parametric and nonparametric tests applicable to testing *statistical* hypotheses. You may find it helpful in selecting the proper tool for the specific situation.

TESTS OF HYPOTHESES

SCALE	HYPOTHESIS							
	Two independent samples have:		Two correlated samples have:	k independent samples have:		k correlated samples have:	Two variables are:	
	Equal variability	Same central tendency or proportion	Same central tendency	Equal variabilities	Same central tendency	Same central tendency	Uncorrelated or independent	Linearly related
NOMINAL		$p_1 - p_2$ is normally distributed with $\sigma_{D_p} = \sqrt{p_a q_a \left(\frac{1}{N_1} + \frac{1}{N_2}\right)}$			Chi-square test for equality of several sample proportions.		Chi-square test of independence. Likelihood-ratio chi-square. If $T = 0$, $1.3863NT$ has chi-square distribution with $(r - 1)(k - 1)$ degrees of freedom.	
ORDINAL	Run test (also sensitive to differences in central tendency).	Run test (also sensitive to differences in variability. Median test. Rank-sums test.	Sign test		Median test Kruskal-Wallis test	Friedman test (sometimes called 'analysis of variance by ranks').	Contingency test of association. Test of hypothesis that $\rho_O = 0$.	
INTERVAL AND RATIO	F test. Assumes normality of populations.	$\tilde{\sigma}_{\bar{X}_1 - \bar{X}_2} = \tilde{\sigma}\sqrt{\frac{1}{N_1} + \frac{1}{N_2}}$ $\frac{\bar{X}_1 - \bar{X}_2}{\tilde{\sigma}_{\bar{X}_1 - \bar{X}_2}}$ has t-distribution with $N_1 + N_2 - 2$ degrees of freedom when samples are from normal populations with equal variances.	Wilcoxon Test for Paired Replicates. For large samples, or small samples from normal populations $\frac{\bar{D}}{sD/\sqrt{N-1}}$ has a t-distribution with N - 1 degrees of freedom.	Bartlett's Test for Homogeneity of Variance.	Analysis of variance. $\frac{\tilde{\sigma}^2_B}{\tilde{\sigma}^2_W}$ has F distribution if samples are from normal populations with equal variances.	Analysis of variance (two dimensional). Assumes normality and homogeneity of variance.	Test hypothesis that $\eta = 0$ by use of F ratio. Test hypothesis that $\rho = 0$ by use of F ratio or t-test.	Test hypothesis that $\rho = \eta$ by use of F ratio.

From *Measurement and Statistics: **A Basic Test Emphasizing Behavioral Science***, by Virginia L. Senders. (Modified at the direction of the author.)

[17] A full explanation of the corner test is given in Albert Rickmers and Hollis N. Todd, *Statistics: An Introduction* (New York: McGraw-Hill Book Company, 1967), pp. 403–405.

Looking Backward

It may be well at this juncture, after what has been a somewhat long and at times involved discussion, to turn to the opening pages of this chapter and to review there what has been the purpose of this discussion: ". . . the purpose is to probe . . . data by means of statistics so that we may infer certain meanings which lie hidden within the data or . . . discern the presence of certain potentials and dynamic forces which may be a clue to areas that warrant further investigation."[18]

It may also be helpful to review the map of the statistical landscape—the flow-chart showing the organization of statistics—also found on page 175. Both of these exercises may help you to see what this chapter has been all about. It may bring into focus the tool of statistics as this handmaiden of the mathematics has been an ancillary servant of research.

Practical Application —

We derive a clear understanding of statistics and statistical procedures by seeing these in actual practice and by encountering them in the literature. To give you an opportunity to see more clearly some of the matters we have been discussing, turn to pages 297–298 of the practicum section. There you will have an opportunity to apply what has here been a theoretical presentation.

— —

FOR FURTHER READING

(See also the Further Readings Section in Statistics at the End of Chapter 2.)

Readings in the Area of General Statistics

Baum, P., and E. M. Scheuer. *Statistics Made Relevant: A Casebook of Real Life Examples.* New York: John Wiley & Sons, 1981.

Box, George E. P., William G. Hunter and J. Stuart Hunter, *Statistics for Experimenters: An Introduction to Design, Data Analysis, and Model Building.* New York: John Wiley & Sons, Inc., 1978.

Brieman, Leo. *Statistics with a View toward Applications.* Boston, Mass.: Houghton Mifflin Company, 1973.

Castle, Winifred M. *Statistics in Small Doses.* New York: Churchill Livingston, Inc., 1977.

Christensen, Howard B. *Statistics: Step-by-Step.* Boston: Houghton Mifflin Company, 1977.

Dapkus, F. *Statistics One: A Text for Beginners.* Elmsford, N.Y.: Collegium Book Publishers, 1979.

Fogiel, Max. *Statistics Problem Solver: A Supplement to Any Class Text.* New York: Research and Education Association, 1978.

Klugh, Henry E. *Statistics: The Essentials for Research.* Second ed. New York: John Wiley & Sons, 1974.

Larsen, Richard J., and Donna F. Stroup. *Statistics in the Real World: A Book of Examples.* New York: Macmillan Publishing Company, Inc., 1976.

Mattson, Dale E. *Statistics: Difficult Concepts, Understandable Explanations.* St. Louis, Missouri: The C. V. Mosby Company, 1981.

[18] See page 173.

Neave, H. R. *Statistics Tables.* Winchester, Mass.: Allen Unwin, Inc., 1977.

Ostle, Bernard, and Richard Mensing. *Statistics in Research.* Ames, Iowa: Iowa State University Press, 1975.

Rowntree, Derek. *Statistics Without Tears: A Primer for Non-Mathematicians.* New York: Charles Scribner's Sons, 1982.

Ukens, Ann S. *Statistics Today.* New York: Harper & Row, Publishers, 1978.

Wonnacott, Thomas J., and Ronald J. Wonnacott. *Statistics: Discovering Its Power.* New York: John Wiley & Sons, 1981.

In the Area of the Behavioral Sciences

Johnson, M., and R. Liebert. *Statistics: Tool of the Behavioral Sciences.* Englewood Cliffs, N.J.: Prentice Hall, Inc., 1977.

Lindner, William A., and Rhoda Lindner. *Statistics for Students in the Behavioral Sciences.* Menlo Park, Calif.: Benjamin-Cummings Publishing Co., 1979.

Mendenhall, William, and Madeline Ramey, *Statistics for Psychology.* North Scituate, Massachusetts: Duxbury Press, 1977.

Palumbo, Dennis J. *Statistics in Political and Behavioral Science.* New York: Columbia University Press, 1977.

In the Area of Biology and the Health Sciences

Bishop, O. N. *Statistics for Biology.* Second ed. New York: Longman, Inc., 1981.

Bliss, Chester I. *Statistics in Biology.* 2 vols. New York: McGraw-Hill Book Company, 1967.

Broyles, Robert, and Colin Lay. *Statistics in Health Administration.* 2 vols. Rockville, Md.: Aspen Systems Corporation, 1980.

Buncher, C. Ralph, and Jai Yeong Tsay. *Statistics in the Pharmaceutical Industry.* New York: Marcel Dekker, Inc., 1981.

Campbell, R. C. *Statistics for Biologists.* New York: Cambridge University Press, 1974.

Colton, Theodore. *Statistics in Medicine.* Boston, Mass.: Little, Brown and Company, 1975.

Finny, D. J. *Statistics for Biologists.* London: Methuen & Co., Inc., 1980.

Goldstone, Leonard A. *Statistics in the Management of Nursing Services.* London: Pitman Books, Ltd., 1980.

Hammerton, Max. *Statistics for the Human Sciences.* New York: Longman, Inc., 1975.

Kviz, Frederick J., and Kathleen A. Knafl. *Statistics for Nurses: An Introductory Text.* Boston: Little, Brown and Company, 1980.

Larsen, Richard J. *Statistics for the Allied Health Sciences.* Columbus, Ohio: Charles E. Merrill Publishing Company, 1975.

Mike, Valerie, and Kenneth E. Stanley. *Statistics in Medical Research: Methods and Issues with Applications in Cancer Research.* New York: John Wiley & Sons, 1982.

Remington, R., and M. A. Schork. *Statistics with Applications to the Biological and Health Sciences.* Englewood Cliff, N.J.: Prentice-Hall, Inc., 1970.

Schefler, William C. *Statistics for the Biological Sciences.* Reading, Mass.: Addison-Wesley Publishing Co., Inc., 1979.

Von Fraunhofer, J. A., and J. J. Murray. *Statistics in Medical, Dental, and Biological Studies.* Montclair, N.J.: Tri-Med Books (England), 1981.

In the Area of Business, Economics, and Management

Ashford, John. *Statistics for Management.* Brookfield, Vt.: Renouf USA, Inc., 1977.

Ben Horim, Mosche, and Haim Levy. *Statistics: Decisions and Applications in Business and Economics.* New York: Random House, 1981.

Chao, Lincoln L. *Statistics for Management.* Monterey, Calif.: Brooks-Cole Publishing Co., 1980.

Clark, John, J., and Margaret T. Clark. *Statistics Primer for Managers: How to Ask the Right Questions about Forecasting, Control, and Investment.* New York: Macmillan Publishing Co., Inc., 1982.

Davies, Brinley, and John Foad. *Statistics for Economics.* Exeter, N.H.: Heinemann Educational Books, Inc., 1977.

Fisher, Walter D. *Statistics Economized: Basic Statistics for Economics and Business.* Lanham, Md.: University Press of America, 1981.

Haack, Dennis G. *Statistical Literacy: a Guide to Interpretation.* Boston: PWS Publishers, 1978.

Heitzman, William R., and Frederick W. Mueller. *Statistics for Business and Economics.* Boston: Allyn & Bacon, 1980.

Lapin, Lawrence L. *Statistics for Modern Business Decisions.* 3rd ed. New York: Harcourt Brace Jovanovich, Inc., 1982.

Levin, Richard I. *Statistics for Management.* 2nd ed. Englewood Cliffs, N.J.: Prentice-Hall, 1981.

Mandel, B. J. *Statistics for Management: A Simplified Introduction to Statistics.* 4th ed. Baltimore, Md.: Dangary Publishing Co., 1977.

Mansfield, Edwin. *Statistics for Business and Economics.* New York: W. W. Norton, 1980.

Matlack, W. F. *Statistics for Public Policy and Management.* North Scituate, Mass.: Duxbury Press, 1980.

McClave, James T., and George Benson. *Statistics for Business and Economics.* 2nd ed. Santa Clara, Calif.: Dellen Publishing Co., 1982.

Mendenhall, William, and James E. Reinmuth. *Statistics for Management and Economics.* 4th ed. North Scituate, Mass.: Duxbury Press, 1982.

Mills, Richard L. *Statistics for Applied Economics and Business.* New York: McGraw-Hill Book Company, 1977.

Plane, Donald R., and Edwin B. Oppermann. *Statistics for Management Decisions.* Rev. ed. Plano, Texas: Business Publications, Inc., 1981.

Sobol, Marion G., and Martin K. Starr. *Statistics for Business and Economics: An Action Learning Approach.* New York: McGraw-Hill Book Company, 1983.

In the Area of Criminal Justice

Griffin, John I. *Statistics Essential for Police Efficiency.* Springfield, Illinois: Charles C. Thomas Publishing Co., 1972.

In the Area of Education

Cohen, Louis, and Michael Holliday. *Statistics for Education.* New York: Harper & Row, 1979.

Crocker, A. C. *Statistics for the Teacher.* Atlantic Highlands, N.J.: Humanities Press, Inc., 1974.

McIntosh, D. M. *Statistics for the Teacher.* 2nd ed. Elmsford, N.Y.: Pergamon Press, Inc., 1967.

Talmage, Harriet. *Statistics as a Tool for Educational Practitioners.* Berkeley, Calif.: McCutchan Publishers, 1976.

Townsend, Edward A., and Paul J. Burke. *Statistics for the Classroom Teacher.* New York: Macmillan Publishing Co., Inc., 1963.

White, David. *Statistics for Education with Data Processing.* New York: Harper & Row, 1973.

In the Area of Geography

Ebdon, David. *Statistics in Geography: A Practical Approach.* Oxford, England: Blackwell Publishers, Ltd., 1977.

Mandal, R. B. *Statistics for Geographers and Social Scientists.* Atlantic Highlands, N.J.: Humanities Press, Inc., 1981.

In the Area of Language and Linguistics

Anshen, Frank. *Statistics for Linguists.* Rowley, Mass.: Newbury House Publishers, 1978.

In the Area of the Physical Sciences

Chatfield, Christopher. *Statistics for Technology: A Course in Applied Statistics.* 2nd ed. New York: Methuen, Inc., 1978.

Martin, B. R. *Statistics for Physicists.* New York: Academic Press, Inc., 1971.

Schaeffer, Richard, and James McClave. *Statistics for Engineers.* North Scituate, Mass: Duxbury Press, 1982.

Wine, Russell L. *Statistics for Scientists and Engineers.* Englewood Cliffs, N.J.: Prentice-Hall, Inc., 1964.

Youmans, Hubert L. *Statistics for Chemistry.* Columbus, Ohio: Charles E. Merrill Company, 1973.

In the Area of the Social Sciences

Bohrnstedt, George W., and David Knoke. *Statistics for Social Data Analysis.* New York: Bantam Books, Inc., 1982.

Cohen, Louis, and Michael Holliday, *Statistics for the Social Sciences.* New York: Harper and Row, 1982.

Hagood, Margaret J., and Daniel O. Price. *Statistics for Sociologists.* New York: Holt, Rinehart and Winston, 1952.

Horwitz, Lucy, and Lou Ferleger. *Statistics for Social Change.* Boston: South End Press, 1980.

Iversen, Gudmund R. *Statistics for Sociology.* Dubuque, Iowa: William C. Brown Company, 1979.

Sharp, Vicki F. *Statistics for the Social Sciences.* Boston: Little, Brown and Company, 1979.

Yeomans, Keith A. *Statistics for the Social Scientist.* Baltimore, Md.: Penguin Books, 1968.

READ THIS—BEFORE YOU READ THE CHAPTER

The experimental method is perhaps the most popular and most commonly understood of all the research methodologies. Test the subject; do something to the subject; test the subject again to see if there is a difference. This, in the popular mind, is the experimental method. And, in a sense, it is. But the experimental method is much more. In this chapter, we shall consider it as a means of attempting to solve many unique research situations for which the methods we have previously considered are totally inadequate. The experimental method has its discrete place, and it contributes a distinctive methodology in the total hierarchy of research approaches.

In the thinking of some, the experimental method is the only pure research method. To them, if the procedure is not experimental, it is not research. This, of course, is a parochial and misunderstood concept of research as a broad inquiry after truth.

The experimental design is a very important method, and for those who find it appropriate to their research needs, a suggestive bibliography at the close of the chapter may provide more in-depth consideration than the overview afforded by this chapter can accomplish.

10
The Experimental Method

GENERAL CONSIDERATIONS

The experimental method is the last major methodological approach in research that we will consider. This methodology goes by various names: the experimental method, the cause and effect method, the pretest-posttest control group design, the laboratory method. By whatever name, the basic idea behind the experimental method is to attempt to account for the influence of a factor or, as in the case of complex designs, of multiple factors conditioning a given situation. In its simplest form, the experimental method attempts to control the entire research situation, except for certain input variables which then become suspect as the cause of whatever change has taken place within the investigative design.

Underlying Concepts

The matter of *control* is, in fact, so basic to the experimental method that we frequently refer to this means of searching for truth as the *control group-experimental group design.* At the outset, we assume that the forces and dynamics within both groups are equistatic. We begin, as far as possible, with *matched groups.* These groups are randomly selected and paired so that, insofar as possible within the limits of the crude evaluative instruments that we have available, especially in the social and humanistic areas of study, each group will resemble the other in as many characteristics as possible and, certainly, with respect to those qualities that are critical to the experiment. Mathematically, we may represent the equivalent status of these groups at the beginning of the experiment as

$$\text{Experimental group} = \text{Control group}$$

And, although we assume that both groups have at the beginning of the experiment identical characteristics, identical values, and identical status, perfect identity is more theoretical than real. In recognition of this fact, therefore, we employ the phrase *matched groups,* or we say that they are "groups matched on the basis of x, y, and z." The x, y, and z are the qualitative parameters which provide the basis for matching.

Perhaps a glance backward will bring into contrast the distinctive nature of the experimental method. Reviewing the various research methodologies, we see that each provides a unique way to handle the data which fall within its methodological boundaries: the historical method deals with the study of documents; the descriptive survey, with the study of observations; the analytical survey, with the investigation of data dynamics and interrelationships of these dynamics through appropriate statistical techniques. We shall now look at the experimental method to see its characteristics.

The Characteristics of the Experimental Method

The experimental method deals with the phenomenon of *cause and effect.* We assess the cause and effect dynamics within a closed system of controlled conditions. Essentially, the basic structure of this methodology is simple. We have two situations. We assess each to establish comparability. Then, we attempt to alter one of these by introducing into it an extraneous dynamic. We reevaluate each situation after the intervening attempt at alteration. Whatever change is noticed is presumed to have been caused by the extraneous variable. Basically, this is the method practiced in research laboratories and is known as the experimental method.

But we must clarify the difference between an *experiment* and the *experimental method.* They are *not* the same. An illustration will suffice to establish the distinction. Consider a problem that arose in the laboratory of Thomas Edison in the early days of the incandescent electric light. Edison had given his engineers the well-known tapering and rounded bulb for them to calculate its volume. They brought to play on the problem all their mathematical knowledge. When they reported to Edison, each of them had a different answer. Edison then went into his laboratory, drew a container of water, measured its volume, immersed the incandescent bulb in it, and snipped off the pointed glass tip. Water rushed into the bulb because it was a vacuum, filling the bulb completely. Edison then measured the difference between the water in the container after filling the bulb and subtracted that volume from the water in the container originally. The difference between the two was the cubic capacity of the bulb.

That was an *experiment.* It was not *research,* nor was Edison's method *the experimental method of research.* Had there been any factual *meaning* behind the experiment and then had this meaning been discovered, the experiment would then have become a *research* experiment. As it was, the experiment merely determined a fact, and for that particular fact there was no further meaning.

Experimental research needs to be planned. We call this planning the *designing of the experiment.* In experimental research, however, the word *design* has two distinct meanings. Because of this, the inexperienced researcher may frequently be confused. In one sense, the word *design* refers to *the propriety of the statistical analysis necessary to prepare the data for interpretation.*

Frequently a student comes to his professor, who advises him that he needs the assistance of a statistician to help him with the "design" of his research. Pick up many tests in psychological or physical or biological scientific research methodology and what you will find is essentially a text in statistics. Hence, what *experimental design* means here is that the proper statistical techniques for analyzing the quantitative data must be properly selected and utilized in accordance with the nature of the data. The meaning of the term in this sense is strictly beyond the province of this text. This is not a text in the teaching of statistical design. We have made reference to proper statistical approaches in the tables of the last chapter and elsewhere. Many statistical textbooks on experimental design are available, and the student should refer to them.

The meaning of the word *design* as it is employed in a purely reseach connotation refers, of course, to *the total architectural plan, the tectonic structure of the research framework.* This goes far beyond the mere selection of statistical tools to process data, test hypotheses, or effect prediction.

We shall explore design in this sense further in this chapter. Where the term *experimental design* is used, it will mean, of course, the architectonics and planning of the entire experimental approach to a problem for research. The statistical aspects are only one phase in that total approach and prepare the data merely so that the researcher may be in better position to assess their meaning and interpret their significance.

Classification of Experimental Designs

Experimental designs have been variously categorized by different writers in the field of research. Perhaps the simplest of these is the dichotomized classification of Wise, Nordberg, and Reitz in which they classify all experimental designs into two types: (1) *functional designs* or (2) *factorial designs.*[1] The difference between the two design types is whether the researcher is able to control the independent variable at will (*the functional*

[1] John E. Wise, Robert B. Nordber, and Donald J. Reitz, *Methods of Research in Education.* (Boston, Mass.: D. C. Heath & Co., 1967), pp. 133-37.

design) or whether, during the course of the experiment, the researcher *cannot* control the independent variable (*the factorial design*). Earlier, we indicated that the matter of *control* was fundamental to the experimental method. So basic is it, indeed, that its presence determines the *nature* of the variable. If the investigator has control over the variable and is able to manipulate it or change it at will, then we say that the variable is an *independent variable.* If, on the other hand, the investigator has no control over the variable and it occurs as the result of the influence of the independent variable, then that variable is known as the *dependent variable.*

To illustrate these two kinds of variables, take a very simple situation. The investigator has a potentiometer connected to a voltage source and, by means of it and by turning a knob, he is able to control the voltage that passes through it. The voltage is the *independent variable.* The potentiometer is in turn connected to a voltmeter. The deflection of the indicator hand on the face of the voltmeter *depends* upon the voltage potential which is controlled by the investigator and is, thus, the *dependent* variable.

We do, however, experiment with factors and forces over which we have no control whatsoever. A person's reaction time, intelligence quotient, age—no investigator can control these.

A more conventional categorization of experimental designs has been made by others. Perhaps the most complete categorization has been made by Campbell and Stanley.[2] They divide experimental studies into four general types: (1) *pre-experimental designs,* (2) *true experimental designs,* (3) *quasi-experimental designs,* and (4) *correlational and ex post facto designs.*

So that we may see the experimental design configurations and the function of each within the context of the experimental method, we present a summary table of the experimental method, according to the schema outlined by Campbell and Stanley. The table is presented on pages 214 and 215. We shall now discuss each of the designs of the experimental method.

Pre-Experimental Designs

★ *The one-shot case study.* The one-shot case study is probably the most primitive genre of observational activity that might conceivably be termed research. For the studies which we shall outline, we will employ a conventional symbolism: When a group, an individual, or an object is exposed to an experimental variable, the letter X will be used. The letter O will indicate an observation or measurement of the data.

The one-shot case study may, therefore, be represented by the following symbolic formula:

Paradigm of Design I: $X \rightarrow O$

This is the simplest and most naive experimental procedure. This is the method behind many superstitious folklore beliefs. We see a child sitting on the damp earth in mid-April. The next day he has a sore throat and a cold. We conclude that sitting on the damp earth causes one to catch cold. According to the above paradigm, the design of our "research" thinking is something like this:

X = exposure of child to cold, damp earth $\rightarrow$ O = observation that the child has a cold.
(*variable*)

[2] Donald T. Campbell and Julian C. Stanley, "Experimental and Quasi-Experimental Designs for Research on Teaching," in N. L. Gage, ed., *Handbook of Research on Teaching.* (Chicago: Rand McNally and Company, 1963), pp. 171-246. Also published separately by Rand McNally and Company, 1966.

SUMMARY OF EXPERIMENTAL METHODOLOGY

Aim of the Research	*Name of the Design*	*Paradigm**	*Comments on the Research Design*
		Pre-Experimental Designs	
To attempt to explain a consequent by an antecedent.	One shot case study	$X \rightarrow O$	An approach which has spawned many superstitions and which is the least reliable of all experimental approaches.
To evaluate the influence of a variable.	One group pretest-posttest design	$O_1 \rightarrow X \rightarrow O_2$	A naive approach which relies upon supposition and coincidence in validating the conclusion
To determine the influence of a variable on one group and not on another.	Static group comparison	Group I $X \rightarrow O_1$ Group II $- \rightarrow O_2$	Weakness lies in no examination of pre-experimental equivalence of groups. Conclusion is reached by naively comparing the performance of each group to determine the effect of a variable on one of them.
		True Experimental Designs	
To study the effect of an influence on a carefully controlled sample.	Pretest-posttest control group design	$R -- \left[\begin{array}{l} O_1 \rightarrow X \rightarrow O_2 \\ O_3 \rightarrow - \rightarrow O_4 \end{array} \right.$	This design has been called by Mouly "the old workhorse of traditional experimentation." Borg and Gall suggest analysis of covariance as best statistical tool for analyzing the data.
To minimize the Hawthorne effect.	Solomon four-group design	$R -- \left[\begin{array}{l} O_1 \rightarrow X \rightarrow O_2 \\ O_3 \rightarrow - \rightarrow O_4 \\ - \quad X \rightarrow O_5 \\ - \quad - \rightarrow O_6 \end{array} \right.$	This is an extension of the pretest-posttest control group design and probably the most powerful experimental approach. Data are analyzed by doing analysis of variance on posttest scores.
To evaluate a situation that cannot be pretested.	Posttest only control group design	$R -- \left[\begin{array}{l} X \rightarrow O_1 \\ - \rightarrow O_2 \end{array} \right.$	To be used in situations that cannot be pretested. An adaptation of the last two groups in the Solomon four-group design. Randomness is critical. Probably simplest and best test for significance in this design is the t test.
		Quasi-Experimental Designs	
To investigate a situation where random selection	Nonrandomized control group pretest-post	$O_1 \rightarrow X \rightarrow O_2$	One of the strongest and most widely used quasi-experimental designs. Differs from experimental designs because test

and assignment are not possible.	test design	$O_3 \rightarrow - \rightarrow O_4$	and control groups are not equivalent. Comparing O_1 with O_3 pretest results will indicate degree of equivalency between experimental and control groups.
To determine the influence of a variable introduced only after a series of initial observations and only where one group is available.	Time series experimental design	$O_1 \rightarrow O_2 \rightarrow O_3 \rightarrow O_4 \rightarrow X \rightarrow$ $O_5^* \rightarrow O_6^* \rightarrow O_7^* \rightarrow O_8^*$	If substantial change follows introduction of variable then variable can be suspect as to the cause of the change. To secure more external validity, repeat the experiment in different places under different conditions.
To bolster the validity of the above design with the addition of a control group.	Control group time series design	$O_1 \rightarrow O_2 \rightarrow O_3 \rightarrow O_4 \rightarrow$ $X \rightarrow O_5 \rightarrow O_6 \rightarrow O_7 \rightarrow O_8$ $O_1 \rightarrow O_2 \rightarrow O_3 \rightarrow O_4 \rightarrow - \rightarrow$ $O_5 \rightarrow O_6 \rightarrow O_7 \rightarrow O_8$	A variant of the above design by accompanying it with a parallel set of observations without the introduction of the variable—the experimental factor.
A variant of the above design with the purpose of controlling history in time designs.	Equivalent time-samples design	$[X_1 \rightarrow O_1] \rightarrow [X_0 \rightarrow O_2] \rightarrow$ $[X_1 \rightarrow O_3] \rightarrow [X_0 \rightarrow O_4]$	This is an on-again, off-again design in which the experimental variable is sometimes present, sometimes absent. Gilbert Sax has extrapolated the design with two extensions (explained in the text).

Correlational and Ex Post Facto Designs

To seek for cause-effect relationships between two sets of data.	Causal-comparative correlational studies	$\overrightarrow{}$ $O_a \neq O_b$ $\overleftarrow{}$	A very deceptive procedure that requires much insight for its use. Causality cannot be inferred to be a *quid pro quo* merely because a positive and close correlation ratio exists.
To search backward from consequent data for antecedent causes.	Ex post facto studies		This approach is experimentation in reverse. Seldom is proof through data substantiation possible. Logic and inference are the principal tools of this design.

*The symbols in each paradigm will be explained fully in the discussion of each design type in the pages following.

This type of "research" is represented in such beliefs as: If you walk under a ladder, you will have bad luck; Friday the 13th is calamity day; thirteen is a number to be avoided; a horseshoe above the doorway brings good fortune to the house.

Someone observed the fact, then observed the consequence and the two were linked together as cause and effect.

★ *The one-group pretest-posttest design.* The one-group pretest-posttest design is a type of experiment where a single group has (1) a pre-experimental evaluation, then (2) the influence of the variable, and, finally, (3) a postexperimental evaluation. The paradigm for this type of research is represented as follows:

Paradigm for Design II: $O_1 \rightarrow X \rightarrow O_2$

A teacher wants to know how effective hearing a story read masterfully on a tape-recorder would be in improving the reading skills of her class. She selects a group of students, gives them a standardized reading pretest, exposes them to daily taped readings, posttests them with a variant form of the same standardized test to determine how much "progress" they have made because of (so she supposes) the tape-recorder technique.

An agronomist hybridizes two strains of corn. He finds that the hybrid strain is more disease-resistant and has a better yield than either of the two parent types. He concludes that the hybridization process has effected the difference.

★ *The static group comparison.* The static group comparison is a familiar control group-experimental group procedure. It is represented by a paradigm as follows:

Paradigm for Design III: Random Group Selection $\left[\begin{array}{ll} \text{Group I} & X \rightarrow O_1 \\ \hline \text{Group II} & - \rightarrow O_2 \end{array}\right.$

Here is a design in which two randomly selected groups are designated by the dictates of chance, one to be a control group, and the other to be the experimental group. The experimental group is exposed to variable X; the control group is not. Control groups in which isolation from the experimental factor is effected are represented in the paradigms as in the paradigm above. At the close of the experiment, both groups are evaluated and a comparison is made between the evaluation values of each group to determine what has been the effect of factor X. In this design, no attempt is made to obtain or examine the pre-experimental equivalence of the comparison groups.

These three designs, although commonly employed in many research projects reported in scholarly journals, are loose in structure and leave much to be desired in terms of factors which, not being controlled, could inject bias into the total research design.

True Experimental Designs

In contrast to the somewhat crude designs that we have been discussing to this point, the *true experimental designs* evince a greater degree of control and refinement and a greater insurance of both *internal* and *external validity.* These are new terms. They have nothing to do with the internal and external evidence with respect to historical research, and which we discussed in chapter 7.

With experimental designs, *internal validity* is the basic minimum without which any experiment is uninterpretable.[3] The question that the researcher must answer is whether the experimental treatment did, indeed, make a difference in the experiment.

External validity asks the question as to how generalizable the experiment is. To what

[3] Ibid., p. 175.

populations, settings, treatment variables, and measurement variables can the effect, as observed in the experiment, be generalized.[4]

Of the two types of validity, internal validity is certainly the more important insofar as the integrity of the study is concerned. The following suggested designs are those that are more likely to be strong in both types of validity, which is certainly the aim of every experimental researcher.

As we emphasized so strongly in the discussion of the descriptive survey method, randomization is one of the greatest guarantees of validity. In each of the three designs that follows, randomization is a necessary and constant factor in the selection of all groups, both experimental and control. In the paradigms, randomization will be indicated by the letter *R*.

★ *The pretest-posttest control group design.* The pretest-posttest control group design is, as Mouly remarks, the "old workhorse of traditional experimentation."[5] In it, we have the experimental group carefully chosen through appropriate randomization procedures and the control group similarly selected. The experimental group is evaluated, subjected to the experimental variable, and reevaluated. The control group is isolated from all experimental variable influences and is merely evaluated at the beginning and at the end of the experiment. A more optimal situation can be achieved if the researcher is careful to match the experimental against the control group and vice versa for identical correspondences. Certainly, where matching is effected for the factor that is being studied, the design is thereby greatly strengthened. For example, if we are studying the effect of reading instruction on the I.Q. level of students, wisdom would dictate that for both control and experimental groups, members of each group should be selected, as nearly as possible, so that a one-to-one correspondence with I.Q. scores be achieved.

The paradigm for the pretest-posttest control group design is as follows:

Paradigm for Design IV:

$$R - - \left[\begin{array}{l} O_1 \rightarrow X \rightarrow O_2 \\ O_3 \rightarrow - \rightarrow O_4 \end{array} \right.$$

The bracketing of both groups shows that R the randomization process, is common to both groups and the $R - -$ shows that before separation these two randomized samples were kept isolated from the influence of the experimental variable X. O_1 and O_2 are the two evaluations of the experimental group, before and after its exposure to the experimental variable X. O_3 and O_4 are the evaluations of the control group.

Campbell and Stanley indicate that good experimental design is separable from the use of statistical tests of significance; but because this is such a common design in the experimental methodology, researchers often use incorrect statistical procedures in an effort to analyze such data. Borg and Gall caution against this and recommend that the best statistical method to use is analysis of covariance, in which the posttest means are compared using the pretest means as the covariate.[6]

★ *The Solomon four-group design.* R. L. Solomon, in 1949, proposed in the *Psychological Bulletin* and "extension" of the control group design, and it is a refinement on the previous design discussed.[7] For the first time, explicit consideration was given to a design which emphasized a regard for factors of external validity.

---

[4] Ibid., p. 175.

[5] George J. Mouly, *The Science of Educational Research,* 2nd ed. (New York: Van Nostrand Reinhold Company, 1970), p. 336.

[6] Walter R. Borg and Meredith D. Gall, *Educational Research: An Introduction,* 2nd ed. (New York: David McKay Company, Inc., 1971), p. 383.

[7] R. L. Solomon, "An Extension of Control Group Design," *Psychological Bulletin,* (1949), 46, 137–50.

The design is obviously an "extension" of Design IV, as is seen from analyzing the following paradigm:

Paradigm for Design V: $R - - \left[\begin{array}{l} O_1 \rightarrow X \rightarrow O_2 \\ O_3 - \rightarrow - O_4 \\ - X \quad \rightarrow O_5 \\ - \quad - \quad \rightarrow O_6 \end{array} \right.$ "extension"

The fact that the pretest disappears in groups 3 and 4 constitutes a distinct advantage. It enables the researcher to generalize to groups which have not received the pretest in cases where it may be suspected that the pretest has had no adverse effect on the experimental treatment. It removes a kind of Hawthorne effect from the experiment. A group of subjects is pretested. The question now is, "What effect does the pretesting have?" It may provide them with additional motivation to do well under experimental conditions. It may contaminate the effect of the experimental variable. The "extension" takes care of these contingencies.

In terms of experimental designs, the Solomon four-group design is probably our most powerful experimental approach. The data are analyzed by doing an analysis of variance of the posttest scores. This rigorous bivariate structure does require, however, considerably larger samples and demands much more energy on the part of the researcher to pursue it. Its principal value is in eliminating pretest influence, as we have previously pointed out, and where such is desirable the design is unsurpassed.

★ *The posttest-only control group design.* We come now to the last of the generally employed true experimental designs. In the thinking of some researchers, especially those in education, psychology, and the social sciences, the phrase *pretest-posttest* has become so habitual that it is inconceivable to many of them to slough off the first half of the phrase and have anything left in terms of scientific research.

Some life situations, however, defy pretesting. You cannot pretest the forces in a thunderstorm or a hurricane; you cannot pretest growing crops or growing children. These phenomena happen only once. The design here proposed may be considered as the last two groups of the Solomon four-group design—the "extension" part. The paradigm for the posttest-only approach is:

Paradigm for Design VI: $R - - \left[\begin{array}{l} X \rightarrow O_1 \\ \\ - \rightarrow O_2 \end{array} \right.$

In order to test for significance in this design, the t test would probably be the simplest and best. Randomness is critical in the posttest-only design and should be carefully considered as an important element in the success of employing such an approach.

Quasi-experimental Designs

Thus far, in the experimental designs, we have been emphasizing the importance of randomness of group composition. Life presents certain situations occasionally where random selection and assignment are not possible. Such experiments, carried on under conditions where it is not possible to guarantee randomness, must rely upon designs that are called *quasi-experimental designs.* In such designs, it is imperative that the researcher be thoroughly aware of the specific variables the design fails to control and to take these into account in the interpretation of the data.

★ *The nonrandomized control group pretest-posttest design.* The nonrandomized control group pretest-posttest design configuration is similar to the first of the true experimental designs that we discussed, except for the lack of randomization:

Paradigm for Design VII:

$$\begin{bmatrix} O_1 \rightarrow X \rightarrow O_2 \\ O_3 \rightarrow - \rightarrow O_4 \end{bmatrix}$$

This design is not to be confused with the pretest-posttest control group design (Design IV) in which the composition of the groups is randomly chosen. The researcher might well consider the employment of Design VII in situations where the true experimental designs (Designs IV, V, and VI) are not feasible.

To minimize the differences that might exist between the experimental and the control groups, the researcher might attempt to match as closely as possible and on as many variables as possible the two groups in a kind of quasi-randomization before beginning the experiment.

Again, the researcher might consider, if feasible, consolidating the so-called control group and the so-called experimental group into one amalgamated group and from this supergroup divide the total number of students into two groups by means of randomization. One of these may then be designated as the control group and the other as the experimental group. Still another way to compensate for initial differences, as suggested by Borg and Gall, is by the analysis of covariance technique. Analysis of covariance reduces the effects of initial group differences statistically by making compensating adjustments of final means on the dependent variable.

★ *The time-series experiment.* The time-series experiment consist of taking a series of evaluations and then introducing a variable or a new dynamic into the system, after which another series of evaluations is made. If a substantial change results in the second series of evaluations, we may assume with reasonable experimental logic that the cause of the difference in observational results was because of the factor introduced into the system. This design has a configuration much like the following paradigm:

Paradigm for Design VIII: $O_1 \rightarrow O_2 \rightarrow O_3 \rightarrow O_4 \rightarrow X \rightarrow O_5^* \rightarrow O_6^* \rightarrow O_7^* \rightarrow O_8^*$

In this paradigm, the O^* indicates that these observations are different in character than those of the series before the introduction of the variable.

This is the design that was formerly widely used in the physical and the biological sciences. The classic discovery of Sir Alexander Fleming that *Penicillium notatum* could inhibit staphylococci is an example of this type of design. Dr. Fleming observed *n* number of times the growth of staphylococci on a culture plate. Then, unexpectedly, a culture plate containing well-developed colonies of staphylococci was contaminated with the spores of *Penicillium notatum.* Dr. Fleming observed that the colonies in the vicinity of the mold seemed to be undergoing dissolution. The experiment was repeated with the bacillus and the mold in company with each other. Each time the observation was the same: no staph germs near the mold. These were the O_5, O_6, O_7, O_8 of the paradigm.

The weakness of this design is in the probability that a major event that may be unrecognized may enter the system along with, before, or after the introduction of the experimental variable. The effects of this extraneous factor are likely to be confounded with those of the experimental factor and the wrong attribution of the cause for the effect observed may be made.

★ *Control group, time series.* A variant of the time-series design is to accompany it with a parallel set of observations, but without the introduction of the experimental factor. This design would, then, take on a configuration like the following:

Paradigm for Design IX:

$$O_1 \rightarrow O_2 \rightarrow O_3 \rightarrow O_4 \rightarrow X \rightarrow O_5 \rightarrow O_6 \rightarrow O_7 \rightarrow O_8$$

$$O_1 \rightarrow O_2 \rightarrow O_3 \rightarrow O_4 \rightarrow - \rightarrow O_5 \rightarrow O_6 \rightarrow O_7 \rightarrow O_8$$

Such a design tends to assure greater control for internal validity. The advantage of a design of this construction is that it adds one further guarantee toward internal validity in drawing conclusions with respect to the effect of the experimental factor.

★ *Equivalent time-samples design.* A variant of the previous design is the equivalent time-samples design. The object of its construction is to control history in time designs. The intervening experimental variable is sometimes present, sometimes absent. Suppose we have a class in astronomy. One approach is to teach astronomy through audiovisual materials; another method is to teach the subject by means of a textbook. An equivalent time-samples design of the teaching method for this class might look like the following:

Paradigm for Design X: $$[X_1 \rightarrow O_1] \rightarrow [X_0 \rightarrow O_2] \rightarrow [X_1 \rightarrow O_3] \rightarrow [X_0 \rightarrow O_4]$$

In this paradigm, X_1 indicates the time when the audiovisual approach was used and X_0 the time when the textbook approach was used. We see also that the instructional cells are such that we can compare observations such as O_1 with O_3, and O_2 with O_4.

Gilbert Sax has suggested two variants of this basic design.[8] One utilizes two variables in the study, so that the schematic of the design looks like this:

Paradigm for Design X_a:

$$[X_1 \rightarrow O_1] \rightarrow X_0 \rightarrow O_2 \rightarrow (X_2 \rightarrow O_3) \rightarrow X_0 \rightarrow O_4 \rightarrow [X_1 \rightarrow O_5] \rightarrow X_0 \rightarrow O_6 \rightarrow (X_2 \rightarrow O_7)$$

If pursued over a long-enough time span, some multivariate comparisons might be made. For example, in the preceding sequence, we could

Compare	with	To explore variable
O_1	O_5	X_1
O_2	O_6	X_0
O_3	O_7	X_2

Whereas in the preceding design Sax introduces a second variable in the time-samples design, he goes even further to suggest an equivalent *materials* design:

Paradigm for Design X_b:

$$[M_a \rightarrow X_1 \rightarrow O] \rightarrow [M_b \rightarrow X_0 \rightarrow O] \rightarrow [M_c \rightarrow X_0 \rightarrow O] \rightarrow [M_c \rightarrow X_1 \rightarrow O] \ldots$$

Sax comments on this design: "This design is exactly the same as the equivalent time-sampling design except that the different materials are introduced throughout the course of

---

[8] Gilbert Sax, *Empirical Foundations of Educational Research* (Englewood Cliffs, New Jersey: Prentice-Hall, Inc., 1968), p. 363.

the experiment. Assuming that these materials are equivalent, experimental controls would seem to be adequate."[9]

Correlational and Ex Post Facto Designs

Correlational designs are usually attempts to establish cause-effect relationships between two sets of data. We might represent the situation by the following diagram:

$$\overset{\longrightarrow}{\underset{\longleftarrow}{O_a \neq O_b}}$$

Correlational studies are always particularly hazardous. So often researchers think that if they can show a positive correlation between two factors which *in their thinking they deem to be related*, then they *assume* the fact of causality (i.e., that one factor is the cause of the other). This is erroneous reasoning. The fact that one can demonstrate a statistically positive correlation between two sets of data in no way implies any causality between them. Remember the Florida orange crop and the elephant population of Thailand![10]

The preceding diagram indicates the possibilities within any correlational situation. We have indicated the observed data with respect to each factor as O_a and O_b. Now, given two variables of this type, with O_a as the independent variable, three conclusions might be drawn with respect to these data:

1. O_a has caused O_b: $O_a \rightarrow O_b$.
2. O_b has caused O_a: $O_a \leftarrow O_b$.
3. Some third variable is responsible for both O_a and O_b: $O_a \neq O_b$.

Perhaps some of the difficulty with the causal-comparative correlational studies has been the fact that we have failed to recognize the structure of the correlational factors with which we work. We have a tendency to simplify. Especially in a research endeavor, we think of a certain effect as having *a* cause when, in fact, because of the complexity of many situations, we are not dealing with *a* cause for a particular phenomenon but with *a constellation of causes*, all of which may contribute to a greater or lesser degree to the effectualization of the phenomenon. Arbitrarily selecting any two or even several factors for any given phenomenon and then attempting to ascribe the causality of the phenomenon to the limitation of *our selection of causative factors* may be both irrational and foolhardy, especially in the face of extremely complex problems whose tributaries of causality may spread far beyond anything that we may have conceived as being remotely relevant to the problem and its co-related data.

Correlation is too simple an answer for most of the complex realities of life, and its simplistic approach disarms the researcher. It is an extremely deceptive tool, and one that the researcher needs to employ with the utmost caution and with maximum sagacity.

★ *Ex post facto studies.* The ex post facto study belongs to a "no man's land" in the discipline of research. Although it is usually considered under the heading of experimentation, by its very nature it has little that is experimental about it. We indicated in the early pages of this chapter that *control* was the one condition that marked the experimental study and that the element of control was characteristic of the experimental method. But after an event has happened, how can it be controlled? Mouly assets

[9] Ibid.
[10] See page 37.

A relatively questionable quasi-experimental design is the *ex post facto* experiment, in which a particular characteristic of a given group is investigated with a view to identifying its antecedents. This is experimentation in reverse: instead of taking groups that are equivalent and exposing them to different treatment with a view to promoting differences to be measured, the *ex post facto* experiment begins with a given effect and seeks the experimental factor that brought it about. The obvious weakness of such an "experiment" is that we have no control over the situations that have already occurred and we can never be sure of how many other circumstances might have been involved.[11]

Strictly because of the lack of the control element, the methodology may be somewhat difficult to classify. Yet it is a method that pursues truth and seeks the solution of a problem through the analysis of data. Science has no difficulty with such a methodology. Medicine uses it widely in its research activities. Physicians discover a pathological situation, then inaugurate their search "after the fact." They sleuth into events and conditions antecedent in order to discover the cause for the illness.

The research which has gone on in laboratories with respect to the moon rocks is a research which is purely ex post facto. So much "post" indeed that the research is separated from the causal fact by millions and even billions of years. Cosmological research which inquires into the origin of the universe is precisely this type of methodology. Yet no one will deny that this is research, that it is oriented to specific problems, supported by specific data, and given direction by underlying hypotheses.

If we were to represent ex post facto research, it might be adequately represented by the following diagram:

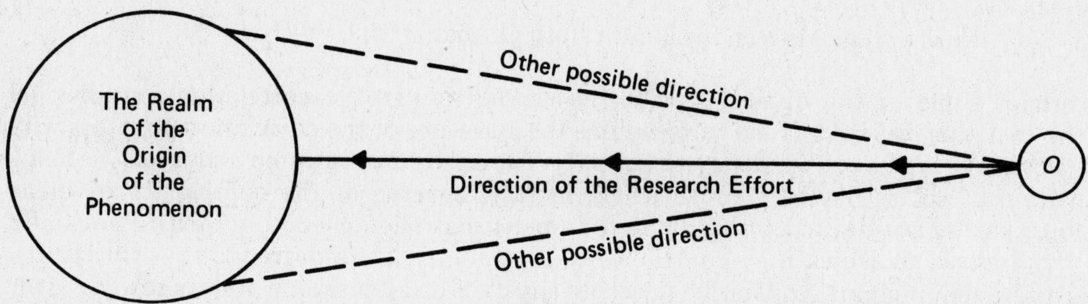

The entry to the diagram is at the right-hand side. Here is where the researcher encounters the observed fact (0). That observed fact originated in a much larger area of factual happening. This is represented by the larger circle at the left: the Realm of the Origin of the Phenomenon, of which the observed fact is but a small part. It is from the area of the observed fact that the researcher must formulate all his hypotheses and aim his research effort. Because of the disparity between the size of the observed instance and the expanse of the possibility out of which the observed fact may have arisen, it is always possible that the direction of the research effort in ex post facto studies may lead nowhere.

We seek the cause of a disease, for instance. Our efforts may come to naught. So vast is the realm of the origin of the phenomenon and so miniscule the single observed fact that to attempt to construct a nexus of cause and effect and to extract meaning from the situation may be very difficult indeed. A cell begins to multiply spontaneously, a neoplasm results,

[11] George J. Mouly, *The Science of Educational Research,* 2nd ed. (New York: Van Nostrand Reinhold Company, 1970), p. 340.

the neoplasm metastasizes. The problem facing the cancer research team is an ex post facto one. What caused the cell to grow inordinately at first? The cytological complexity of the cell is such that careful as the aim of our research effort may be, we are like hunters drawing the bead of a rifle on a little bird, flitting in a thicket a mile away. We are indeed doing, as Mouly has suggested, "experimentation in reverse."

Conclusion

Let us conclude this broad section of the book, which has dealt generally with methodology, with a word about methodologies other than those we have been discussing here. In any new area—and research is a relatively new academic discipline—there is always confusion of terminology and many names for the same process.

The methodologies that we have suggested in this chapter have been broad generic ones within which other types of methodological approach can be accommodated. These are sometimes discussed separately as discrete methodologies in themselves. Inspected closely, you will usually find that these minor methodologies take on definite characteristics of the broader forms discussed here.

One author, for example, indicates that predictive methods are a separate type of methodology.[12] But we have chosen to discuss prediction as an aspect of analytical statistics and to consider it under the analytical survey method. Others have decided to include the case study method as a discrete methodology, but because it is an approach which keeps observational details of the behavior of one or more individuals, we have deemed it appropriate to include the discussion of this research approach under the heading of the descriptive survey method.

Other writers have chosen to indicate still other methodologies: the cross-cultural method, the developmental method, the causal-comparative method, the correlational method, the statistical method, and even the so-called philosophic method.

You should not be disturbed, therefore, if you find some disagreement and some discrepancy in the terminology and organization of the discipline of research. Some academic areas, notably in the physical and natural sciences and English and the languages, do not have a discrete and identifiable methodology associated with their research efforts; other areas such as education, psychology, nursing and the social sciences have a well-defined and recognized academic discipline of research which is found in the curriculum as educational research, psychological research, nursing research, or social research.

Research, in a very real sense, is a new discipline. It is also a chaotic discipline. We pointed out in the first chapter the multiple meanings that the word *research* has. It is used almost to mean all things to all men. Little wonder then that the divisions, the discussions within the larger framework, the terminology, the basic viewpoints, and individual opinions should differ so widely. Unsettledness is characteristic of youth; this is true of both young people and young disciplines. Some writers on research do not mention any discrete methodologies. Many think of statistics as being synonymous with research and vice versa. Some will quarrel violently with some positions that are taken and some of the concepts that are articulated in this book. This may not be too serious. It is but an indication of the growing pangs of a discipline which is as yet very young and of indecisive mind. So long as we are fair in our judgments and respect the honest convictions of others, and are willing to consider *both* sides of any question, little harm can come from sincere differences of viewpoint. We now turn to a pair of chapters devoted to some suggestions on presenting the results of the research effort.

---

[12] Ibid., pp. 357-376.

Practical Application ---

Turn to the practicum section at the back of this book. On page 298-299, you will find a practical application of some of the matters we have been discussing in this chapter.

FOR FURTHER READING

Anderson, Virgil L., and Robert A. McLean. *Design of Experiments: A Realistic Approach.* New York: Marcel Dekker, Inc., 1974.

Campbell, Donald T. "Factors Relevant to the Validity of Experiments in Social Settings." *Psychological Bulletin* 54 (1957): 297-312.

Campbell, Donald T., and Julian C. Stanley. *Experimental and Quasi-Experimental Designs for Research.* Boston: Houghton Mifflin Co., 1966.

Christensen, Larry B. *Experimental Methodology.* 2nd ed. Boston, Mass.: Allyn & Bacon, Inc., 1980.

Coombs, Clyde H. *A Theory of Data.* New York: John Wiley & Sons, Inc., 1967.

Edwards, A. L. "Experiments: Their Planning and Execution." In G. Lindzey, ed., *Handbook of Social Psychology.* Vol 1. Cambridge, Mass: Addison-Wesley, 1954, pp. 259-88.

———. *Experimental Designs in Psychological Research.* New York: Holt, Rinehart and Winston, 1972.

Fairweather, George W., and Louis G. Tornatsky. *Experimental Methods for Social Policy Research.* Elmsford, N.Y.: Pergamon Press, 1977.

Hulica, Irene H., and Hulica, Karel. "To Design Experimental Research." *Americal Journal of Nursing* 62 (February 1962): 100-103.

John, J. A., and M. H. Quenouille. *Experiments: Design and Analysis.* 2nd ed. New York: Macmillan Publishing Co., Inc., 1977.

Myers, J. L. *Fundamentals of Experimental Design.* Boston: Allyn & Bacon, Inc., 1966.

Natrella, Mary G. *Experimental Statistics.* Washington, D.C.: Government Printing Office, 1963.

Peng, K. C. *The Design and Analysis of Scientific Experiments.* Reading, Mass.: Addison-Wesley Publishing Co., Inc., 1967.

Ridgman, W. J. *Experimentation in Biology: An Introduction to Design and Analysis.* New York: John Wiley & Sons, Inc., 1975.

Robinson, Paul W. *Fundamentals of Experimental Psychology.* Englewood Cliffs, N.J.: Prentice-Hall, Inc., 1976.

Rosenthal, Robert. *Experimenter Effects in Behavioral Research.* New York: Halstead Press, 1976.

Rubin, Z. "Designing Honest Experiments." *American Psychologist* 28 (1973): 445-48.

Sidman, Murray. *Tactics of Scientific Research.* New York: Basic Books, 1960.

Sidowski, Joseph B., ed. *Experimental Methods and Instrumentation in Psychology.* New York: McGraw-Hill Book Company, 1966.

Winer, B. J. *Statistical Principles in Experimental Design.* New York: McGraw-Hill Book Company, 1971.

PRESENTING THE RESULTS OF RESEARCH

READ THIS—BEFORE YOU READ THIS CHAPTER

Research—everything that we have considered in these pages, to this point—is useless unless it is communicated. What we have done, what we have discovered, and the conclusions we have reached with respect to a particular problem must be shared with others. That sharing is accomplished through the writing of the research report.

The report is a communicative document, well organized, whose logic and divisional discussion is announced to the reader by a universally accepted set of format conventions.

In the following pages, we suggest a form of research report. It is presented only as a guide and as a suggestion of the form that most reports generally follow. Nothing is intended to be arbitrary, and at the close of the chapter you are encouraged to inspect many reports to appreciate the way others have told the world what they have done.

The bibliography at the close of the chapter will suggest a group of readings that cover a broad spectrum of report writing. This list may be very helpful to those writing research reports in specialized areas.

11

Writing the Research Report

THE REPORT AS A COMMUNICATIVE DOCUMENT

The research report is a straightforward document that sets forth clearly and precisely what the researcher *has done* to resolve the research problem. In structure, it is factual and logical. It makes no pretense at being a literary production. It must, however, be readable, which is another way of saying that the writer of the research report must know how to communicate clearly.

Many reports suffer because those who attempt to write them may need greater skill in English expression. The basics of sentence and paragraph structure must be thoroughly mastered. Unity, coherence, and emphasis are rhetorical principles with which every writer needs a functional acquaintance. Punctuation, also, facilitates the expression of thought. All of the nine marks of punctuation should be ready expressional tools of those who would write communicative and easily read reports. But we shall say more of matters of style and readability in the next chapter.

The Parts of a Research Report

The research report has a relatively simple format. In general, it should achieve three objectives:

1. It should acquaint the reader with the problem that has been researched and explain its implications adequately enough so that all who read the report may have a clear orientation to the problem.
2. It should present the data fully and adequately. The data within the report should substantiate all the interpretations and conclusions which the report contains.
3. It should interpret the data *for* the reader and demonstrate exactly how the data resolve the problem which has been researched. A report which merely *presents* the data as raw and uninterpreted fact (in the form of tables, graphs, histograms, and other data-summary devices) is of little help to the reader in providing *meaning* from those data.

Briefly, we shall discuss each of these matters and amplify their significance insofar as they relate to the writing of the research report.

Acquainting the Reader with the Research Problem

The first section of the research report should have but one purpose: to create between the writer of the report and the reader of the report a meeting of minds. The reader should be able to comprehend through the merits of the report alone what the problem and its several ramifications are. The reader should appreciate the setting in which the problem was conceived. Much report writing is of poor quality because the writer has not approached the task of writing the report from the standpoint of reconstructing for the reader the problem and setting it forth clearly and adequately. Often the reader may not grasp the precise concept that was in the mind of the writer. We cannot assume that the reader will be aware of important facts that the writer has never set forth.

At the outset, after perhaps a few paragraphs of introductory remarks stating the rationale, the background or the relevance of the study, the document should set forth clearly and unmistakably the problem that has been researched. This might be further emphasized for the reader if it is announced with a proper subheading. This has presumably been done already in the proposal. The statement of the problem as well as other essential information needed to understand the problem comprehensively should comprise the first chapter of the final report.

At this juncture, it may be well for you to turn again to the sample proposal in Appendix A to review there the section entitled "The Problem and Its Setting." The final report will in a sense merely amplify what is set forth here, and its contents will be identical.

If the problem has been divided into subproblems, these should be stated following the statement of the problem and, likewise, announced with a proper subhead. The object of the first section of the research document is to present the reader with as clear an understanding of the *principal* thrust of the research effort as possible. By so doing, the reader will then be in a better position later on to understand the interpretation of the data and to judge the merits of the research. The research methodology is also stated and justified in the opening pages of the report.

Terms which may be ambiguous, or which may be used in a specialized sense, must be defined. For a meeting of minds, it is imperative that the reader and the researcher be concerned with precisely the same orientations to the problem, the same concepts, the same ideas. This is accomplished by a careful definition of any terms within either the problem or the subproblems which may be open to varied interpretation. In case you have forgotten what we said earlier about these matters, it may be well for you to review Chapter 4.

Any delimitations should also be clearly set forth. It is well for all who read the research report to know precisely how far the research effort extended and where the limits were set. Into what areas relevant to the problem did the research effort not intrude? What aspects of the problem have not been studied? Readers want answers to these questions, and they should be provided with them in the opening pages of the study report.

The research report provides no opportunity for imprecise thought or inexact expression. We should see explicitly what hypotheses have been tested; we should know exactly what the assumptions were upon which the researcher has relied.

In addition, the first chapter of the research report should indicate the importance of the study both to the academic audience and to the practical reader in the broad world of affairs. And, perhaps, it should end with a section bearing a heading such as "The Organization of the Remainder of the Study" in which, chapter by chapter, the writer of the report delineates what the organization of the remainder of the study will be. This prepares the reader with a summary in advance and a prediction of things to come.

These matters might well comprise the first chapter of the research report, the thesis, or the dissertation. It is presumed, of course, that the organization will be indicated by the use of appropriate headings, subheadings, and sub-subheadings. Because some students may never have acquired the habit of using headings and subheadings to articulate the outline of the thought, we shall take a brief detour at this point to discuss the proper use of such format devices. On page 107, we indicated that we would discuss this matter at an appropriate place, and there you were referred to this chapter and these pages.

Headings Show Organization

The outline of the thought is indicated by the headings in the document. The most important of all headings is, of course,

THE CENTERED HEADING

which appears in the manuscript exactly as we have represented it here, centered on the central axis of the type page and typed in *all capitals*. In manuscript writing, it is always reserved for announcing the major divisions of thought. The printer, because of the wide variety of type weights and faces to choose from, can be much more versatile in heading style and placement than the writer of manuscript, who must rely upon the limitations of the typewriter alone to express the thought and its relative degrees of importance.

In printed material, centered headings are usually set in the largest type size and, although the printer may place them variously and not always center them, they are always the main divisions of the textual matter such as chapter headings and other divisions of prime importance in the document. In outline style, such headings would ordinarily correspond to those parts of the outline which would be assigned the importance of Roman numerals: I, II, III, and so forth.

The Free-Standing Sidehead

Here it is printed to show exactly how it would appear in typescript. This heading is written in capitals and lowercase letters with each word of the heading underscored. No punctuation follows the free-standing sidehead. The initial letters of the principal words of the heading are capitalized, the rest of the word and the prepositions and articles (except, of course, unless these are the first words of the heading) are typed in lowercase.

In print, free-standing sideheads are commonly italicized; they are *always* italicized in typescript. Italicization in typescript is indicated by underlining the words to be italicized. Note that the spaces are *not* underlined. The reason is obvious: you cannot italicize a blank space!

In importance, the free-standing sidehead is next below the centered heading. In an outline this level would ordinarily be represented by the captial letters: A, B, C, of the first indentation under the Roman numerals. Usually free-standing sideheads are set four single spaces below the preceding text and three single spaces above the text that follows, and are placed flush with the left-hand margin of the textual material—exactly as we have done here.

The paragraph sidehead. The paragraph sidehead, as the term indicates, is a heading set into the paragraph, as we have done here. It is always indented to line up with the other paragraph indentations of the page, and it always has a period as a terminal point of punctuation. Only the *first word* of the paragraph sidehead is capitalized; the rest of the words of the heading are in lowercase. The heading indicates the next lesser degree of thought subordination under the free-standing sidehead, and would normally correspond to the 1, 2, 3 level in the conventional outline. The paragraph sidehead is *always* italicized (underlined), as we have done here. Normally in typing and for ease of reading, three spaces usually follow the period of the paragraph sidehead before the paragraph proper is begun.

In this text, to call attention to the paragraph sideheads we have preceded them with a ★ symbol. Generally, in scholarly papers no such device is appropriate.

The use of these three types of heading is illustrated on page 257 of the sample proposal in Appendix A.

Should you desire a *fourth-level-of-importance heading*, such further diminution of thought importance is indicated by a centered heading, but this time quite different from the heading-of-first-importance discussed above. We have shown this type of heading in the sample proposal in Appendix A. It is typed in captials and lowercase and centered on the text page as follows:

The Fourth-Level Heading

Note that it is *not* italicized, and when placed in the text four single spaces should intervene between the text above and three single spaces below the heading. Such a heading would indicate an importance of thought corresponding to the a, b, c level in the conventional outline.

The treatment of the fourth-level heading will be fully appreciated by referring to page 270 of the sample proposal in Appendix A, where it is used in connection with the free-standing sidehead and the paragraph sidehead. This, incidentally, is the professional manner in which fourth-level headings are indicated and it differs somewhat from some academic style book recommendations.

The purpose of headings is to show the outline of thought and, at the same time, to keep the left-hand margin of the type page straight. Outlining has its place, but with headings of the type described above, there is no need to accompany these with the conventional outline symbols: I, A, 1, a, and so forth. That is tautology. Avoid it.

We are back from our detour and will discuss one further matter under the general heading of acquainting the reader with the research problem.

In the document or dissertation, the matter of the review of the related literature should probably be given the status of a major division of the document and be dignified with a centered first-importance heading. Such divisions always begin on a new page and generally a more-than-usual amount of space is left before the heading to mark it as a new major division of the document.

The section entitled the review of the related literature is designed to acquaint the reader with the corollary literature of research. We need, at times, to see a particular research endeavor against the broad background of the efforts of others. This gives us a better understanding of the orientation of the problem to the larger general research environment. We have discussed previously the function of the review of the related literature. What has been said there is highly appropriate to the writing of the report document. In this connection, it may be well, therefore, for you to review Chapter 4.

The Presentation of the Data

After we appreciate fully just what the problem is and the research setting in which it has been investigated, the next question is, "What are the facts?"

The research document is not a unique production that only you can write. It is, instead, a report that, being given your problem and your data, *anyone* should be able to write. As a matter of fact, that is one of the criteria that is frequently cited by which to judge the adequacy of the research proposal: the proposal should be so self-contained that, should you be unable to complete the research, anyone with the requisite skill and ability could, by virtue of your proposal and the facts which you have amassed, carry the research to its completion.

The data are presented *in terms of the problem*. The researcher has gathered a mass of data. These were then codified, arranged, and separated into segments, each of which corresponded to a particular section of the problem which was being studied. The sectionalization of the problem has been presumably expressed in the form of appropriate subproblems in order to facilitate the management of the problem as a whole. There is, then, a one-to-one correspondence: certain data which relate to each subproblem. These are then exhibited in logical sequence within the report. As each subproblem with its attendant data is discussed, it may be helpful to restate, at the beginning of such discussion, the subproblem in its exact wording in which it appears both in the proposal and in the first chapter of the study. To do so will keep your reader oriented to the progress of the research as it is being reported; and it will, likewise, focus the attention of the reader on the specific subtopic of the research problem under discussion.

Generally, the report is divided into chapters. A logical division is to devote one chapter to each subproblem and its pertinent data. The subproblem is presented, the data germane to it are then presented, and then those data are analyzed and interpreted and the conclusions that are warranted by the data are presented in resolution of the subproblem. Each chapter normally ends with a summary section in which the findings of that particular chapter are shown in relationship to the general problem and the previous subproblems. In this way, a tightly woven web of communication is established throughout the report.

The data should be presented *completely*. They may, of course, be organized and summarized into charts, tables, graphs, statistical summaries, lists of responses to questionnaire inquiries, and so on, but it is imperative that the data be exhibited as evidence for the conclusions that the researcher draws from them. Where the data are extensive and the researcher presents them in summary form in the body of the study, they are then presented in full array in an appendix. In this way, anyone wishing to take the same data should be able to replicate the results of the research effort and should be able, therefore, to reach substantially the same conclusions as those reached by the researcher.

Let us not forget that we are also testing a hypothesis. Somewhere, therefore—probably in the closing paragraphs of the chapter—some indication should be given as to whether the data did or did not support the hypothesis being tested. The hypothesis should be restated and the fact of its support or nonsupport by the data should be stated clearly.

Where the data were subjected to statistical analysis, a rationale for employing the particular statistical approach should be presented. It is important to know, for example, not *that* one employs a particular correlational technique but *why* that particular correlational technique was used. In fact, throughout the entire research process, it is well for you to keep in mind that generally the answer to the question "What?" is not nearly so important as the answer to the question "Why?" One of the weakest links in research is frequently the failure to substantiate *what* one has done with a solid rationale as to *why* one has done it. We shall have more to say about this in the next section.

The Interpretation of the Data

All too frequently, researchers feel that having once presented the facts and figures, they have done all that needs to be done. This is self-delusion and a misunderstanding of the research process. To do only that is to have done nothing more than a grand exercise in compiling minutiae. To display the data is certainly important, but it is the *interpretation of the data* which is the *sine qua non* of research.

In *Teaching for Thinking*, the following passage epitomizes the point: "The teacher who asks what the data are (the *who, what, when, where* questions) is concerned with a lower mental process, albeit he elicits the responses with pedagogical flourish. The teacher who gives the student some data and then asks what they *mean* is concerned with a higher mental process."[1] In fact, without inquiring into the intrinsic meaning of the data, no resolution of the research problem or its attendant subproblems is possible.

Many researchers, however, fail to exploit the data fully. One cannot turn over the facts too often; look at them from too many angles; chart, graph, and arrange them in too many ways, inspect them from too many vantage points. Don't be satisfied. Ask simple questions of those facts. "Doodle" with them. This is not to suggest a superficial or trifling approach. It is, however, to indicate that sometimes very simple questions, very naive approaches will afford you startling insights. Have you thought of plotting the data? What has caused the plotted data to "peak"? To reach a plateau? To dip or plummet? Does the behavior of the data have any relationship to events which lie outside the data—a question the historical researcher should ask as a standard procedure.

---

[1] Louis E. Raths, Selma Wasserman, Arthur Jones, and Arnold Rothstein, *Teaching for Thinking* (Columbus, Ohio: Charles E. Merrill, 1967), p. 117.

Questions like these may sometimes crack the shell of the data and reveal the meaning within. Every data configuration may not be meaningful, but that is beside the point. What is important is that the researcher leave no stone unturned, no data unnoticed, no arrangement untried. As a general rule, data have many more meanings than most researchers discover. This is because having processed the data by one means only, many researchers are unaware that other processes applied to the same data may refine additional meanings from those same facts.

This discussion also suggests another matter. Researchers are sometimes so intent on "proving their point" that their enthusiasm takes control of their better judgment. In the last analysis, *the facts must speak for themselves*. The researcher is only the mouthpiece. You may not like what the facts say. They may not confirm your fondest hopes or support your preconceived opinions, but the researcher is the servant of the scientific method and that method looks at facts squarely and without subjective prejudice; and it reports candidly and precisely what the impersonal fact affirms.

There is danger here. Every beginning researcher needs to ferret out every generalization, underscore it in red, and then be sure that the facts in the tables, graphs, and other exhibits will solidly support what those words, underlined in red, declare.

It is an academic tradition to defend one's research effort. *Defend* in this sense means "to justify one's conclusions, to support one's statements with the backing of solid fact that has been presented in the document." Nothing short of this will suffice.

As a final section to the interpretation of the data, the report should close with a chapter entitled "Summary, Conclusions, and Recommendations." In this chapter, all loose threads should be gathered together. Here is the place for looking backward, for distilling into a few paragraphs precisely what has been accomplished in each phase of the research activity. One should be able to see the research endeavor as through the wrong end of a telescope: clearly, minutely, and at some distance, with all significant aspects brought together in proper perspective. On the basis of this summary, the researcher should state very clearly the findings and the conclusions reached with respect to the problem and the subproblems that have been studied. The conclusions should be entirely supported by the facts previously presented. Then, the researcher is ready for two final steps: (1) to state whether the hypotheses have been supported or not, and (2) to make recommendations for further study, perhaps in those areas related to the problem which, during the research, the researcher has recognized as worthy of further investigation.

A word should be said about summaries. One of the weakest aspects of all research report writing is the failure of report writers to summarize adequately. They forget human psychology. They overlook the psychological necessity of the reader who comes to the report "cold." The whole research project—the problem, the organization of the data, the facts, the figures, the relationships and interrelationships—these are all so clear in the minds of those who have been involved with the research that they sometimes give little thought to the fact that the reader is not so intimately acquainted with the project and its several parts. Researchers should always be mindful of the fact that through their long acquaintance with their study they have an awareness which sees plainly the master plan, the relation of each component to the total study, the parts as they fit into the whole.

Readers, however, are not so fortunate. They need to stop occasionally as they proceed through the report, to orient themselves with respect to the totality of the investigation. To this end, guideposts in the form of headings, transitional words and paragraphs, and other means of directing the reader are helpful. Instead of a long rambling discussion of related literature, the writer may help the reader to keep oriented by employing any of the several means that we have mentioned. One of the best directive devices is a summary at the close of each extended discussion. By the writer pausing long enough to summarize for the reader what has been happening and what relevance such discussion has to the larger considerations within the report gives a unity to the whole which is highly desirable; and is tantamount to keeping one's eye on the goal post when, in the frenzy of the game, we need orientation and reference points. Pure frenzy can leave us greatly bewildered. Discussions that ramble on and on tend, in like manner, to produce psychological numbness, bewilderment, and confusion. Summaries avoid such reader disorientation.

A Schematic Model of the Research Report

The writer of a research report needs to visualize clearly the total schema of the report. What is central needs to be distinguished from what is peripheral; what is basic, from what is ancillary. The writer should understand the dynamics of the report and, seeing these matters, should never leave the reader in doubt for a moment as to what is happening during the entire discussion.

At the close of Chapter 1, we presented a diagram showing the cyclical nature of research. At this point, we are presenting the same schema only in a slightly different form.

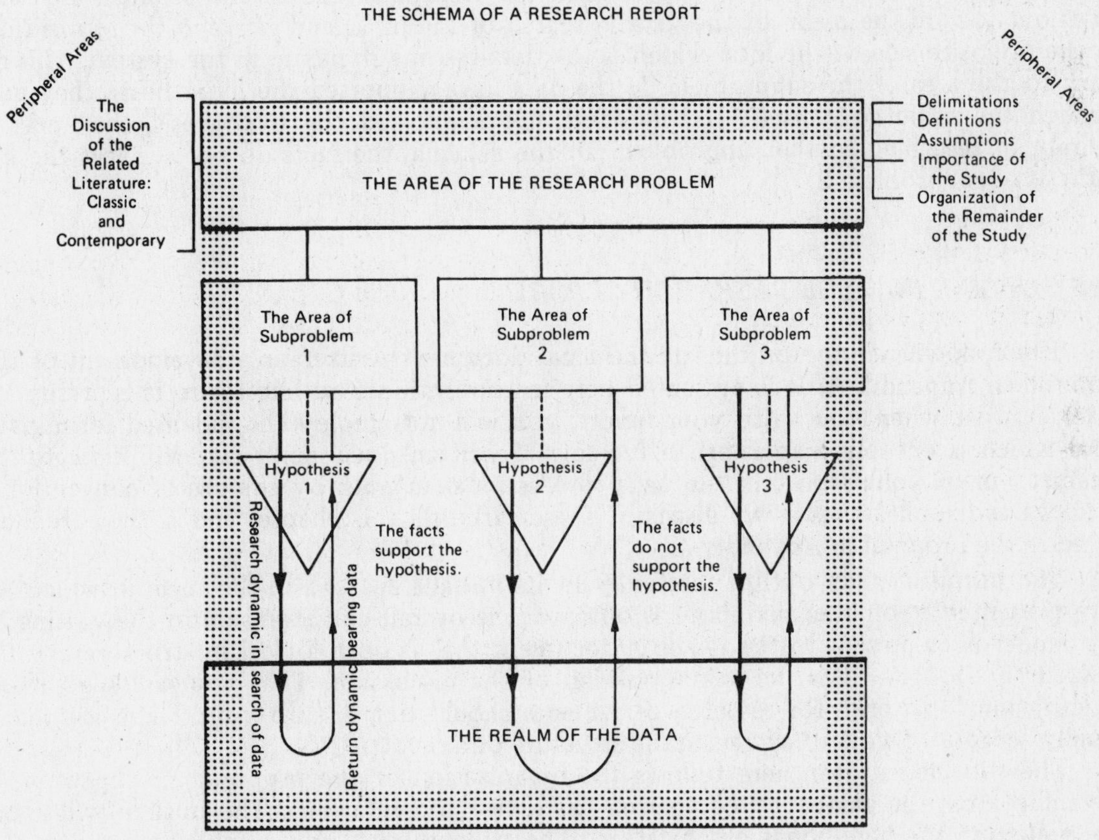

Let us conceive of the research problem as metaphorically covering a certain "area" of investigation. The subproblems, then—and we will assume that we have three of them—will each cover one-third of the area occupied by the problem. The main dynamics of the research effort will take place in a more or less vertical system of activity localized under the area indicating the "spread" of the problem. Peripheral to the problem will lie those other items whose principal function is to throw light on the problem by explaining the meaning of its terms, delimiting the extent of its boundaries, presenting the assumptions that the researcher has made, delineating the importance and the relevance of the study, and outlining the remainder of the report organization. These matters help us to understand the problem, but they are not an integral part of it.

In quite the same peripheral relationship is the review of the related literature. This discussion, although helpful in causing us to see the problem under study in relation to other studies, classical and contemporary, merely orients us within the total research environment. It does for us what a map does for the traveler. Below is a schema of a research report. It indicates within the dotted boundary lines what is essential to any research activity. It places outside those boundaries that which is necessary for an intelligent reading of the research report but which has not been a part of the activity itself. At the top of the diagram is the area of the unsolved research problem; at the bottom is the realm of the data where the potential for solving the problem lies. In vertical paths which originate in the problem, but principally in the subproblem areas, is the research activity itself. This activity passes through and is focussed in the direction of the facts by the hypotheses. The hypotheses point in the direction of the data. The activity loop contains two types of energy: *efferent*, the activity that originates in the researcher and in the problem area and flows out toward the realm of the data in search of the facts, and *afferent*, the return flow on the opposite side of the loop which is the data-bearing dynamic in the system. This returns to the area of the subproblem. If the data have supported the hypothesis, they pass through the hypothesis itself. If they have not supported the hypothesis, they miss it entirely in returning to the subproblem. In the schema, the facts do not support the hypothesis of subproblem 2.

THE OUTLINE FOR THE RESEARCH REPORT

The following is the outline of the final document written as a development of the proposal in Appendix A. It is presented here in conventional outline form. It is presumed, however, that when you write your report, you will not employ the indented form given here—which is entirely inappropriate for formal written documents—but will indicate the organization of your report in the usual professional manner by the use of conventional headings and subheadings as we discussed these earlier in this chapter and as they are illustrated in the proposal in Appendix A.

The purpose of an outline, certainly in its initial stage and in the form in which we have presented it on the next page is obvious: the overall consideration in the writing of any report is to present to the reader a document that is both logical in structure and organized in thought. It is the spinal column of the discussion. That you will see variant organizational patterns for research documents should not disturb you. There are many equally acceptable ways of arranging the structure of a report.

The outline as given here follows the organization of the proposal in Appendix A. Advantage may be gained by comparing these two presentations. The outline will show the skeleton: the bare-bones organization. The proposal will add some substance to the skeletal structure; the complete report will present the body of research, fully developed, muscular with facts, and dynamic because of the mental processes of the researcher, who has taken those facts and *interpreted* them so that they manifest their meaning to the reader of the research report.

Of particular interest is the material which the researcher of this project proposes to present in the eight appendices, A through H. By including these data the researcher invites those who read the study to check the validity of the conclusions against the facts. This augurs well for the integrity of the research and the honesty of the researcher. It is a forthright presentation of the raw data, insofar as this is feasible, so that those who read the research may follow the footsteps of the researcher as he conducted the research.

Preliminaries

Title Page	Table of Contents
(Copyright Notice)	List of Tables
Acknowledgments	List of Figures

Text

Chapter

I. THE PROBLEM AND ITS SETTING
- The Problem
- The Subproblems
- The Hypotheses
- The Delimitations
- The Definitions of Terms
- Abbreviations Employed in the Dissertation
- The Assumptions
- The Need for the Study
- The Organization of the Remainder of the Study

II. THE REVIEW OF THE RELATED LITERATURE
- Interests as Theoretical Concepts
- Interests in Counseling and Vocational Choice
- The Measurement of Interests
- The Strong Approach
- The Measurement of Interests among Cartographers

III. THE POPULATION OF CARTOGRAPHERS
- The Population of Cartographers; Distribution and Genesis
- The Criterion Group
- The Cross-Validation Groups

IV. GENERAL PROCEDURES
- Response Data
- Collection Procedures
- Treating the Data

V. THE RESULTS
- The Criterion Group Returns
- The Cross-Validation Group Returns
- The Cartographer Scale
- Other *SVIB* Scores of Cartographers
- The Test of the Hypotheses
  - Hypothesis 1
  - Hypothesis 2
  - Hypothesis 3
  - Reliability and Validity
- Other Findings
- Summary of Results

VI. SUMMARY, CONCLUSIONS, AND RECOMMENDATIONS
- Summary
- Conclusions
- Recommendations

The Preliminary Matter and Appendix Content

The preliminary matter is all of the material of an introductory nature that precedes the actual text of the study. This includes the title page and, on the page following, the copyright notice. Following this is a page for the dedication (if any), a section of prefatory remarks and acknowledgement of indebtedness to those who have assisted in the research, the table of contents, the list of tables, and the part-title page (if any), in that order.

Perhaps a word should be said about copyright. Copyright is the protection given by law (U.S. Code, Title 17) to the authors of literary, dramatic, musical, artistic, and other *intellectual* works. Because of the great expenditure of time, effort, monetary resources, and other investment in a scholarly work such as a thesis or dissertation, it would seem only prudent to protect that investment by copyright. Formerly, the first term of statutory copyright ran for 28 years and could be renewed for a second term of 28 years. Under the current law, which took effect in 1978, copyright protection lasts for 50 years following the author's death, and is not renewable. For full information, write to the Copyright Office, Library of Congress, Washington, D.C. 20540.

Some theses and dissertations have later been turned into very remunerative and well-known books. Consider John Livingston Lowes' *The Road to Xanadu*[2] or Rudolf Flesch's many books on readability. Sometimes, under pressure of writing a dissertation, a student may not realize how important or publishable one's efforts may be. For the low cost of protective literary insurance, it may be well, therefore, to have the dissertation or the thesis copyrighted—just in case.

The acknowledgments page is usually a gracious acknowledgment of the assistance of those through whose kindness, the research effort, has been made possible. This assistance may include those who are responsible for providing the researcher with an entree to persons or data sources which have aided in completing the research, those who have guided the study and have given counsel—an academic dissertation committee or similar mentors, a faithful typist and proofreader, and those in one's own family who have encouraged and assisted in the research effort so that, with their cooperation, it could be brought to a suc-

[2] See previous reference to this work, page 91.

cessful conclusion. The guild mark of education is to say "thank you" to those who have given their time and their assistance to forward your efforts and your aspirations. The acknowledgments page is the proper place for the gracious expression of such indebtedness and the courtesy of recognition.

The rest of the "front matter" of the document is largely material intended to indicate the content and organization of the body of the text. The most important of this category of material is the table of contents. The table of contents is merely a bird's-eye view of what the document contains and its organizational structure. The illustrative material appearing in the manuscript is indicated by two types of lists: a list of tables and a list of figures. A *table* is usually an arrangement of words, numbers, signs, or combinations of them in parallel columns for the purpose of exhibiting certain information in compact and comprehensive form. A *figure*, on the other hand, indicates any kind of graphic illustration other than a table: a chart, photograph, schematic, drawing, sketch, or other illustrative or graphic device to convey an idea by other than verbal means.

The "back matter" usually contains supplementary aids or addenda which may be valuable in understanding the text material more completely but which are not absolutely essential to the comprehension of the body of the report. A rule of thumb is that the material appearing in the appendix enables one to "go further" with the document, if that is so desired. In the dissertation whose contents we cited, the appended data are largely numerical scores, statistical computations, mean values, and other similar data, so that if the reader wishes to do so, he can "check" the statistics of the researcher to confirm their accuracy or the statistical procedures to determine their appropriateness. In reporting research, nothing is hidden. All the data are laid before the reader. The researcher's integrity is, thus, preserved and the results and conclusions of the study can be readily verified.

The bibliography is likewise a part of the back matter and also is in the nature of reference material. Should one wish to read further in the area of the problem or in corollary areas, the bibliographical items provide directions and suggestions. The bibliography likewise speaks pertinently of the researcher's awareness of the literature in the field of investigation and his own critical evaluation of that literature. A glance at the bibliography is usually enough to convince us that the researcher knows the principal scholarly works underlying the entire area of the study. Bibliographic materials usually may be categorized into two principal classes: the "classic" studies that one might find almost invariably appearing with respect to any particular area and the highly relevant items that are especially appropriate to the specific problem under investigation.

Learn by Looking

Perhaps the best way to appreciate the nature and the various forms of research reports is to inspect a number of them. Any university library will have a collection of theses and dissertations. State and federal agencies issue reports of research in many areas. Certain notable reports available are the reports of the Surgeon General of the United States on smoking, the numerous reports on research issued by the National Institutes of Health, the American Medical Association, the many learned societies, professional associations, and occupational and trade groups.

You need only to let your imagination roam, to inquire, and to request; and soon a research report will be reaching you in the mail. Not all reports will follow the somewhat formal and academic format and style we have outlined here. All of them, however, should exhibit essentially the basic characteristics of a research report. Perhaps the best way, therefore, to become acquainted with what a research report is—and, conversely, to become aware of what a research report is not—is to learn by looking, keeping in mind the guidelines presented in this chapter. In your looking, and bearing in mind that they are nothing more than *abstracts*, not full-blown reports, you might profit a great deal by spending several hours perusing the research as reported in *Dissertation Abstracts International*.

Also, the United States Government Printing Office, Public Documents Department, Washington, D.C. 20402, issues a free periodical listing of published governmental research in a leaflet entitled *Selected U.S. Government Publications*. You should request it from The Superintendent of Documents.

FOR FURTHER READING

Allen, Eliot D. *A Short Guide to Writing a Research Paper, Manuscript Form and Documentation*. Deland, Florida: Everett Edwards, 1976.

Barzun, Jacques and Henry Graff. *The Modern Researcher.* 3rd ed. New York: Harcourt Brace Jovanovich, Inc. 1977.

Cooper, Bruce M. *Writing Technical Reports*. Baltimore, Md.: Penguin Books, 1964.

Cummins, Martha H., and Carole Slade. *Writing the Research Paper: A Guide and Sourcebook*. Boston, Mass.: Houghton Mifflin Company, 1979.

Davis, Gordon B., and Clyde A. Parker. *Writing the Doctoral Dissertation.* Woodbury, New York: Barron's Educational Series, 1979.

Doubleday, Neal F. *Writing the Research Paper.* Rev. ed. New York, D. C. Heath & Company, 1971.

Gallagher, William J. *Writing the Business and Technical Report.* Boston, Mass.: CBI Publishing Co., 1981.

Harris, M. B. "Accelerating Dissertation Writing: Case Study." *Psychological Reports* 34 (1974): 984–86.

Hauser, Travis, and Lee L. Gray. *Writing the Research Term Paper.* New York: Dell Publishing Co., 1965.

Hubbell, George S. *Writing Term Papers and Reports.* 4th ed. New York: Barnes and Noble, 1969.

Jones, Paul W., and Keen, Michael L. *Writing Scientific Papers—Reports.* 8th ed. Dubuque, Iowa: William C. Brown Company, 1981.

Koefod, Paul E. *The Writing Requirements for Graduate Degrees.* Englewood Cliffs, New Jersey: Prentice-Hall, Inc., 1964.

Lester, James D. *Writing Research Papers: A Complete Guide.* 3rd. ed. Glenview Ill.: Scott Foresman and Company, 1980.

Martin, Roy. *Writing and Defending a Thesis or Dissertation in Psychology and Education.* Springfield, Ill.: Charles C. Thomas, Publisher, 1980.

Morse, Lawrence. *Writing the Economics Paper.* Woodbury, N.Y.: Barrons Educational Series, 1981.

Nelson, Joseph R. *Writing the Technical Report.* 3rd ed. New York: McGraw-Hill Book Company, 1952.

O'Connor, Maeve, and F. Peter Woodford. *Writing Scientific Papers in English*. Amsterdam: Elsevier, 1976.

Samuels, Marilyn S. *Writing the Research Paper.* New York: AMSCO School Publications, Inc., 1978.

Scientific Writing for Graduate Students. Rockville, Md.: Council of Biology Editors, 1968.

Sternberg, Robert J. *Writing the Psychology Paper.* Woodbury, N.Y.: Barrons Educational Series, 1977.

Stromberg, M. and Jo Ann Wegmann. "The Fine Art of Writing Research Abstracts." *Oncology Nursing Forum* 8 (Fall 1981): 67–71.

Weidenborner, Stephen, and Domenick Caruso. *Writing Research Papers: A Guide to the Process.* New York: St. Martin's Press, Inc., 1982.

Willis, Hulon. *Writing Term Papers: The Research Paper—The Critical Paper.* New York: Harcourt Brace Jovanovich, Inc., 1977.

Winkler, Anthony C., and Jo Ray McCuen. *Writing the Research Paper: A Handbook.* New York: Harcourt Brace Jovanovich, Inc., 1979.

Woodford, F. P., ed. *Scientific Writing for Graduate Students.* New York: Rockefeller University Press, 1968.

"Writing a Market Research Report." *International Trade Forum* 16 (October-December 1980): 22–27.

READ THIS—BEFORE YOU READ THIS CHAPTER

Finally, we come to the minutiae: those little details that make all the difference between a job well done and one marked by mediocrity. Michelangelo is reputed to have said, "Trifles make perfection, but perfection is no trifle!" In preparing the report, the attention one gives to technical details and stylistic convention will clearly separate those who know and those who don't. And for those doing theses or dissertations, unless you are willing to endure long delays and much extra work, it is better to know before you start.

Typing the report can sometimes be a decided ordeal for those not experienced in secretarial skills. The suggestions in this chapter may make that phase of report writing much less onerous.

Finally, a few words are offered about style. Nothing can take the place of a crisp, direct, and interesting presentation of fact. To think of research reports as dull reading is to misconceive the nature of research. Those who really do research find it exhilarating and full of excitement. Those who write about what they have done should not lose the thrill of that excitement when they report to others what their efforts have revealed.

12

The Style, the Format, the Readability of the Report

TECHNICAL DETAILS AND STYLISTIC MATTERS

We have discussed in the previous chapter and at various other places throughout the book matters of style and format as these have seemed appropriate to the discussion at hand. This chapter will be devoted to methods of presenting the thought upon the page, and to some suggestions of practical importance that will facilitate the production of the document.

Write on the Right Side of the Paper

Few students know that there is a right and a wrong side of a sheet of paper. Every piece of paper has one side which has a smooth felt-like appearance. This is called the *felt side*. This is the side on which the typing is done. Typing on the felt side of the paper gives the manuscript a soft clean appearance, with the letters having a sharp, clear configuration. The reason for this will be seen by taking any sheet of paper and looking carefully at one side and then at the other with a high-powered magnifying glass. One side will be, as we have said, soft and felty in appearance. The other side, under magnification, will look like a window screen, or it will have a rough fibrous appearance. In fact, this side is called the *screen side*.

In the paper-making process, the pulp and rag issue from the Jordan macerating machine and flow onto the first stage of the paper-making machine as a thin milklike fluid. This stage uses an oscillating trough where the water carrying the fibers is drained away, the shaking orients the fibers, and the soft pulp comes to rest upon a very fine screen bed. The impression made by the webbing of the screening is never entirely eradicated from the surface of the paper in the processes that follow. Because of its pitted texture, the screen side of the paper does not register the full force of the typed character as well as the felt side, and although the difference is miniscule, to those who observe closely there *is* a difference. Papers typed on the screen side do not have the snap, the vitality, or the finesse of appearance that those written on the felt side do.

With watermarked paper, it is a very simple matter to identify the felt side. Hold up the paper to the light, looking at the watermark. When the watermark is oriented in the proper right-side up reading position, you are facing the felt side of the paper on which you should type. For papers without watermark, the outside wrapper of the package will usually bear the words "felt side," to identify it, but inspection under magnification will always reveal one side as more granular than the other. The granular side, the "dead"-looking side, is *not* for typing.

A further word about paper. In making paper, both wood pulp and rags are used. Wood pulp paper, sometimes merely called pulp paper, is cheaper, less durable, and after a time has a tendency to turn yellowish or brown and become brittle. Other types of paper are composed of various proportions of rag content. Rag content in the paper gives the paper durability and a flexibility that pulp paper lacks. The proportion of rag content is usually indicated as 25, 50, 75, or 100 percent rag. Many universities specify a particular make and proportion of rag content for their dissertations. You should check with your university librarian, registrar's office, or the office of the graduate dean to ascertain whether, indeed, a special paper requirement is designated for your thesis or dissertation. If it is, it will doubtless be watermarked. Check the orientation of the watermark before you begin typing.

Follow Accepted Guidelines

If you are writing a thesis or a dissertation, be sure to check with the office of the graduate dean to ascertain whether the university has a prescribed set of guidelines for writing theses. Check such matters as paper size, width of margins, and size and style of typeface. (Some universities specify only 12 point pica, others will accept either pica or elite face.) Double spacing of manuscript is a universal requirement. Stylistic customs differ. What is permitted in one institution may be entirely unacceptable in another. You should make sure, then, whether your university has a style manual for writing research documents or whether it recommends that you follow a particular style manual and, if so, which one. Some of the principal manuals of style are the following:

A Manual of Style. 12th revised edition. Chicago: The University of Chicago Press, 1969.

Manual for Authors of Mathematical Papers. Providence, Rhode Island: The American Mathematical Society, 1979.

Campbell, William G., Stephen V. Ballou and Carole Slade. *Form and Style: Theses, Reports, Term Papers*. 6th ed. Boston, Mass.: Houghton Mifflin Company, 1982.

CBE Style Manual. 5th edition. CBE Style Manual Committe. Bethesda, Maryland: Council of Biology Editors, 1983.

MLA Handbook for Writers of Research Papers, Theses, and Dissertations. Edited by Joseph Gibaldi and Walter S. Achtert. New York: Modern Language Association of America, 1977.

Parker, William Riley, compiler. *MLA* (Modern Language Association) *Style Sheet*. Revised edition. New York: Modern Language Association of America, 1954.

Publication Manual of the American Psychological Association. 2nd ed. Washington, D.C.: The American Psychological Association, 1975.

Trelease, Sam F. *How to Write Scientific and Technical Papers*. Cambridge, Mass.: MIT Press, 1969.

Turabian, Kate L. *A Manual for Writers of Term Papers, Theses, and Dissertations*. Fourth edition. Chicago, Ill.: The University of Chicago Press, Phoenix Books, 1973.

United States Government Printing Office. *Style Manual*. Revised edition. Washington, D.C.: Government Printing Office, 1973.

Words into Type. Third ed. Englewood Cliffs, New Jersey: Prentice-Hall, Inc., 1974.

Publication Style Manual for Authors and Editors. Washington, D.C.: American Bankers Association, 1977.

Footnotes and Documentation

We shall not prescribe any footnote form here. There are too many styles. Almost every academic discipline has its own preference for footnote and bibliographic documentation. But beneath all of them lie some basic principles of reference notation. What you need is to grasp the *purpose* of the footnote that lies behind the variant forms.

First, we shall discuss the general idea of documentation. The documentary footnote has two principal functions. One of these is to invest the footnoted statement with an aura of authority. You buttress your statements with an authoritarian source to establish their validity. Again, the footnote acknowledges your indebtedness for quoted material or data appropriated. Ethics among writers requires that if material is borrowed from any source, whether a direct quotation or not, and if those who know the source would recognize the appropriated material, then both author and source should be acknowledged by footnote citation. Where the quotation is extensive and the writer is contemplating having his document published in any form, or copyrighted, he should secure *in writing* from the publisher or the author of the material—whoever holds the copyright to the material—permission to reprint the material. In addition to the footnote citing the source, the words *Reprinted by permission of the publisher* (or author—whichever may be the case) should be added to the footnote.

The purpose of the footnote is to convey information. That information may generally be categorized as follows:

1. The authorship data.
2. The source data.
3. The publication data.
4. The chronological data.
5. The locational data.

We shall discuss each of these items briefly.

★ *The authorship data.* Generally, in footnotes the author's name is listed in the natural order: given name and surname. In bibliographic entries, the author's name is usually reversed: surname, given name, and middle initial or middle name. Where multiple authors are involved, the names are separated by commas with *and* joining the name of the last author to the series. Except for the first author's name, the others in the series are usually presented in given name-surname sequence. Academic degrees or titles of respect are always deleted in listing authors' names.

★ *The source data.* The source data tell the source of the information. From what *source* did you get the information? A book? A journal? An interview? An address? Acknowledge it. Generally, the complete title of the source is listed as it appears on the title page of the book or in the masthead of a journal. The rule is: put the title in *italics* when the source document is a separate publication. In typing, italics are indicated by underscoring the words with a straight line. When the reference is a part only of a larger published whole (such as the title of an essay within a book of essays, the title of a poem in a volume of poetry, or the title of a chapter within a book or an article within a journal), then put the title in quotation marks. Titles of books and journals are *never* enclosed with quotation marks.

The misuse of the quotation mark is a common fault among writers who do not know how this punctuational device is used. The quotation mark has five specific uses. Any dictionary with a section on punctuation will give you these uses. Quotation marks are not to be inserted at the whim of the author, nor are they to be scattered willy-nilly. Learn to employ them properly.

★ *The publication data.* With books, the publication data usually consist of the city and state in which the publisher is located and the full corporate name of the publisher. The place of publication is available from the title page of the book or the masthead of the periodical. In the case of books, the title page may carry a list of cities; for example, Van Nostrand Reinhold Company, New York, Cincinnati, Toronto, London, Melbourne. The place of publication is always the first city mentioned in such an array—in this case, New York.

The publication information for a periodical, in addition to the title, is the title of the article being cited, the volume—usually with the month and date in parentheses, following the volume—and the page or pages on which the citation appears. With some periodicals issued quarterly the quarter of publication is also included among the publication information: e.g., winter, spring, summer, fall.

★ *The chronological data.* With books, chronological information is the year of publication as indicated on the title page or, if it does not appear there, the date of copyright is used as indicated on the copyright page. The chronological information usually follows immediately after the name of the publisher and is separated by a comma. With periodicals, the chronological data are usually the year, the month, and in the case of daily or weekly periodicals, the day of the month. Newspaper citations usually also include section, page, and, at times, column location.

The purpose of all documentation is to permit the reader, if he wishes, to go with the least difficulty to the source cited. To that end, the documentary data should assist the reader.

★ *The locational data.* The locational data identify the reference by its page location within the book or the periodical. Usually this information is the last item cited in the footnote. A widely used convention is to include the abbreviation *p.* or *pp.* for page references with *book* citations and to *omit* the page abbreviations for periodical citations—for example: *Research/Development* 24:33 (1973). In this citation, 24 is the volume and 33 is the page. Many journals number their pages consecutively throughout all the issues in a year.

Think of each issue of a periodical as one section of a bound volume. A journal which is issued monthly will have twelve sections which are often compiled into a single volume. These volumes will be found on the bound periodicals shelves or the reference shelves of the library. The spine of the volume will show the title of the periodical and the volume number.

Bibliographies are usually appended to extended discussions either as a recapitulation of the works cited in the document or as an additional reading list of related literature for the reader who wishes to pursue the subject at greater length.

Two other types of footnotes that we have not mentioned are the *informational footnote*, in which supplementary information (considered by the author as not particularly appropriate for inclusion in the text proper) is placed in footnote position, and the *internal reference footnote*, in which the reader is referred to a page earlier or later in the same work in which a particular topic is discussed.

The Prose Style of the Report

The research report is precisely that—*a report*. It is the researcher reporting upon what he has done in the progress of his research effort. As we have said earlier, the researcher is acquainting the reader with the problem, with the data he has brought to bear upon the resolution of that problem, the means he has employed in gathering those data, the processes of analysis to which he has submitted them, and the conclusions that he has reached. All of this, from the actual research effort standpoint, is history.

Because the researcher is reporting upon what has already happened, *the manuscript should be written in the past tense.* The document will also be restricted by another convention of document writing; namely, that—except for the title page or the by-line—*the researcher, qua researcher, should be anonymous.* The use of the first personal pronoun in any of its forms or the reference to the researcher in any other way is particularly taboo. Research permits only one "character" upon the stage: *the facts!* All of the action within the drama of research revolves around *the data*; they, and they only "speak."

This, however, creates a concomitant problem: it forces the writer to employ the less forceful, more impersonal *passive voice* style of writing. In case you are uncertain on matters of grammar, do not confuse the *past tense* with the *passive voice*. They have nothing in common. Past tense relates events as happening in time past: "The Treaty of Paris *brought* the Revolutionary War to an end." That is a simple statement of an event which happened in the past. The passive voice, on the other hand, is used to indicate that no identifiable subject is performing the act. It is a kind of ghostly form of the verb that causes events to happen without any visible cause being present. We assume that someone or something caused the events to occur; but on the face of the record no evidence of it appears. Note the passive voice construction in this sentence: "A survey *was made* of the owners of the Rollaway automobiles." We have no indication of *who* made the survey, only of *the fact* that the survey "was made." The passive voice plays down the person; it emphasizes the fact. We might indeed have said, "A survey was made *by the researcher* of the owners of the Rollaway automobiles" or *The researcher made* [here we have the active voice] a survey of the owners of Rollaway automobiles." But both of these versions are unacceptable. Here we have a quasi-first-person intrusion of the researcher and some readers may frown upon it; but mainly, the best research reporting does not use it.

The passive voice is always identifiable by two features: it always contains some form of the verb *to be*; it always contains a past participle of a verb. It need not suggest events happening in past time at all. We can suggest events that will happen in the future, without any indication of who will do them, by using the *future* passive form of the verb. Take, for example this statement: "The test will have been given before the students are permitted to read the novel." The underscored words indicate the essential verbal components of the passive voice construction: a part of the verb *to be* (*been*) + a *past* participle (*given*).

The general rule for the style of the research report is, therefore:

1. Write it in the past tense as a report of events which have already happened.
2. In the interest of keeping the person of the researcher subdued upon the face of the report, employ the passive voice in writing the report.

THE TYPING OF THE REPORT

The report should be a clean, neat, attractive document. City planners are conscious of "open spaces" in the design of urban communities. Research report writers should be no less aware of their importance. Between text and free-standing sideheads, ample space should be allowed. Four single spaces between the end of the text material and the sidehead, then three single spaces between sidehead and the continuing text, give an openness to the discussion which suggests a definite break in the pursuit of one topic and a turning to another matter. Margins are probably the most important factor in creating the impression of uncrowded open space. Leave two inches at the top of the paper, one inch at the bottom, 1.75 inches on the left, and one inch on the right to be devoted to margin. To do so will give your page an atmosphere of spaciousness and will conform to the best typographical quality standards.

Such a page fulfills the specifications laid down by typographers and printers of quality books. The following sets forth the principle clearly:

> Enough of the paper is exposed to make its contribution of a surface sympathetic to the type, texture, and pliability pleasant to the touch, and color pleasing to the eye. The classic page relationships are in the neighborhood of 50 percent for type page and paper respectively. The Gutenberg 42-line Bible has 45 percent for type, 55 percent for paper page area.
>
> The distribution of margins from the esthetic viewpoint is governed by the principles of design relating to spatial areas. This means simply that there should be a pleasing difference between front and back and top and bottom margins.[1]

[1] *Typography and Design: United States Government Printing Office Training Series* (Washington, D.C.: United States Government Printing Office, revised 1963), p. 66.

The proportions of type page suggested above are well proportioned from an esthetic standpoint and the left margin is wide enough to allow room for binding in the case of theses and dissertations. Also a textpage area which is 5.75 × 8 inches on an 8.50- × 11-inch sheet covers slightly more than 49 percent of the total page area.

Chapter headings should be dropped approximately 3.5 inches from the top of the page. The first line of text of the new chapter begins six single spaces below the chapter heading. On the first page of the new chapter, the text extends to within 2 inches of the bottom of the page. The first page of the chapter is drop-folioed; that is, the page number is typed at the bottom of this page, centered, 1 inch from the lower edge of the typing page. All chapter headings are typed in capital letters, centered on the page.

Perhaps one of the most useful devices for typing a manuscript is an easily made typing guide. It is placed under the page upon which the manuscript will be typed, and aligned at the top, bottom, and left side. Both guide sheet and typing sheet are then inserted into the typewriter together.

The guide sheet measures 2 inches wider than the standard typewriter page. On this extra 2-inch extension to the right of the page, the important page features are noted. Also in diminishing sequence, beginning with the maximum number of lines which will be assigned to each page—25 in this instance—and descending in reverse order to 1, each double spaced line is numbered. The typist knows, therefore, at any given time just how many lines are left. The page is also divided within the print area into half-sections by both vertical and horizontal lines. An elongated box is provided for chapter headings and a pair of parallel starting lines for the first line of the text in the new chapter. In the upper right-hand corner is a small box which indicates the placement for the page number for all pages of the chapter except the first.

As we approach the bottom of the page an additional device comprised of ∇ symbols warns us of the approaching end of the page. The first triangular symbol appears ten lines from the lower margin of the type page. We are further alerted by the word *Caution* beginning at line 8. The last five lines are marked by ever-widening rows of inverted-triangular symbols. See the reduced illustration of the typing guide on the next page.

A page typed with such a guide will be well proportioned, neat, and attractive. The boundary and guide lines are drawn in India ink, or with a black magic marker. Delineated thus, the guidelines are faintly visible through the typing sheet and serve to keep the text material within bounds.

When the text matter is typed on the page overlaying the typing guide, if we could see both pages with x-ray vision, the relation of text material to typing guide lines would appear as we have represented it on page 248.

Before you begin typing your final draft of the manuscript, be sure that you have a well-inked ribbon and that you have thoroughly cleaned your type characters. Nothing so confirms your meticulousness in research as your fastidiousness in these mechanical incidentals. Clogged dirty type characters hint at an insensitivity to quality work which all careful placement of text upon paper cannot dispel. N●thing leaves a w●rse impressi●n than a page typed with ink cl●gged characters, with lines that c●me ●ut l●●king like this specimen.

A stiff bristle brush and a can of lighter fluid can correct such a condition.

And, Finally, the Research Report Need Not Be Dull Reading!

There is no reason why a report should be dull—anymore than there is a reason why a textbook should be dull. Both of them deal with the excitement of human thinking prompted by the fascination of facts in the world around us. It is unfortunate that the research report, the academic thesis, and the dissertation have been considered an almost certain cure

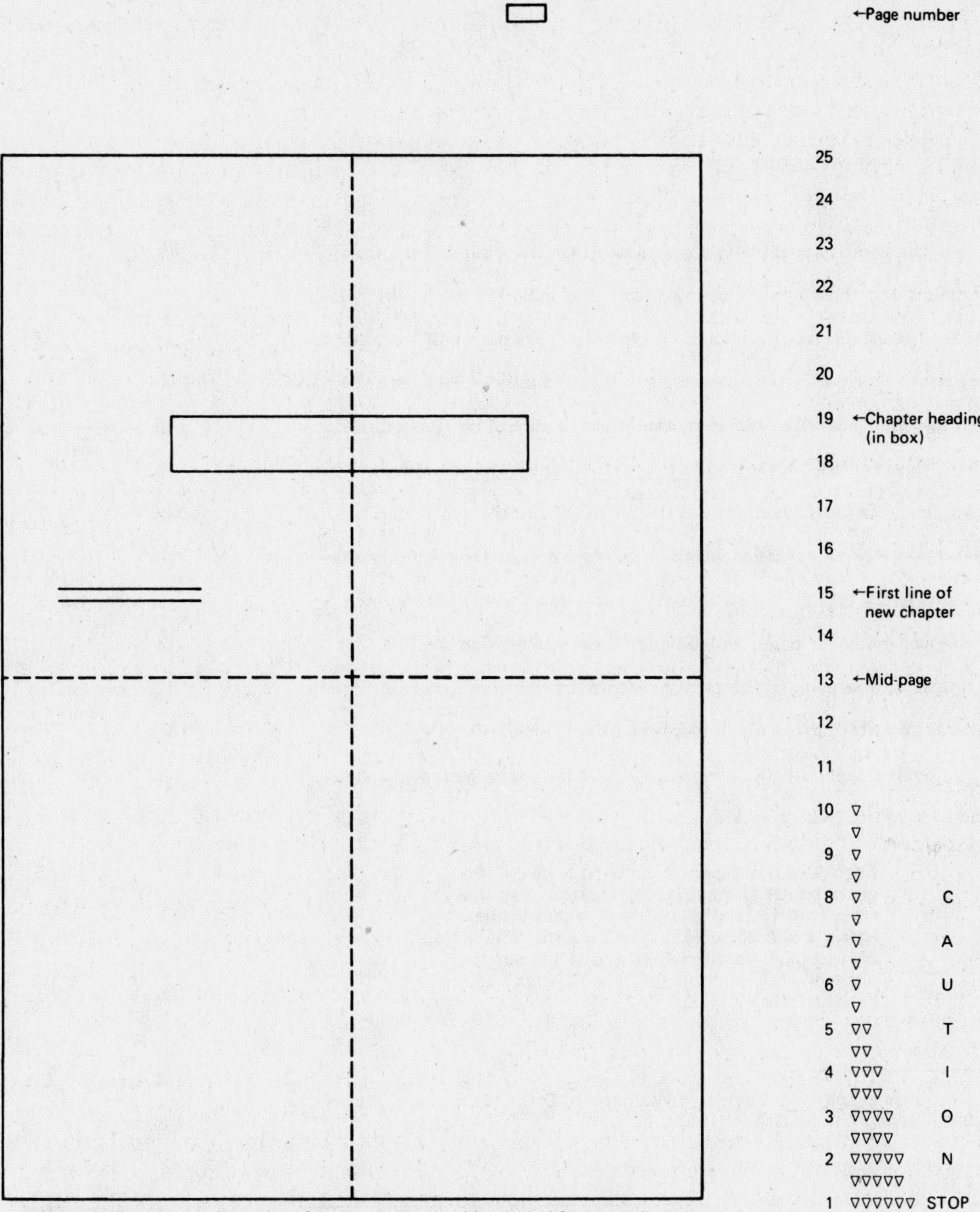

The lay-out of a guide for the typing of manuscript pages, with principal features indicated at the proper locations.

for insomnia. The only reason research reports are dull is because they are the products of dull writers. Phlegmatic attitudes and unimaginative minds will never set ablaze dry lifeless fact.

Discovery is one of the most exciting of human activities. And research is discovery! It is sailing upon seas where no man has ever been before. It is looking across vast wastelands of mere data and seeing in them features previously missed by other observing eyes and characteristics hitherto unnoticed by any human mind. Imagine the thoughts of the

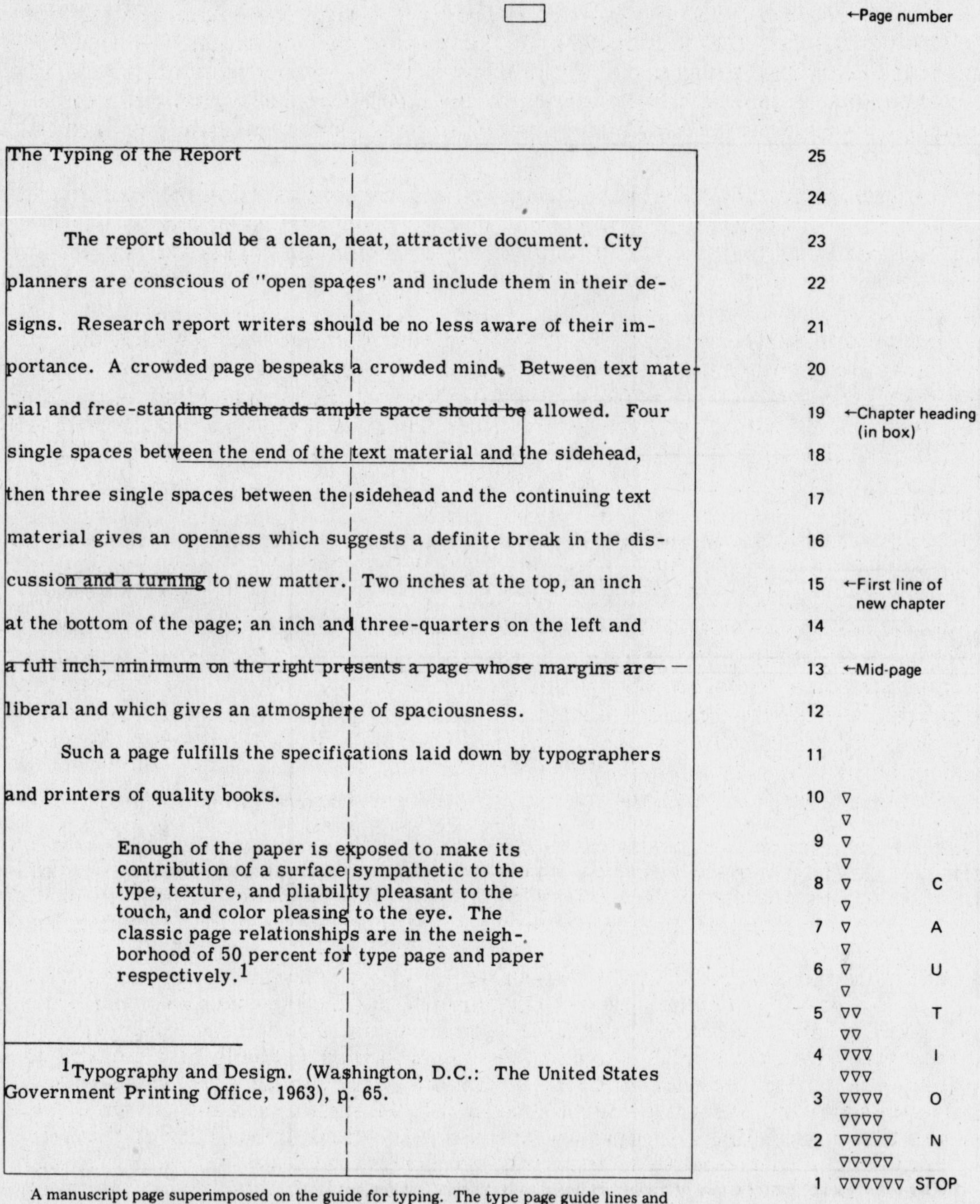

←Page number

The Typing of the Report

The report should be a clean, neat, attractive document. City planners are conscious of "open spaces" and include them in their designs. Research report writers should be no less aware of their importance. A crowded page bespeaks a crowded mind. Between text material and free-standing sideheads ample space should be allowed. Four single spaces between the end of the text material and the sidehead, then three single spaces between the sidehead and the continuing text material gives an openness which suggests a definite break in the discussion and a turning to new matter. Two inches at the top, an inch at the bottom of the page; an inch and three-quarters on the left and a full inch, minimum on the right presents a page whose margins are liberal and which gives an atmosphere of spaciousness.

Such a page fulfills the specifications laid down by typographers and printers of quality books.

> Enough of the paper is exposed to make its contribution of a surface sympathetic to the type, texture, and pliability pleasant to the touch, and color pleasing to the eye. The classic page relationships are in the neighborhood of 50 percent for type page and paper respectively.[1]

[1]Typography and Design. (Washington, D.C.: The United States Government Printing Office, 1963), p. 65.

←Chapter heading (in box)

←First line of new chapter

←Mid-page

C A U T I O N STOP

A manuscript page superimposed on the guide for typing. The type page guide lines and center division broken lines are visible under the manuscript text.

men who walked upon the moon. To them it was a thrilling adventure: not because it was the moon, but because in that dull and lifeless world lay the facts that might provide evidence for the birth and age of the earth, the origin of the solar system, and the birth of the moon itself. It offered a means of testing our theories. It was the end of an observation that began in Padua in the seventeenth century when Galileo, with a 32× telescope first discovered the mountains of the moon! In the gray and lifeless dust, more completely dead than anything that man has ever looked upon in all his long history, lay exciting facts, pregnant with the possibilities of extending human knowledge.

There is no such thing as a dull and lifeless fact. When facts die, something more important than the fact has first succumbed: the imagination, the insight, the excitement of discovery, the creative thought within the mind of the researcher. When this goes, all goes; when this goes, research dies. The writing of the report then becomes a dull exercise that produces an uninspired account of the researcher's efforts and the garnering of his factual quarry.

We have come full circle. Now we understand why the selection of a problem which fascinates the researcher is so important. Only by being engrossed with a problem that captivates him will the reserarcher be able to keep his enthusiasm until the last word of the report is typed. And that enthusiasm is infectious. It will spread to the words of the report itself.

The author many years ago started to find the origins and investigate the influences which have been contributory or ancillary to the history and development of reading improvement as an instructional subject at the college level. He expected that his quest would take him back perhaps a quarter of a century and that the causes would have shallow roots. Instead, his study became a quicksand, taking him down, down, down into a historical abyss for which he had not bargained and of whose cavernous reaches he had little dreamed.

Coming back from the historical depths, he brought with him data. In writing the research report, the author was faced with essentially the task of uncovering a hitherto undiscovered chapter in American higher education. A few paragraphs indicate what the author did with what was otherwise pedestrian and uninspiring fact. These paragraphs probably illustrate that the difference between the soporific narrative and one alive with the dynamic force of imagination is not so much *that* you present the facts but, rather in the *way in which* you present the facts. Unless the author—the researcher—is alive with enthusiasm for the newly discovered fact, the thought will be delivered to the page stillborn: dull, uninteresting, and prosaic.

Here are some of the dullest data with which the author had to deal.

> Many reasons contributed to the discouragement of reading in the mid-nineteenth century college. The libraries grew slowly, and even the oldest—and, presumably, the best—fell far short of what a college library might have been. Harvard and Yale had, doubtless, the acme of collegiate libraries in America; but even they left much devoutly to be wished by men of vision who saw what books and reading could mean in the educational program of the American college. . . .
>
> While no particular data can dichotomize the moment when the old order ceased, giving way to the new, 1876 seemed an especially noteworthy year. Influences which accumulated strength for years seemed suddenly of a moment to materialize into concrete fact. When this happens, certain historical moments become pivotal. In retrospect, 1876 seemed to be such a moment. . . . In 1876, the American Library Association was formed. Perhaps in the light of this fact, Shores says that modern librarianship generally dates from 1876. In this year also R. R. Bowker became the first editor of the newly founded *Library Journal*, a publication that was to voice again and again in its columns the pertinency of reading to higher education. On the first of January of this year, Daniel C. Gilman, the new president of The Johns Hopkins University, issued his first annual report.[2] In this initial report to the trustees of the new university, President Gilman said,
>
>> The idea is not lost sight of that the power of the university will depend upon the character of its resident staff of prominent professors.

[2] Refer to Chapter 7, pages 127–128, where we discuss the keeping of a multiple-file of the same data. Unless the author had a chronological file of data, these facts would probably have not been noticed.

> It is their researches in the library and the laboratory . . . which will make the University in Baltimore an attraction to the best students and serviceable to the intellectual growth of the land.

And the University in Baltimore did, indeed, have a far-reaching effect upon the "intellectual growth of the land."[3]

The Elements of Style

The elements of style are there: readability, topic sentences. These are developed and the facts are documented. See what variety of structure the author has used. The first three sentences are normal subject-predicate order. The fourth sentence begins with a dependent clause. Then sentence five assumes the subject-predicate form again. In succeeding order sentences begin with a phrase, an adverb, another phrase. Variety is the spice of life; it is also the life of a readable style. Short sentences alternate with longer ones. These are all features that make for easy interesting reading.

You might do well, if you are not sure what makes writing readable, to study two books: *The Elements of Style*[4] and *The Art of Readable Writing.*[5] Eschew the exaggerated expression; look sharply at your ill-advised and thoughtlessly chosen adjectives. Stick to the facts. Report them accurately; but, in so doing, enliven your prose with a variety of sentence structure, sentence length, and precision of verb and noun. You may have to write your report in the unappealing passive voice, but there is much compensation in the skill and art of readable writing.

More do's and don'ts are probably to no avail. Distilled into a brief stanza by an anonymous hand is a broad guideline for all your writing. Follow it.

> The written word
> Should be clean as bone:
> Clear as light,
> Firm as stone;
> Two words are not
> As good as one.

FOR FURTHER READING

Barzun, Jacques. *Simple and Direct: A Rhetoric for Writers.* New York: Harper & Row, Publishers, 1975.

Barzun, Jacques, and Henry E. Graff. *The Modern Researcher: A Manual on All Aspects of Research and Writing.* 3rd ed. New York: Harcourt Brace Jovanovich, Inc., 1977.

Baker, Sheridan. *The Practical Stylist.* 3rd ed. New York: Thomas Y. Crowell Company, 1973.

Cather, Willa. *On Writing.* New York: Alfred A. Knopf, Inc., 1949.

DeBakey, Lois. "Literacy: Mirror of Society." *Journal of Technical Writing and Communication* 8 (1978): 279–319.

———. "Medical Writing: Let Thy Words Be Few." *International Journal of Cardiology* 2 (1982): 127–32.

---

[3] Paul D. Leedy, "A History of the Origin and Development of Instruction in Reading Improvement at the College Level" (unpublished doctoral dissertation, New York University, 1958), pp. 94, 97–98.

[4] K. W. Strunk, Jr., and E. B. White, *The Elements of Style*, 3rd ed. (New York: Macmillan Publishing Co., Inc.), 1979.

[5] Rudolf Flesch, *The Art of Readable Writing* (New York: Harper & Row, 1949).

——. "Medical Writing: Grammar. Word Order: the Misplaced Modifier." *International Journal of Cardiology* 1 (1982): 447-48.

DeBakey, Lois, and DeBakey, Selma. "Syntactic Orphans and Adoptees: Unattached Participles. I. Mischevous Intruders." *International Journal of Cardiology* 3 (1981): 67-70.

——. "Syntactic Orphans and Adoptees: Unattached Participles II. Medical Misconstructions." *International Journal of Cardiology* 3 (1983): 231-36.

Koefod, Paul E. *The Writing Requirements for Graduate Degrees.* Englewood Cliffs, N.J.: Prentice-Hall, Inc., 1964.

Mandel, Siegfried. *Writing for Science and Technology: A Practical Guide.* New York: Dell Publishing Company, 1970.

Words into Type. 3rd ed. Englewood Cliffs, N.J.: Prentice-Hall, Inc. 1974.

SAMPLE PROPOSAL AND PRACTICUM IN RESEARCH

Appendix A. Sample Proposal for a Research Project
Appendix B. Practicum in Research

Appendix A

Sample Proposal for a Research Project

On the pages that follow is an exact reprint of the text for a doctoral research project submitted to the faculty of the School of Education of The American University, Washington, D.C.

The proposal is presented here to give the student a clearer concept of precisely what a proposal is, the form it should take, and a suggested arrangement of its several parts. The proposal is shortened, since it is unnecessary and uneconomical to present the entire document.

Every proposal is essentially the same whether it is an outline for a thesis or a dissertation or an application for a grant to underwrite an independent research endeavor. Especially should you notice the degree of fullness and the precise care with which the details are spelled out.

The greater the investment of time, money, and effort, the fuller and more specific the proposal should be. Certainly there are variations to the format as here presented. No brief is made for the form of the proposal as presented here over any other equally logical presentation.

Underlying the proposal as here presented was a substratum of reasoning similar to this: Everyone desires to succeed. People are more likely to succeed if they are engaged in work they like to do. If one, therefore, can find a key to a person's interests, it is in part at least a key to the probability of vocational success. One must do what one is interested in doing. Interests are identified objectively by measuring the degree of like or dislike with which a person reacts to a vicarious activity.

Of the several general interest inventories, the *Strong Vocational Interest Blank* has been one of the most widely used and intensively studied. Interest scales have been developed on the Strong inventory for 54 occupational groups. No scale has ever been developed for cartographers, however, either on the Strong or on any other interest-measuring instrument.

Cartographers, and the nature of their professional activities as map makers, are little known to the general public. Furthermore, the annual production of cartographers is only 1 percent of the annual requirement.

If, therefore, some way could be found to match people who have kindred interests to those of cartographers with vocational opportunities in which there is a 99 percent demand, we may have come to grips with a very practical problem: the supplying a professional group with needed personnel and the guidance of individuals who have particular skills and aptitudes for cartography into a satisfying and rewarding profession. Here is the researcher's problem. Here is even a broader problem for an entire profession. It is to seek a possible solution to this problem through the medium of research that this proposal addresses itself.

One further word should be said about the form in which the proposal is presented here. As we have said earlier, the typescript is *a verbatim reprint of the proposal as it was presented by the student.* Its value to the user of this book will lie in two ways: (1) in seeing its original form, and (2) in seeing how, excellent as it is, even this proposal might have been improved.

Two conventions have, therefore, been employed in this presentation: (1) the usual proofreading marks to indicate editorial changes, and (2) a running commentary in the right-hand margin, pointing out both the excellent features of the proposal and, likewise, indicating those areas in which improvement might have been made to make the proposal even more effective.

The proposal is not meant to be slavishly emulated. It is presented in the hope that it will crystallize the material presented in Chapter Six of the text in a specific document which *demonstrates* in concrete form the features of a practical and successful proposal dealing with a very pragmatic and substantial problem.

A STUDY TO IDENTIFY AND EVALUATE THE EXISTING DISCRETE INTERESTS AMONG FEDERALLY EMPLOYED MALE CARTOGRAPHERS AND TO DEVELOP A SCALE FOR THE STRONG VOCATIONAL INTEREST BLANK TO AID THE RECRUITMENT OF CARTOGRAPHERS INTO FEDERAL EMPLOYMENT

This is the title page for the study. Note that what is given here is a title for the study and not the statement of the problem. Note also the spacing, the balance, the eye-appeal in the format of the page.

A Dissertation Proposal

Presented to

the Faculty of the College of Arts and Sciences

The American University

This section explains what the document is and for whom it is written. The solid line above separates the one type of material from the other.

In Partial Fulfillment

of the Requirements for the Degree of

Doctor of Philosophy

This section explains the rationale for the document and its function.

---

by

Arthur Louis Benton

December 1969

The author's name completes the essential information on the title page.

COMMENTS ON ITEMS WITHIN THE PROPOSAL

THE PROBLEM AND ITS SETTING

Note the use of the headings to indicate the organization and outline of the proposal. Refer to the discussion of this matter in Chapter 11 (pp. 228-230).

The Statement of the Problem

This research proposes to identify and evaluate the existing discrete interests among Federally employed male cartographers and to develop a scale for the revised *Strong Vocational Interest Blank* to aid recruitment of cartographers into Federal employment.

The phrase "existing discrete" is useless verbiage. If they are "discrete interests," they do "exist."

Note the underscoring, indicating italics, for published titles.

Note also that only the words are italicized. It is impossible to italicize spaces. Hence, the line is broken and not solid as so often written.

The Subproblems

1. *The first subproblem.* The first subproblem is to determine whether male cartographers employed by the Federal government have a discrete pattern of interests different from those of men in general as measured by the *Strong Vocational Interest Blank.*

The numbering here is superfluous. The ¶ sidehead makes it clearly apparent that this is the first subproblem. No need, therefore, to number it 1.

2. *The second subproblem.* The second subproblem is to construct a scoring key for the Strong Vocational Interest Blank to differentiate ^the interest of^ cartographers from ^those of^ men in general and ^also from the interests of^ other occupational groups.

Here the researcher is not thinking what he is saying. What he says is that he wants to differentiate cartographers. That is not so. He wants to differentiate the interests of cartographers. The edited additions bring the thought into correct perspective.

3. *The third subproblem.* The third subproblem is to analyze and ^to^ interpret the treated data so as to evaluate the discovered interests in terms of their discreteness in recruiting cartographers.

Note the correction in syntax. A correlative connects two like constructions; thus the insertion of the to.

Note that the three subproblems add up to the totality of the problem.

Note the spacing between the freestanding sidehead and the first line of text. Such spacing causes the heading to stand out prominently for ease of reading. Crowding is the worst typing fault of most students.

The Hypotheses

The first hypothesis is that male cartographers employed by the Federal Government have a discrete pattern of interests different from those of men in general.

Note the position of the hypothesis section. It immediately follows the

The second hypothesis is that the Strong Vocational Interest Blank can identify the existing discrete interests of cartographers differentially from those of men in general and those of other occupational groups.

The third hypothesis is that the development of an interest scale can aid the recruitment of cartographers into Federal employment.

The Delimitations

The study will not attempt to predict success of cartographers.

The study will not determine nor evaluate the preparation and training of cartographers.

The study will be limited to male cartographers who have attained, within the U.S. Civil Service classification system, full performance ratings of GS-09 or higher in Occupation Series 1370.

The study will not evaluate any cartographers who may be also uniformed military personnel.

The Definitions of Terms

Cartographer. A cartographer is a professional employee who engages in the production of maps, including construction of projections, design, drafting (or scribing), and preparation through the negative stage for the reproduction of maps, charts, and related graphic materials.

Discrete interests. Discrete interests are those empirically derived qualities or traits common to an occupational population that serve to make them distinct from the general population or universe.

Abbreviations

SVIB is the abbreviation used for the Strong Vocational Interest Blank.

USATOPOCOM is an acronym for the U.S. Army Topographic Command.

CIMR is an abbreviation used for the Center for Interest Measurement Research.

SD is the abbreviation used for standard deviation.

subproblems. It facilitates seeing the one-to-one correspondence between subproblems and hypothesis pertaining to that subproblem.

"Edited-in" words express precisely what the writer of the proposal means.

This hypothesis goes beyond the limits of the problem. The researcher does not intend to investigate the actual recruitments of cartographers, yet, unless he does he cannot know whether his hypothesis will be supported or not.

Delimitations indicate the peripheral areas lying contiguous to the problem which the researcher expressly rules out of the area of his investigation.

Again, the researcher is not saying what he means precisely. What he intends to say is: The study will not evaluate any cartographers who may be uniformed military personnel.

Note that the word to be defined is given in the ¶ sidehead. Then follows a complete definition comprising the three parts discussed on p. 63. The small numbers over the first definition indicate: 1 = the term to be defined, 2 = the genera, 3 = the differentia.

Again the definition is formal in that it begins with the term to be defined (discrete interests); it states the genera to which the term belongs (empirically derived qualities or traits); and then the differentia (e.g., common to an occupational population).

This section was not discussed in the text, but it is perfectly appropriate. Whatever makes for ease of reading and aids in giving the problem an appropriate setting is worthy of inclusion in this part of the proposal.

Note that the assumptions are set up with appropriate paragraph subheads. Perhaps this is one feature which might have enhanced the presentation of the hypotheses. Had they been set up, as, for example, The first hypothesis, each section would have been parallel in format.

Assumptions

The first assumption. The first assumption is that the need for cartographers in Federal service will continue.

The second assumption. The second assumption is that the revised Strong Vocational Interest Blank will continue in use as a vocational guidance tool.

The third assumption. The third assumption is that the recent revolutionary advances in the cartographic state of the art will not alter the interests of persons in the employment of the Federal Government as cartographers.

The fourth assumption. The fourth assumption is that the criterion group consisting of the population of catographers employed by the USATOPOCOM at Washington, D.C.; Providence, Rhode Island; Louisville, Kentucky; Kansas City, Missouri, and San Antonio, Texas, is representative of the universe of Federally employed cartographers.

Note that the assumptions are set up with appropriate paragraph subheads. Perhaps this is one feature which might have enhanced the presentation of the hypotheses. Had they been set up, as, for example, The first hypothesis, each section would have been parallel in format.

As we said earlier, clarity is most important in the writing and structuring of a proposal. The writer of this proposal has presented his material in a delightfully clear manner.

Note that again and again the writer of this proposal gives evidence of working with care and precision. He does not try to cut corners. Here he spells out fully the name of the state, rather than employing abbreviations.

The Importance of the Study

Cartographers and the nature of their work is little known in American society. The total annual production of graduates, at the bachelor's level, with competence in the broader field of survey engineering within which cartography is subsumed, is currently less than one per cent of the annual requirement. The addition of a cartographer scale to the occupations routinely reported for the Strong Vocational Interest Blank would potentially bring to the attention of everyone involved with the existing vocational guidance system the opportunities within the field of map-making and serve to attract serious and capable students into the appropriate preparatory college programs.

This section gives the reader of the proposal a practical rationale for undertaking the study. It shows a utilitarian connection between the problem for research and the exigencies of real life.

Here the researcher points out that chance produces less than 1 per cent of graduates required for the demand of the cartographic profession. If he can find a way to identify potential candidates for the profession in terms of their discrete interests on the SVIB, it may attract serious and capable students into courses which might prepare and lead them toward cartography as a life's work.

This section makes no attempt to present a complete discussion of the related literature with respect to this problem. It does, however, select a representative sampling of each section from the complete discussion so that the student may see how the discussion of related literature is presented.

THE REVIEW OF THE RELATED LITERATURE

Note the centered heading, all caps. This is the second main division of the proposal, a fact which the position and all-capitalization of the heading indicates. (See p. 228.)

A Historical Overview

The reader is introduced to the problem through the perspective of its historical background. Note that the discussion begins with the earliest reference to interests in the eighteenth century and progresses strictly chronologically from J. J. Rousseau (1712-1778) to Guilford (1965).

The role of interests within the behavioral sciences is not new. Rousseau (1712-1778) in the eighteenth century spoke to the matter of interests:

> . . . Education . . . is a development from within, not an accretion from without; it comes through the workings of natural instincts and interests and not in response to external force; it is an expansion of natural powers, not an acquisition of information; it is life itself, not a preparation for a future state remote in interests and characteristics from the life of childhood.[1]

Extended quotations are single spaced, indented. Ellipsis is indicated by three periods alternating with single space distances (. . .). Ellipsis indicates that words, or perhaps even sentences, have been deleted from the original text. If an entire paragraph is omitted, such omission is marked by an entire line of double-spaced periods:

. . . .

Herbart (1776-1841) stressed virtue as the ultimate purpose of education but recognized the need for arousal of interest in order to secure the attention and appropriation of new ideas.[2]

Herbart is discussed as having been interested in the subject of interest.

---

[1] Paul Monroe (ed.), History of Education (New York: The Macmillan Company, 1909), p. 566.

[2] Ibid., p. 752.

Here the author should have gone to the original sources,—to the writings of J. J. Rousseau (definitive edition) and cited the location of the quotation from the work in which it appears.

Again the reader should be referred to the specific location in Herbart's writings where the idea discussed is found.

Within the same context of educational and psychological thought, James (1842-1910) said:

> Millions of items of the outward order are present to my senses which never properly enter into my experience. Why? Because they have no interest for me. My experience is what I agree to attend to. Only those items which I notice shape my mind -- without selective interest, experience is utter chaos. Interest alone gives accent and emphasis, light and shade, background and foreground -- intelligible perspective, in a word.[3]

Note that here the author of the proposal does cite the prime source of the quotation (footnote 3). This is the way the Rousseau and Herbart quotations should have been cited.

Note again that an extended quotation is single spaced, and indented from both margins of the page.

Psychologists and educators alike have sought to define the desires, interests, and satisfactions that initiate behavior and have applied the term motivation to the concept. Ryan remarked that a postulated "X" which energizes and directs behavior is still the common core across widely different theories of behavior.[4]

Guilford perhaps ~~comes~~ came close to explaining motivation in terms of his informational psychology when he addressed the Nebraska Symposium on Motivation in 1965, saying ". . . there is goal information and this is in the form of the product of anticipation. Human goals are almost entirely developed by experience in the form of anticipated values, and anticipations are implications."[5]

Ryan and Guilford are cited and the footnotes refer the reader to the original sources.

Note the change in tense. Precision of expression is paramount in research writing and reporting. The broad rule for tense usage is generally that since a research report recounts what has been done, the tense employed should generally be the past tense. If present or future tenses are used they should represent facts that will be true at any time the document is read. Here comes is inaccurate. Guilford came close to explaining motivation in 1965 at the Nebraska Symposium. Other changes in tense will be made where necessary.

---

[3] William James, The Principles of Psychology (New York: Henry Holt and Company, 1908), Vol. I, p. 402.

[4] T. A. Ryan, "Drives, Tasks, and the Initiation of Behavior," American Journal of Psychology, LXXI (January, 1958), 74-93.

[5] J. P. Guilford, "Motivation in an Informational Psychology," David Lewine (ed.), Nebraska Symposium on Motivation (Lincoln: University of Nebraska Press, 1965), pp. 313-333.

Since interests involve reactions or inclinations to specific things, then it would appear that they must be learned. Within that field of psychology identified as learning theory, motive ed is crucial for Hul ndike,[7] Lewin,[8] and others amo ed incidenta tensive ng

ysis is

usly app geneous scale

ure research that "after forty years of fact gathering we come organizing theory, especially since the computer has made it possible to carry empiricism to ridiculous extremes.

Here the discussion continues for several more pages, dealing with the "Historical Background." We have given enough for you to appreciate how the material is handled. We have, thus, represented a tear in the manuscript and, after the hiatus, we shall take up the next division of the discussion.

This may be a proper place to point out the organization of the discussion of related literature. Note how it proceeds, from the standpoint of the problem, from the broadest consideration—the historical overview—to the specific construction of a scoring key for the SVIB. Here is the organization as represented by the subheadings:

The Historical Overview
Interest Measurement in Counseling and Guidance [in general]
Measurement of Interests among Cartographers [in particular]
The Strong Vocational Interest Approach [Now, a specific way of measuring interests]
The Validity and Reliability of the Strong Approach [a discussion of a particular phase of the Strong approach]
The Construction of a Scoring Key [And so, the discussion of related literature has come full circuit. Refer to the problem and you will see that this is the object of the research: "to develop a scale" for the SVIB].

Note how each section becomes of narrower and narrower scope. (See pp. *72-73.*)

Interest Measurement in Counseling and Guidance

There appears to be universal agreement in the relevance of interest measurement as a guidance technique. In the words of Cronbach:

> . . .Historically, interest tests have always been a method for helping the individual attain satisfaction for himself rather than a method for satisfying institutions. . . . The aim in counseling should be to give the student a more sophisticated view of the world of work, of the choices open to him, and of his own range of potentials for achievement and satisfaction.[12]

Although there is agreement on the use of interest inventories, preferences vary when it comes to the selection of a specific instrument. Perhaps even more important, however, is how the results obtained through the instrument are used in counseling situations. Again quoting from Cronbach:

> . . . It is most unwise to concentrate the interview upon an analysis of scores for specific occupations . . . It is absolutely essential that the student go beneath occupational labels and stereotypes, that he should understand the variety of roles different members of the same occupation play, that he should understand the differences between the demands of the occupations, and that he should recognize the shifting nature of occupations.[13]

Here is a second extended quotation from Cronbach. The source is the same, except for the page location, as the previous quotation; hence, the footnote reference Ibid. [<L. ibidem = the same].

Routine interest testing, as a part of college entrance programs is a relatively recent development. The University of Minnesota was among the early institutions to add interest testing; first appearing in the 1940's so as to provide students with the opportunity to consider

[12]Cronbach, op. cit., pp. 431-432.

[13]Ibid., p. 433.

Op. cit. [<L. opere citato = the work cited) is an abbreviation meaning "in the work already cited by the author whose last name is given."

vocational alternatives.[14] The function of guidance at the college level, according to Humphreys and Traxler, should be to assist the student to (1) recognize the need for fundamental skill improvement, (2) choose an appropriate curriculum of studies, (3) select a vocation wisely and with insight, (4) make better social and personal adjustment.[15]

Mild dissent ~~comes~~ came from Ginzberg, who ~~feels~~ felt that difficulty is encountered in the translation of interests into realistic choices compatible with goals and values, ~~contending~~ having contended that the individual is not necessarily unaware of his interests. He ~~does~~ did agre hat

the indivi osess such as of

r vocati

ests ~~are~~ were so ed in counseling

rea of guidance and vocational guidance which has been extensi

has devoted an entire volume to the Counseling Use of the Strong Vocational Interest Blank.[19]

Again, to be absolutely accurate in expressing the thought, the verb must be in the past tense because it was actually in 1951 that Eli Ginsberg voiced his "mild dissent" in a book entitled Occupational Choice, published by the Columbia University Press.

Again, a hiatus in the manuscript.

In the previous section, we were discussing "Interest Measurement in Counseling and Guidance" generally. Now the subject narrows to the measurement of interests among a specific occupational group, viz., cartographers.

Measurement of Interests Among Cartographers

The literature ~~contains~~ contained no references directly to the measurement of interest among cartographers nor to the skills subsumed therein, i.e. photogrammetrist, map-analyst, geographer, surveyor, geodesist, or compiler.

Note tense change. When the researcher searched the literature (in the past) the literature "contained."

Research done with the SVIB has resulted in some fragmenting of the broader vocational fields. The physician scale, for example, ~~is~~ was based upon a composite made up of nine specialties plus interns.[20] Similarly, the engineer criterion group ~~includes~~ included mining, mechanical, civil, and electrical engineering.[21] In the latter case, Dunnettee has

Note the footnote form here for citations with reference to journals. Here for the volume the writer uses Roman numerals, the date in parentheses, and merely the numbers—without pp.—for the pages. There are several forms for footnote citation which we shall discuss later in the text.

Note that the author cannot use ibid. here. He is referring to two different works by Campbell: one published in 1968, the other in 1966.

---

[14] Ralph F. Berdie, "Guidance Between School and College," College Admissions, III (1956), 99-100.

[15] J. Anthony Humphreys and Arthur E. Traxler, Guidance Services (Chicago, Illinois: Science Research Associates, 1954), p. 14.

[19] W. L. Layton, Counseling Use of the Strong Vocational Interest Blank (Minneapolis, Minnesota: University of Minnesota Press, 1958).

[20] Campbell (1968), op. cit., p. 26.

[21] Campbell (1966), op. cit., p. 59.

compared the responses of several types of engineers to the SVIB and concluded that the SVIB potentially ~~can~~ could discriminate between the fields within the engineering disciplines.[22]

Note that the tense has again been changed to the past: could is the past tense of can. Also, would, should, and might for will, shall, and may.

In present practice, Campbell ~~reports~~ reported that counselors usually extrapolate from the available SVIB scales to occupations not listed on the profile.[23] This technique, although weak, might be appropriate to parcel out the geologist from potentially relevant engineer and chemist scales. However, to apply the technique when a larger number of existing scales appear applicable to the occupation would considerably weaken any resulting interpretation. The presently available scales ~~do~~ did not identify a single occupation even remotely related to cartography.

The Kuder Preferential Record, the Minnesota Vocational Interest Inventory, the Guilford-Sheidman-Zimmerman Interest Survey, the Occupational Interest Inventory, and the Vocational Interest Analysis ~~are~~ were not scored for cartography nor for any related occupation.

Again, the discussion narrows from the broad discussion of "measurement of interests among cartographers" to a particular method or means of measuring interests among cartographers; namely, the Strong Vocational Interest approach."

The Strong Vocational Interest Approach

The research generated by the SVIB ~~is~~ was probably exceeded only by that of the Rorschach.[24] The SVIB is so well known as to need no description in detail. To repeat here all the information available on the construction of scoring keys for particular occupations does not seem at all pertinent. But the necessary information which is relevant to the

When the research "generated by the SVIB" was superseded by the Rorschach was in 1969, when Benton wrote his proposal.

Also note the insertion of "that of" expresses precisely the thought the author wished to express.

---

[22]M. D. Dunnette, "Vocational Interest Differences among Engineers Employed in Different Functions," Journal of Applied Psychology, XLI (October, 1957), -273; see also M.

Another hiatus in the manuscript.

procedures to be used in this research were also used by Roys to construct a scoring key to identify potential male administrators in community recreation.[31]

The Validity and Reliability of the Strong Approach

Now the author discusses the matter of validity and reliability of the Strong approach to assessing interests.

The criteria for judging the value of a test have long constituted a controversial issue and are beyond the scope of this review. The American Psychological Association, attempting to aid both the test-maker and the test-user, has published a helpful document, "Technical Recommendations for Psychological Tests and Diagnostic Techniques."[32] Cronbach also ~~includes~~ included an excellent coverage of the subject of test evaluation in his work on psychological testing which has been mentioned earlier in this review.[33]

Note the way in which the author has delimited the discussion by openly stating whatever he feels is beyond the province of his discussion.

Note the general discussion of test validity here.

There are three validities of concern to the test user: content, concurrent, and predictive validities. The validity of the SVIB in each of these traditional areas ~~is~~ was discussed in detail by Strong,[34] by Campbell,[35] and by others.[36] Campbell, in his recent report of factor analysis study found occupational choice determinative.

Now the topic narrows to three validities.

Then we come to Strong and the discussion of these validities as they apply to the Strong approach.

---

[31] K. B. Roys, op. cit.

[32] American Psychological Association, "Technical Recommendations for Psychological Tests and Diagnostic Techniques," Psychological Bulletin Supplement, LI (March, 1954), 1-34.

[33] Cronbach, op. cit.

[34] E. K. Strong, Jr., Vocational Interests Eighteen Years after College (Minneapolis, Minnesota: University of Minnesota Press, 1955).

[35] Campbell (1966), op. cit.

[36] Buros, op. cit.

The degree of separation between scales of the SVIB is generally indicated by a determination of the per ce f overl ping occasioned

If we go back to reread the problem for this research effort we will see how the author has kept his goal constantly in mind while planning his discussion of related literature. In the statement of the problem the author specifically announces as one of his research objectives is to "develop a scale for the revised Strong Vocational Interest Blank to aid recruitment of cartographers."

That is precisely what he is discussing here, "the construction of a scoring key—the developing of a scale—to aid in isolating the interests of cartographers from men in general.

The Construction of a Scoring Key

Although Strong has published his procedures for the construction of keys for the SVIB, the literature indicated that refinements in techniques have subsequently occurred. The blanks in scoring and in the weighting system; the format and the items were relatively unchanged.[44] Originally weights of 30 were used. Subsequently, they were reduced to 15; then to 4, and with the current edition, to 1.

Here is a discussion of the evolution of the "revised" SVIB key.

The rationale for adoption of unit weights and reduction in the number of items scored from 400 to 298 ~~is~~ was fully discussed in Strong's last contribution to the literature, published posthumously.[45]

The current procedures, and those to be used in this study, for constructing a scoring key are: first, the SVIB is administered to a criterion group of people in a specified occupation. Length of time employed and the individual's liking of the work are specific requirements for the criteria. Second, the percentage responses for the group

The author finally comes to the announcement of the procedures, following those of Strong, that he proposes to use in his study.

[44] E. K. Strong, Jr., et al., "Proposed Scoring Changes for the Strong Vocational Interest Blank," Journal of Applied Psychology, XLVIII (April, 1964), 75-80.

[45] Ibid.

are determined for each response and contrasted to men in general. Item choices different for the criterion group and also for the men-in-general group are separated out for use in the scale. Third, all members of the criterion group and the men-in-general group are scored on the new scale. Fourth, the norms and standard scores are established if the scale has adequately separated the two groups.

In the original document, the discussion of the construction of a scoring key runs on for several pages.

Until the current revision, the weighting system in use employed a mathema cal proce re to load the data prop tional to

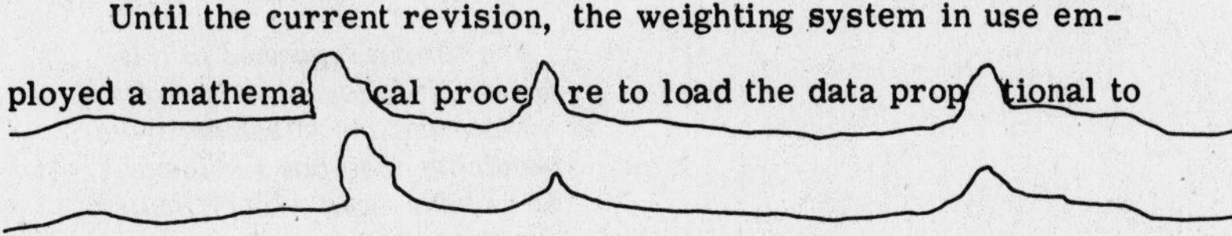

Summary

The extent of research done with the SVIB and its value and reliability as a counseling aid ~~is~~ was well stated by Cronbach in his summary of the application of interest inventories:

> The Strong blank is undoubtedly the most highly developed and best understood of the inventories; indeed it ranks near the top among psychological tests of all types . . . The great number of keys make interpretation both rich and complex . . . But its length and complexity, together with its research foundation, make the Strong the preferred instrument of most highly trained counselors and psychologists.[56]

The heading of this section is somewhat of a misnomer. Actually this is not so much a summary of the discussion of the related literature as it is a justification, by citing an authoritative opinion, for the choice of using the Strong approach over and against any other approach which might have been selected.

[56] Cronbach, op. cit., p. 434.

THE DATA AND THE TREATMENT OF THE DATA

The Data

The data of this research are of two kinds: primary data and secondary data. The nature of each of these two types of data will be given briefly below.

The primary data. The responses to the SVIB by cartographers are one type of primary data. The demographic responses to the questionnaire appended to the SVIB comprise another type of primary data.

The secondary data. The normative data and current occupational scales for the SVIB constitute one type of secondary data. The published studies and texts and the unpublished dissertations and theses dealing with interest measurement are another type of secondary data.

COMMENTS ON THE TEXT OF THE PROPOSAL

We have now come to the section of the proposal which is its very heart. This section should, indeed, be the strongest of all the sections of the research proposal in setting forth precisely what it is that the researcher intends to do and precisely how he intends to do it.

The format suggested in this section, if followed scrupulously, will prevent the researcher from becoming nebulous and inexact when he is faced with difficult problems to solve.

The researcher should begin by describing broadly the types of data he plans to use in the study. The statements are direct and informative: "The data of this research are of two kinds. . . ." Each type of data is then clearly described.

The study will utilize two categories of primary data.

The secondary data are described. More detail with respect to both of these types of data will be given later under the heading in each subproblem entitled "The Data Needed."

This is the first page of a new section of the proposal. Note the format, and the very effective way in which "open space" has been used.

First pages of chapters and new sections place the folio (page number) at the bottom, centered.

The Criteria for the Admissibility of the Data

Only the revised SVIB for men, completed in accordance with the test publisher's instructions, will be used in the study.

Only responses from criterion group cartographers with three or more years of cartographic experience and who indicate on the SVIB that they like their work will be used in this study.

For the researcher merely to amass data is not sufficient. Data in its raw form is frequently defective or contaminated. The researcher should, therefore, state unequivocally what standards his data must meet or under what conditions he will accept the data that comes to his attention. Here the researcher has provided a screening process through which the data must pass in order to be acceptable for use in the study.

Immediately after stating what the data are, we state the standards which they must meet to be acceptable.

The Research Methodology

Having presented the types of data and their refining criteria, the next item to be settled is the methodology which will be chosen for handling or processing those data. That is the purpose of this section on the "The Research Methodology."

Although Hillway pointed out that vague description of the approach to research is indicative of poor understanding of what is to be done and such research potentially will be ineffectual, the classification of educational research method is essentially an arbitrary process.[1] Identification of the method or techniques must also include a description of the schema if ambiguity is to be avoided. The classification system suggested by Barr[2] includes the grouping of data-gathering techniques and data-processing methods among others. Within that framework, this research uses the survey method for data gathering and actuarial prediction for data-processing.

Here is the statement of methodology: the survey method will be used. Now we know the methodological framework within which we are operating.

Further description of the data-gathering procedures is suggested by Mouly.[3] His system would classify the data-gathering method proposed for this research as a self-report descriptive survey and the data-processing methods as statistical empiricism.

Now the author goes one step further and suggests that the method will be more closely pinpointed as a descriptive survey—using Mouly's definition—and that the data processing methodology will be "statistical empiricism."

---

[1] Tyrus Hillway, Introduction to Research (Boston: Houghton Mifflin, 1956), p. 126.

[2] Arvil S. Barr, "Research Methods," Chester W. Harris, (ed.) Encyclopedia of Educational Research (New York: The Macmillan Company, 1960), pp. 1160-1166.

[3] George J. Mouly, The Science of Educational Research (New York: American Book Company, 1963), pp. 300, 301.

The author has buttressed his comment on method by citing from a standard text on research methods.

A second citation justifies his own choice of method.

The methods and procedures used in this study are those developed by E. K. Strong, Jr. over a period of forty years and continued by David P. Campbell, Director of the CIMR. Interest measurement research continues to evolve, however; and in spite of the prolific literature centered on the SVIB, the current procedures for scale development are not in print.

Here is an interesting comment. The author indicates that the methods and procedures used in this study are those that the developers of the instrument that he is using have developed "over a period of forty years." He also lets the door open for new developments.

Now we come to the heart of the proposal: the specific treatment of the data for each subproblem. Until now we have been dealing in generalities. No more! Now we cannot be too specific.

Specific Treatment of the Data for Each Subproblem

Subproblem one. The first subproblem is to determine whether male cartographers employed by the Federal Government have a discrete pattern of interests different from men in general as measured by the SVIB.

The author begins by restating the subproblem. Let's get it before our eyes and know precisely what it is we are attempting to resolve.

Each subproblem will be considered under four headings:
The Data Needed
Where the Data Are Located
How the Data Will Be Secured
How the Data Will Be Treated.

The Data Needed

The data needed for the solving of subproblem one are (a) the names of the cartographers within the employ of USATOPOCOM who meet the criteria established earlier in this proposal, (b) the responses of the criterion group to the SVIB, and (c) the responses of the normative men-in-general group to the SVIB.

Here the author states what data he needs to solve the subproblem. Note how specific he is in specifying the data needed.

He is in the same position as a builder who must specify exactly what materials he needs to construct the part of the building he is erecting.

While some researchers may feel that the format that we have suggested here is somewhat pedantic, it may be well for you to force yourself to articulate precisely where the data are located which you will need. The author of this book has seen entirely too many students who know what data they need but when asked where the data are located, they bewilderingly begin: "Well, I guess it is in. . ." Let's not guess. There is no guessing in this proposal. We should know with such precision where the data are located that we could send another to get the data for us with specific instructions as to where to get it.

The Location of the Data

The identification data are located in the personnel files of the USATOPOCOM, Washington, D. C.

The responses of the criterion group are located within that population.

The responses of the normative men-in-general group are located at the CIMR, University of Minnesota.

Here we could go to the personnel files of USATOPOCOM (if we had proper credentials) and to the office of CIMR at the University of Minnesota. We know where the data are.

The Means of Obtaining the Data

The identification data will be requested of the Personnel Officer, USATOPOCOM. Prior verbal permission for release of the data has been obtained. Appendix A exhibits the letter requesting these data.

All right; you know what data you need and where they are located. The next question is: How will you secure them?

The responses of the criterion group will be obtained by written request from the Commanding General, USATOPOCOM, accompanying the mailed SVIB to the individual members of the criterion group. Appendix B contains a copy of the cover letter. In order to preclude possible compromise and to avoid infringement of copyright, a copy of the SVIB is not included in the appendices to this proposal.

This section spells out the answer to that question without any ambiguity.

Note that for even the criterion group provision is made for obtaining the data. No loose ends remain!

If you are tempted to pass any of these sections off with a generalized comment such as, "The data will be obtained from the sources where they are located," be suspect of such an answer. It usually indicates either that you don't know how you will get them, or that you are too careless to bother to spell it out. Either situation will defeat you finally.

The responses of the normative men-in-general group will be obtained from Dr. David P. Campbell, Director, CIMR, University of Minnesota, 101 Eddy Hall, Minneapolis, Minnesota 55455. Appendix C contains the prior letter offering assistance, and Appendix D displays the letter requesting the data.

The student should study the format of the headings in this section of the proposal. Note that the centered heading, unitalicized, follows the paragraph sidehead, and that the next paragraph sidehead has its principal words capitalized to distinguish it from the first paragraph sidehead format. Read the headings consecutively under "The Treatment of the Data" and you will see how logically the author of this proposal proceeds.

The Treatment of the Data

How the Data Will Be Screened. The completed blanks returned by the criterion group will be screened to eliminate those where the respondent fails to meet the criteria for experience and job satisfaction and those forms improperly filled out.

How the Item Analysis Will Be Made. The criterion group response data will be treated by performing an item analysis to determine which of the three responses, i.e., "Like," "Indifferent," or "Dislike," have been made to each of the 298 items on the blanks that are currently used in scoring. The number of persons among the total group selecting each response to each item will be converted to a per cent value, and this value will be numerically compared with the responses of men-in-general.

The subsection on "The Treatment of the Data" is the vital center of the proposal. Unless this section spells out without any equivocation or ambiguity precisely what the author of the proposal intends to do, the proposal is a failure.

The criterion for this section should be that it ought to explain accurately precisely what is to be done to the data so that, were you inaccessible, anyone competent to do the research could carry out your research project without your assistance.

Scoring weights will be assigned for each item where the difference in response between cartographers and men in general is 20 per cent or greater. The items will be assigned positive values whenever the difference is in the direction of the cartographers and minus values when the reverse is true.

What is the rationale for 20 per cent? The researcher should tell us. Why not 10, 15, 25, 30 per cent instead of 20?

Table I is hypothetical so far as the data it exhibits, but it is illustrative of the way the data will be treated.

Note the inclusion of Table 1. Many students will say: "A table will be presented," and nothing more. It is not enough to know that a table will be presented but precisely, what the table will indicate, and what will be its data components. To show this treatment of the data, the skeletonized "hypothetical" table is presented on the next page.

TABLE I

DETERMINATION OF WEIGHTS FOR CARTOGRAPHER SCORING KEY FOR THE SVIB

(Hypothetical Data)

Items on SVIB	Percentage of Men in General Tested			Percentage of Cartographers Tested			Difference in Percentages Between Groups			Scoring Weights for Cartographers		
	L	I	D	L	I	D	L	I	D	L	I	D
Architect	37	41	22	63	31	7	25	-10	-15	1	0	0
Zoologist	27	41	32	87	11	1	60	-30	-31	1	-1	-1

Note the format of the table. It is entitled TABLE I (all capital letters). Roman numerals are used to number tables. Double lines indicate the boundary top and bottom of the table with the column headings separated from the data arranged under them by a single line.

Perhaps an asterisk after the first "L I D" would explain these cryptic letters for those who do not know the SVIB. These letters are three choices which the respondent has to the item: L = "Like," I = "Indifferent," D = "Dislike."

How the Data Will Be Interpreted. The data will be interpreted by counting the number of weighted items and comparing the resulting total to Strong's criterion.[4] That is, weighted response variance on the last forty items will be construed to mean that cartographers possess a discrete pattern of interests as measured by the SVIB.

Note that we have come full circle. The subproblem sought to determine whether cartographers possessed discrete interest patterns as compared to men in general.

After you have finished with the "Treatment of the Data" section it is always well to go back to read your subproblem again to see if what you have done does indeed provide an answer to the subproblem.

Subproblem two. The second subproblem is to construct a scoring key for the SVIB to differentiate cartographers from men in general and also from other occupational groups.

Now under the "Treatment of the Data," we come to the second subproblem. As before, it is stated (repeated) here so that the reader does not lose sight of what it is we are structuring a solution for.

The Data Needed

The data needed are the scoring weights for the 298 items of the cartographer-criterion group, their original responses to the SVIB, as well as responses from a separate group of male cartographers in the Federal employ, the scoring keys for all other available occupational groups, and their normative data.

Again we go through the same ritual as with subproblem one. The careless researcher will not have the patience and precision to work out each subproblem with meticulous detail. If not, it is an unhappy augury for the remainder of his research effort. All that he does will probably be careless and imprecise. A proposal carefully and meticulously worked out is 50 per cent of the research effort completed.

[4] E. K. Strong, Jr., et al., "Proposed Scoring Changes for the Strong Vocational Interest Blank," Journal of Applied Psychology, XLVIII (April, 1964), 75-80.

The Location of the Data

Data collection and treatment to be conducted as part of subproblem one will obtain the responses of the cartographer-criterion group and produce, in Table I, the scoring weights. The response data from a separate group of cartographers are located among the male cartographers employed by the U.S. Navy Oceanographic Office, Washington, D.C., and the U.S. Air Force Aeronautical Chart and Information Center, St. Louis, Missouri. The other available occupational scales and their normative data are located at the Center for Interest Measurement Research, the University of Minnesota, Minneapolis, Minnesota.

So accurate are these locations that, again, we could send another with proper credentials to get the material for us.

The Means of Obtaining the Data

The responses of the cartographer-criterion group and the scoring weights will be available at the conclusion of the prior subproblem. The respective commanders of the U.S. Navy Oceanographic Office and the U.S. Air Force Aeronautical Chart and Information Center will each be requested by letter to furnish Strong Vocational Interest Blank responses from a selected sample of sixty cartographers meeting the established experience criterion. A visit will be made to each of these installations to select randomly from the personnel files every fourth name and to facilitate the distribution and return of the blanks. Appendix E contains the letter requesting the data.

Note the way in which the researcher has provided has provided for randomization of his sample: every fourth name in a file.

The other available occupational scales and their normative data will be requested from David P. Campbell, Director, Center for Interest Measurement Research, University of Minnesota, 101 Eddy Hall, Minneapolis, Minnesota, 55455. Appendix C contains the letter requesting this data.

Letters are important. Note that the researcher exhibits the letter in Appendix E which he will use requesting the data. This gives us an opportunity to see the whole process of selection of the data.

Another letter is spread upon the record.

The Treatment of the Data

Scale Construction. The new cartographer scale will be construed by selecting those Strong Vocational Interest Blank response items from Table I that discriminate with a 20 per cent or greater variance. The scoring key will be comprised of all items having weights of +1 or -1.

The researcher might have strengthened his proposal at this point by giving us the rationale for setting 20 per cent as as arbitrary—or seemingly arbitrary—figure.

Normalizing. Norms for the cartographer scale will be established by:

(1) scoring the criterion group of answer sheets on the new scale,

(2) computing standard scores for the results,

(3) assigning letter ratings to appropriate ranges of standard scores for the criterion group.[5]

Note how clearly the author of this proposal outlines his next three steps. We shall now note each of these steps with specific emphasis.

The criterion-group answer sheets will be scored to obtain the algebraic sum of the previously selected items. Their range and arithmetic mean score will be determined. The standard deviations will be computed by the formula:[6]

←STEP 1

Where statistics are involved it is well to give the formulas that will be used, together with the meaning of each symbol employed in the formula. This was not done here. The authority or origin for the formula should also be given (here Downie and Heath; see footnote).

$$s = \sqrt{\frac{x^2}{N-1}}$$

A slight weakness is discernible at this point in the proposal. The researcher should have told us not only what he was doing statistically, but why he needed to do it. Why does he need the standard deviation?

The raw scores will be converted to standard scores by the formula:[7]

←STEP 2

$$\text{Standard score} = \frac{(x - \bar{X})}{s}(10) + 50$$

Of course, we see why he needed the "s" in the next formula: to derive the standard score.

Where

x = an individual raw score

$\bar{X}$ = criterion group raw-score mean

s = criterion group raw-score standard deviation

Here the researcher does give us the symbols and their meaning. This is always a desirable practice.

Letter ratings will be assigned to the distribution of standard scores expressed as percentages in the manner developed by Strong.[8,9] The data will appear in Table II and Table III.

←STEP 3

---

[5] Campbell (1966), op. cit., p. 9.

[6] N. M. Downie and R. W. Heath, Basic Statistical Methods (New York: Harper and Row, 1959), p. 45.

[7] Ibid., p. 61.

[8] Strong (1943), op. cit., p. 64.

[9] Campbell (1966), op. cit., p. 9.

TABLE II

CARTOGRAPHER-CRITERION-GROUP-LETTER-GRADE DISTRIBUTION

Rating	Standard Score	Per Cent of Normal Distribution	Value in S.D.	Per Cent of Cartographers
A	45 & above	69.2	-0.5 and above	- - -
B+	40-44	15.0	-0.5 to -1.0	- - -
B	35-39	9.2	-1.0 to -1.5	- - -
B-	30-34	4.4	-1.5 to -2.0	- - -
C+	25-29	1.6	-2.0 and below	- - -

Again, a skeleton table shows exactly how the data which have been assembled from "raw" sources will be displayed.

No researcher should ever be content merely to say: "A table will be presented. . ." Always that table should be shown in sufficient fullness for the reader to appreciate precisely what the table will show and, thus, be in a position to judge whether, with such data, the subproblem can be solved or the research goal achieved.

The criterion group answer sheets will be scored for each available occupational scale, converted to standard scores and percentages as was previously done for the cartographer scale. The results will appear in Table III.

To avoid unnecessary repetition, the researcher may refer back to the description of a data treatment which was delineated in an earlier subproblem.

The object of a proposal is not to make it repetitious, but clear.

Cross Validation. The responses of the cross-validation group will be screened to eliminate those blanks where: (1) the respondent failed to meet the previously established criteria for experience and job satisfaction; and (2) the respondent filled out the forms improperly.

The responses will then be scored with the newly developed (Table I) cartographer scale and all other available occupational scales. The results will be converted to standard scores and percentages. The data will appear in Table III.

Note the progress through this section of the Treatment of the Data for the second subproblem: The research task as enunciated by the subproblem is to construct a scoring key. The author, therefore, constructs the new cartographer scale, establishes norms for it (presenting the statistics for so doing) and now cross-validates the scale, and—as we shall see next—establishes the validity and, finally, the reliability for the newly developed scale. Read the subheads. That is the complete story. No researcher could do more than that.

The statistical nature of the data will be determined by comparing the difference between the means by using the z test:[10]

Note how carefully the author of the proposal spells out precisely how the statistical matters will be handled.

He also footnotes the authority for each statistical operation. There is, therefore, no question about the appropriateness of the statistic for the research task in which he is applying it.

Scale Group	Cross-validation Group
$\overline{X}_1$ = ________	$\overline{X}_2$ = ________
S_1 = ________	S_2 = ________
N_1 = ________	N_2 = ________

All of the values which will be later employed in the formulas are presented here for each group.

Standard error for $\overline{X}_1$ | Standard error for $\overline{X}_2$

$$S_{\overline{X}_1} = \frac{S_1}{\sqrt{N_1}} \qquad S_{\overline{X}_2} = \frac{S_2}{\sqrt{N_2}}$$

Now the computation of the standard error of the mean for each group takes place.

Standard error of the difference between the means:

$$S_{D_{\overline{X}}} = \sqrt{S_{\overline{X}_1}^2 + S_{\overline{X}_2}^2}$$

Then the computation of the standard error of the difference between the means.

$$z = \frac{\overline{X}_1 - \overline{X}_2}{S_{D_{\overline{X}}}}$$

And now, the computation of the z test.

[10] Downie, op. cit., pp. 124-125.

The resulting data will appear in the $\tilde{z}$ column of Table III.

And, finally, an indication of the disposition of the data in Table III.

Validity. The similarities between cartographers and other occupational groups will be determined by the degree and direction of of correlation between the standard scores of the criterion group on their own scale and their scores on other scales. The responses, after scoring, will be converted to standard scores by the use of the previously stated formula. The standard scores will then be used to compute the Pearson's product-moment by the formula:[11]

Now, the validity of the new scale will be determined by comparing by means of the Pearson product moment correlation technique the similarities between cartographers and other occupational groups.

Note that the author of this proposal is careful to footnote his source of even so common a technique as the Pearsonian r formula. No opportunity is given for the reader of the proposal to question the integrity of the research approach.

$$\underline{r} = \frac{\Sigma xy}{\sqrt{(\Sigma x^2)\ (\Sigma y^2)}}$$

The data will be included in Table III.

The amount of overlap between the criterion group and other occupational groups will be determined using the method devised by Tilton:[12]

Here, then, is the statistical procedure to determine the amount of "overlap" between the two groups—again, firmly documented to establish the validity of the statistical tool.

$$Q = \frac{M_1 - M_2}{\frac{SD_1 - SD_2}{2}}$$

Where

M_1 is the mean of group one,

M_2 is the mean of group two.

SD_1 is the standard deviation of group one.

SD_2 is the standard deviation of group two.

The resulting data will appear in Table IV.

Again, the writer indicates the disposition of the statistical data by showing in skeletonized form how he will present them in the research report.

---

[11]Downie, op. cit., p. 127.

[12]Tilton, op. cit.

TABLE III

SIGNIFICANCE OF THE DIFFERENCE BETWEEN THE SVIB MEAN STANDARD SCORE FOR CARTOGRAPHERS AND MEN-IN-GENERAL SCORED WITH THE CARTOGRAPHER SCALE

Group 1 (Criterion)	Group 2 (Cross Validation)	$X_1 - X_2$	$\tilde{z}$	Significance	Pearsonian Correlation Coefficient
Criterion	Men-in-General				
Criterion	Navy Cartographers				
Criterion	Air Force Cartographers				

A $\tilde{z}$ value of 1.96 is significant at the .05 level.

In this table all of the data are gathered together which have been drived during the treatment of the data for subproblem two.

With a design such as this, all the researcher needs to do now is to gather the data, process it statistically as he has indicated earlier, and fill in the table at the appropriate places with the appropriate data.

With a carefully thought-out proposal design the research is as good as completed!

Recall what we said earlier: A proposal is like the plans for a house. If the plans are carefully worked out, the contractor has no trouble in constructing the building. The simile is equally appropriate for the research effort.

TABLE IV

MEANS AND STANDARD DEVIATIONS OF RAW SCORES OF THE CARTOGRAPHER GROUP ON OTHER CURRENT OCCUPATIONAL SCALES AND THE PERCENTAGE OF OVERLAP

Scale	Mean	Standard Deviation	Percentage Overlap
Actor	- -	- -	- -
Architect	- -	- -	- -
Artist	- -	- -	- -
- -			
- -			
- -			
- -			
- -			
- -			
Zoologist			

The table will present data comparing the cartographer group on other current occupational scales and the percentage of overlap.

Obviously the occupations are to be arranged alphabetically in this table and the respective values for each column will be entered, from Actor to Zoologist.

Reliability. The reliability or internal consistency of the newly developed cartographer scale will be determined by computing a Pearson product-moment correlation between odd-even split halves and correcting the correlation by applying the Spearman-Brown formula:[13]

Where many a less experienced researcher would have stopped, the writer of this proposal carries his data one step further: he establishes by statistical means the reliability or internal consistency of his newly developed cartographer scale.

$$r_{tt} = \frac{2r_{oe}}{1 + r_{oe}}$$

Where

r_{tt} = the reliability of the original test

r_{oe} = the reliability coefficient obtained by correlating the odd items with the even items

Meaning of symbols is again given.

Interpretation of the data. The discreteness of cartographer's interests derived from responses to the SVIB will be interpreted in statistical terms by comparing the resulting numerical values of validity and reliability with standards established through precedence in similar research.

Finally, subproblem two is wrapped up in the final step which describes the manner in which the statistical data will be interpreted. This is the capstone for all that has gone before. Here we see an indication for the use of the "other" data, which the researcher indicated he needed back on page 272. "The other available scales and their normative data. . . ."

Note also that the researcher has used the data in this subproblem in the order in which he listed having need for it. (See page 272.)

Subproblem three. The third subproblem is to analyze and to interpret the treated data so as to evaluate the discovered interests in terms of their discreteness in recruiting cartographers.

We come now to the third and last subproblem.

As with the other two, it is stated at the beginning of the section on the treatment which the researcher will give to the data pertaining to it.

The Data Needed

The data needed are: (1) all treated data developed in previous subproblems, (2) pertinent and selected secondary data gleaned from the literature, and (3) the normative data for the SVIB.

Again he states clearly the data he needs to solve this subproblem.

The Location of the Data

The data will be contained in Tables I, II, III, and IV of the study.

He indicates where the data are found.

[13]Downie, op. cit., p. 192.

The secondary sources -- textbooks and journals containing reports and research conducted with the <u>SVIB</u> -- are located at the Library of Congress, the Battelle-Tompkins Library on the campus of The American University, and in the microfile publications of University Microfilms, Inc., Ann Arbor, Michigan (which may be secured at the Library of Congress or at the Battelle-Tompkins Library, The American University).

On page 268, we indicated the need for secondary data. The reader may have thought that the researcher had forgotten about those data. Not so! Here is the subproblem in which those data will be appropriate. Now we see the comprehensiveness with which he planned. This is the way proposals should be.

The Means of Obtaining the Data

To many readers this section may seem superfluous. Not to this researcher. He is entirely too careful for that. The section takes only a few sentences and he deems these well worth while in order to present the information <u>completely</u>.

No problems exist with obtaining the primary data for this subproblem. All of the data are those which have previously been secured, and reside in treated form within Tables I, II, III, and IV.

The secondary data will be secured at the Library of Congress and from the stacks of the Battelle-Tomkins Library, The American University. The material will be reviewed in place and xerox copies of whatever materials requiring further study will be secured.

A <u>complete</u> statement of how the data will be secured.

Pertinent unpublished dissertations and theses have been obtained through interlibrary loan or purchased from University Microfilms, Inc., Ann Arbor, Michigan.

The section in the Selected Bibliography will indicate the meaning of <u>pertinent.</u> Here those dissertations are fully listed.

The normative data for the <u>SVIB</u> will have been obtained from the CIMR.

The Treatment of the Data

The most as well as the least descriptive discrete interest characteristics of cartographers will be selected from the scoring weight data contained in Table I. Similar and dissimilar occupations will be identified from the data appearing in Tables III and IV. Descriptions of allied and alien occupations will be extracted from the literature.

The researcher will now deal with extremes in terms of cartographer interests.

He will also analyze the data in Tables II and III for similar and dissimilar occupation interest patterns.

The data will be interpreted by consolidating the discrete characteristics into a composite and elucidative description of cartographer interests as compared to and contrasted with other occupations.

Now comes a synthesizing of all of the data into "a composite and elucidative description of cartographer interests."

Turn at this point to page 257. Read again what the purpose of the research was as stated in the problem. We have indeed come full circle!

THE OUTLINE OF THE PROPOSED STUDY

PRELIMINARIES

- The Preface and the Acknowledgments
- The Table of Contents
- The List of Tables
- The List of Figures

I. THE PROBLEM AND ITS SETTING

- The Statement of the Problem
- The Statement of the Subproblems
- The Hypotheses
- The Delimitations
- The Definitions of Terms
- Abbreviations Used in This Study
- The Importance of the Study

II. THE REVIEW OF THE RELATED LITERATURE

- Interests as Theoretical Concepts
- Interests in Counseling and Vocational Choice
- The Measurement of Interests
- The Strong Approach
- The Measurement of Interests among Cartographers

III. THE POPULATION OF CARTOGRAPHERS

- The Population of Cartographers: Distribution and Genesis
- The Criterion Group
- The Cross-Validation Groups

IV. GENERAL PROCEDURE

- Response Data
- Collection Procedures
- Treating the Data

Many beginning researchers seem to feel that the outline of the proposed study is nothing more than the outline of the proposal. Nothing could be further from the truth.

You do in this section what the architect does when he draws an elevation of the various exposures of the building before a shovel of dirt has been lifted from the site for the foundation.

You envision what the completed study will be. What will you have in Chapter I, Chapter II, Chapter III, etc.?

Note how the outline of the study departs from the outline of the proposal.

The first chapter is fairly consistent with the proposal, merely because we need the same information to orient us to the problem and to give us its setting.

The review of the related literature section is also almost comparable to what we have done in the proposal with the exception of its updating with recent studies.

Now organizationally we depart from the proposal. Chapter III of the proposed study will describe the population of the study and the various subgroups within the population.

Chapter IV will outline the general procedures by which the data will be handled. If the data were to be computerized, here would be a full discussion of the computerization process and the programming of the data.

V. THE RESULTS

The Criterion Group Returns

The Cross-Validation Group Returns

The Cartographer Scale

Other SVIB Scores of Cartographers

The Hypotheses

Hypothesis 1

Hypothesis 2

Hypothesis 3

Other Findings

Summary of Results

In this chapter the results of processing the data are set forth. It will doubtless consist of many tables of summarized data.

Now we come to seeing whether the data have supported the hypotheses.

There are always miscellaneous findings. These are presented.

Finally, the summary.

VI. SUMMARY, CONCLUSIONS, AND RECOMMENDATIONS

Summary

Conclusions

Recommendations

This chapter brings the research to a resolution point. Here we have summarized for us the findings, the conclusions reached, and the suggestions for further research in the area.

BIBLIOGRAPHY

The bibliography is always an indispensable part of any study. It lists all of the literature referred to in the study.

APPENDIXES

A. Letter of Transmittal

B. Follow-up Letter

C. Item Count and Differences in Group Percentages and Scoring Weights Assigned to the SVIB Key for Army Cartographers

D. Standard Score Means and Standard Deviations of the Cartographer Groups on Other Current Scales of the SVIB

E. Significance of the Differences between Cartographer Group Means on Other Scales of the SVIB

F. Percentage Overlap of Cartographers on Other Current Scales

G. Pearson Product Moment Correlations between Scores of the Cartographer Criterion Group on the Cartographer Scale and Other Occupational Scales Incorporated in the 1971 Revision to the SVIB

H. Significance of the Differences between the Mean SVIB Scores of Cartographers and other SVIB Occupational Groups

The appendixes contain the very important matter which has facilitated the research.

The appendixes also contain a set of displays of the "raw" data and the statistical computations that are so necessary if anyone would wish to check your results, redo the study, or compare point for point the results of a later study to your data.

This material, too bulky for inclusion in the main study, is extremely valuable for anyone who might wish to check your statistics or do other computational study on the basis of your data.

SELECTED BIBLIOGRAPHY

Books

Blum, Milton L., and B. Balinski. Counseling and Psychology. New York: Prentice-Hall, Incorporated, 1951.

Buros, Oscar K. (ed.). The Sixth Mental Measurement Yearbook. Highland Park, New Jersey: The Gryphon Press, 1965.

Campbell, D. P. (revised from E. K. Strong, Jr.). Manual for the Strong Vocational Interest Blank for Men and Women. Stanford, California: Stanford University Press, 1966.

Clark, K. E. Vocational Interests of Non-professional Men. Minneapolis, Minnesota: University of Minnesota Press, 1961.

Clark, K. E., and D. P. Campbell. Minnesota Vocational Inventory. New York: Psychological Corporation, 1965.

M. N. Appley. Motivation, ry and Research. New York: ley & Sons, 1964.

This is but a partial page of the Selected Bibliography section. This section is indicated as dealing with books. Other sections of the bibliography deal with periodical and journal materials; publications of government, learned societies, and other organizations; and unpublished materials (dissertations, theses, etc.).

Note: For personal reasons, the section preceding the Selected Bibliography entitled "The Qualifications of the Researcher" has been omitted. It forms, however, an essential part of every research proposal. Information concerning the competence of the researcher to engage in the research (and in professional research vitas of the participants) is always an expected component of every proposal. This material usually precedes the bibliographical material.

Appendix B
Practicum in Research

This manual will give you an opportunity to develop those skills which are the mark of a qualified researcher. To be able to recognize genuine basic research from pseudo-research is one of the first abilities of any researcher. To develop this skill, you should read critically and evaluate already existing research studies dispassionately and according to the criteria by which genuine basic research is tested.

PROJECT 1: PART 1

Making an Evaluative Survey of Recent Research

Your first project in research is to make a survey of various types of existing research studies and to evaluate them against a checklist of the criteria discussed in Chapter 1 (pages 4–7).

Select fifteen to twenty studies which purport to be research—dissertations, theses, articles which appear in recent professional journals that report research. By using the following checklist, which contains those features which should generally appear somewhere in the study, evaluate each of the studies you inspect to determine how closely each approximates the criteria for basic research.

If you wish, you may use regular 8.5 × 11-inch sheets of manifold (onion skin) paper. Each piece will then be the size of a page in this book. Place a sheet of this thin manifold paper over the printed evaluation form on p. 284. The items on the form and the check columns may then be easily seen through the paper.

Always keep the paper aligned. Place the manifold paper on the page and mark on it a + and - directly over those same marks in the book. When checking each item, be sure that the two marks are always directly over their corresponding marks in the book. If you then wish to refer to the checklist after you have removed the manifold copy from the book, all you have to do is to reposition the + and - marks over the corresponding ones in the book and you will have the check sheet in an exact position for reading.

At this point, turn to page *284* where you will find the checklist.

PROJECT 1: PART 2

Conclusions with Reference to the Above Survey

You have made a brief sampling of some research studies. At this point, look over your findings. What conclusions can you reach in terms of what you have discovered?

1. How much of the research that you reviewed seemed to have the qualities of genuine basic research? (Average the scores of all your samples.)

☐ 100%   ☐ 80%–90%   ☐ 50%–70%   ☐ 30%–50%
☐ 10%–30%   ☐ None of it.

2. What were the areas of greatest weakness in the studies which you reviewed?

☐ Failure to state the problem clearly.

☐ No subproblems stated.

☐ Research poorly planned and organized.

(Continued on page 285.)

Locational [+] Mark

Locational [-] Mark

CHECKLIST FOR EVALUATION OF RESEARCH

Author ____
Last Name First Name Initial

" ____ "
Title of research report/thesis/dissertation

appearing in ______________________________, (______, ______), ______.
Journal (title) Volume Month Year Pages

Directions: Place a check mark in the appropriate column after carefully inspecting the research report to see if it contains the item designated.

Factor	*Yes*	*No*	*Comment*
1. Is the central problem for research clearly stated?			
2. Are the subproblems clearly stated?			
3. Does the research evidence plan and organization?			
4. Has the researcher stated his hypotheses?			
5. Are the hypotheses related to the principal problem or the subproblems of the research?			
6. Is the research methodology which has been employed clearly stated?			
7. Did the researcher interpret the data, i.e., tell what the facts mean?			
8. Are the conclusions which the researcher presents justified by the facts presented?			
9. Is there any indication whether the hypotheses are supported or rejected?			
10. Is there any reference to or discussion of related literature or studies by other researchers?			
Number of tally marks in each column (Enter these here) ⟶			
Multiply the total of each column as follows	x 10	x 0	
Total Score (Column 1 only)		0	

- ☐ Hypotheses were not stated.
- ☐ No seeming connection between problem being researched and hypotheses stated.
- ☐ No research methodology is indicated.
- ☐ Data are poorly presented.
- ☐ Data are merely presented; no interpretation of what data mean.
- ☐ Conclusions do not seem to be justified by facts presented.
- ☐ No indication of support or rejection of hypotheses.
- ☐ Related literature is not discussed.

3. Which factors seem to be most generally present in these studies?

☐ Problem statement	☐ Methodology stated
☐ Subproblems stated	☐ Data clearly presented
☐ Good organization	☐ Data clearly interpreted
☐ Hypotheses present	☐ Conclusions logical outcome of facts
☐ Problem-hypothesis closely related	☐ Hypotheses supported or rejected
	☐ Relevant literature discussed

4. From your review of the studies as a whole, what conclusions can you formulate about the studies in general? ______________________________

____

____

5. Additional comments (list in space below):

PROJECT 2

Discovering the Resources of the Library

The library is, perhaps, the universal tool of research. Every scholar needs its assistance. Every scholar should be self-sufficient when it comes to using its resources.

On pages 17-18, we listed eight master keys as master guides to the basic reference literature of the world. Go to your library; do the following:

☐ 1. Check the card catalog to see how many of the eight master keys your library owns.

☐ 2. In your text, in the left-hand margin, opposite each of the eight titles, jot the call number of the volume.

☐ 3. Go to the reference shelves; inspect each of the works, beginning with the preface and the table of contents. Then, look in the section of the volume which contains the major reference works appropriate to your own area of specialization.

☐ 4. Go to the reference stacks where the reference works pertaining to the area of your specialization are located. Browse. Spend time merely thumbing the volumes. Get acquainted with what is available.

☐ 5. If you feel that you are unacquainted with the total resources of the library, go to the reference desk or the circulation desk and ask whether there is a printed "Guide to the Library" which many college and university libraries issue. Get a copy. Study it; then, go on an exploration tour of your library.

As you accomplish each of the above objectives, check the box before the item number. Done conscientiously, there are many hours of work in this project.

PROJECT 3

Stating the Problem, the Subproblems, the Definition of Terms, Assumptions and Hypotheses

1. Write a clear statement of a problem for research.
   A. Is your problem fully stated in a complete, grammatical sentence? (See pages 55-56)
   B. Is the fact of interpretation of the data apparent in the statement of your problem? ☐ Yes ☐ No.
   C. If yes, quote the section of the statement of the problem which implies interpretation of the data: ______________________________

   ____

   D. If no, rephrase the problem, or revise it, or get a new problem so that you can fulfill the demands of B and C above.
   E. Have you said precisely what you mean to do in your research endeavor? ☐ Yes ☐ No.
2. Have you edited your problem? ☐ Yes ☐ No.
   If yes, write your problem in its original statement; write it immediately below as the edited version.
3. Now, evaluate your problem according to the following Checklist for Evaluating the Problem.

CHECKLIST FOR EVALUATING THE PROBLEM

The following checklist will assist you in evaluating your problem. It may indicate to you those aspects of your problem that need further refinement. In using the following checklist, *be realistic*. Read the problem as you have it written; read the checklist statement; then, to the best of your ability, try to decide whether the checklist item is applicable. There is no value at this point in wishful thinking. Either the item is applicable or it is not. Check the appropriate column.

Faults Resulting from Lack of Understanding of the Nature of Research

	Yes	No
1. Problem seems to be merely an exercise in gathering data on a particular subject. ("I don't know anything about the subject; I'd like to learn more by 'researching' it.")	____	____
2. Problem seems to be little more than a simple comparison.	____	____

3. Problem can be resolved finally with a yes or no answer. ____ ____
4. Problem seems to indicate that all you will have ultimately is a list of items. ____ ____
5. Problem seems to indicate that your study will be little more than an exercise in finding a correlation coefficient—the discovery that there is a relationship between various data. ____ ____
6. Problem has no identifiable word within it which indicates the need for interpretation of the data. ____ ____

Diagnosis of your difficulty: If you have checked any items in the yes column, you need to go back to the text and study pages 4–7 and pages 53–59. After you have read these pages and restudied your problem again in terms of the items 1-6, check this box. □

Faults Relating to Pseudoproblems

Yes No

7. You do not have a problem *per se* but rather an expression of an opinion which you would like to defend or "prove." ____ ____
8. Your problem does not focus on *one* research aim or goal but rather diffuses into several problems. ____ ____
9. The problem is too broad; it attempts to research too much; too large a geographical area, too great a population. ____ ____
10. The problem seems to suggest that you wish to learn more about the particular area you propose to "research" and that you are using the research project as a means of gathering such information. ____ ____
11. The problem seems to be more in the area of *applied* research than in that of *basic* research: you wish to research the problem merely because it has a practical application—"it needs to be done"—rather than because it seeks to discover the basic truth underlying the practical application. ____ ____

Diagnosis of your difficulty: If you have checked any items in the yes column in the preceding section, you need to go back to the text and study pages 3-4, 53-57. After you have read these pages and restudied your problem again in terms of items 7-11, check this box. □

Faults Relating to the Language and Manner in Which You State the Problem

Yes No

12. Problem statement is a meaningless fragment: you have no sentence. ____ ____
13. Read your problem *literally, phrase by phrase.* Are there any areas in the wording where the words do not say precisely what you *mean?* Is there any "fogginess" in the statement? ____ ____
14. Problem is stated in clichés or in other inexact or involved language which does not communicate clearly. ____ ____

15. You use reference words which have nothing to which they refer: pronouns without antecedents. ____ ____

16. You have additional discussion: a preamble, apology, statement why you have an interest in the problem area, or other discussion. You have written more than simply the statement of the problem. ____ ____

Diagnosis of your difficulty: If you have checked any items in the yes column in the preceding section, you have trouble in an area which is corollary to the domain of this book: you need to learn some matters pertaining to written English. Many people have difficulty in putting their thoughts in written form. Read again pages 58-59 in the text and follow the suggestions given there. ____ ____

After you have read the preceding pages (and whatever other sources were necessary) and have edited your work and are satisfied with it—and do not be too easily satisfied with your own efforts—check this box. □

Now rewrite the statement of your problem, if necessary, precisely as you wish it to stand after checking it out and editing it according to the preceding sixteen criteria.

PROJECT 4

Stating the Subproblems (See pages 60–62.)

On a separate sheet of paper, copy the problem for research that you have written on the previous page. Allow considerable space between the lines. Now do the following, after inspecting the problem carefully:

1. Box off within the problem those areas that must receive in-depth treatment if the problem is to be fully explored. Number each of the boxed-in areas consecutively.
2. Enclose within dotted lines those specified words within your statement of the problem which indicate your intention to interpret the data.
3. Below the problem, which has been thus treated, write in complete sentences the several subproblems for your study.

The Other Items to Complete the Section Entitled "The Problem and Its Setting."

Now having stated the problem and the subproblems, you are ready to finish the entire first section of your proposal. Turn to the sample proposal and study it carefully. Note especially the running comments in the right-hand column. These comments will guide you with respect to important points to be observed. Note carefully the use of the headings in presenting the material in a clear, logical format.

Now do the following:

□ *Write the hypotheses.* Read again what has been said about hypotheses in the body of the text (pages 5-6, 64-65). Study the way in which the author of the sample proposal posited his hypotheses. They are precisely parallel with his subproblems.

Write the delimitaions. Review again what was said on pages 62-63. Study the way in which the author has ruled out in the sample proposal those areas which, although contiguous to his research effort, his study will not consider.

□ *Write the definitions* of terms. Before writing your definitions read again page 63. It may help to number 1, 2, 3 the parts of the definition as we did in the text or to "box in" the several parts of your definition, labeling each as "term," "genera," or "differentia." Study the handling of the definitions section in the sample proposal. (Take out the numerals in the final draft of the proposal.)

Write the assumptions. Read again pages 6, 63-64, and study the section of the sample proposal dealing with assumptions.

□ *Write the section dealing with the importance of the study.* In a short succinct statement point out to the reader the importance of your study. Generally, you will not need more than two or three well-written paragraphs. Edit out all but essentials. Study the section which establishes the importance of the study of the sample proposal.

As you complete each item, check the box preceding the directive.

Using now the sample proposal as a format, type up *your* proposal, observing the amenities of style and format as suggested by the sample proposal.

You now have the first section of your research proposal completed. After you have your proposal typed and positioned on the page, compare the appearance of your page with that of the sample proposal. Do they resemble each other? They should.

PROJECT 5

Defining the Scope and Indicating the Sources of the Related Literature

The purpose of this project is to help you plan in a systematic and organized manner the search of the related literature with respect to the problem that you delineated in Project 4.

The literature that you will review is related only to your problem and to nothing else. In order to keep that fact foremost in your mind, write your problem in the following space:

Step 1

Step 2. Now read the problem analytically and insert 1 , 2 , 3 , 4 , and so on, before each separate subarea of your problem, thus isolating the several subareas of your problem into topics under which you might look in indexes, abstracts, bibliographies, and similar reference works in order to find specific items related to your problem. List the key words or phrases which will guide you in your search in the following spaces:

__________ __________ __________ __________

__________ __________ __________ __________

__________ __________ __________ __________

__________ __________ __________ __________

Step 3. Begin your search of the related literature by consulting the following eight keys to reference materials (see pages 17–18), noting in each instance they library where the book was consulted, the edition, the pages on which relevant material was found, and any comments that you may wish to make.

MASTER KEY TO REFERENCE MATERIALS*

Title	Library	Edition	Pages	Comments
Burke & Burke, *Documentation in Educ.*				
Hillard, James M., *Where to Find What.*				
Murphey, Robert W., *How and Where to Look. . .*				
Prakken, Sarah L., *et al.* *The Reader's Adviser*				
Sheehy, Eugene P., *Guide to Reference Books*				
Walford, Albert J., *Guide to Ref. Material*				
Walsh, John J., *Guide to Microforms . . . .*				
Wynar, Bohdan S., *Amer. Ref. Bks. Annual*				

*See pages 17–18.

Step 4. On the basis of the references suggested to you in the several master reference works, represented in the preceding chart, make up a bibliographic reference card similar to the following and duplicate it in sufficient quantities for your use. This is the first step in locating specific items: to go to the indexes, abstracts, bibliographies, and similar works to find the particular bibliographic item in the literature. A suggested 3- × 5-inch bibliographic reference card might contain the following information:

BIBLIOGRAPHIC REFERENCE CARD
For Abstracts, Bibliographies, Indexes, etc.

Type of Reference

Title ______________________________ Abstract (Check) [ ]

Volume ________ Date ______________________ Bibliography [ ]

Categories consulted: Index [ ]

Library ______________________ Book call number ______________________

See other side for additional notes

Step 5. Finally, using the suggested bibliography card given on page 71 copy down the specific references in the literature as given in the abstract, bibliography, or index. Use one card for each item. Fill in the author's name, the title of the article, the title of the journal in which the article is to be found, together with the volume of the journal, the pages, and the month and year of publication, and finally the source of your information (the bibliographic reference that you are using). You are now ready to go to the library to begin reading.

A reduced copy of the bibliography card follows. It may be well for you to read the section in the text entitled "How to Begin a Search for Related Literature," pages 70–72, before you actually begin collecting the data for the related literature discussion.

Serial No. ______

Author(s) ______
(Last names first, first name, initial)

Title of article ______

Journal title

Volume ______ Pages ______ Month ______ Year ______

Place of Publication, Publisher, date (books only) ______

______ Edition ______

Source of bibliographic information ______

Library where information is located ______

Call number of book ______

How item relates to problem: ______

______

Use reverse side for additonal comment. (If used, check here ☐.)

PROJECT 6: PART 1

Understanding the Nature of the Data

We have been discussing the care with which a researcher regards data. A study of the diagram of how we receive data, page 88, suggests many alternatives to a unilateral interpretation of any quantum of data.

Let us take a specific instance:

A woman screams.

Now with the philosophical structural diagram of the research process, let us fit the happening (the data) into the research structure:

Absolute Truth of the Situation	*The Impenetrable Barrier*	Data Reaching the Observer	*First Barrier: Single Sensory Channel (Hearing)*	Channel of Perception	*Second Barrier: Limitations of Human Ear*	Limits (Barrier) of the Channel	*Third Barrier: Data Beyond Reach of the Observer*	Meta-* perceptual Data (Confirm-atory)	*Fourth Barrier: Human Reason and Deductions from Data*	Probable Meaning of the Perceived Data
?		Scream		Human ear (hearing).		Frequency limits of hearing. Human hearing can perceive only within certain limits.		Blood pressure rise. Muscular tension. Adrenalin content.		Fear motivated the scream.

*Meta is a combining form from the Greek which means "beyond." Metaperceptual data, therefore, are those available data which are beyond the receptive and sensory channels available to the observer.

Perhaps it should be pointed out that the last column contains only *one* deduction which the observer has made. It could be that this deduction is entirely wrong. The woman may have screamed in surprise; she may have screamed in delight, or in laughter. We cannot be sure, merely by *hearing* a woman scream—without other confirmatory data—that she indeed has screamed in fright.

The following is a list of data-bearing situations. Using the skeleton table which follows, try to consider each of these situations in terms of its possible interpretation.

Data Reaching the Observer	Observer's Channel of Perception	Limits of the Channel	Metaperceptual Data*	Probable Meaning of the Situation	Other Conceivable Meanings

*Metaperceptual data are those data beyond the sensory mode through which the data reach the observer. They are confirmatory data which may assist in substantiating the probable meaning that he deduces from the available data that he has.

Here is a list of situations. Fit each into the preceding table format:

A low moan.
A fireball in the night sky.
The smell of acrid smoke.
A man collapsed on the sidewalk.
The wailing of a siren.
A slight tremor of the house.
A distinctly bright spot on the equator of a newly discovered planet.
All of the lights in a room go out.
A sudden flash in a dark area.
An automobile which suddenly swerves off the road into a ditch.

PROJECT 6: PART 2

Establishing Research Criteria and Justifying the Methodology

This part of the project will continue the writing of your research proposal for which you developed the review of the related literature section in Project 5 (pages 289-291). In this part of Project 6 you will want to make a four-level display of the manner in which you will treat the development of each subproblem. In the form below (and this will not be adequate for your purposes but is presented here merely to show you how to present these data), you will write your problem across the page over the two columns. In the left-hand column, write the subproblem; and, indented, immediately below it write the description of the data you will need to solve that subproblem. In the right-hand column, write the criteria which you will establish for the admissibility of those data into your research design. Be very specific. Avoid generalized statements. Here is the manner in which you should set these matters forth:

<table>
<tr><td colspan="2">The Problem: (Write is as you stated it on page 000.)</td></tr>
<tr><td>A Statement of Each Subproblem Together with a Description of Those Data Needed for Its Solution.

Subproblem 1:

The Data Needed for Its Solution:</td><td>The Criteria Which Will Govern the Admissibility of the Data into the Research Design.

Criterion 1:

Criterion 2:

Criterion 3:</td></tr>
</table>

PROJECT 6: PART 3

Justifying the Research Methodology in Terms of the Characteristics Exhibited by the Data

Refer to page 92. There you will find a description of the four methodologies which are appropriate to the four types of data. In this part of the project,

1. Describe the characteristics that the data in your research project will exhibit.
2. Indicate with those data that you have just described the methodology that would be most appropriate for the processing of such data. Justify your choice.

PROJECT 7

Practicum in Historical Research Writing

Historical research evidences broad variations, depending upon the historian and his style of writing. We make the point in Chapter twelve (pages 246–250) that research writing need not be dull. This statement is certainly obvious when reading some historians. Their pages are as varied and as interesting as life itself.

To appreciate how various historical scholars have handled the same subject matter, take *one* significant event in history—the Peloponnesian War, the Sacking of Rome by Alaric in 410 A.D., the Battle of Tours, the march of Hannibal across the Alps—and compare the treatment of the event by various historical writers. In view of the matters discussed in Chapter 7, compare the various historical accounts of the basis of the following criteria.

Criterion or Evaluative Standard	Yes	No	Your Comment Based on Your Observations
Are the accounts essentially the same? If not, what is the difference between them?	___	___	
The accounts reveal some attempt at textual criticism of sources.	___	___	
The accounts show an awareness of "historical space."	___	___	
The accounts show some awareness of "historical space."	___	___	
The account is a prose form of chronology.	___	___	
The account is interspersed with interpretations of the historical data presented.	___	___	

General critical reactions:

Author: ______________________ Author: ______________________

Title: ______________________ Title: ______________________

Source 1 Source 2

Perhaps for the preceding project it may be well to look up some event in the *Cambridge Ancient (or Medieval, or Modern) History* and to choose the identical event in, for example, Will Durant, *The Story of Civilization.* The purpose of this project is to give you an opportunity to develop a critical evaluation of historiography and historical research.

PROJECT 8: PART 1

The Descriptive Survey: Questionnaire Construction

If your research methodology falls within the area of the descriptive survey and you intend to gather some or all of your data by means of a questionnaire, you should duplicate as many of the forms for the construction of a questionnaire as you will need to accommodate all your questions. Beginning in the left-hand column with the statement of the question which you should write out clearly and completely, you should then proceed to analyze that question in terms of the following channels, moving toward the right. With an analysis of each question in this manner, there will be much less chance that you will produce a questionnaire that may be grossly faulty or that may have in it major defects that might impair your study and cast a shadow of credibility upon you as a researcher. The following form is merely to help you to put into practice some of the principles discussed in Chapter 8.

GUIDE FOR THE CONSTRUCTION OF A QUESTIONNAIRE

Write the question clearly and completely in the space below	What is the basic assumption underlying the reason for this question? How does the question relate to the research problem?	Type of question				How do you expect to relate this question to the research effort?
		Multiple Choice	Yes/No Answer	Comple-tion	Counter-check*	

*A "countercheck" question is one included to countercheck the reply given on another question in the questionnaire.

PROJECT 8: PART 2

The Descriptive Survey: Population Analysis

Take any population and make an analysis of its structure and characteristics. First, identify the population on the following line:

____

Now ask the following questions with respect to the *structure of the population:*

	Yes	No
1. Is the population a conglomerate mixture of homogeneous units?	____	____
2. Considered graphically, could the population be considered as consisting generally of equal "layers" each of which is fairly homogeneous in structure?	____	____
3. Considered graphically, could the population be considered as being composed of separate homogeneous layers but differing in size and number of units comprising them?	____	____
4. Could the population be envisioned as isolated islands or clusters of individual units, with each cluster apparently the same or similar to every other cluster, but upon close inspection being composed of distinctly heterogeneous units?	____	____

What is the *randomization process,* i.e., the means of extracting the sample from the total population? (Describe on the following line:)

____

____

By referring to the table on page 155 is the technique of randomization appropriate to the characteristics of the population?

Has the maximum of fortuitousness and at the same time the equality of representativeness of the various components of the population been guaranteed? ☐ Yes ☐ No

If the preceding answer is yes, indicate *how* this has been done. Explain simply on the following lines:

____

____

____

Indicate what means will be employed to extract the "hard facts" from the sample:

____

____

____

What are the weaknesses inherent in this method of securing the data?

____

____

____

What safeguards have you established to counteract the weaknesses of the data extraction approach? Be specific.

____

____

____

____

PROJECT 9

Guide to the Management of Data for the Analytical Survey

If your research methodology falls within the area of procedure normally considered to belong to the analytical survey methodology, the following guide to the consideration and management of the data will help you with the necessary groundwork for such a study.

The Characteristics of the Data

1. Are the data ☐ discrete or ☐ continuous?
2. What are the characteristics of the data? Are they
   - ☐ nominal
   - ☐ ordinal
   - ☐ interval
   - ☐ ratio
3. What do you want to do with the data?
   - ☐ Find a measure of central tendency? If so, which? ______________
   - ☐ Find a measure of dispersion? If so, which? ______________
   - ☐ Find a coefficient of correlation? If so, which? ______________
   - ☐ Estimate parameters? If so, which? ______________
   - ☐ Test the null hypothesis? If so, at what confidence level? ______________
   - ☐ Test of significance? If so, which? ______________
   - ☐ Other (specify) ______________
4. With respect to correlational techniques, what are the characteristics of the variables?
   Independent variable: (identify) ______________
   Nature of the data? ______________
   Dependent variable: (identify) ______________
   Nature of the data? ______________
   Correlational technique for dealing with these types of data: ______________
5. State clearly your rationale for planning to process the data as you have indicated you intend to do in sections 3 and 4:

The Interpretation of the Data

6. After you have treated the data statistically to analyze its characteristics, what will you then have? (Explain clearly and succinctly.)

7. Of what will your interpretation of the data from a research standpoint consist? What has the statistical analysis done in terms of solving any part of your research problem? (Explain precisely.)

8. What yet remains to be done before your problem (or any one of its subproblems) can be resolved? In other words, what further needs to be done so that the data will result in a resolution of the problem or any of its integral parts?

9. What is your plan of procedure for further carrying out this interpretation of the data? (Explain clearly.)

PROJECT 10

Practicum with Respect to the Experimental Method

1. You have a pretest-posttest control group design. When you have the statistical data collected, what statistical treatment of the data would be the recommended procedure to use?

2. Researchers talk so much about the importance of the "pretest" in the pretest-posttest design experiment. Name ten instances where life phenomena do not lend themselves to pretesting techniques.

3. In such instances as those cited above, indicate how you would employ the experimental method of research to resolve problems associated with them.

4. We have cited the instance of Fleming and experimentation with penicillin as an example of the

$$O_1 \rightarrow O_2 \rightarrow O_3 \rightarrow O_4 \rightarrow X \rightarrow O_5 \rightarrow O_6 \rightarrow O_7 \rightarrow O_8$$

design. Name some other experimental situations that would be appropriate for testing by the same design structure.

5. You have two types of material (conventional textbook and programmed textbook). You wish to test experimentally the effectiveness of the use of the one type of material as against that of the other type. Indicate what experimental research design you would employ and give the procedure in paradigm form.

Index

D

VERMONT STATE COLLEGES
0 0003 03028070 0